Corruption, Contention, and Reform

Michael Johnston argues that corruption will persist, and even be the rule rather than the exception, until those with a stake in ending it can act in ways that cannot be ignored. This is the key principle of "deep democratization," enabling citizens to defend their interests by political means. The author analyzes four syndromes of corruption in light of this principle: Official Moguls in Egypt and Tunisia; Oligarchs and Clans in the Philippines; Elite Cartels in Argentina; and Influence Markets in France, Australia, and the USA. Johnston argues that different kinds of corruption require distinctive responses, each bearing specific risks. Focusing on recent events, including the global economic crisis and the Arab Spring, he shows that we can assess vulnerabilities to corruption and the effects of reforms, and use this information to identify new practices. His book offers a fundamental reappraisal of ways to check abuses of wealth and power.

MICHAEL JOHNSTON is the Charles A. Dana Professor of Political Science at Colgate University.

Corruption, Contention, and Reform

The Power of Deep Democratization

MICHAEL JOHNSTON

CAMBRIDGE
UNIVERSITY PRESS

University Printing House, Cambridge CB2 8BS, United Kingdom

Cambridge University Press is part of the University of Cambridge.

It furthers the University's mission by disseminating knowledge in the pursuit of education, learning and research at the highest international levels of excellence.

www.cambridge.org
Information on this title: www.cambridge.org/9781107034747

© Michael Johnston 2014

This publication is in copyright. Subject to statutory exception and to the provisions of relevant collective licensing agreements, no reproduction of any part may take place without the written permission of Cambridge University Press.

First published 2014

A catalogue record for this publication is available from the British Library

Library of Congress Cataloguing in Publication data
Johnston, Michael, 1949–
Corruption, contention and reform : the power of deep democratization / Michael Johnston, Colgate University.
   pages   cm
Includes bibliographical references and index.
ISBN 978-1-107-03474-7 (hardback)
1. Corruption.   2. Political corruption.   3. Democracy – Moral and ethical aspects.   I. Title
JF1525.C66J637   2014

2013032786

ISBN 978-1-107-03474-7 Hardback
ISBN 978-1-107-61006-4 Paperback

Cambridge University Press has no responsibility for the persistence or accuracy of URLs for external or third-party internet websites referred to in this publication, and does not guarantee that any content on such websites is, or will remain, accurate or appropriate.

*For Betsy,
and for our family,
past, present, and future*

Contents

List of figures		*page* ix
List of tables		x
Preface		xi
Acknowledgments		xiv
1	Reform in an imperfect world	1
2	"Deep democratization" and the control of corruption	29
3	First, do no harm – then, build trust: reform in fragile and post-conflict societies	57
4	Official Moguls: power, protection … and profits	86
5	Oligarchs and Clans: high stakes and insecurity	119
6	Elite Cartels: hanging on with a little help from my friends	151
7	Influence Market corruption: wealth and power versus justice	186
8	Staying power: building and sustaining citizen engagement	220
Appendix. Recognizing the syndromes of corruption		241
References		252
Index		285

Figures

2.1 The changing reform agenda: primary tasks of deep democratization, by corruption syndrome *page* 50
A.1 "Forced-choice" method of classification 250

Tables

1.1	Four syndromes of corruption	*page* 20
3.1	Qualitative indicators of positive trends in expectations and corruption	82
7.1	Scores on major governance indices	190
7.2	Transparency International "Bribe Payers Index" scores, selected years	201
8.1	Varieties of incentives and target constituencies	228
A.1	Recognizing corruption syndromes in practice	244
A.2	Examples of corruption syndromes	246

Preface

Today a child will not be vaccinated against contagious diseases. A family will not have clean water. A young university graduate will not be given a fair shot at a job for which she is well trained. A small business owner will pay inspectors to avoid large fines for health and safety violations that do not exist, while a nightclub owner across the street pays other inspectors to ignore the fact that fire exits are blocked. A journalist with solid evidence about problems in regional government will wonder why his editor shows no interest in publishing the story. A local investor with a plan for improving a poor neighborhood will be denied essential licenses and permits – again. A young opposition leader will search for support against long-time incumbents who have campaign budgets several times as large as his. A researcher whose university laboratory is funded by a large corporation will publish findings friendly to that company's interests. A banker with a track record of making bad loans will be thinking about ways of spending a large bonus. A general from a developing country will close the deal on the purchase of a townhouse in the 16th *arrondissement* of Paris – using funds intended to support vaccinations for small children.

These scenarios and many more like them will play out in societies around the world, rich and poor, democratic and authoritarian. More often than in years past they may eventually make headlines, and draw the attention of citizens, journalists, organizations, and officials determined to reduce abuses of wealth and power. In time a few of the perpetrators and beneficiaries of such schemes might even go to jail. Yet the overall pattern of benefits for the "haves" at the expense of the have-nots is unlikely to change. Corruption is far from the only cause of that pattern; perfectly honest and transparent government might become a global reality tomorrow, and yet the next day, or next year, would not necessarily be very different. Indeed, some of the events above do not clearly fit most people's conceptions of corruption, although I will try to make a case in chapters to come that they have key elements in common.

Doing research on corruption is a humbling process in at least two ways. One has to do with the sheer tenacity of the problem, and the speed at which it can spread and change forms. The other is that the more closely I look at the problem the more respect I have for those who are living with, and resisting, serious corruption in circumstances far more difficult and risky than anything I encounter in a small village in upstate New York. I have had the privilege of working with many such people, and seeing a little of what they confront, in Thailand, the Philippines, Colombia, Ghana, and many places in between. While our analytic schemes require the best theory and data we can assemble, corruption itself, and the challenge of reform, will always have a human face.

In the pages to come I am at times critical of the past generation's anti-corruption movement, but it is criticism from a friend. Anti-corruption efforts would not have gotten as far as they have were it not for the efforts of innumerable smart, hard-working, and courageous people. That they – we – are still searching for ways to control corruption in diverse societies does not mean the movement has failed: after all, a generation ago corruption was not even widely discussed, and certainly received little attention from any but a handful of researchers and institutions. Today's heightened awareness, in itself, is a major accomplishment. But after such an eventful generation it may be time to take a step back, look again at the bigger picture, and think about reform in new ways.

This book builds upon my 2005 work *Syndromes of Corruption*, carrying forward its fourfold scheme of contrasting types of corruption problems. This time the issue is what they might tell us about reform – what to do, what not to do, and how we might judge whether we are having any effect. Two key arguments run through these pages: first, that lasting corruption control requires deep democratization – not building democracy in an electoral or constitutional sense, but rather enabling and encouraging citizens to check abuses of wealth and power through political advocacy of their own interests. That challenge will take on contrasting forms depending upon the syndrome of corruption that confronts us in a given time and place, and what may be a fine idea in Country A may be a very unwise measure in Country B. The second argument is that instead of building a grand public reform strategy and then trying to rally citizen support for it, we should select (and at times defer) specific reforms depending upon which ones will best help citizens become effective advocates for their own interests and well-being. The reform scenarios that result are more indirect and gradual than many (including me) might wish. But they seem likely to be more sustainable than short-term anti-corruption projects implemented from above and, in many parts of the world, driven more by the interests of well-meaning donors than by those at the grassroots. They may also emulate the much longer historical experiences of many of today's apparently well-governed societies, many of which brought serious corruption under control in the course of contention over other issues. That does not mean those societies have solved the corruption problem; indeed, in Chapter 7 I will argue that corruption in – and emanating from – the world's market democracies may be among the most worrisome and elusive of all. It does, however, serve as a reminder of important issues of fairness and justice, which is why corruption is worth our attention in the first place.

Acknowledgments

My previous book brought me an impressive amount of useful feedback, both critical and positive. It also brought surprising and, again, humbling recognition: in 2009 *Syndromes of Corruption* received the Grawemeyer Award for Ideas Improving World Order, presented by the University of Louisville. That response to the previous book does not necessarily imply any sort of endorsement of this one, but the gratifying and, to me, amazing vote of confidence it conveyed did much to sustain my more recent work. I thank all who were associated with the Award, including first and foremost the Grawemeyer family, President James Ramsey and Allan Dittmer of the University administration, Professor Rodger Payne of the Louisville Political Science Department, Arlene Brannon, and Denise Fitzpatrick.

In March of 2010 I had the opportunity to spend a few weeks at the Quality of Government Institute at the University of Gothenburg, Sweden. In addition to a pleasant stay in a handsome old university city, that visit offered numerous chances to try out ideas with a large number of accomplished researchers who shared my interests but also possessed a range of experiences far greater than my own. Sincere thanks to Professor Bo Rothstein for that invitation, and for the hospitality and support so freely given by his colleagues and team.

Many others – and I sincerely hope I have remembered them all! – contributed to this project in various ways. Some crunched their way through draft chapters, others influenced the work through their own research and suggestions, and still others included me in various projects or gave essential advice on research that shaped these chapters. In many cases they did all of those things. For their good advice, and for their ability to withstand my academic prose, I thank Ronnie Amorado, Cleo Calimbahin, Jaime Faustino, Angela Garcia, Aranzazu Guillan Montero, Jerry Hyman, Jennifer Kartner, Lawrence Lessig, Luigi Manzetti, Illan Nam, Steven Rood, Bruce Rutherford, Frederic Schaffer, Viviana Stechina, Hana Takada, and Maryse Tremblay.

Acknowledgments

Participants in a long series of seminars for United States Government agencies, similar sessions at the World Bank, the Fulbright/Hubert H. Humphrey Fellows program at Syracuse University, and a seminar on Argentina at Georgetown University have helped improve these chapters in many ways. Roderick M. Hills, founder of the Hills Program on Governance, Center for Strategic and International Studies, in Washington, DC, provided support, encouragement, and access to a long list of knowledgeable people. Sahr J. Kpundeh and Steve Ndegwa have enabled me to participate in research projects, and hosted discussion sessions of our findings, at the World Bank. Janos Bertok and his colleagues at the Organization for Economic Cooperation and Development (OECD) in Paris were kind enough to invite me to spend a few weeks in residence working on ideas that figure heavily into Chapter 3 of this book. A portion of the research behind several chapters was funded by the United States Government; the findings reported here do not necessarily reflect its views or policies.

I am also indebted to many people at Cambridge University Press, including John Haslam, Carrie Parkinson, Fleur Jones, Christina Sarigiannidou, and Sarah Turner, for their help and unfailingly good advice, and to two anonymous reviewers for their useful criticisms and suggestions.

Colgate University provided research support via the Faculty Research Council and, most of all, time for reading and reflection during a recent sabbatical term – as well as a generation and more of able and curious students in my Political Corruption lecture course. Cynthia Terrier of the Colgate Political Science Department brought her formidable energies to a number of clerical tasks; it should also be noted that she is the only person on earth who knows every quirk and nuance of Microsoft Word and how to live with both. All of these people and more have contributed to this work in ways too numerous to name; all are, of course, blameless for its errors, oversights, and gaps in analysis.

To all, and to those who, today and every day, give the challenge of reform its compelling human dimensions, huge thanks.

1 | Reform in an imperfect world

If men were angels, no government would be necessary. If angels were to govern men, neither external nor internal controls on government would be necessary. In framing a government which is to be administered by men over men, the great difficulty lies in this: you must first enable the government to control the governed; and in the next place oblige it to control itself.

– James Madison, *The Federalist Papers*, 51

Restraining power

Let us begin with a simple proposition about a complicated problem. Corruption will continue – indeed, may well be the norm – until those with a stake in ending it are able to oppose it in ways that cannot be ignored.

Corruption is tenacious – often sustained by powerful incentives and, at times, protected by violence. The contemporary anti-corruption movement enjoys broad-based support, and can point to genuine accomplishments in terms of analysis and public awareness over the past generation. Yet particularly where reform has been most urgently needed, lasting reductions in corruption have been elusive (Mungiu-Pippidi 2006; Birdsall 2007; DFID 2009; United Nations 2010). The difficulty of measuring corruption makes any such judgment impressionistic: we can never know just how much corruption a society experiences, and tracing trends is even more difficult. Still, despite successes at the level of specific programs and agencies it is difficult to point to sustained and significant reductions in corruption in whole societies. Hong Kong and Singapore have had widely recognized success, but both are city-states whose undemocratic regimes could force extensive change, and where the economic benefits of reform could rapidly become apparent. Botswana teaches us important lessons about the value of socially rooted leadership but its population, spread over a large area, is just a quarter of Hong Kong's. Japan and Belgium are perceived as having made steady progress, but already had solid national institutions in place. Korea, Indonesia, Ghana, and Taiwan are promising cases worth watching closely. Overall, however, the results of a generation's hard work in pursuit of reform are not encouraging.

At the same time, a longer view shows that entrenched corruption need not be a permanent condition. Had there been corruption rankings in the seventeenth century England would have been near the bad end of the scale. At times during the eighteenth century Denmark and Sweden were seen as extensively corrupt (see Rothstein 2011, discussing Rothstein 1998; Heidenheimer 2002: 4, 5; Frisk Jensen 2008). In the nineteenth century the United States and the United Kingdom again with its electoral "Old Corruption" (O'Leary 1962; Rubinstein 1983; Summers 1993) would have received poor ratings. Australia's first seventy years were marked by frequent scandals, and the following half-century featured a long struggle for reform (Curnow 2003). Chile, Canada, Finland, and the Netherlands – all, like Australia, well-regarded today – have experienced times of significant corruption too (Kernaghan 2003; Tiihonen 2003; van der Meer and Raadschelders 2003; Rehren 2004; Kerkhoff 2012). Progress usually was slow (although on Sweden's "big bang," see Rothstein 2011: 111–18) and indirect, driven by interests and ideas that had as much to do with self-interest as with civic virtue. Even where laws and accountability measures hold corruption in check today, those safeguards are not what brought the problem under control in the first place. More often those reforms were outcomes of political contention over questions of who is to govern whom, by what right, through what means, and within what limits.

Most effective limits emerged over generations or centuries. Today's highly corrupt societies have not got that much time. They exist in a different world – one in which risks and opportunities emerge rapidly and external influences are impossible to ignore (Rose-Ackerman 1999). If reformers wish to emulate the historical processes of checking power with power, and if they did so in ways that reflect the contrasting realities of diverse societies, what might reform look like? How could we know whether we were succeeding? Do we risk doing harm in the course of seeking better government? And how can we ensure that support for reform will last?

Deep democratization

This is a book about the politics of corruption control. It does not propose strikingly new corruption controls, but rather offers a different perspective on reform as a long-term social and political process. In that connection it develops two parallel arguments: first, that even the best anti-corruption ideas need strong political and social foundations – the support of people and groups with lasting reasons, and the ability, to defend themselves politically against abuses by others or, as Madison had it, to "*oblige* [government] to control itself."[1] Second, corruption itself, like the societies in which it occurs, comes in contrasting forms, confronting us with qualitatively different challenges and opportunities. Some situations are so fragile that reforms may be more of a stress than a benefit. Others, including the affluent market democracies that have been the source of most reform ideas, can experience corruption that is embedded in legal activities – and those are just two possible contrasts. Thus reformers must have political strategies as well as good ideas for corruption control; and as for the latter, what might seem to be a good reform idea in country A may well be impossible in B, irrelevant in C, and downright harmful in D.

Where do those arguments lead us? I will offer an argument that lasting corruption control is more likely to succeed as a part, and outcome, of *deep democratization* (an initial discussion appears in Johnston 2005a: Chapter 8). "Deep democratization" does not mean that democracy itself, or processes like competitive elections, will control corruption. Like many others (Philp 2001) I have argued that democracies have their own distinctive varieties of corruption (Johnston 2005a: chapters 3, 4). India's history suggests not only that democracy, in itself, is unlikely to control corruption, but also that where economic development – not just growth, but also workable economic institutions – is strikingly uneven or lacking, democracy can make some varieties of corruption worse (Sun and Johnston 2010).

---

[1] Italics added. Madison's immediate point was the separation of powers envisioned within the proposed United States Constitution, but in both Federalist 10 and 51 he emphasizes that countervailing political forces and interests are essential sources of vitality for that scheme. In the latter, for example, just before the passage quoted at the beginning of this chapter, Madison argues that "Ambition must be made to counteract ambition. The interest of the man must be connected with the constitutional rights of the place" (cf. "Publius" 1987: 319).

Moreover, corruption control has at times been built on undemocratic foundations: Pinochet's Chile and Lee Kwan Yew's Singapore come quickly to mind.

Instead, deep democratization is a continuing process of building workable rules and accountability by bringing more voices and interests into the governing process. It is "deep" in a double sense: it draws force from many levels of society, reflecting the lasting interests of the humblest as well as the elites; and it extends deep into the institutions and processes of government, making those social interests a factor in policy-making and implementation, not just slogans at election time. The clash of interests and values; contention over the acceptable sources and uses of wealth and power, and over accountability; and disputes over the nature and significance of rights are of the essence in deep democratization and, I will suggest, in checking corruption. Those sorts of political energy are not easily sustained solely through appeals to virtue; the defense of one's own interests – property, rights, personal safety, the chance to earn a living – is a more lasting motivation when it comes to confronting the wealthy and powerful.

Deep democratization is a long and complex process involving the mutual interplay of many motivations and activities. Societies do not vary, in corruption terms, on a more-versus-less continuum only; there are, instead, contrasting syndromes of corruption (Johnston 2005a), and change among them is qualitative as well as (or instead of) just quantitative. Similarly, the essential tasks of deep democratization change and evolve in different sorts of settings (see Chapter 2). Some of the key processes are economic: material well-being is a strong motivating interest, and we have good reason to think that controlling corruption can help build more prosperous, open, and fair economies. At the same time diversification of economic activities can help intensify demands for better government (Chavez 2003). Similarly, bringing more voices to the table can help build more open institutions and processes. There is no single starting point: change, particularly where there are significant corruption problems, takes many paths from numerous points of departure – deep democratization is unlikely to reach any definitive end point. Indeed, today's liberal democracies are hardly reform ideals; I will suggest in Chapter 7 that they confront us with particularly difficult corruption challenges. The political malaise seen in many of today's established democracies suggests that they fall well short of the ideals sketched out above.

Deep democratization amounts to gaining meaningful influence in processes of rule-making (for a similar argument see Acemoglu and Robinson 2012). Any such process is likely to be contentious – after all, agreements strong enough to protect one group will likely restrain someone else – and disorderly, but broadening the range of groups that must be heard and interests that must be considered is a democratizing process. Deep democratization will more likely revolve around countless group and personal grievances than any overriding vision of good government. In extensively corrupt societies deep democratization is unlikely to attain breakthroughs in political morality or anything like fully open, rational government. It *can* (though by no means must) culminate in settlements and accommodations that institutionalize accountability and limits on power (Ostrom 1990). Where such arrangements acquire legitimacy and credibility it is primarily because, from the standpoint of those who built them, they work.

We will explore these themes at several levels. In this opening chapter I will consider basic definitions and revisit the idea of contrasting syndromes of corruption. Chapter 2 expands on the notion of deep democratization to identify four key tasks it involves: increasing pluralism, opening up safe political and economic space, reform activism, and maintaining accountability. Those tasks vary in importance across societies depending upon the particular syndrome of corruption they experience, as well as upon their degree of fragility. Chapter 3 takes up that issue of fragility, not as a fifth corruption syndrome (fragility in various forms may be linked to at least three of the four syndromes) but rather as a set of circumstances that must be addressed before many of the four tasks above can be launched. That chapter considers societies where a functioning state and legal frameworks are lacking, where social and political trust are weak, and where reform itself can be a significant systemic stress, at times doing significant damage. It proposes two rules for reformers: "first, do no harm"; then, by providing some basic services, begin to build trust. It also takes up the critical issue of assessing progress, or lack of it – suggesting, not that we devise yet another corruption index, but rather that we gather and benchmark indicators of government performance, wherever possible working with citizens.

In chapters 4–7 the emphasis shifts to the four contrasting syndromes of corruption – Official Moguls (Egypt and Tunisia), Oligarchs and Clans (the Philippines), Elite Cartels (Argentina), and Influence Markets

(Australia, France, and the United States) – and their implications for deep democratization and reform. In a chapter considering each syndrome I will examine one or more societies, identifying the major challenges of deep democratization as well as steps to be avoided. The cases collectively do not cover all regions of the world, if only because the emphasis is on examples of the four syndromes rather than on geographical categories. However, I have made some effort to take up regions not extensively discussed in the earlier 2005 volume; thus, that book did examine cases from Africa (Botswana) and East Asia (China, Japan). This book will include North Africa and the Islamic world, via discussions of Tunisia and Egypt, as well as Latin America (Argentina). The final chapter, on Influence Markets, does devote more attention to the United States than to other societies; that is so because some of the possible implications of that syndrome of corruption – notably, growing economic inequality and distortions of democratic processes – are arguably on display more vividly in the American case than in most others (on that comparative claim see Hacker and Pierson 2010; see, more generally, Lessig 2011). A final chapter examines the challenges of maintaining support and coherence for reform over the long run, and discusses challenges confronting the next generation of reformers.

What do we mean by "corruption"?

What is corruption, and what do diverse types have in common? Those questions are hardy perennials; indeed, in its own way defining corruption is as difficult as controlling it (landmarks in the debate include Nye 1967; Heidenheimer 1970; Scott 1972; Thompson 1993, 1995; Philp 1997, 2002; Warren 2004). For the complex comparisons to come we need a systemic view that is not restricted to a few specific kinds of conduct, that accommodates divergent outlooks on how wealth and power should and should not be used, and yet is not so general that it lacks meaning.

Corruption implies deterioration or impropriety as judged by some set of standards, and is thus an inherently normative idea (see Johnston 2005b). Most uses of the term, but not all, apply to the roles and powers of government, and in practice the issues of standards and transgression can be matters of much dispute. The idea is thus inevitably political as well. Most contemporary definitions apply to specific actions or people, but it was not always thus: at times corruption was seen as a collective state of being. Thucydides, in his accounts of the Peloponnesian War, tells us that Athens as a whole fell into a state of corruption when its leaders, betraying the values by which they claimed the right to lead, invaded the island of Melos (Thucydides 1954; Dobel 1978; see also Warren 2004). In this "classical" view, when leaders or citizens undermine society's claim on the loyalty of citizens, its basic system of order has been corrupted (Dobel 1978). That outlook seems quaint in an age when the state is often viewed, factually and normatively, in liberal terms – as an arena in which people and groups pursue their own interests, and in which collective well-being is a byproduct of individual choices rather than an overarching good. In that setting political ethics are usually seen as having more to do with process than with goals and outcomes, or the overall moral state of society.

When a public trust is abused for private gain, most would agree that corruption has occurred. In day-to-day terms that makes sense: most notions of corruption emphasize rules for the process of governing, not what government ought to accomplish. But because of that implied neutrality with respect to specific people, interests, and outcomes, those standards are often assumed to be non-political – as serving all, rather than reflecting anyone's particular (in more than one sense) interests. Ironically, both scoundrels and reformers frequently reaffirm that view – the former, when they dismiss allegations of corruption as "politically motivated" and therefore as bogus, and the latter with their longstanding insistence that good government requires keeping administration and politics separate. But *where do those standards come from*, and who has a stake in seeing them upheld? Can they really be anything *but* political? These questions underlie the basic of deep democratization as a way to check corruption.

In fact the contemporary behavior-oriented conception of corruption has limitations and problems. Even the most outwardly successful liberal states, with their relatively strong institutions and well-defined rules, have governance problems. Their "Influence Markets" syndrome of corruption (Johnston 2005a, chapters 4, 7 of this book) is fraught with subtleties: it can be hard to say whether those societies have limited their corruption or whether they have merely removed most of the remaining restraints on the uses and pursuit of wealth. Ironically, it is in those societies – supposedly, where law and accountability are strongest and public–private distinctions clearest, that it can be most difficult to say what, exactly, is corrupt (see Chapter 7). What constitutes the "abuse" of power, or unacceptable connections to wealth – *and who gets to decide?* Even in relatively settled societies those standards are open to dispute, manipulation, and change. In the global arena that has emerged over the past generation, many of the most controversial uses of wealth and power take place in sectors, and involve roles, that are neither clearly public nor private, and that are so rootless it is hard to claim they are accountable to anyone (Wedel 2009).

Perhaps the notion of corruption as a systemic or collective attribute is not as *passé* as it seems. In American politics, for example, large-scale flows of political money have persuaded solid majorities that democracy has been fundamentally corrupted. That the overwhelming portion of such funds are given, spent, and disclosed in completely legal ways does not change the fact that the popular credibility of important guarantees and institutions is under threat. Perhaps we should look beyond specific actions to include more systemic aspects of governance and justice – to contemplate the sorts of issues Mark Warren (2004: 329) raises by arguing that in a democracy corruption fundamentally means "a form of duplicitous and harmful exclusion of those who have a claim to inclusion in collective decisions and actions." A "claim to inclusion" is central to deep democratization; perhaps (to pursue the American example a bit further) the core corruption problem is not whether specific funds are raised and spent legally, but whether citizens believe they still have a place at the table. That sense of corruption, and the question of what to do about it, points directly to whether people and groups can assert and defend their interests politically, and suggests that our definition of corruption must explicitly make room for disagreement and contention.

Two aspects of any definition are *conceptualization* (sometimes called an "essential" definition) – the basic idea we have in mind – and a *nominal definition*, or an expression of that idea in words. As for conceptualization, I do not find it useful to limit corruption to a characteristic of a particular action. So many historical, political, cultural, and situational considerations enter into that sort of judgment that we must analyze the issues and disagreements they raise, rather than attempt to resolve such differences in advance. Instead, I suggest that corruption is a continuing *systemic* problem: that of delineating acceptable domains, uses, and connections between power and wealth. That can be a controversial issue; it confronts every society, and can be resolved in a variety of ways, yet is unlikely ever to be settled once and for all. Within that conceptual frame, my nominal definition of corruption is *the abuse of public roles or resources for private benefit* – but, with those contrasting values, situations, and interests very much in mind, emphasizing that in practice "abuse," "public," "private," and even "benefit" are very much open to dispute.

For answering precisely questions like "what is a corrupt act," that definition will be unsatisfying. But disagreements over the meaning of "abuse," for example, are not just noise. They are manifestations of the clashing interests, standards, and conceptions of power that bring the basic idea of the abuse of power to life in the first place. And they can signal important underlying problems: disputed or shifting boundaries between the "public" and the "private," for example, may reflect weaknesses in key institutions, the effects of important changes in policy, or deep social divisions over the role of government. As Acemoglu and Robinson (2012: 332) note, "Inclusive economic and political institutions do not emerge by themselves. They are often the outcome of significant conflict between elites resisting economic growth and political change and those wishing to limit the economic and political power of existing elites." If we wish to understand corruption issues in real societies – that is, if we want to know how and why those with wealth and power are, or are not, called to account – political contention is not a definitional complication but rather a prime concern.

What our definition loses in terms of precise boundaries may thus be regained by the way it points out key questions: where *the basic idea of limits* upon power originates, who sets and contests those limits, and how accountability becomes credible, valued, and effective. Those issues will never be settled once and for all, any more than corruption will ever be defined to everyone's satisfaction or completely eradicated. Why reform entails fundamental political changes, what "deep democratization" means in practice, and how we get there from here[2] will be central questions in the chapters to come.

Why is corruption so tenacious?

The contemporary anti-corruption movement does not lack smart, committed leadership or supporters. In many societies people fight corruption imaginatively and, sometimes, at considerable personal

---

[2] I thank an anonymous reviewer for suggesting that way of framing the argument.

risk. Nor is there a dearth of knowledge or good ideas: new research and data have advanced our understanding dramatically over the past generation. Still, a generation of reform effort has produced mixed results at best. Let us consider three basic reasons for that: problems inherent in corruption activities themselves; gaps in our understanding of political dimensions of the issue, including difficulties of collective action and trust; and the fact that corruption can occur in contrasting forms, reflecting different combinations of causes, across diverse societies.

Deeply rooted, yet often elusive

One inherent difficulty in checking corruption is that, as we have seen, there is no consensus as to what the term means. It is used so indiscriminately in politics that it is easily dismissed as a big word for "people and policies I don't like." Not surprisingly, therefore, people disagree about what "better government" would mean in practice and how we might put it in place.

Other issues have to do with power and political economy. Reformers often confront powerful, wealthy interests all too willing and able to defend their advantages. At the highest levels modern corruption increasingly respects no international boundaries, feeds upon new technologies, and evolves far more rapidly than can our efforts to contain it. Similarly, there is a pervasive imbalance of incentives. Corruption generally benefits the "haves" and their clients at the expense of the have-nots, offering gains that are tangible, immediate, highly concentrated, and sometimes quite large. The harm, by contrast, is often widely shared, long-term, and/or intangible. Corruption hurts most people most of the time, but for any one citizen on any one day there may seem little point in fighting it – particularly where doing so can be dangerous. As we saw in the "Arab Spring" uprisings of 2011, and as we will discuss in later chapters, when the issue *does* become compelling in such risky settings, it is often part of a sweeping range of accumulated grievances, and may be touched off by symbolic events.

At times corrupt benefits trickle downward to some of the population. The cost of those crumbs from the high table usually outweighs their value, particularly over time, as they are often distributed in order to control rather than to help. It is hardly surprising that people in need will accept them, but they help corrupt leaders buy support, compromise or misuse the courts and law enforcement, and divide the opposition. When threatened, some may back down, but others will resort to rapacious theft – or to violence.

Global dynamics play a critical role too. Societies today, and particularly those depending upon natural resources, are far more exposed to global forces than were most affluent market democracies during their own emergent phases. Liberalization and integration into wider markets may limit corruption in some ways (Sandholtz and Koetzle 2000; Treisman 2000; Larraín and Tavares 2004; for qualifications to that argument see Zhu 2009), but it creates new risks too (Warner 2007). Until recently, governments of several affluent democracies gave their "home" corporations political cover and substantial tax incentives for bribing officials in the developing world (OECD 2008). Some continue to halt inquiries into such cases, or maintain legal barriers to effective prosecutions (*Forbes* 2007; *Financial Times* 2008; Guardian Unlimited 2008; House of Lords 2008; Beck 2012; Carnegy 2012). Banks and markets in affluent countries provide safe havens for the proceeds of corruption elsewhere. In the face of such challenges and dangers the wonder is not that corruption is extensive, but rather that anyone at all steps forward to fight it.

Misunderstanding the problems?

Other difficulties originate in the ways we think about corruption. In an era when international rankings of more or less everything have become popular, we rely extensively on corruption indices ranking entire societies along one dimension. As a consequence we implicitly view corruption as essentially the same wherever it occurs, varying in extent but not in nature. Not surprisingly, reform strategies tend to be similar from one case to the next. Often we envision reform as a cumulative, additive process – in effect, of stacking one administrative "best practice" upon another until national corruption levels subside. But a "best practice" here may be a bad idea there. Corruption is not an aggregate national attribute like GDP per capita; much more often it originates in highly specific dealings among particular people in specialized niches and situations. Discontinuous change, be it in the form of "big bang" reform success (Rothstein 2011) or spikes in corruption, is common.

In keeping with the idea of a single, more-versus-less, dimension of corruption we all too often estimate the effects of corruption and benefits of reform by comparison to a corruption-free state of affairs.

But there has never been such a society nor will there ever be one, which raises questions about what success might look like in practice. Calls for "political will," or for throwing the scoundrels out and replacing them with good honest folks (usually, people like ourselves) begin to look like comprehensive reform. The claimed benefits of a rational and completely honest government are powerful appeals, but in the worst cases corrupt networks and processes do not threaten the system; instead, they *are* the system. A perverse equilibrium of high corruption, low accountability, distorted development, and low expectations can become a quite durable state of affairs (Johnston 1998; Rose and Shin 2001; Mishra 2008). If corruption were suddenly to vanish it is hard to say what would take its place.

It is one thing to speak of "systematic" and "systemic" corruption, but most reform thinking still treats it as a form of deviance, or as an illness: corruption-as-cancer is a popular metaphor. A deviance perspective encourages us to overemphasize crime-prevention approaches, even where police, the courts, and the broader legal system are deeply compromised and political pressures for better performance are weak. In affluent market democracies corrupt actions may in fact be deviance from both formal and de facto norms, and crime-prevention approaches may work fairly well – particularly if wealthy and well-connected interests seldom find themselves constrained by the law. Even there, however, laws need social and political support.

The role and importance of politics

Another gap in anti-corruption thinking has been a tendency to see politics as corrupting and, more recently, to denigrate the role and value of the state. Generations of reformers, particularly in the Anglo-Saxon world, have made separating politics from administration an article of faith. Particularly in emerging democracies "good governance" has been envisioned in narrowly technical and administrative terms – in ways that Rothstein (2011: 5) describes as "normatively barren" – and the state's role has been seen essentially as a referee of sorts for liberalized economies. Politics was reduced to a feedback mechanism aiding the state's few administrative functions – as a kind of parallel market mirroring the economy. It was common to portray politics, and many distributive and regulatory policies, as a drag on governance – the latter being conceived of as a matter of sustaining economic growth – as it emphasized private-regarding demands over rational, minimalist administration, and diverted economic resources into popularity-building programs.

A key critique of the state was that rent-seeking officials interfered in markets and distorted administration in order to enrich themselves, and on a day-to-day basis that argument was right on target. More debatable, however, were the remedies it suggested: get government out of the economy, the argument ran, and officials would have nothing to sell or rent. Firms in newly freed-up markets would have little reason to pay up, drying up the "supply side" of corrupt dealings. The markets that would result would be undistorted, essentially self-regulating, and largely free of corruption. By the late 1990s, however, the desperate experiences of transitional states required a reassessment. The contention that markets, if left to themselves, would not only benefit participants but also drive broad-based development *and* be fair and open looked more like a wish (on the lineage of such views see Warner 2007: Introduction, chapters 2, 4; for empirical tests see Gerring and Thacker 2005; general critiques appear in Sampson 2005; Bukovansky 2006; and de Sousa, Larmour, and Hindess 2009).

Minimalist views of the state and the denigration of politics underestimate the value of both, not only for governing but also for reform. Missing from that view, Rothstein rightly points out, was "a normative standard for the proper role of the state, and [of] what type of moral standards citizens have the right to expect when public power is exercised" (Rothstein 2011: 6; see also Thompson 2005). Conversely, "running government like a business" may be an attractive slogan, but it is neither possible nor desirable. It is impossible because governments, where they hold meaningful power, are monopoly institutions, possessing unique powers of coercion and sources of revenue. They perform an extraordinarily broad range of functions – many of which cannot be provided by markets and many of which have important symbolic and moral dimensions – and they contend with a wide range of expectations and values that are complicated and contradictory yet (outside autocratic settings) cannot be completely ignored. Business-style government is undesirable because governments should be accountable, and political processes open, to far broader segments of the population than most businesses must (or can) deal with. Citizens, in democracies at least, possess inherent rights for which there are no direct counterparts in economic dealings, where rights and standing are generally grounded in ownership. Politics is driven not by the convergence of interests – in its simplest form, A wants what B wishes to sell – that facilitate market transactions, but more often by contention and the clash of interests. The "contagion of conflict," as Schattschneider (1960) memorably described it, is regarded by many as a drawback of political life or as noise in the policy-making system. But it is in fact a critical source of political energy and accountability. Indeed, in democracies it is the essence of public life (a classic, albeit more extreme, statement of that outlook appears in Bentley 1908).

Looked at that way, political pressures driven by self-interest are not inevitably corrupting; instead, they can create sustained incentives to check abuses of power. Reform should not merely be a matter of persuading people to "be good" or to set self-interest aside. Nor should we expect political parties and interest groups to put civic goals first: as Van Biezen (2004) points out, too often we treat the political parties of emerging societies as though they were "public utilities" established to serve democracy as a grand public good, rather than to energize it by advocating real social interests. Parties and interest groups can help people defend and better themselves, and demand fair treatment, by political means.

Collective action and trust

Given the harm corruption does to the vast majority of people, it ought to be easy to mobilize opposition to it – but it is not. Reforms that do not connect to citizens' sense of their own best interests and of fairness, or measures requiring sacrifice and risk in the pursuit of uncertain benefits, will often win little lasting support. Two difficulties are particularly acute: low levels of trust, and collective-action problems.

Successful reform requires a working level of trust, both among citizens and in those who govern (the most extensive work on those issues is that of Eric M. Uslaner; see, for example, Uslaner 2004; see also Rothstein 2011). Trust should not be confused with blind faith or total political loyalty; it need not require that we believe others are virtuous, but rather that they will keep their promises. Trust cannot be commanded or proclaimed; it reflects our understanding of the past, the intentions we attribute to others, and our expectations. Even in well-ordered societies trust, beyond a small number of primary acquaintances, is likely to be complex and conditional. Indeed, the sort of trust that best aids deep democratization and corruption control will be selective, linked to self-interest as well as to mutual benefit, and built through day-to-day experience. Its relationship with reform is reciprocal, for good government performance can build confidence and trust (Mishler and Rose 2005; Rothstein and Uslaner 2005; Espinal, Hartlyn, and Kelly 2006; Clausen, Kraay, and Nyiri 2009; Turner and Carballo 2009) – a theme to be explored in greater depth in Chapter 3, which takes up the question of building trust in fragile situations.

Without a workable level of trust, reformers have little hope of overcoming collective-action problems, which occur in two forms (this discussion draws upon Rothstein 2000, 2011; see also Ostrom 1998; Uslaner 2004; Teorell 2007). The *first-order* collective-action problem is the familiar free-rider situation (Olson 1965): fighting corruption is hard work, can be dangerous, and often involves giving up benefits now (or others anticipated) in exchange for improvements that may or may not materialize – someday. Citizens who doubt others will make such commitments are less likely to make sacrifices themselves. That is particularly likely with respect to any benefits they may be receiving from corruption – not only petty patronage, but perhaps a sense of prestige, protection, or at least predictability flowing from connections to the "big man." Moreover, reform is often portrayed as a public good: check corruption and everyone will be better off. That may well be true – someday – but many citizens will leave the heavy lifting to others, believing that they stand to benefit from any successes reformers might have on their own.

The second-order collective-action problem relates even more directly to trust. We might overcome free-rider difficulties by entering into mutual compacts; credible institutions and guarantors might persuade us that the burdens and the benefits of reform will be distributed fairly. But building such institutions and enforcing shared commitments are collective-action challenges too. Why should I pay my taxes, refuse to pay bribes, and decline petty benefits from the local warlord or political boss if I do not trust others to do the same? Low levels of trust and collective-action problems will be particularly intense in post-conflict and transitional societies, but anyone who has tried to organize a good-government group in a democracy knows these difficulties firsthand too. How lasting political settlements and credible institutions might emerge from conflict and contention will be an important concern in Chapter 2.

In chapters to come I will suggest that building trust and avoiding harm requires medium-term, indirect strategies, many of them emphasizing unexciting but demonstrably fair and effective government functions. That does *not* mean we ignore corruption or wait for perfect conditions before taking action. Some corruption controls must be launched early and pursued with diligence, as the case studies to come will emphasize. And in no way does this approach disregard the sorts of administrative improvements that are the heart of most contemporary anti-corruption efforts. But those measures must be integrated with broader efforts to build trust, and to win sustained support and credibility not only for the reforms but for effective governance itself.

Contrasting syndromes of corruption

A final, and major, complication is that corruption is not the same thing everywhere it occurs. It reflects contrasting origins, opportunities, and costs, and affects societies in quite different ways, depending upon a number of deep-rooted influences as well as more recent trends. For those reasons differing societies' corruption problems require responses appropriate to their histories, realities, and prospects.

Some time ago I explored contrasting corruption problems in a book (Johnston 2005a) analyzing statistical indicators and then testing proposed categories of corruption through case studies. It offered the argument that four major syndromes of corruption can be observed in countries around the world:

- **Influence Markets:** in a climate of active, well-institutionalized markets and democratic politics, private wealth interests seek influence over specific processes and decisions within strong public institutions, not only bribing officials directly but channeling funds to and through political figures who put their access and connections out for rent. The United States, Japan, and Germany were discussed as case studies (Ibid.: Chapter 4).
- **Elite Cartels:** in a setting of only moderately strong state institutions, colluding elites – political, bureaucratic, business, military, and so forth – maintain high-level, collusive networks by sharing corrupt benefits, and thus stave off rising political and economic competition. Examples presented were Italy, South Korea, and Botswana (Ibid.: Chapter 5).
- **Oligarchs and Clans:** a small number of contentious elites backed by personal or family followings pursue wealth and power in a climate

of very weak institutions, rapidly expanding opportunities, and pervasive insecurity, using bribes and connections where they can and violence where they must. Opponents of corruption, and of oligarchs and their factions, face major risks and uncertainties. Distinctions between public and private sectors, and between personal and official loyalties and agendas, are very weak in this syndrome. Case studies included Russia, the Philippines, and Mexico (Ibid.: Chapter 6).

- **Official Moguls:** powerful individuals and small groups, either dominating undemocratic regimes or enjoying the protection of those who do, use state and personal power – at times, a distinction of little importance – to enrich themselves with impunity. The primary loyalties and sources of power are personal or political, rather than official in nature; anti-corruption forces, like opposition to the regime generally, are very weak. In this final group China, Kenya, and Suharto's Indonesia were examined in detail (Ibid.: Chapter 7).

These four syndromes are "ideal types" (see Coser 1977: 223–4) highlighting important similarities and contrasts, and do not necessarily describe any one country's corruption problems exactly. Moreover, some generic problems, such as police corruption, occur everywhere. The syndromes are not "system types": countries that differ in important ways may be found within each group, a given society can move from one to another over time, and while they are meant to highlight a society's dominant corruption problems we might find more than one syndrome at work in various regions, economic sectors, or levels of government. They do not embody a developmental sequence in which countries move from Official Mogul corruption through intermediate stages toward Influence Markets; change of several sorts is possible. Nor do they point to "high" versus "low," or "bad" versus "good" or "functional" corruption by other names: contrasts among the four syndromes are qualitative rather than matters of degree.

The various syndromes reflect underlying trends in, and balances or imbalances between, participation and institutions: how people pursue, use, and exchange wealth and power, and the social, political, economic, and state institutions within (or outside of) which they do so. Participation involves not only the liberalized markets and politics seen in so many places over the past generation, but also a society's balance between political and economic opportunities. As Huntington (1968: 59–72) suggested years ago, where economic opportunities are more plentiful than political ones, people will likely use wealth to buy power, while in places where political opportunities outnumber the economic, power will more often be used to pursue wealth. The key point is relative balance, not whether it is easy in any absolute sense to win power or to get rich; thus, sizeable imbalances and associated corruption problems can arise in established market democracies. Institutions can be of several types: social, such as customs of reciprocity, the values and strength of civil society, and systems of norms; political, as for example parties, electoral systems, and patterns of leadership and followership; and public institutions broadly defined, including not only laws, courts, police, and bureaucracies, but also banking systems, capital markets, economic regulatory bodies, and so forth. Strong and legitimate institutions can build predictability and trust, serve as guarantors for commitments, cut transaction costs, improve government performance, and protect vigorous political and economic activities while restraining their excesses. Weak or illegitimate institutions are not only likely to fail at such tasks; they can also be used to pursue and protect a variety of corrupt and unjust activities.

Participation and institutions vary in many ways, but as shown in the earlier data analysis (Johnston 2005a: Chapter 3) certain combinations of attributes are more common than others. Affluent market democracies, for example, feature mature economies in which liberalization is largely a fait accompli; competitive politics and markets have been in place for a long time, and their institutions are generally strong. They are likely to be home to the Influence Market syndrome of corruption – one that is more complicated and worrisome than is often recognized. But there are also consolidating or reforming societies in which political and market competition is gradually increasing; institutions in such settings, while moderately effective, are generally weaker than those in the first group. There we often find Elite Cartels: interlocking networks of elites in several spheres, their common interest in fending off rising political and economic competitors cemented by sharing corrupt benefits. Elite Cartel corruption can create de facto institutionalization from above, as we shall see, but may not adapt well to changes over the long run.

Countries in a third group are often coping with major upheavals. Opportunities in both politics and the economy are proliferating in a setting of very weak and disorderly institutions. Relationships between state and society are unpredictable and open to manipulation by a few powerful players and their followings, operating in both the political and economic arenas at once – domains that may substantially overlap. Politics, the economy, and private life are marked by insecurity. Such uncertainty means that these Oligarchs-and-Clans cases suffer greatly in terms of development; because the oligarchs function in a climate of insecurity too, where gains may be difficult to protect, corruption-related violence may well be common.

The final group is made up of undemocratic regimes that by definition offer few political opportunities. Those that do exist are either tightly controlled or, because they involve challenging a regime that makes its own rules, risky; countervailing forces – civil society, parties, interest groups – will be weak, manipulated from above, or absent. Strong, independent economic institutions are uncommon in most such places, in part because fair play is the last thing powerful figures wish to see. In part because of international pressures, and in part because of rulers' prospects for personal enrichment (legitimate and otherwise), the economies of many authoritarian countries have liberalized at least slightly over the past generation, but the resulting wealth opportunities are held in relatively few hands. The result is often corruption with impunity – exploitation by a dictator, inner circle, and/or political clients, with access to economic opportunities, legitimate or otherwise, being allocated to personal favorites.

Table 1.1 (based on Johnston 2005a: Chapter 3) summarizes these broad patterns.

What are the connections between these general categories and qualitative contrasts in corruption?

Influence Market corruption

Most Influence Market societies are mature, well-institutionalized market democracies offering extensive political and economic opportunities. Competition is relatively orderly in each arena, and legitimate paths of access exist between them. Neither politicians nor wealth interests are clearly dominant – yet each side has things the other wants. Businesses, wealthy individuals and well-funded interest groups have the money politicians and parties need (or simply want); political figures have influence over policy within legislatures and bureaucracies. Private parties can bid for influence, while politicians can put their connections out for rent. Some money finds its way directly into the

Table 1.1 *Four syndromes of corruption*

Syndrome	Participation		Institutions		Examples
	Political opportunities	Economic opportunities	State/society capacity	Economic institutions	(cases in **bold** were case studies in *Syndromes of Corruption*)
Influence Markets	Mature democracies Liberalized, steady competition, and participation	Mature markets Liberalized, open; steady competition; affluent	Extensive	Strong	**United States, Japan, Germany**, Australia, France, UK, Uruguay
Elite Cartels	Consolidating/reforming democracies Liberalized, growing competition, and participation	Reforming markets Largely liberalized and open; growing competition; moderately affluent	Moderate	Medium	**Italy, South Korea, Botswana**, Argentina, Belgium, Brazil, Israel, Poland, Portugal, S. Africa, Zambia
Oligarchs and Clans	Transitional regimes Recent major liberalization; significant but poorly structured competition	New markets Recent major liberalization; extensive inequality and poverty	Weak	Weak	**Russia, Philippines, Mexico**, Bangladesh, Bulgaria, Colombia, India, Malaysia, Niger, Senegal
Official Moguls	Undemocratic Little liberalization or openness	New markets Recent liberalization; extensive inequality and poverty	Weak	Weak	**China, Kenya, Indonesia**, Algeria, Chad, Haiti, Iran, Kuwait, Nigeria, Rwanda, Syria, Uganda

hands of bureaucrats too, via bribery, but most of the action comes in the form of competition over influence and access. Influence Market corruption is unlikely to disrupt development or destabilize politics, but it remains a serious – and, as we shall see in Chapter 7, a surprisingly complex – concern both domestically and internationally.

Constitutional frameworks, political competition, free news media, secure property rights, strong civil societies, and relatively open economies in Influence Market settings do check some of the worst abuses of wealth and power. They do that in part via laws, public opinion, and institutions, but also because they create numerous legal ways to seek economic and political advantage. In fact it can become difficult to say just what is, and is not, corrupt in an Influence Market setting. Abuses are often a matter of pushing legal, even desirable, activities and connections to unacceptable extremes. Contributions to election campaigns, for example, are an accepted part of the democratic process, but contributions that are too large will strike many as corrupt; lobbying is not corrupt in itself, but can be done in ways most would regard as abusive. Precisely how large a contribution is too large, and what lobbying techniques are and are not abusive, can be a matter of contention. Most Influence Market dealings revolve around specific outcomes – winning a contract or an election, or rewriting a regulation, not looting the national treasury – although some of those specific outcomes can be very valuable and have far-reaching social implications. In fact, the very strength of public institutions raises the value of influence: favorable decisions, once made, will likely be implemented effectively. Influence Market corruption works through the system in many ways, rather than undermining it fundamentally: after all, those who trade in wealth or power are generally well served by existing arrangements.

Many Influence Market societies are seen (or offer themselves) as international models of reform, and receive good scores on international rankings. But in no way have they "solved" the corruption problem. More often they have finessed the issue by developing policies and institutions that are quite accommodating to business interests and incumbent politicians, thus reducing incentives to resort to blatantly corrupt tactics. Most economic dealings take place entirely within the private sector, under rules less restrictive than those of the public sector, and legitimate channels exist for both political influence and funding. Such factors contribute to relatively favorable corruption perceptions, but other problems – abuses at lower levels of government, as well as questions of equity and justice that have in effect been privatized – are less likely to be reflected in the indices.

Thus Influence Market corruption is well worth our concern. The banks and well-institutionalized markets in affluent democracies can be the repositories, or participate in the laundering, of corrupt gains from elsewhere. Their multinational businesses make deals abroad that would be prohibited at home. Other problems are domestic: both economic and political interests have a stake in limiting competition and protecting their advantages. The costs of their dealings may thus come in the form of political competition that is more apparent than real, economic and policy alternatives that are kept off the public agenda, policy changes and innovations that do not occur, and private advantages that get written into public policy – factors concentrating wealth and power in fewer and fewer hands. Reform, in such settings, can be challenging indeed: anyone seeking significant change or challenging the prerogatives of the well-connected will have to do so through a political system already extensively shaped by wealth and its interests.

Elite Cartel corruption

In other societies – many of them reforming, or moving into post-conflict or post-dictatorial stages – politics and markets are gradually becoming more competitive, yet institutions are only moderately strong. Political, business, bureaucratic, military, media elites, and others, unable to capitalize upon a strong institutional framework, yet constrained by increasing openness from dominating through sheer intimidation, still seek to stave off rising competitors. They do that, often, through pervasive collusion – sharing corrupt rewards to maintain networks strong enough to hold onto power. In some cases those elite networks are strong enough to govern relatively effectively, at least as compared to the likely, as opposed to ideal, alternatives.

In Elite Cartel settings power and wealth are in flux, creating both new opportunities and risks. More than in our other syndromes, corruption often is a defensive game: continued power and self-enrichment depend upon protecting existing advantages and alliances. Official positions will be valuable because state institutions, while less secure than in Influence Market cases, are not wholly ineffective. But corrupt linkages bridge public–private divides, linking top figures in many segments of society, because such collusion is strategically useful.

Laws, bureaucracies, political processes, and rights that have only moderate credibility make life more difficult for would-be competitors, and weaken anti-corruption efforts as well. Particularly in post-conflict and post-dictatorial situations civil society will likely be weak, manipulated from above, and riven by distrust.

Elite Cartels can maintain a working order of sorts and a gradual pace of change, even if they accomplish both out of self-serving motives. On the whole the societies they rule are more successful economically than Oligarch-and-Clan cases (Johnston 2005a: Chapter 5), if only because their predictability attracts some investors and lenders. Several such countries, including South Korea, Botswana, Israel, Spain, South Africa, and some of the formerly communist states of East Europe have built sustainable democracies too, while others hold regular elections that are less competitive. Reasons for such success vary from case to case, but will be further explored in Chapter 6; for now it is worth suggesting that an Elite Cartels alignment might, for a time, be a useful "halfway" situation for countries seeking to bring corruption within workable limits.

Still, Elite Cartels are in no way the "good cholesterol" of the corruption world. They can delay or distort democratic trends precisely because they have a stake in fending off competing political interests. Confronted with stress, they may not so much bend as break: during the 1997–8 Asian financial crisis, for example, the unaccountable business practices of Korea's politically privileged *chaebols* (huge family-owned industrial combines), protected by preferential lending practices bought from top leaders, were revealed as an economic house of cards. Likewise, Italy's political party system – long held together by collusion among ostensibly competing non-Communist parties – collapsed in the wake of the *Tangentopoli* scandals of the early 1990s. For those reasons, how we understand Elite Cartel corruption is critical from a reform standpoint: particularly in post-conflict and post-dictatorial societies an excessive emphasis on liberalization, and insufficient attention to institution-building – and specifically, to credible *informal* institutions – can make a bad situation far worse.

Oligarch-and-Clan corruption

In other societies rapid change – in many cases, simultaneous, if poorly integrated, political and economic transitions – and very weak institutions put immense opportunities on the table in a setting with few meaningful constraints. Would-be business people and political leaders (categories that may extensively overlap) have much to gain and, potentially, everything to lose – at times, very quickly – in a setting of profound insecurity. A variety of oligarchs and their "clans" – mass followings, judicial or organized crime connections, a bureaucratic fiefdom, or a powerful family – are among the strongest forces, at times dominating official institutions; official bodies have little credibility, and citizens who might elsewhere build a strong civil society find it prudent to keep their heads down and try to survive.

Corruption in such settings is likely to consist of a disorderly, sometimes violent scramble among contending oligarchs. In a setting of high stakes, few rules, brutal competition, and porous boundaries between the public and private sectors, contending elites parlay personal influence into wealth *and* power. Indeed, each is needed in order to win and protect the other: power is profitable but often depends upon a following that must be continually paid off and placated, for followers too are in the game for their own benefit and (outside of cases where clans are literally extended families) have many options. Unlike Elite Cartel situations, power is not centralized into an overarching network, and corruption is anything but stabilizing. Indeed, the difficulties of protecting one's gains, collecting debts, and enforcing contracts make violence, organized crime, and protection rackets integral parts of the corruption picture (Varese 2001).

The unpredictable corruption that results is not only extensive but also particularly disruptive to development (Campos, Lien, and Pradhan 1999). Investors in Elite Cartel or Official Mogul societies (more on the latter below) confront extensive corruption, but can anticipate at least some aspects of the situation. As we shall see in Chapter 5, however, Oligarch-and-Clan settings feature unpredictable, even conflicting, corrupt demands, and there may be little assurance that paying up will produce lasting benefits; yet business people risk violence if they do not comply. That state of affairs can devastate economic development: many entrepreneurs will direct their capital elsewhere or maximize short-term profits (Keefer 1996). Both corrupt and legitimate gains will often be shipped out to places with harder currencies and safer banks. Anyone confronting the oligarchs will be taking on powerful factions answerable to no one but themselves, and will have few resources or meaningful rights to fall back upon. Poverty and insecurity further disrupt alternatives, and resistance, to corruption. Shaky, oligarch-dominated institutions make administrative reforms, privatizations, transparency measures, and law-enforcement strategies ineffective, or even vehicles for further abuses. Unlike Elite Cartels and their collusion, oligarchs are unlikely to cooperate for long, if at all. They are oligarchs in the sense that much of the most significant competition occurs – often in ungoverned and intensely personal ways – among relatively few players, at times on zero-sum terms. Oligarchs may be victims as well as perpetrators of corrupt deals, depending upon who commands which advantages. Indeed, it may be difficult to say just what is public and what is private, who is a politician and who is an entrepreneur, or even who is corrupt and who is an innovator.

Post-conflict and post-dictatorial societies in a state of overall insecurity, with weak institutional frameworks and high levels of distrust, will be particularly vulnerable to Oligarch-and-Clan corruption, and thus to self-perpetuating cycles of insecurity, corruption, poverty, and violence. The problems of Russia in the years following the fall of communism are well known (a particularly tragic account, based on diaries of a murdered journalist, is found in Politkovskaya 2007; see also Freeland 2000; Hoffman 2002; Goldman 2003; Ledeneva 2006; Åslund, Guriev, and Kuchins 2010). Mexico arrived in a similar dilemma by a different route. As recently as the mid 1980s it was an Elite Cartels case, but economic liberalization and electoral reforms undermined the nation's strongest political institution – the Institutional Revolution Party (PRI) – hastening the rise of the Oligarch-and-Clan corruption that is now aggravated by the power and violence of drug cartels. Mexico's economic and political reforms were well worth doing, but careful attention must be paid to what can be put in place when less desirable institutions are dismantled. The Philippines offers a somewhat different case of Oligarchs and Clans: there, the clans are actual families, their power often reaching back over generations (McCoy 2009; Quimpo 2009).[3]

---

[3] As we shall see in a later chapter, the role of Filipino oligarchs and families should not be oversimplified: not all have been perpetrators of corruption, most have been victims of it at various points, and some of those families most prominent in politics and the economy have extensive histories of philanthropy as well. The idea is not that political families or clans are inherently corrupt, but rather that where political and economic opportunities are plentiful and formal institutions are very weak, they can embody a particular structure of corrupt dealings.

Official Mogul corruption

A final group of countries is characterized by undemocratic rule, economic opportunities that are growing at greater or lesser rates, and – again – very weak institutions. While Oligarch-and-Clan cases can be confusing in terms of who, if anyone, is in charge, Official Mogul settings are dominated from the top. Political opportunities are few; those in the economy are controlled by a few powerful figures. A few may pursue pro-growth policies, but others plunder the economy, distributing economic opportunities to family or personal favorites. Opposition forces and civil society, to the extent that either term is meaningful, are weak, intimidated, or manipulated. In smaller or more unified societies the key figures may be a dictator, family, or tight ruling circle, and power is personal in its sources and use. In larger or more fragmented countries multiple people or groups can monopolize fragments of state authority, exploiting them more independently. Of our four syndromes, Official Moguls is least focused upon influence *within* official processes: state institutions and offices may be merely useful tools in the search for wealth.

Economies in most such societies are liberalizing in limited ways, if only in response to global pressures and incentives. Officials can exploit emerging economic opportunities with impunity if they enjoy top-level status or protection; in more fragmented settings they can wheel and deal independently to the extent that they do not exceed general limits set from above. Integration into the world economy may check corruption to some degree, as noted above. But authoritarian rulers just beginning to open up markets, and facing little competition from a domestic private sector, can monopolize flows of goods, capital, and aid, cutting lucrative deals with international businesses. Corruption is scarcely the sole cause of poverty in these societies: often they depend upon primary exports such as oil, a situation widely thought to distort development (Barro 1999; Leite and Weidmann 1999; Sachs and Warner 2001; Papyrakis and Gerlagh 2004; Dietz, Neumayer, and de Soysa 2007; Shaxson 2007; for a dissent see Brunnschweiler and Bulteb 2008). Even in poor countries a political monopoly can be the source of great wealth.

Mature market democracies resemble each other in many ways, but in Official Mogul cases much depends upon the personalities and agendas of those in power. Some may seek reform or at least refrain from the worst corruption, and where that is the case considerable growth may occur. Others ruthlessly exploit both state and economy, with devastating results. Official Mogul societies are not necessarily stable, however: those who hold power without rules may face enemies, rather than competitors or political oppositions, who are similarly unconstrained save by the threat of violence. That sort of insecurity may drive egregious "hand-over-fist" corruption (Scott 1972) as leaders under threat take as much as they can, as fast as they can take it. Governance and development trends within this group of countries can thus vary widely. Several Middle Eastern states fit this pattern, to varying degrees, along with a number of African countries (particularly those marked by military rule and internal strife). China's explosive growth and its corruption are well known; there, officials and favored business cronies at several levels, often operating within local or regional bailiwicks, exploit an increasingly fragmented party and state apparatus. Pre-1998 Indonesia, by contrast, was in some respects a national patronage system dominated by Suharto, his family and protégés (Johnston 2005a: Chapter 7; see also Liddle 1985, 1996; Vatikiotis 1998; Robertson-Snape 1999).

In Official Mogul cases most reforms accomplish little without the backing of top figures, for there are few independent political forces to demand accountability. Privatizations, high-level commissions, and intensified bureaucratic oversight can become the means of top-down political discipline, revenge against critics, or smokescreens for further abuses. Reforms without solid social and institutional foundations may make matters worse: Kenya's rapacious corruption during the 1990s was exacerbated, if anything, by the launching of competitive elections, because systems of legitimate political funding and mobilization were lacking. The main effect was to create political uncertainties for Daniel arap Moi and his ruling circle, who responded with egregious high-level theft and deal-making designed to keep key political leaders on board (Klopp 2000, 2002).

None of these four syndromes of corruption will fit a country's situation exactly, and in practice it may not be easy to categorize a case (an Appendix to this book suggests ways to recognize various syndromes in action). Even if the specific categories are unconvincing, however, the main points they make – that corruption problems can vary in kind, and that a good idea in one case may not be applicable elsewhere – deserve careful thought. More detailed discussion of corruption, deep democratization, and reform in the context of each syndrome appears in chapters 4 through 7.

Conclusion

But what is deep democratization in practice, and what are its prospects – particularly in the more unpromising situations discussed here? Is there really reason to think that reform based on the contentious advocacy of groups' own interests will produce anything other than more contention – or, indeed, more corruption? After all, many of the societies we are most concerned about in corruption terms are fragile in various ways – dealing with the aftermath of conflict or dictatorships, suffering from very weak institutions and low levels of social and political trust, and trying to make their way in a world dominated by powerful and intrusive forces that may be scarcely accountable themselves. And what of the established democracies? I have suggested that they, too, could benefit from deep democratization. But what do those ideas mean in practice? In Chapter 2, exploring the deep democratization idea in more detail, and in Chapter 3, considering the problems of fragile societies, we will consider those issues in more detail.

2 | "Deep democratization" and the control of corruption

Right, as the world goes, is only in question between equals in power, while the strong do what they can and the weak suffer what they must.
– Thucydides, the Melian dialogue

Why isn't there *more* corruption?

Corruption is often portrayed in terms of infection, deterioration, or plague, spreading relentlessly and threatening societies with collapse. We are told that it is on the rise around the world, even though we have no real way of showing that that is true, and often it is implied that there was a time when there was far less of it – or maybe even none.

But maybe the real question is not why there is so much corruption, but rather why there is not *much more* of it? Maybe we should ask how it was that the powerful and wealthy were ever brought within limits, and how the idea that rulers should be answerable to others took root and became credible. After all, politics and government did not originate in a civic Eden. For centuries, governing consisted of swinging the biggest stick. Power and its rewards justified more or less any action, to the extent that justification was needed at all, and notions of a "public" – much less, one with any rights overriding the personal interests of rulers – were illusory. The remarkable thing may not be that elites stray from the straight and narrow, but rather that anyone has ever been able to call them to account.

In this chapter, I will lay out the notion of deep democratization – processes whereby citizens become able to defend themselves and their interests by political means. It is "democratization," not in the sense of establishing formal democratic institutions for their own sake, but rather in the sense of broadening the range of people and groups with some say about the ways power and wealth should – and should not – be pursued, used, and exchanged. After a brief thought experiment that builds upon that idea, I will examine historical anti-corruption struggles in England, and in American cities during the heyday of machine politics. In both cases contentious factions defending their own interests succeeded in imposing limits upon power, often in the course of contention over other issues. In contemporary societies, of course, the path from here to there is rarely clear; progress is contentious and difficult to define, much less measure, and it can be hard to tell good news from bad. The fundamental challenge, I will suggest, is to help create situations in which citizens can control corruption in the course of asserting their own interests and defending their own well-being. The latter part of this chapter will identify four basic reform tasks, varying in importance depending upon the syndrome of corruption in question, that are essential if deep democratization is to take root.

That approach to reform is long-term in nature, even though it may well include episodes of sharp change. It is indirect: often the emphasis is less upon attacking corrupt people and practices – in many cases, a matter of mobilizing the weak against the strong – than upon building social and political foundations for such challenges and limits in the future. It has no single end point – I will suggest in Chapter 7, for example, that today's affluent democracies face particularly serious corruption problems – and provides no guarantees against backsliding. That does not mean we do nothing until all elements of reform are fully in place: specific corruption controls will figure into the process during all phases. But there is little point in mobilizing citizen support, and wasting scarce reform opportunities, to fight battles we are doomed to lose. Rather than devising a grand corruption control strategy and then seeking citizen support for it, we will be far better off pushing for those reforms and controls most likely to strengthen citizens' ability to defend their own interests at any given time. It follows that the overall emphasis of deep democratization is upon political contention, driven by citizens' own problems and interests. That may make it unappealing to anyone seeking broad moral consensus, but those seemingly minor issues and interests both energize the process and are essential to sustaining any progress. Values and beliefs about good government and political morality will undeniably be important to some participants, and will be strategically useful for encouraging alliances among partially overlapping interests and outlooks. But while such values may help build and focus the effort, self-interest is more likely to sustain it.

Power, countervailing forces, and accountability

Political contention is not only central to reform, but also shapes basic notions of corruption. In contemporary societies we take for granted that leaders and officials ought to serve interests above and beyond their own. But where do such ideas originate, how do they gather credible strength, and what forces reshape them over time?

Instead of visualizing a corruption-free society, imagine another, equally improbable oversimplification – albeit one with more historical resonance. Imagine an absolute, utterly unchallenged autocrat. No laws or countervailing forces restrain that ruler's actions. The right to rule flows from having the biggest army and following, taking the most ruthless attitude toward possible challengers, claiming divine blessing, or – via hereditary succession – a lucky dip into the gene pool. Notions of "the public" and its interests mean nothing; what *we* might think of as "the public" is, in this imagined case, just there to be exploited. Because of the absolute nature of our imaginary autocrat's power, any views those people might have regarding right and wrong, wealth and power, or legitimacy matter not at all.

In what sense can our autocrat be corrupt? There are no rules to break. No one else's well-being matters. There are no collective principles of loyalty, no constraints, and no principles transcending the ruler's whims. We can easily judge the autocrat corrupt by our standards – standards that he or she is free to ignore – or as morally corrupt in the eyes of God, a definitive judgment for some but not much of a restraint in the here and now. Is there corruption here in the classical sense of a collective state of being? Dobel (1978) emphasizes the loss of a ruler's or regime's ability to inspire loyalty – an acknowledgment that others do matter. But as our absolute autocrat can rule through fear, loyalty is beside the point. Contemporary meanings of corruption resting upon rules, checks and balances, duties of office, the public interest, or positions of trust have no meaning in our imaginary case.

This example, obviously, is a caricature. But it elaborates on a key aspect of the definition of corruption proposed in Chapter 1 – the systemic and essentially *political* challenge of delineating domains for, and boundaries around, the acceptable pursuit, use, and exchange of power and wealth. However much we may justify them in terms of fundamental values, such limits are not natural features of the political landscape. They exist because someone demanded them – most likely, because they had a significant stake in upholding some limits – not just because they were good ideas. At some point rulers found it advantageous to abide by such limits, and to take others' views and well-being into consideration. The path to such developments is usually contentious, for as we have noted, a rule or agreement strong enough to protect someone will usually restrain someone else. To build such limits citizens need basic security and a measure of liberty (Isham, Kaufmann, and Pritchett 2000), as well as political resources of their own.

Rules and values

For centuries, having "a role in politics" meant being a relative, retainer, or crony of some powerful person, and thus having a share of loot or favor. Political propriety often began and ended with what Friedrich (1974: 102) calls "The ancient rule that 'the King can do no wrong.'" Theobald adds that "If we go back to the pre-modern era ... the state is not regarded as an impersonal legal entity but as the living embodiment of an inheritance which reached into the dim and distant past" – in many cases, as personal property in the sense both of a claim to territory, and of office as private property (Theobald 1990: 19–20). Further justifications of power and its benefits, save perhaps placing both beyond debate by claims of divine right, were rarely required.

The evolution of a "public" domain, and of a state that was owned by no one, passed through a variety of intermediate stages. In England from the eleventh through the seventeenth centuries, for example, practices like tax- and customs-"farming," whereby revenue functions were in effect franchised out to entrepreneurs who recouped their investments by keeping all or part of the revenues, provided income and status to officials and more predictable revenues for the sovereign (Ashton 1956). There and elsewhere, what would later become public offices were treated as personal property, openly bought and sold (Peck 1990; Swart 1949). No notions of merit, save perhaps loyalty, were involved, although any attempt at merit selection might well have recruited many of the same people. Such "freehold offices" were defended by Montesquieu and Bentham on grounds of efficiency, and by Burke as a legitimate property right (Scott 1972: 89–90, 93). In France, Spain, England, and to a degree China, networks of "freehold bureaucrats" supplied their patrons with revenue, political support, and an intelligence network (Ibid.: 89–94). By the sixteenth and seventeenth centuries English monarchs were regarded as "the fountain of virtue" – a notion that not only conveyed moral force but also, in the fountain metaphor, reflected the ways they bought support through patronage (Peck 1990). Ideas like these were quite practical ways of projecting power, backed up by symbolic and normative claims.

Such practices had their drawbacks, however. Once an office changed hands it was generally sold for good. To supplant a freeholder by creating a rival or superior office could mean a fight. Moreover, as societies expanded, would-be elites became too numerous to be bought off. In Elizabethan England, for example, university graduates had long been accustomed to obtaining church or state offices via personal preferment. But when Oxford and Cambridge began to turn out graduates in unprecedented numbers, those who were left out took the lead in objecting to what had been an accepted and, for their predecessors, an advantageous system of patronage (Hurstfield 1973: 155–6). Similarly, various estates, or what Van Klaveren (2002) termed "intermediary groups," tended to advocate interests of their own. They included, among others, the clergy, military officers, civil servants, merchants, and eventually members of guilds and professions. While such groups were in some respects precursors of civil society they were scarcely tribunes of the people or moral innovators; Van Klaveren notes that they frequently encouraged corruption as they sought advantages for themselves (Ibid.: 88). Still, via stalemate and obstinacy, if not through any official powers, they could be a counterweight to the sovereign's day-to-day power, their tenacity reflecting their lasting interests in protecting wealth and status while expanding their own autonomy.

Those convoluted, back-and-forth processes of contention, resistance, and stalemate followed no grand overall design or any single direction. They varied considerably from place to place, and while idealism was by no means absent – consider the Putney Debates or the *Déclaration des droits de l'homme et du citoyen* – more often than not there was nothing noble about the tactics and motives involved. For both the Putney debaters and the *Déclaration* property – and the rights that should or should not be linked to it – were major concerns. As Kettle has pointed out, Putney was really driven by contention over who should, and should not, be allowed to vote, and while Thomas Rainborough memorably proclaimed that "[T]he poorest he that is in England hath a life to live, as the greatest he," that idea excluded women (Kettle 2007).

Still, as societies grew and diversified, political interests proliferated and helped bring a different conception of government into being, as Scott (1972: 96) notes:

[I]n the nineteenth century, when the more democratic form of government limited the aristocracy, and the modern idea of the State came into existence, the conception of public office as private property disappeared. The State became considered as a moral entity and the exercising of public authority as a duty.

We invoke such notions today when we speak of "the rule of law," not just as a good way to do public and private business, but as a matter of justice. But fundamental as those ideas may seem today, they are products of political struggle and contention.

Thus what we may see as bedrock civic values are as much the outcomes of democratization as they were its causes. Years ago Rustow made a similar argument: the rise of democracy, he wrote, required "prolonged and inconclusive political struggle ... [T]he protagonists must represent well-entrenched forces ... and the issues must have profound meaning to them" (Rustow 1970: 352). In those struggles, "Democracy was not the original or primary aim; it was sought as a means to some other end or it came as a fortuitous byproduct of the struggle" (Ibid.: 353). There is nothing inevitable or irreversible about it, but over time political settlements among contending groups – even if compromised and conceded only grudgingly – can solidify into institutions made legitimate and effective by the fact that they protect real interests. Similarly, Rustow concluded that factors sustaining democracy where it is strong – literacy, affluence, multi-party politics, or a middle class, for example – are not necessarily the ones that created it. An analogous argument can be made with respect to corruption control: checks and balances, mechanisms of transparency and accountability, the values they reflect, and the rules that delineate them may be expressed in the impersonal language of legality and morality. But they came from somewhere – from people and groups defending themselves from abuses by others. Where they work, they are effective because significant parts of society have a stake in their success. Where the active groups and interests making up such social and political foundations are weak or absent, even the best anti-corruption ideas will likely fail. Our challenge in controlling corruption, therefore, is not just to come up with better rules, administrative procedures, and incentives. We must first build the political foundations they require.

Drawing the lines: historical examples

Deep democratization is often disorderly, involves many reverses, and is driven by what appear to be narrow interests. It does not necessarily culminate in democracy itself in any formal sense; indeed, as we shall see in later chapters, most of today's established democracies have deep democratization challenges of their own, while we can identify some less-than-optimal "halfway" situations that offer real opportunities for progress. Instead the core idea is political contention leading, over time, to settlements with the potential to become the basis of institutions setting workable standards for the ways governing power is taken and used. Rothstein makes that sort of argument about the "quality of government":

> democracy, which concerns *access to government power*, cannot be a sufficient criterion of quality of government. If quality of government merely equaled democracy, the importance of *the way power is exercised* by government authorities would be left out (Rothstein 2011: 6; emphasis added).

Lessig (2011: 1–39), too, provides a telling critique of the ways both public institutions and many business and professional associations in the United States systematically deviate from citizens' expressed will or best interests – the service of which being, after all, the basis of the popular trust they enjoy – because of the influence of money, much as a compass exposed to a magnet will deviate from true north. That the mechanisms of influence and funding involved are usually fully legal – indeed, in many cases enjoying constitutional protection – does not negate the fact that public power, resources, and trust are being abused, and that unfair and unearned advantages are being won, in the process.

For Rothstein, impartiality is a far more important criterion of the quality of government than democracy as such. In a strict sense impartiality means that official decisions and actions "shall not take into consideration anything about the citizen/case that is not stipulated beforehand in the policy or the law" (Strömberg 2000, as quoted in Rothstein 2011: 13). In terms of how contention might eventually lead to political settlements and institution-building, impartiality embodies a useful point of convergence among contending groups who, after all, might not trust each other any more than they trust the rulers they seek to check. Goodin (2004: 100) makes a similar point by a different route, arguing that the "antithesis of justice is favouritism" (see also Dworkin 1977; Barry 1995; Kurer 2005). Impartiality as a criterion for the quality of government has its critics (Rothstein 2011: 24–30), but among its virtues is the fact that impartiality does not impose any particular kind of policy or institutional framework as a further criterion. Governments drawing upon a wide range of mandates and pursuing contrasting policies might still be impartial; democratic majorities, on the other hand, often are not, and democratic institutions can and do act in partial and corrupt ways.

Deep democratization might, then, be thought of as a political process by which impartiality can be sought as a working principle. It is not "democracy" but rather democratization in a simpler sense – broadening the range of groups and outlooks shaping basic rules of power. As Acemoglu and Robinson (2012: 79) put it, "Politics is the process by which a society chooses the rules that will govern it."

How have such processes played out in practice?

Confronting the King

Consider the case of Magna Carta (see, for example, Drew 2004). Readers of a certain age may recall civics lessons portraying England's Great Charter of the early thirteenth century as heralding the dawn of modern democracy. But it was really a list of grievances, and a set of demands for limits upon royal power, drawn up by a small number of barons who were fed up with King John, and with his demands for funds and foot soldiers for his wars in France. The King was over a barrel: unless he agreed to the Charter he would be hard put to continue his quest for land. So he signed – with what actual intentions, we can only guess – agreeing to limits regarding property, taxation, trials and the treatment of prisoners, and other concerns. Democracy or "good government" had little to do with the deal; the barons spoke primarily for themselves. The restrictions imposed by the Charter had to be reasserted many times; they eventually took hold because people with meaningful political resources, including monarchs themselves after a time, had good reasons to see that limits be honored.

King John was not one of today's constitutional monarchs, but neither was he our imaginary autocrat. The authors of Magna Carta had resources and social standing of their own and, given the King's immediate dilemma, enough security and political "space" to put their influence to use. Monarchs of the day were not accountable to "the public"; as they made their progress around the countryside they and their minions often commandeered whatever they pleased. But those monarchs also had burdens of sorts: they occasionally faced rivals, and conflict could be risky and expensive. They were responsible for defending the realm, if only because major segments of it were their own. As territories expanded and societies grew larger and more differentiated, factions and networks of influence multiplied. Sovereigns increasingly needed money, not only for its own sake but also to fund their emerging government-like activities and buy the support of those they could not easily oversee or coerce. Where the money came from, who got pieces of it, and what was expected in return became matters of continuing conflict. By the early seventeenth century, those conflicts contributed to systemic change and new ideas about accountability.

Stuart England: Crown, Parliament, and power

Sometimes the key parties to contention are other office holders. In Stuart England, Parliament took the lead in resisting what it saw as abusive uses of royal power. Both the House of Lords and the Commons spoke for segments of society, but Parliament was also defending itself in a struggle over issues including religion, taxation, and its own autonomy.

By the 1620s Parliament's influence had been significantly undercut by generations of royal patronage (Roberts 1980; Peck 1990). Tudor and Stuart monarchs, while far more powerful than those of the modern era, still had to go to Parliament to request tax levies, backing for wars, and the like. That was of particular urgency for Stuart monarchs such as James I, who was chronically short of cash and who, as a newcomer from Scotland, could not take political backing for granted. Because an uncooperative Parliament could frustrate monarchs in a variety of ways, they found it useful to buy support, or neutralize opposition, by handing out gifts and privileges to members and others. Parliament debated anti-bribery bills and measures to forbid or control the trade in offices in 1621, 1625, 1626, and 1628 (Peck 1990: 196). Such initiatives were proposed as checks on power but were also attempts by Parliament to protect itself in the larger power struggle. Proposals to extend the franchise similarly were envisioned as broadening Parliament's political base; they were backed by "(s)urprisingly radical arguments ... about the need to involve as many men as possible in elections to withstand the threat from the great to parliament's existence" (Hirst 1986: 136). Corruption provided much of the vocabulary of those struggles, but issues of money, power, and prerogative gave them their energy.

Under the ancient doctrine that "the King can do no wrong," legislating limits directly on the sovereign was out of the question at that point, but Parliament could move against the counselors through whom he acted. Thus during the years before the civil wars of the 1640s, Parliament revived its old thirteenth-century powers of impeachment. In ways that are familiar to many countries today, a list of charges was drawn up against the accused, who was then summoned to Parliament for trial. Unlike today's impeachments, however, conviction could lead not just to loss of office but to execution (Peck 1990). The sensational impeachments of royal protégés such as Francis Bacon, Thomas Howard, Lionel Cranfield, and the Duke of Buckingham (Doig 1984: 37–42; Hirst 1986; Peck 1990) featured charges of misconduct, but were also battles in the larger war between Parliament and Crown. Not only were evidence, laws, and procedures hotly contested; new ideas about accountability emerged in the course of the struggle. In 1640–1, for example, Parliament impeached and tried the Earl of Strafford on various charges of corruption and influence-dealing, threatening to send him to the Tower (this discussion draws upon Roberts 1980). Accusers, looking to strengthen their hand against a royal protégé, claimed that despite his role of counselor to the sovereign, Strafford was accountable to Parliament, and could thus be charged and tried despite royal objections. Strafford responded with an idea of his own: Parliament could not impeach him on its own, because both Parliament and royal counselors were accountable to the electors.

Those are quite recognizable notions of accountability today, but they came into being as clubs to swing in a bitter political fight. Parliament was trying to protect itself from the influence of the King while Strafford was fighting for his life; neither side was proposing plans for good government. The electorate in question was very small and frequently manipulated by local landowners; many locations did not even have MPs of their own. Nonetheless, ideas formed in the heat of conflict eventually became principles of the Constitutional Monarchy that emerged – after three civil wars, a regicide, a restoration, and an "abdication" by James II that was in fact a convenient fiction created by Parliament – from the political settlement of 1688–9. The Bill of Rights enacted in 1689 not only settled the issue of William and Mary's succession, but also defined and restated the rights of Parliament itself, as well as those of citizens, as Parliament spoke for them (Lock 1989). Behind the façade of a reshaped monarchy, both Parliament and royal advisors came to hold accountable roles with real, yet limited, powers. Later parliaments still had to resist inappropriate influence, and in the early seventeenth century the House of Commons established a Committee on Privileges to defend its independence. Until the changes following the 1995 Nolan Report (House of Commons 1995), that Committee was its anti-corruption watchdog. It defended the principle that a member's first loyalty is to the House itself – an ethical doctrine, to be sure, but reflecting practical political calculations that would be recognized instantly by those who fought Crown patronage in the seventeenth century (Jordan 1998).

Fighting the bosses: anti-machine reformers in American cities

The struggle against machine bosses in American cities during the nineteenth and early twentieth centuries was a self-conscious campaign for better government. Reformers tapped into powerful moral sentiments; one stream of the movement flowed directly out of Civil-War-era Abolitionism (Anechiarico and Jacobs 1996), while the Anti-Saloon League and the early stirrings of the women's rights movement added broad-based popular support on many issues (Kerr 1980; Okrent 2010). Social reformers, urban planners, and anti-slum activists also backed the reform coalition, while anti-immigrant and anti-Catholic groups joined in for reasons of their own.

So powerful were reform appeals – and so blatant were the abuses by city bosses and their minions – that it is tempting to view the anti-machine movement through its own images of good versus evil. But like the barons who drew up Magna Carta and the parliamentary forces which contended with Stuart kings, many reformers were motivated by their own interests as well (Hofstadter 1955). Once-powerful native or "Yankee" ethnic groups and businessmen, many of whom had amassed considerable wealth, resented the bosses for pushing them out of their "natural" positions of political privilege – all the more because the machine built its electoral base in immigrant and poor neighborhoods. Later-arriving immigrants, who might have welcomed the boss's patronage, saw it continue to flow disproportionately to earlier arrivals; like the sixteenth-century Oxbridge graduates noted above, they railed against a spoils system in large part because it short-changed them. Resentment of high taxes, the waste and theft of public funds, poor-quality services and facilities, costly demands for bribes and kickbacks, and favoritism in law-enforcement and regulatory functions drove many business people into the camp of reform. Anti-immigrant groups feared the boss's immigrant backers would take over their jobs.

Andrew Dickson White's classic anti-machine statement from 1890 reflects that mix of idealism and resentment:

> Without the slightest exaggeration we may assert that, with very few exceptions, the city governments of the United States are the worst in Christendom – the most expensive, the most inefficient, and the most corrupt. The city halls of these larger towns are the acknowledged centers of the vilest corruption ... As a rule, the men who sit in the councils of our larger cities dispensing comfort or discomfort, justice or injustice, beauty or deformity, health or disease, to this and to future generations, are men who in no other country would think of aspiring to such positions. Some of them, indeed, would think themselves lucky in keeping outside the prisons ... [W]e are attempting to govern our cities upon a theory which has never been found to work practically in any part of the world ... What is this evil theory? It is simply that the city is a political body; that its interior affairs have to do with national political parties and questions. My fundamental contention is that a city is a corporation; that as a city it has nothing whatever to do with general political interests; that party political names and duties are utterly out of place there ... The work of a city being the creation and control of the city property, it should logically be managed as a piece of property by those who have created it, who have a title to it, or a real substantial part in it ... Under our theory that a city is a political body, a crowd of illiterate peasants freshly raked in from Irish bogs, or Bohemian mines, or Italian robber nests, may exercise virtual control. How such men govern cities, we know too well; as a rule they are not alive even to their own most direct interests (White 1890: 357, 358, 368).

White's inflammatory language should not distract us from the fact that machine governments were wasteful and corrupt (Caro 1974: Chapter 18). Industrialization and immigration were turning many small cities into major urban centers, overwhelming existing municipal and charitable institutions while creating opportunities for anyone willing to play political hardball. Machine politicians took advantage of chaotic electoral laws and administrative procedures to take power, where necessary through vote-buying, fraud, and intimidation. Once in office, bosses used all the resources of government – personnel, contracting, policing, inspection functions, and franchising of utilities and rapid transit – to reward themselves and their friends while penalizing their enemies. The resulting facilities and services were often of poor quality, and were apportioned on the basis of political loyalty rather than need; meanwhile, municipal payrolls, budgets, and debt mushroomed.

The battle between bosses and reformers may have been expressed in terms of corruption and virtue, but the underlying conflict was about power and self-interest. Arguments that city government should be non-political were not just an objection to mismanagement; they were also a complaint by those who had once dominated local politics but could no longer win. Municipal payrolls fed the "spoils system" (Arnold 2003) that rewarded the machine's friends and sustained its army of political foot soldiers. Smaller benefits – food, help with the police and landlords, and occasional bits of cash – flowed to voters who had nowhere else to turn for help (Merton 1957). But the boss was no friend of the poor, and his help came at a price, for the point was not social uplift. Rather, it was control. Loyal backers could hope for benefits but others, no matter how needy, were out in the cold (Stave 1972).

Businesses, too, were treated as political friends or enemies. Some business leaders actually helped consolidate rising machines (Shefter 1976). Many had backgrounds and interests different from those of the old patricians; political influence could be good for business. But as the machine's political monopoly hardened, business became just another target for exploitation. The price of favors rose, bosses took larger cuts of each major deal, and harassment of uncooperative businesses intensified. The lack of accountability, and the weakness of the forces confronting the machine, that defined the heyday of boss rule was symbolized by one of Thomas Nast's most famous anti-Tammany Hall cartoons: a huge hand held New York City under its thumb, and the caption – a quotation from boss William M. Tweed – read, "What are you going to do about it?"

By the end of the nineteenth century, business people in many American cities had moved solidly into the camp of reform. They sought fair treatment, lower taxes, better public services, and an end to bribes and kickbacks – not just as good ideas in themselves, but as changes that would also make business more predictable and profitable. Upper-status groups sought to regain lost influence. Less-favored ethnic communities, many of them poorer than those that had first been drawn into the machine, sought help on a basis of need, not political loyalty. Ending machine corruption might build a better city, but there were personal stakes on the table as well.

The reform movement did not end corruption, but in many places it helped uproot the machines. Some victories happened at the polls, although reformers learned that bosses could easily make a comeback. Others took place in state legislatures, where anti-urban sentiment could be mobilized against bosses and immigrants. Civil service codes attacked the spoils system. The non-partisan ballot and at-large elections of city councils (two of White's primary prescriptions),[1] new forms of government such as the City Manager plan, and a shift toward bureaucracy and "scientific management" all chipped away at the boss's monopoly and discretion. Reformers were also aided by post-World-War-I restrictions on immigration, the advent of the New Deal and its need-based benefits, and post-war suburbanization. By the mid twentieth century full-blown machine politics was but a memory in many American cities, even if some of its practices did survive in many places.

But while good-government measures were cloaked in the symbolism of the public interest, in no way did they benefit all. In general they favored the literate, English-speaking, relatively affluent types whose interests drove reform in the first place. At-large elections and the non-partisan ballot depressed turnouts in poorer and working-class districts while favoring candidates with money and elite connections, again diluting the voting power of ethnic enclaves (Arnold 2003). Civil service examinations channeled jobs to the educated. City manager systems were more responsive to those with bureaucratic and professional skills. Bureaucracies, even if well-managed internally, became autonomous islands making it difficult to govern (Lowi 1968). In many places reform imposed controls so extensive that agencies became inefficient, inflexible, and hostile to innovation (Anechiarico and Jacobs 1996). A reform

---

[1] White also urged the creation of powerful Boards of Control to be made up solely of property owners. While that idea did not gain currency, many reformed cities did create Boards of Estimate to oversee expenditures, taxation, and budgeting. In some instances those Boards were appointed, not elected, and in many cities they primarily served the interests of property owners (Rubin 1998).

movement that sought to insulate administration from political influence – an understandable reaction to the bosses' politicization of virtually everything – succeeded in many ways. But in the process it produced isolated, unresponsive governments (Lineberry and Fowler 1967; Arnold 2003).

"Good government" and "the public interest" were both powerful symbols and, for a portion of the anti-machine movement, genuine goals. But reformers built governments that best served people like themselves. The movement claimed to drive politics out of local government, but in its origins, its sustaining incentives, and the changes it produced, it was profoundly political.

From contention to convergence: renovators, coalitions, and useful stalemates

Self-interested political contention thus would seem to be essential to reform. But how might contention, particularly when driven by issues people care about and will take risks to pursue, lead toward agreement – and then, to the emergence of legitimate institutions? If anti-corruption advocates encourage such contention, how can they steer it toward some sort of convergence?

The simplest answer is that there is nothing inevitable about contention leading to agreement and institutions. More often than not, contention leads to more contention, often with the initial issue and participants getting lost in a larger, shifting process. "Steering" contention, in the sense of keeping it contained and focused, is even less likely, if only because the essence of deep democratization is people acting on their own interests in their own ways. Institution-building as a dedicated activity can be costly and uncertain, particularly in fragile or low-trust situations; for that reason it is central to Rothstein's (2011) "second-order" problems of collective action.

Still, as our historical examples suggest, sometimes contention does lead to political settlements, and to new or renewed institutions that serve various interests tolerably well and thus acquire legitimacy and credibility. That they may be far less than ideal is both inevitable and a secondary concern, at least initially; the essential accomplishment will be new rules and procedures for politics and governing that engage a broad range of interests. How might that come to pass?

Reaching political settlements

Exploitation at the hands of the powerful can be an intolerable state of affairs, and it is not surprising that people will often resist it. Similarly, those on top of the situation will resist challenges to their power, for they have much to lose. But contention has its costs for all sides as well: in addition to the direct costs of taking action – finding resources for a group of angry farmers, or deploying police or soldiers to resist them – there are also more general costs such as risk, uncertainty, and danger. The disruption of life and the economy, or the opportunity costs of forgoing other activities, are real. There is also sheer fatigue and exhaustion, particularly where contention has been protracted. While those under challenge – the rulers, who are quite possibly also exploiters – have more to gain or lose in the conflict and possess more resources, often extracted from others, they too may well find continuing contention and repression costly in a variety of ways. The stress of facing enemies, rather than just competitors who must play within certain agreed rules, can be considerable.

At times, anti-corruption forces may win clear victories; perhaps more frequently, they will see their efforts come to naught. But in some cases we will see stalemates, and a point at which it becomes more attractive to go forward under a few rules rather than in a setting of continued tension. For those confronting the rulers, the resulting agreements are likely to be far from perfect but can still be a way to realize *some* benefits or protection. Therein lies the importance of self-interest – "get your hands off my land" – in sustaining deep democratization, rather than only seeking public goods such as "better government for all." Elites facing challenges may accede to agreements with little real intention of honoring them – or if they do honor them, may well do so reluctantly rather than face an even more uncertain future. During the agitation that led to the first of the great Reform Acts in the United Kingdom in the early nineteenth century, Earl Grey, the Prime Minister, had little affection for the idea of broadening the franchise, but nonetheless acquiesced:

There is no-one more decided against annual Parliaments, universal suffrage and the ballot, than I am. My object is not to favour but to put an end to such hopes and projects ... The principle of my reform is, to prevent the necessity of revolution ... reforming to preserve and not to overthrow (quoted in Acemoglu and Robinson 2012: 311).

Most political settlements are just that – parties agreeing to settle for something. They contain little magic: convergence on some points may fall apart or merely shift the focus of contention to other grievances. In other cases, however, agreeing to make taxation more predictable, to honor property rights, or to restrain a president's gangs of thugs may, over time, reshape mutual expectations. Regularized taxation may give those in power more predictable revenues, stronger property rights can contribute to general prosperity and reduced violence, and the former thugs may evolve into a militia or police force useful to many segments of society. It is less important that emerging institutions embody "best practices" than that, in the eyes of engaged groups and interests, *they work*.

Three scenarios

Such desirable outcomes are far from inevitable, and there is no simple path from here to there. Acemoglu and Robinson (2012: 79) argue that "When there is conflict over institutions, what happens depends on which people or group wins out in the game of politics – who can get more support, obtain additional resources, and form more effective alliances. In short, who wins depends on the distribution of political power in society." That point is persuasive, although the cases to come will show that it is not always clear who is winning, or whether contention has actually led to a stalemate. Still, there are ways in which political settlements and institutions enjoying significant support might emerge.

One such possibility, central to many mainstream anti-corruption scenarios, is a broad-based good-government movement led by renovators who have an overall institutional design in hand. As the American anti-machine movement illustrates, such movements can produce major changes, although they likely require unusually favorable circumstances – a generally sound legal and legislative system, a free press, and leaders possessing major resources and skilled at making broad moral appeals. Too often, however, such circumstances are not in place; moreover, the grassroots connections of that sort of movement may be more apparent than real (the business elites who led the reform movement in many American cities were themselves targets for challenges by workers and social reformers, regarding other issues).

A more likely outcome – one more effective in broadening the range of views around the table – is the growth of diverse coalitions of people and groups with partially overlapping agendas, pursuing what are likely to be less coherent but mutually agreeable changes. Acemoglu and Robinson (2012: Chapter 3 *et seq.*) outline the ways such coalitions have helped build more "inclusive" political and economic institutions – as opposed to "extractive" institutions by which a small elite exploits the rest of society – and significantly improved social outcomes. Those coalitions can be a delicate balancing act among people who may not completely trust each other, and who agree more about what they oppose than about what they want in its place. Collective-action problems, as well as the costs and fatigue that accompany extended contention, may become acute. But in some cases they can lay the foundations for new, and more broadly legitimate, ways of governing. England's Glorious Revolution, for example,

> was not the overthrow of one elite by another, but a revolution against absolutism by a broad coalition made up of the gentry, merchants, and manufacturers as well as groupings of Whigs and Tories ... The rule of law also emerged as a by-product of this process. With many parties at the table sharing power, it was natural to have laws and constraints apply to all of them, lest one party start amassing too much power and ultimately undermine the very foundations of pluralism. Thus the notion that there were limits and restraints on rulers, the essence of the rule of law, was part of the logic of pluralism engendered by the broad coalition that made up the opposition to Stuart absolutism (Acemoglu and Robinson 2012: 306).

Finally, and perhaps most likely, are what we might call "useful stalemates": situations in which a long struggle proves inconclusive, yet going back to the old ways is unacceptable. There, participants might simply look for some way out of a deadlock. Such stalemates might look like failures of deep democratization at any one time, but viewed another way they could be the basis of agreements made out of expediency, yet closely watched by numerous parties. Like the pluralistic victory described above, stalemates too can put Rothstein's values of impartiality on the table, to the extent that participants insist that new ways of doing things, even if unsatisfying in some ways, at least not leave them worse off than anyone else.

None of those three scenarios will take place in the same ways everywhere, but they do illustrate how contention, low levels of trust, and significant collective-action problems *might*, over time, give way to political settlements that have a chance of solidifying into institutions. They may also help us understand the significance of shifting processes of contention in real societies, and to break the broad notion of "deep democratization" down into more specific tasks and challenges. Those tasks are discussed in the next section; how they might play out in contemporary situations will be a key issue in the case studies of chapters 4–7.

Deep democratization as a political agenda

Hindsight has a way of clarifying complicated events – often, excessively. Our historical cases do show how past efforts to limit and contrive new rules for power were sustained by self-interest, not just by commitment to better government in general. But they also raise significant questions. Which issues and aggrieved groups might help build foundations for reform? Who is a sincere reformer, and who is using "reform" to build an image, obtain aid, or jail the leaders of the opposition? How can we prevent contention, and any new limits on power, from creating new problems? Most societies today are far more exposed to global influences and interference than were Stuart England or nineteenth-century urban America. They cannot wait for generations while needed political changes percolate through society. Worse yet, it is quite possible to do harm in the name of seeking good. In the worst of cases, urging citizens to confront their leaders can produce bloodshed and repression. Developing societies often lack institutions strong enough to counterbalance their own internal stresses, much less deal with added contention touched off by well-meaning corruption fighters.

Deep democratization, then, may be an interesting way to understand past processes of reform. But it also suggests that today's reform opportunities may come disguised as political dilemmas, fraught with risk and uncertainty. Does the idea offer any useful guidelines for today's societies?

Four major tasks

There is no tried and true plan for deep democratization, but we can specify four major, long-term tasks that are essential if a society is to move toward the situation sketched out above. They are:

- *increasing pluralism*: increasing the number and diversity of socially rooted groups, interests, and viewpoints politically active in society;

- *opening up safe political and economic "space"*: creating an open and valued public arena in which people can act, advocate their interests, and take issue with others – including rulers – without significant concerns about their own safety, and an economy in which property rights, enforcing agreements, settling disputes, and the exercise of official power are matters of law rather than of sheer power;
- *reform activism*: enabling and encouraging people sharing grievances to act on those concerns, voice opinions and demands, safely and with some chance of having real effects; and
- *maintaining accountability*: insisting that powerful people and organizations in both the public and private sectors respect rights and liberties, laws, limits on their powers, and their own social commitments, and being able to seek redress when they do not.

A few caveats are in order here. First, each of these tasks is a continuing challenge in all manner of societies, not an item on a democracy-promotion checklist: many established democracies fall short on these criteria (more on that point in Chapter 7). The point is the *political process* of increasing pluralism, advocating interests, and so forth – processes driven by socially rooted interests and citizens themselves. A society's performance on one or more tasks may also deteriorate, sometimes very rapidly. In addition, we should not expect to see one task "completed," followed by the beginning of the next; a better way to put it is that substantial progress on one task can pave the way for others. Brave citizens and groups can and do demand accountability in undemocratic societies, but they are likely to be more effective where a wider range of political grievances can safely be given a public airing. Each task can be a contentious proposition – indeed, *must* be so; accountability is not a destination but rather another process needing continuing energy and contention. Finally, as we will see in Chapter 3, some societies are so fragile and deeply divided that *none* of the four tasks can be addressed until a workable level of trust has developed, and governing elites and institutions have earned some credibility.

The changing context

A key argument in chapters to come will be that the emphasis on the various tasks, and the ways in which deep democratization and reform might develop some synergy, will vary depending upon the syndrome of corruption in question. Direct demands for accountability, for example, may be risky in an Official Moguls setting, premature where Oligarchs and Clans leave it unclear whether *anyone* is in charge of a particular function, and yet essential where we encounter Influence Markets. The implications of the four syndromes are illustrated in Figure 2.1; in chapters 4–7 we will consider those connections in the context of specific societies.

Figure 2.1 oversimplifies complex contrasts and issues, but it does point out how the basic tasks of deep democratization will be shaped by the four syndromes of corruption. Official Moguls corruption, as the discussion in Chapter 1 indicates, is dominated by a dictator, tight ruling circle, or other sort of undemocratic regime; those top figures engage in corruption with little real opposition. Building pluralism – enabling more people and groups to act and gain some visibility publicly, whether or not their agendas are linked to corruption in any direct way – is no simple task: in some places latent oppositions may exist (consider Egypt or Tunisia), while in others it may be unclear just where pluralism might emerge (Cuba and Myanmar are possible examples). Too much emphasis on confronting such regimes directly could well result in repression – or, could induce insecurity among elites and thus encourage rapacious hand-over-fist corruption in the here and now (Scott 1972: 80–4). The worst outcome might be the abrupt collapse of the regime, with the society – still lacking credible institutions – possibly lapsing into the disorder of Oligarchs and Clans. A related, and secondary, challenge is to begin to open up safe political and economic space, which again must be done judiciously; for that space to become meaningful in deep democratization terms, however, there must be groups and interests to use it.

In Oligarch-and-Clan corruption pluralism abounds; indeed, it can be hard to say who, if anyone, is really in charge, and corruption, like many legitimate activities, is loosely structured, risky, unpredictable, and susceptible to violence. Directly confronting the oligarchs, or competing with them economically, may be so dangerous that few will take the lead – consider the numerous murdered journalists in Russia – and formal political processes may be largely irrelevant to the real exercise of power and influence. The most pressing need is for safe political and economic space: a reduction of violence; credible law enforcement, courts, contract enforcement, property rights, and civil liberties; elections with real

Tasks / syndromes	Official Moguls	Oligarchs and Clans	Elite Cartels	Influence Markets
Increasing pluralism	Primary			
Opening safe political and economic space	Secondary	Primary	Secondary	
Reform activism		Secondary	Primary	Secondary
Maintaining accountability				Primary

Emphasis on task	Primary	Secondary

Figure 2.1 The changing reform agenda: primary tasks of deep democratization, by corruption syndrome

choices, in which votes are cast and counted honestly; and a free or freer press are some of the major elements. As a workable measure of security begins to emerge, we might encourage groups to build networks, reach out to those with complementary interests and grievances, share information and ideas, and begin to change expectations for the better.

Elite Cartel cases, as the discussion in Chapter 1 suggests, also present significant potential and risks. Institutions are stronger than in the other two syndromes just discussed and corrupt figures, rather than exploiting society in a setting of impunity or chaos, are in a more defensive posture, resisting rising competitors in politics and the economy. While political life and the economy may be far from fully open and competitive, elections are likely to be more meaningful, laws and courts somewhat stronger, and civil society and opposition groups more autonomous. There is a possibility that Elite Cartel cases can slide back into Oligarch-and-Clan disruption – consider Mexico's journey from the 1980s through to today (Johnston 2005a: Chapter 5) – or into an authoritarian Official Moguls situation. But cases like Korea and Taiwan suggest that there are also prospects for greater prosperity and democracy. Thus deep democratization in Elite Cartel cases will involve continued effort to open up and protect safe political and economic space in the face of possible pressures from elites. But the central challenge is reform activism – enabling people, motivated by their own shared problems and aspirations, to assert and defend their autonomy while pressing for better official treatment and policies. Civil-society organizations of all sorts – not just anti-corruption groups, but more or less *any* self-organized "bridging" activity (to borrow from Putnam's bridging/bonding distinction; see Putnam 2000) that brings people together around shared problems and interests – can build mutual trust, diffuse organizational skills, extend networks, and deepen social capital. In Chapter 8 I will discuss the diverse ways of sustaining such efforts. Political parties may be important as well, depending upon the range of interests they might bring together. By contrast, reform crusades or other broad-based movements drawing much of society out into the streets, on the "colored revolutions" model seen in many post-communist countries, are far less promising. Such upheavals are difficult to sustain and are open to manipulation (Curry and Göedl 2012), and are often ill-suited to address people's more specific grievances even if they do succeed in changing the leadership (an outcome that might well encourage more disruptive varieties of corruption).

Influence Market corruption, even though it tends to be found in relatively settled and affluent market democracies, is a serious concern. And it is different: more often it involves economic interests seeking to affect specific processes within relatively strong public institutions, rather than unconstrained political leaders who reach out and plunder the economy. Many corruption issues do not involve clearly transgressive behaviors like bribery or extortion, but rather private advantages gained at the public expense through legal political processes and economic advantages that are written into laws and policy (see Chapter 7). Here, political space is open and relatively secure, even though many citizens may not see the political process as reflecting their outlooks. Formal mechanisms of accountability are in place, but citizens seeking to use them must work through political, economic, and administrative processes extensively shaped by the wealthy, and by their interests. Pluralism of varying sorts is a fact of life, and mobilized interests abound in politics, but the overall system of influence generally favors elite viewpoints over those of other citizens. Reform activism, often in the form of reviving civil society and grassroots groups, will often be on the agenda, however, as many of the contemporary democracies experiencing the Influence Markets syndrome are contending with a democratic malaise of sorts (Pharr and Putnam 2000). Accountability, in such a setting, cannot be taken for granted – and many of these societies have a great deal of deep democratization work to do.

Longer trajectories of change

Figure 2.1 may, if only at a stylistic level, convey the sense of an underlying developmental path or trajectory, but any such interpretation must be highly qualified at best. With respect to the syndromes of corruption themselves, there is no such presumption at all. As we have seen, societies do not "start out" as Official Mogul cases, then move through Oligarchs-and-Clans and later "stages." Not only is change of many sorts possible (Mexico, as noted earlier, would have been an Elite Cartels case in the early 1980s but now experiences Oligarchs-and-Clans corruption), but it is also important to remember that the four syndromes do not embody relative amounts or strengths of any one underlying dimension. Official Moguls and Oligarchs and Clans, for example, differ qualitatively from each other; in the former it is usually quite clear who is in charge while pluralism is weak, while in the latter pluralism abounds – indeed, may be out of control in some sectors – and it may be not at all clear who, if anyone, governs society. Elite Cartels and Influence Markets likewise present their own distinctive sets of relationships between state and society, and their own profiles of participation and institutions.

From the standpoint of reform, by contrast, there may be something more of a sequence. If Official Moguls cases can pluralize, confronting elites with greater competition and contention, and if Oligarchs and Clans can be gradually contained by stronger state, political, and social institutions, both types of cases may move toward the Elite Cartels situation, where a collusive ruling elite fights a rear-guard action against rising competition and increasing institutional constraint. More will be said about such possibilities in Chapter 3, with its discussion of fragile situations, and indeed such trends might be a workable halfway state of reform for a time. Because of their de facto institutionalization and predictability, many Elite Cartel societies are moderately, or more, successful economically (Johnston 2005a: Chapter 5); some have moved on to greater levels of overall democracy, as noted above. Few would recommend Elite Cartels as an ultimate goal, and there is nothing absolutely preventing a lapse into the bad old ways; but such a situation *might* be a good way for anti-corruption forces to consolidate and catch their breath for a time, while citizens in general benefit from improved living standards and fewer political disruptions and intrusions. Still, there is nothing inevitable about "passing through" an Elite Cartels "stage"; in some societies – perhaps, smaller, more homogeneous and non-mineral-dependent – Moguls or Oligarchs might give way more or less directly to Influence Markets. Further, for an Official Moguls case Oligarchs and Clans are something to be *avoided*, if possible. Finally, Influence Market corruption is emphatically not an end stage of reform, good corruption, or anything of the sort; it has real costs, particularly for other countries, and represents participation and institutional problems all its own.

All of these questions will be revisited in chapters 4–7, when we consider a number of case studies. For now, three general points are worth noting. One is that if Figure 2.1 has any validity, it is striking how some of the key elements of the mainstream anti-corruption playbook not only reflect the experiences and outlooks of affluent market democracies, but also seem to assume that many essential democratic developments have already taken place. In other societies a number of more basic tasks must be accomplished, at times in the face of considerable resistance, in order to give conventional corruption controls the social and political foundations they need. Absent those foundations, such efforts are not only more likely to fail, wasting scarce reform support and opportunities; they may also do considerable damage, not least by putting reform advocates at great risk.

Second, one way to think of the tasks of deep democratization taken as a whole is that they represent the opportunities and challenges of building, or rebuilding, the key institutions and linkages of pluralistic, open, and accountable states in places where such developments never took root because of, or have been supplanted by, corrupt networks and ways of getting things done.[2] That perspective might not only reiterate the longer-term logic of deep democratization, but also serves as a useful reminder of the sheer scale of difficulty of the tasks in question, and of the tenacity with which existing corrupt leaders and their clients will resist our efforts.

Third, the tasks identified in Figure 2.1 point toward ways of choosing specific corruption controls in various situations. While our emphasis here has been on interest-driven political contention, that does not mean we should ignore or tolerate corruption, or that judiciously chosen anti-corruption measures have no place in the deep democratization process. Rather, instead of laying out a reform agenda and then seeking citizen support for it, we should emphasize those reforms that seem most likely to aid the deep democratization tasks at hand. In an Official Moguls situation, a national anti-corruption commission might be vulnerable to elite interference, but we can still push for police reforms (to cite just one example) to reduce torture and arbitrary arrest, in the process helping more people and groups enter the public arena. In a deeply insecure Oligarchs-and-Clans setting, setting up broad-based citizen anti-corruption organizations might be an act of futility or even quite risky, but court reforms to open up lines of recourse from crime and arbitrary administrative treatment are a step toward safe political and economic space. Elite Cartels may be sufficiently entrenched in some societies to see off many specific demands for accountability, but reforms to electoral procedures may over time give citizens enough choice and autonomy to undercut the cartels politically. Those are but

---

[2] I thank Bruce Rutherford for suggesting that way of thinking.

a few possibilities; more will be explored in the case-study chapters to come.

Conclusion: lessons and challenges

I began this chapter by suggesting that the remarkable thing may not be that there is so much corruption, but rather that there is not much more of it. Even when we rule out imaginary absolute autocrats, throughout history the person with the biggest stick has often had things pretty much his own way. Restraining the powerful has never been easy.

Lest the argument so far seem speculative or fanciful, it is worth noting that some aspects of it can be seen in action today. What checks abuses in many of the societies generally seen as less corrupt today? It is not only fear of punishment; indeed, in most such countries major corruption prosecutions are fairly unusual. Many other forces are at work: social standards and disapproval; a degree of consensus over basic rules and fairness, if only because they offer greater security and reduced levels of conflict and contention to both rulers and ruled; a widespread sense of having personal stake in government, and in the rule of law; and a belief that existing systems of order, however imperfect, promise a better life.

To pursue reform via the long road of deep democratization is to set the bar very high. But to think that way is also to take seriously Warren's (2004) arguments about inclusion and exclusion, and to begin developing a good working definition of justice. Justice is not just an abstract goal, a set of process standards, or a slogan. It is more than merely an instrumental sense that following rules A, B, and C will raise one's income or ward off crime. It is instead a sense of confidence that our rights, interests, outlooks, and security matter – and that others' do, as well; that even the most powerful and wealthy must respect those limits and values; and that they can be called to account if they do not. Justice is the linchpin between, or a way of reconciling, self-interest and our obligations to fellow citizens and society. It is an essential link between self-interested contention and the broader social value of corruption control. It requires, and over time can reinforce, a working level of mutual trust. It is precisely these values and linkages that corruption undermines, and that reform, if it is to be sustainable over time, must give credible promise of building and upholding.

It is relatively easy, with the advantage of hindsight, to identify such developments and motivations in historical cases. But contemporary cases are far more confusing, and it can be difficult to tell the good news from the bad. Among other things, it may not always be clear which syndrome of corruption is on display (an issue addressed in a variety of ways in the Appendix of this volume). Trusting the market-like aspects of formal democracy to bring "the public interest" into reality is trusting too much: reform activism and demands for accountability are often responses to the shortcomings of liberal politics and markets, and to aspects of both that endanger important values (Sandel 2012). Deep democratization may come disguised as social upheaval; Zuern (2006), for example, sees in South Africa's churning social movements a process of "contentious institutionalization spurred by the contradictions of inequality and liberal democracy" (see also Zuern 2011). Wood (2001) has termed the same processes an "insurgent path to democracy" and draws comparisons to El Salvador.

On the way to such optimistic outcomes, however, lie serious practical challenges. Many societies – particularly those emerging from conflict or dictatorships – are in situations too fragile to withstand much political contention. Fragility is not a "fifth syndrome" – as we shall see, it arises in many forms, and aspects of fragility can be found in at least three of our four syndromes of corruption. But it is a reason why *none* of the four tasks might be a wise option in some places – at least, not until workable levels of trust and basic government performance have been put in place. Fragility, and ways of addressing it, are the central issue in Chapter 3.

3 | *First, do no harm – then, build trust: reform in fragile and post-conflict societies*

All happy families resemble one another; every unhappy family is unhappy in its own way.

– Lev Tolstoy, *Anna Karenina*

Fear and, quite possibly, loathing too

Any anti-corruption strategy – particularly one emphasizing political contention – faces two sobering facts. First, many of the societies where corruption problems are worst are fragile in fundamental ways. Reform is difficult enough in sound, established states. In societies emerging from conflict or dictatorship, and in those where social divisions and distrust, poverty, or natural disasters have undermined leadership and citizenship, too much contention too soon could invite disaster. Second, at some point reformers must show that their efforts are producing benefits. What, if anything, can be done to build institutional and social foundations strong enough to withstand the stresses of reform? Are there ways to demonstrate results to enough segments of society to avoid intensified distrust or violence?

This chapter offers two arguments. First, reformers confronted with fragile situations must avoid making things worse in the name of doing good. Some good ideas may have to be deferred for a time while a

---

Portions of this chapter are adapted from Michael Johnston, "First, Do No Harm – Then, Build Trust: Anti-Corruption Strategies in Fragile Situations," a background analytical chapter for the *World Development Report 2011*. Washington, DC: The World Bank. Online at http://siteresources.worldbank.org/EXTWDR2011/Resources/6406082-1283882418764/WDR_Background_Paper_Johnston.pdf (viewed February 6, 2013). Special thanks to Steve Ndegwa, Sahr J. Kpundeh, and their colleagues for their excellent advice as that project developed.

foundation of trust – both among citizens, and between them and government – can be laid down. To that end, emphasis should be upon providing some basic services in a demonstrably fair and effective manner. Second, showing that positive changes are underway, and that citizens thus have a stake in reform, can be done by gathering and publishing indicators of government performance. That process can also point out vulnerabilities to corruption, and the effects of reform, in a wider variety of settings.

Fragility

Like corruption, fragility comes in many forms with contrasting causes and implications. One way to think of a fragile situation is as one in which key institutions, including but not limited to the state, lack capacity, credibility, and/or resilience. Those ideas are helpful but, at another level, amount to replacing one metaphor with others. Moreover, by emphasizing what such societies seem to lack, they tell us relatively little about what is actually going on, or about possible sources of strength.

In practice fragility can originate in the state and its key institutions; the personalities, and relationships among, key leaders; a range of divisions and disputes among people; identities, culture and value systems; the type and strength of a society's economic base; relations with neighboring states and factions, including not only armed conflicts but also refugee flows (Murshid 2013); and technological or economic changes more rapid than people and institutions can withstand – all parts of an incomplete list. The Tolstoy quotation above suggests a double truth of sorts: solid or integral societies have much in common, suggesting to some the possibility of a standard set of anti-corruption reforms, but fragile societies pose diverse and even unique combinations of problems. Even if they aspire to broadly similar sorts of outcomes their journeys can follow quite different paths.

Therefore, my deliberately broad definition of a fragile situation will be one in which the boundaries and identity of society, basic operations of the state, essential public services, and the day-to-day security of citizens cannot be taken for granted. Like the metaphors noted above, this definition points out deficiencies and difficulties, but it is also intended to indicate key dimensions on which fragile situations might vary, improvements are most urgent, and some sources of strength might exist. The final phrase of the definition introduces a key aspect of both fragility and reform – expectations. The key issue is governance in its most fundamental sense: can a society sustain itself with some degree of peace, order, and justice, given its stresses and resources – and do people act and make choices in the belief it will do so?

Fragility does not necessarily signal a society's endgame or an imminent "failed state" (Fund for Peace 2013). In some ways it might be a function of new opportunities, such as the fall of a dictator – of "an open moment in history" (Ghani and Lockhart 2007) – disrupting the bad old ways of doing things. Some fragile situations are linked to valuable resources: the familiar "oil curse" is but one example. Furthermore, trust may not be completely absent: it is easy to imagine a situation in which state functions are unreliable, yet trust is strong at the family or small-group level. On the other hand, animosities among tight-knit social groups can add to overall fragility. Fragility not only complicates the question of what to do about corruption. It also poses tough questions of what *not* to do, for poorly thought-out attempts at reform may only make matters worse.

Moreover, fragility is not a fifth syndrome of corruption. It is, first of all, not the same thing as corruption, and like so many other issues in this book, fragility varies significantly across categories. It is most likely in Oligarch-and-Clan cases, where the economic and political stakes are large and institutions are very weak. But it can arise in Official Mogul situations too, particularly where the ruling group becomes factionalized, isolated from society (on trade-offs between coercion from above and the flow of information from below see Apter 1971), and face enemies rather than competitors. When key personalities pass from the scene in such situations there may be little left to hold old arrangements together. Fragility is not synonymous with either of those corruption syndromes: Albania, Benin, and Thailand, to name three examples, are Oligarch-and-Clan cases (Johnston 2005a: Chapter 3 and pp. 221–4) that have seemed fragile at times over the past generation, but others in that category – consider Bulgaria, Ghana, Malaysia, and Turkey – have proven stronger. Similarly, in China, Iran, and Uganda, Official Moguls are securely in charge for now, while the events of 2011 in Tunisia, Libya, and Egypt show how they can become surprisingly vulnerable.

Elite Cartel corruption creates a de facto institutionalization, or at least predictability, as elites collude to defend their positions. But there, too, elite isolation can make for a fragile situation; moreover, if the flow of corrupt gains is disrupted or competition reaches critical mass, elite alignments may be less likely to bend than to break (on that point see Johnston 2005a: Chapter 6). Countries in the Influence Market group – most of them established liberal democracies – have generally been able to cope with scandals, even on a major scale, and few if any have slipped into other syndromes. That such societies can deal with corruption from positions of relative strength is one factor, perhaps, encouraging their reform advocates to pursue anti-corruption strategies elsewhere without enough regard for fragility issues. On the other hand, to the extent that Influence Market corruption makes those societies less open and adaptive, worsens economic and political inequalities, and encourages mass political disengagement, well-established market democracies, too, can experience a political malaise that hollows out democratic values and political trust.

Make haste slowly

Would-be corruption fighters must move cautiously in fragile situations, particularly if their prescriptions include greater political contention. Reform, after all, has costs for citizens – usually in the here and now – while its benefits may seem remote. Where trust is weak, anti-corruption efforts are likely to have little credibility at the outset, and may appear to be – indeed, may *be* – just another way for a political faction to gain or keep the upper hand. If people benefit from corruption, even in very small or symbolic ways, if they expect to benefit over time, or if they simply believe reform (like many other developments in a fragile setting) will make a bad situation worse, fighting corruption may be an unattractive prospect.

But reform cannot simply wait until all stars are in perfect alignment. They never will be – even if we did know enough to recognize such circumstances if we saw them. The challenge, I will suggest, is to avoid major mistakes while building a basic level of trust among citizens, and in those who govern. Urgent as grand assaults on corruption may seem, it is possible to do considerable harm in the process of seeking better government. Threatening entrenched corrupt elites without strengthening countervailing forces and key institutions may encourage corrupt elites to shift thievery into overdrive, or push societies toward even more disruptive syndromes. Direct, high-profile attacks on corruption may raise expectations that cannot be met, further undermining the credibility of well-meaning officials and the next round of reforms. In an Oligarchs-and-Clans situation the result may be intensified violence, while in an Official Moguls case top figures may step up repression.

Some of the most familiar ways to deal with corruption can, in such situations, be less than helpful. As we will see in the case of the Philippines (Chapter 5), "frying a big fish" – prosecuting and imprisoning prominent ex-politicians – is a popular option. That impulse is understandable, but should not be confused with building institutions and changing expectations for the long term. At best the fry-a-big-fish strategy may open the door for such measures by demonstrating determination, and have some temporary demonstration effects for potential bad actors, but often corruption will return once the excitement has subsided. In post-conflict situations frying a big fish might be a matter of basic justice with respect to the conflict itself, but in other fragile cases it may only intensify factional animosities.

Another tempting approach is to set up an anti-corruption agency, perhaps patterned on the famous Hong Kong Independent Commission Against Corruption (ICAC). Again, the key issue is follow-through. Where other institutions are weak and resources are scarce, ICAC-style strategies are unlikely to receive the backing they need; where they have been tried repeatedly, expectations will be weak or negative. If such commissions can be used to pursue corruption in service delivery, and be headed by leaders enjoying significant social trust, they might be effective. But it is worth noting that the most successful commissions have been created in relatively small, undemocratic societies where a regime's hold on power is secure, and have been closely linked to rapid improvements in the quality of life (Hong Kong, Singapore) – or in jurisdictions where accountability and institutional quality are not seriously in question (New South Wales). The broad visibility they can attract can make ICACs an attractive strategy of first resort, but in fragile situations they may only add to the overall stress on society. Much the same is true of national morality campaigns: they are difficult to sustain, and are often a kind of default option where capacity for more complex and detailed reforms is weak.

Complicating matters further is the risk that fragile societies – be they formerly solid Influence Market or Elite Cartel cases that are coming unstuck, or Official Moguls facing social or economic stress – might fall into the highly disruptive Oligarchs-and-Clans syndrome. Indeed, the wrong reforms at the wrong time may push them in that direction. A rapid push for transparency and institutional change can increase the oligarchs' sense of insecurity, increasing violence, repression, the rapid export of assets, and rapacious corruption. Civil-society strategies may expose well-meaning citizens to danger or add to mutual distrust. Liberalization, decentralization, and aggressive privatization can further weaken such institutions as still matter, making it easier for would-be oligarchs to move in on key sectors of the state and economy.

Reformers, then, must think in terms of the possible rather than the ideal: Grindle's (2004, 2007) notion of "good-enough governance" can be very instructive. Perhaps fragile societies should not try to become Denmark or New Zealand, at least not yet; in any event, Influence Market societies have significant corruption problems of their own. Emulating the Elite Cartels of South Korea, Italy, or Botswana might be a better interim goal – a possibility to be discussed in greater detail later on. Those halfway situations cannot be engineered with any degree of predictability, and they will be an unpopular recommendation to anyone understandably frustrated by the tenacity of corruption. But their de facto institutionalization can make way for increased legitimacy, economic growth, levels of trust, and the chances for workable social compacts (Johnston 2005a: Chapter 5), and unlike ultimate governance goals they may be attainable over the medium term.

Improving government performance to build trust

Trust cannot be created by proclamation or calls for idealism. People in fragile situations will have seen and experienced too much, and received too little; for many, a flood of rumors and resentments make trust an unaffordable luxury – or, a bad joke. And as we have seen, where trust is weak neither individual anti-corruption commitments nor collective action will gain much strength. For those reasons, reform in fragile situations must often be selective, indirect, and deliberately unexciting – performing a few basic public functions fairly, and doing them well. The goal is to show that better government is possible, and that people have a stake in helping build it.

A related point has to do with matters of style. The language of corruption abounds with "hot" language ("graft," "kickbacks," crooks and thieves, terminal-illness metaphors, and the like) that engage not only the specifics of corruption but can also crystalize more general emotions and grievances (the classic argument is by Edelman 1985). It also is rich in euphemisms and evasions ("tea money," "sweeteners," "commissions") that reflect and encourage continued cynicism – often, well-founded – about leaders, governance, and politics. Reforms are sometimes described as "wars on graft," crusades, moral uplift, and national redemption, any of which might revive all-too-recent resentments and fears in post-conflict societies and could foster expectations that cannot be met. Further – perhaps a cynical view – such language suggests leaders with a sense of urgency but with little idea of what should be done.

Thus most of the recommendations that follow are deliberately unexciting. Rather than further turning up the heat, they are intended to reduce social tensions and build up expectations that leaders and governments can actually govern. Further, they are intended to show citizens that they are not competing with each other in zero-sum games. Getting to those goals is far from simple, however, and as noted can involve considerable risk. Why might an emphasis on basic services, expectations, and trust make a positive difference?

Doing what governments do: the importance of basic services

Fragile societies often exist in situations so desperate that the idea of providing basic government services on a fair, effective basis seems far-fetched in itself. Particularly in post-conflict situations, the notion that such services offer a way to build trust may seem to be a stretch. For those seeking high-profile anti-corruption offensives, upgrading basic services as a first step will likely be quite unsatisfying. But basic services – day-to-day public safety, improved utility services, workable education and road systems – emphasize demonstrable performance that can positively affect citizens' lives. Further, they are a way to put Rothstein's principle of impartiality, as a marker of high- or better-quality government, into practice. One serious objection to the basic-services approach might be that such improved performance requires precisely the kinds of effective institutions that are absent in fragile societies, more or less by definition. That is likely to be true at the outset, so it is important to start small by doing a few things well – or, at least, noticeably better than they have been done in the past. In addition, choosing a few strategic functions provides clear targets for resources, and for administrative and institutional improvements – much more so than pledging to fight all corruption, and associated pathologies, everywhere at once.

Basic day-to-day security for citizens, and for their homes and property, may be the most pressing challenge, particularly in post-conflict and Oligarch-and-Clan cases. Attaining that goal will not be easy. But it may help reduce tensions, ease the sense that governing is a zero-sum fight among opposing factions, and enable people to plan for a longer timespan as they make important choices. Basic order and security are also particularly sensitive areas when it comes to showing that impartiality is not just a slogan but a fact of life. Provision of water, electricity, and fuel can be similarly large challenges: after all, a distressingly large number of people around the world, many of them living in the sorts of Oligarch-and-Clan or Official Mogul situations most closely linked to fragility, have never had access to clean water. Fairness may be harder to demonstrate as well, inasmuch as such utilities must usually be restored or instituted on a geographical basis, but an approach that spreads progress across major segments of society, be they communal or geographical, as much as possible will be useful. Basic schooling, road-building, and health services offer similar challenges and opportunities.

Visible improvement in the effectiveness and fairness of just one or two of these key service sectors can drive a process of institution- and trust-building. It is true that expanded activity and budgets in service agencies will likely attract the attention of corrupt actors, particularly where opportunities in the wider economy are scarce; for that reason, familiar corruption controls in areas like procurement, personnel, budgeting, and disbursements may well be needed. But those efforts, too, should receive greatest emphasis in the service sectors chosen for visible upgrades. As with the services themselves, effective controls in just one or two important agencies can, over time, have important demonstration and deterrent effects for would-be manipulators in other parts of government. How any improvements can be demonstrated, and what they can tell us about "hot spots" for corruption and reforms, will be discussed in a later section of this chapter.

All well and good: but do improvements in services actually build trust and change expectations? Acemoglu and Robinson (2012: Chapter 13) note that credible state authority (as opposed to the exercise of personal power), a workable level of order and security, and basic services are often missing in countries dominated by extractive institutions and government practices, and few key leaders or interests have any incentive to provide them. Is the connection reversible – that is, can maintaining the peace and keeping the lights on for all really build support for better government performance? Rothstein and Uslaner (2005) provide evidence that the answer *could* be yes (possible connections are also explored in Fischer and Schmelzle 2009; McKechnie 2009; Turner and Carballo 2009). Their data from sixty-three countries suggest that universal social policies – not those targeted at the poor, but rather at those distributing resources and increasing opportunities across whole societies – help build trust:

> We argue that social trust is caused by two different, yet interrelated types of equality, namely, economic equality and equality of opportunity. This argument has important implications for public policy because universal social policies are more effective than selective ones in creating both types of equality and thereby social trust (Rothstein and Uslaner 2005: 42–3).

Rothstein and Uslaner also note, however, that low-trust societies – particularly those emerging from conflict – are less likely to enact such policies on their own.

Some analysts (Delhey and Newton 2005; Rothstein and Stolle 2008) have found that improved quality of government, and better day-to-day performance, help build social capital over time, and an important line of argument in the post-Cold-War years had it that poor state performance was a prime cause of ethnic and communal conflict, as well as an effect (Diamond and Plattner 1994). Espinal, Hartlyn, and Kelly (2006: 200), studying survey data from the Dominican Republic, conclude that "trust in government institutions is shaped primarily by perceptions of economic and political performance by government." Mishler and Rose (2005), using data from Russia, find that solid economic and political performance by government and key institutions is a critical influence upon levels of diffuse support – an idea they regard as closely linked to trust. Dix, Hussmann, and Walton's analysis of fragile situations (2012) sees solid government performance as contributing to stability and state legitimacy. Marquette's (2012) discussion of the particularly complex Afghanistan case suggests that that country's Performance Based Governance Fund has begun to show positive results in terms of building trust and citizen involvement in public life, as well as improving government performance in several provinces. The Fund commands significant resources and evaluates the quality of provincial governance via regular, published performance evaluations that influence subsequent allocations of funds. The uses and value of such performance indicators are explored later in this chapter.

Such evidence is suggestive at best, and causal connections are complex and reciprocal. It would be over-optimistic to see the provision of basic services as a direct path to good government and a trusting society. It is safer to say that without such changes, political and social trust become even harder to build, and credibility much more difficult for institutions and leadership to earn. Still, poorly performing government is one reason why we worry about corruption to begin with, and it does seem plausible that when citizens consider whether or not leaders can be trusted, better government is a real possibility, and reform might serve their own interests and needs, they will consider how they are treated by, and the benefits they do or do not receive from, agencies charged with basic services. If the answers to those questions are positive, or even just if expectations are improving, people may bring their problems into the public arena rather than seeking the help of fixers, patrons, or local warlords.

A final advantage of emphasizing the provision of good basic services is that measuring levels and trends of such performance can tell us a great deal about specific vulnerabilities to corruption, targets for reform, and countermeasures that are most needed. Those advantages are the focus of the following section.

Show, don't tell: tracking corruption, making reform real

No matter which syndrome of corruption reformers confront, at some point they must assess the scope and trends of corruption problems and estimate the effects of their reforms. As a practical matter, they must show political backers, officials, citizens, business people, and potential wrongdoers that reform is for real. They also need sound evidence to decide which problems to attack, in what specific parts of government, using what tactics. Further, if corruption control is to be sustained by

This section draws upon research that is also reported in Johnston 2009a, 2010. I gratefully acknowledge comments, advice, and encouragement received from Janos Bertok and his colleagues at OECD in Paris, where I spent time in early 2008 working on an extended report (Johnston 2009a).

citizens defending their own interests, the links between reform and the problems of daily life must become more than an abstraction. If those connections are not clear, collective-action problems and low levels of trust will likely inhibit reform. For all of those reasons, those seeking to check corruption need valid and reliable measures of corruption vulnerabilities and the effects of reform.

Few existing methods of measuring corruption will help us much at those levels. The most widely published corruption indices are based wholly or largely on perceptions, assign a single number to whole societies, and are of debatable use at best when it comes to tracking trends (more complete critiques of existing indices, and of the ways they affect societies struggling for reform, can be found in Sampford et al. 2006; Andersson and Heywood 2008; Johnston 2009a). Ultimately, all encounter problems inherent in attempting to measure corruption itself: we have no agreed definition or dimension of comparison, some unknown percentage of cases remain secret, and corruption can occur in diverse and contrasting forms.

More useful would be assessments that are detailed; based on verifiable evidence; non-invasive, as far as possible, with respect to administration and officials' personal rights; policy-neutral, in the sense that they not encourage some kinds of policies or discourage others (Manning, Kraan, and Malinska 2006); inexpensive to gather and publish; transparent and easily understood; linked to positive accomplishments, rather than just labeling societies or broad segments of government as corrupt; trackable over time; supportive of trust between citizens and government; and actionable – not only indicating problems but also pointing toward what should be done. Clearly, those criteria set the bar quite high.

This section offers an approach that does not claim to measure corruption itself, and will not yield yet another set of rankings, but rather looks at what governments do, and how well they do it, over time. Gathering and publishing evidence on government performance, I will suggest, can give us a highly detailed view of the effects of past corruption, the incentives that sustain it, and responses that would be effective. Indicators could focus on a very wide range of activities, but in fragile societies the emphasis might well be on law enforcement and basic security, utility provision, schools, and taxation, for example. Improvements in those areas, difficult as they may be, would not only be good things in themselves; for citizens who see government as ineffective and riddled with favoritism, for those who see neighbors as competitors for basic services, and for those who see no alternative to dealing with "fixers," credible evidence of improved government performance might change expectations.

Indicators and benchmarks

The core idea is to gather and publish readily understood indicators of government performance – how long it takes to get a license, how much agencies pay for diesel fuel or concrete, whether promised roads are actually built and to what standards, to name some examples – on a regular basis. Those data would be benchmarked, not only for given functions over time but also, ideally, against data from comparable agencies and jurisdictions, to help us interpret the indicators and demonstrate trends. That strategy can be a low-cost way to track the impact of reforms at a detailed level, and to spot likely vulnerabilities to corruption. Many such indicators can also tell us where the profitability of corrupt schemes is being squeezed out of the system. Ultimately, the goal is government that serves its citizens well, and is *seen* to serve them well – reasons why we worry about corruption in the first place.

Measuring and reporting levels and trends in government performance is in no way "the answer" to corruption, or even to the measurement problem, nor does it guarantee greater anti-corruption activity among citizens or officials. It is, however, essential to basic notions of accountability and has a surprisingly long pedigree. D. Allen (2012), for example, provides a fascinating account of the ways in which better measurements of activity and performance helped build the modern British Civil Service in the years between about 1500 and the mid nineteenth century. Measurement was a way to move beyond older, personal forms of accountability – master–servant or patron–client relationships, for example – and beyond "venal institutions" that did at least involve personal incentives (think tax- and customs-farming), to more modern ways of assessing merit and accomplishment, identifying problems, and fixing blame or assigning credit. In modern societies where face-to-face accountability is impossible, and in which a large and complex administrative apparatus is essential, measuring levels of performance is essential to accountability, effective administration, due process, and fairness. Thus the scheme to be discussed in this section is not so much a new anti-corruption idea as a way of bringing broader segments of society into the assessment process.

What should we measure? Indicators

Consider, as an example, data on bureaucratic delay. Assume that in City A getting a building permit involves thirty-three steps and takes seven weeks, while in City B the same process typically involves four steps and takes three days. We cannot measure corruption in those two agencies directly, and in no way is it necessarily the cause of all difficulties there. Still, the numerous steps and long delays in City A seem likely to be, at least in part, effects of past corruption: bureaucrats have found they can make money by contriving new requirements and delays. Even more clearly, convoluted processes create incentives sustaining them, and creating vulnerabilities: contractors facing numerous bureaucratic "toll gates" and long delays may find it quicker and cheaper to pay up. In City B, by contrast, officials have fewer opportunities to demand payments and contractors have less incentive to bribe. Even if bureaucrats demand payments, resulting delays are more likely to become visible, and intolerable, in an otherwise expeditious process. Further, if City A reduces the number of steps and amount of time involved in its process, opportunities for corruption and incentives to pay are likely to be reduced too. A relatively[1] fast government process, all else being equal, can signal that interference and corruption are less common and, in all likelihood, less tolerated. While it is possible that the faster process could be of lesser quality, with substandard construction projects slipping through for lack of scrutiny, that risk can also be assessed through examination of outcomes: independent inspections of randomly selected projects, and keeping track of citizens' and others' complaints, offer possible reality checks.

Similar connections can be made in other policy areas. Whether or not the police come when they are called, and how long it takes for them to arrive; the availability and dependability of electrical service,

---

[1] "Fast" is obviously a sliding scale: taking ten weeks to issue a passport is poor performance, while approving a proposal to build a nuclear power plant in only ten weeks would for most people qualify as extreme (and unwise) haste.

and the percentage of paid connections made by utility operators versus those rigged informally by residents; percentages of children attending schools and, of those, the share having a chair and the right textbooks; and taxes levied and actually collected in various communities are examples of data that can help assess and demonstrate the coverage and fairness of public services. That the relevant authorities in many places might not be able – or willing – to produce such evidence is itself a symptom of fragility; so too is the likelihood that they believe they can falsify such evidence, or refuse to cooperate at all. At those levels, regularly gathering and publishing data on government performance can be seen as a better-government strategy in its own right.

Data on government functions, gathered and published on a regular basis, can be easily understood and verifiable. An agency can compile them from its own records, while investigators, news media, and citizen groups might send individuals through various administrative processes in order to gather their own data. Results can be compared over time and among jurisdictions. Unlike broad-scale corruption indices, such data can target specific agencies, programs, and locations, identifying especially urgent problems.

Many other indicators could be similarly useful. A few examples might include:

- time, expense, and the number of steps involved in registering a business, obtaining utility service, or appealing a tax assessment;
- the frequency of, and trends in, discretionary practices and exceptions in hiring, procurement, and taxation;
- modifications of public contracts once they have been awarded;
- speed and accuracy with which vendors' invoices are paid;
- time and charges for access to public information;
- time, number of steps, and frequency and range of variations involved in business dealings with regulatory agencies;
- trends in the numbers of licenses and permits, or in subsidy and benefit payments, granted by a given agency;
- whether government purchases are delivered in the quantities, quality, and places intended, and in a timely fashion; and
- the number of employees included on an agency's payroll versus the numbers participating in specific activities (a possible signal of "ghost workers").

Show, don't tell: tracking corruption, making reform real

A consistent logic underlies such measurements: if one unit of government pays 50 percent more[2] for fuel than do others; charges unusually high (or low) royalties for extracted natural resources; needs ten employees to accomplish tasks performed elsewhere by four; publishes budgets that are routinely far off the mark in terms of actual revenues and expenditures; has a high percentage of variances in zoning and regulatory decisions, or in tax exemptions and collections; or conducts far more (or many fewer) regulatory inspections than other comparable locations, such variations may well reflect the effects of past corruption and incentives and gaps facilitating further abuses – among other difficulties.

The data in question are verifiable, not perceptual. They point to sensible countermeasures: slow processes can be streamlined, excessive prices brought into line with appropriate norms, the frequency of inspections and variances examined for abuses of discretion, and payments to vendors and employees audited. None of these countermeasures are anything new, but an indicators-and-benchmarks system can tell us where they are most urgently needed and whether they are having positive, or any, effects. Other useful evidence might be subjective but still draws upon actual experience; asking officials whether and how often they see corruption in their agencies may be a useful cross-check for process-oriented data. Similarly, citizens and advocacy groups can provide direct evidence on treatment by government officials, verify the quality and completion of construction projects and facilities (such activities in the Philippines are discussed in Chapter 5), and give feedback on the quality of services – all concerns linked to their quality of life.

Compared to what? Benchmarks

By itself a given indicator says little about whether performance is good or poor, and nothing at all about trends. Performance must be assessed against benchmarks – valid and reliable evidence allowing repeated comparisons. Among the most important are self-to-self comparisons within a function or program over time, which can provide the sorts of

---

[2] Perhaps surprisingly, paying strikingly *low* prices can be a sign of trouble too, if one bidder (perhaps with official connivance) under-charges to drive out competitors, in anticipation of charging much higher prices later on.

evidence on trends reformers often find elusive. Other useful benchmarks might assess positive accomplishments – speed, for example, or the quality of specific services – across comparable jurisdictions and over time. Like the indicators themselves, benchmarking does not measure corruption or other problems directly nor, again, can all contrasts or problems be attributed to corruption. It can, however, specify realistic standards against which to judge the indicators and assess the direction and scale of changes.

Benchmarks should not be confused with "targets" which, once attained, tend to acquire an air of finality. They are much more likely to be moving standards based on a range of observations that will change as government practices evolve and diffuse. Improvements across several jurisdictions can produce gradually rising benchmarks; declines can also be made apparent, at which point the most appropriate first step may be to give administrators opportunities to explain observed differences and help formulate responses. The indicators-and-benchmarks strategy does not equate high-quality government (much less integrity) with "efficiency" alone: it is entirely possible for an agency to be so efficient that public input is disregarded, or that flawed policies rapidly and consistently produce lamentable results. Nor is the speed of a process always a virtue: a one-step licensing process, for example, might amount to one-stop shopping for venal clients, and become the most corrupt of all. Benchmarking will be most meaningful when considered in light of evidence on public satisfaction with government, facilities, and services.

Benchmarks are quite specific, and thus multiple benchmarks are not only possible but necessary. Over time we can watch for very low numbers (a deliberately sluggish process designed to extract bribes), very high figures (frequent inspections as a form of bureaucratic or political harassment), "spikes" in prices paid, and so forth. Such findings, as noted, help identify "hot spots" – a locality that pays far too much for concrete, for example, or a contracting agency with very frequent renegotiations of specifications – where the scope and incentives for corruption are likely to be great. Subsequent trends in indicators and benchmarks can tell us much about whether reforms and controls are working. No corruption index now available can provide that sort of guidance and feedback.

Benchmarks can come in several forms and may be drawn not only from agency data but also from a variety of surveys (Reinikka and

Svensson 2003, 2006). Some possible examples follow, each of which can in turn refer to a variety of indicators and functions.

- **Statistical norms based on multiple government organizations** – Does registering a business in one community take significantly longer than the median across a number of others, or is a given function significantly more expensive to perform (see, for example, Golden and Picci 2005; Olken 2005)?
- **Norms in private-sector organizations or market transactions** – Some administrative functions, though not all, can be compared to private-sector benchmarks. Payment of invoices might be an example, although many other functions (e.g. licensing) will have no direct private-sector counterpart.
- **Expert assessments** – Where comparable jurisdictions or private-sector processes do not exist – for example, in a newly liberalized economy, in a city that is by far the largest in a country, or in an agency implementing highly technical policy – expert panels might define reasonable performance benchmarks.
- **Statistical projections** – Statistical models might also yield useful benchmarks. Policing in an exceptionally dense urban area might be inherently more expensive than similar functions performed elsewhere, but statistical models can estimate a reasonable range of costs and services (see, for example, Dincer, Ellis, and Waddell 2010).
- **Comparisons in light of agency resources** – Many processes and outputs should be judged in the context of resources – funds, staffing, and so forth – that are available. An agency whose indicators improve by 5 percent might seem to be doing well until those results are judged against its 10 percent growth in resources, for example.
- **Comparisons of substantive outcomes** – Is a health department in one city that conducts unusually frequent restaurant inspections just highly conscientious, or is it running a shakedown operation? One clue that additional scrutiny might be in order is data on actual levels of cleanliness, as assessed by citizen surveys, or from public health statistics.

All such indicators and benchmarks should be gathered, published, and opened up for discussion among citizens and officials on a regular basis.

A final benefit of the indicators-and-benchmarks strategy is that it can send important signals to potential bad actors. If an agency that had been paying 30 percent over market for diesel fuel is now paying, say, 5 percent over market, it is a reasonable guess that there is less money to be made via corruption in that particular area. Sustained improvements would suggest that the scope for corruption is being squeezed out of the system. Draining the incentives out of corruption is, at the least, an essential counterpart to investigations and prosecutions, and over the longer term may be even more effective.

Implementing indicators and benchmarks

There is no magic to indicators and benchmarking. Even though the focus is on basic operations of government, cooperation and evidence may be difficult to come by, particularly where they might reveal major corruption vulnerabilities. In order to be meaningful, data must be gathered, assessed, and reported on a regular basis, and the benchmarks themselves will need to be reassessed from time to time. While benchmarking strategies can point to remedies, somebody must assume the risks and responsibilities needed to make them happen. Leadership, backed by political and social support, and a judicious mix of incentives will all be needed. Citizen backing and participation will be a particularly difficult challenge where the Official Moguls or Oligarchs-and-Clans syndromes are entrenched; there, the initial impetus may depend on outside reform and aid partners, perhaps via conditionality rules. In Oligarch-and-Clan cases, however, gathering and publishing indicators of performance in basic service functions might well enhance the strength and coherence of citizen participation in politics. Demonstrated improvements, over time, could begin to replace the pervasive insecurity of that syndrome with at least a limited sense that pushing for better government can have positive results.

Indicators and benchmarks need not be technologically complex or expensive; moreover, they are a better-government strategy in their own right. Developing leadership, cooperation, institutional capacity, and the willingness to make such information public – and then, to respond positively to what the process reveals – is no small challenge, but *any* strategy that does not push for such developments will have few benefits. Convincing officials that positive as well as negative results will have real consequences, and that assessments of their work will be based on verifiable data rather than on politicized criteria or the whims of higher-ups, will be essential. A few targeted projects might be a good way to begin, particularly if positive results can be visibly linked to favorable publicity, higher salaries, and enlarged budgets. Rank-and-file employees may resist as well, particularly if monitoring is intrusive or seen as an early sign of impending job cuts. There, too, rewards and positive incentives can be essential.

Will agency managers "game the indicators" (Hood 2006; *New York Times* 2008), and will they follow through on what the results tell them? Hood (2006: 514) identifies three classic types of "gaming" – the "ratchet effect" whereby managers, knowing that future targets are likely to be based on current levels of performance, restrain those levels so that standards rise less rapidly; "threshold" phenomena, in which similar targets across multiple groups reduce the incentive for any of them to excel; and output distortion, in which statistical results have little to do with actual outcomes (as a civil servant quoted by Hood put it, "hitting the target and missing the point"). Hood identifies four other common practices as well: changing the focus of service provision, "storming" to meet targets in the short term, quietly removing a target after performance declines, and outright fabrication of results (Ibid.: 518–19). Broad-based consultation regarding methodology, cooperation, and the eventual uses of data, along with clear-cut connections between valid results and any available rewards (even if intangible), will be essential. Benchmarks, as opposed to targets, may offer some checks on gaming: if nothing else, manipulating many of the standards they set would require extensive collusion across jurisdictions.

Assessments of facilities and services should bring citizens into the process too, as noted. But citizen input must not be an empty exercise, nor should it become monopolized by a few organized groups or their leaders. Social media and crowd-sourcing techniques can help maintain the vitality and openness of citizen participation; while such activities tend to make every list of recommendations, if only on grounds of trendiness, there are nonetheless serious pilot projects in numerous countries based on citizen reports of corruption and poor services submitted by texting and over the internet, or gathered face-to-face: "I Paid a Bribe," Bribespot, and Shudify are examples.[3] Such information may be less systematic than large-scale probability surveys, but it can be

---

[3] See www.ipaidabribe.com/, and its Facebook page and postings; http://bribespot.com; and http://www.shudhify.org/ (all viewed January 2, 2013).

up-to-date and inexpensive to gather, as well as a way to encourage a sense of participation and efficacy among citizens.

Important caveats

A particularly important caveat, already noted, is that poor or declining performance might be caused by many difficulties other than corruption. Resource problems, poor recruitment and training, insufficient data-gathering and analysis, low official pay and morale, unclear goals and lines of accountability, weak citizen input, and other factors can cause delays, overpayments, frequent exceptions in implementation, and the like. In practice such problems may well be related to corruption, but poor or declining performance by itself does not prove such a link. Just as vulnerabilities to corruption are deeply embedded in society, reform will require not just a hunt for "bad guys" and "big fish" but rather comprehensive improvements in the ways agencies and officials do their work.

This strategy will be less suitable and effective for some public functions and corruption problems than for others. It works best with routine functions, and as such will not tap into large, one-time, or high-level "grand corruption" transactions. Some agencies will deal with qualitative or technical decisions, or with cases that vary widely among themselves, that are less easily compared with others – planning permission applications are an example. Similarly, priorities among service functions, how much (if at all) budgets or staffing ought to be cut, how much workers ought to be monitored on an hour-by-hour basis (Anechiarico and Jacobs 1996), and how many inspections a staff member should be expected to perform, are examples of policy questions for leaders to decide, not just extensions of the benchmarking process. Just as not all performance problems flow from corruption, we should not assume ourselves that all improvements correspond to reductions in it, or that corruption controls can somehow make performance ideal. From an analytical standpoint we will never know exactly how much of any improvement is attributable to reduced corruption versus other causes. But from a reform standpoint, we may not particularly care: if administration and services are being improved, scarce resources are going to better use, and government is doing a better and more responsive job of serving citizens and society, key goals of reform are being attained.

A crisis may arise if performance data indicate severe problems, as indeed they are likely to do in many fragile situations. At that point action will be required, and that may well be politically challenging. Still, reform advocates will be acting on the basis of sound evidence, not hearsay or politically driven scandal. Second, in most instances they will be able to act against highly specific problems – a slow process, excessively high prices paid in procurement – in targeted areas, rather than taking on major segments of the political leadership and public service. Third, the public credit that accompanies any progress can be a significant political incentive to cooperation; even where political or administrative elites are deeply factionalized, demonstrated improvements in services to the public across the board will be difficult for any faction to discredit or stigmatize.

A few hopeful examples exist of how such appeals to leadership can produce positive results. Since 2003 the Burundi Leadership Training Program (BLTP) has addressed deficits of trust directly. Groups of thirty to thirty-five local and regional leaders, nominated in large groups by their own communities but chosen individually by BLTP leaders in order to maximize group diversity, participate in six-day retreats and then a series of subsequent workshop sessions. The emphasis is upon "how-to" skills of problem-solving and intergroup relations; organizers make it clear to participants that they have been chosen because of their current and potential significance as leaders. Skills are presented to participants as ways of heightening their own effectiveness and of solving citizen problems. As Wolpe and McDonald (2006: 133) describe the BLTP approach,

> Democratic nation-building is not simply a matter of persuading political leaders to subordinate their parochial interests to those of the nation. Real transformation requires not greater altruism from leaders and citizens, but rather a new recognition that their self-interest can be more effectively advanced through collaboration and inclusive political processes.

Police and military officials have requested BLTP programs for themselves, with generally positive results: participants from differing regions and backgrounds interact with much greater trust and skill. Burundi has scarcely solved its challenges of trust-building and reconciliation, but it is building a foundation for better governance (Wolpe et al. 2004; Wolpe and McDonald 2006, 2008; Margolies 2009; United Nations 2010: chapters 7, 9; Burundi Leadership Training Program 2012; Woodrow Wilson Center 2012).

For the longer term

The argument so far has been that in fragile situations – which can arise in many forms, in the context of at least three syndromes of corruption – building trust in government, and among citizens, is our first priority if those societies and their institutions are to cope with the stresses of reform. The delivery of basic services on a fair and effective basis is critical to that process, both showing citizens that government can govern fairly and effectively, and that they can demand, and get, help with the problems of daily life. Indicators and benchmarks of government performance are a way to make those accomplishments visible, and to assess vulnerabilities to corruption and identify effective responses in highly targeted ways.

The expectations dilemma

But those steps, challenging as they are in their own right, will only pave the way for reform if they change *expectations* among citizens, officials, investors – and those contemplating corrupt deals. Citizens may take note of a generally improved climate of order, more reliable utility services, and the re-opening of local schools, and they may note that officials seem more receptive to grassroots issues and demands; but will they become more accustomed to solving problems through official channels rather than via local "fixers"? Whatever the actual incidence of corrupt dealings, the expectation that playing by the rules is futile is a critical problem (Oldenburg 1987; Khanna and Johnston 2007). Will they decide that cooperation with their neighbors is worth the effort? Do officials see any point in trying to improve government performance, and do they and their political counterparts think they can earn a living wage and avoid reprisals as they do so? Do investors expect corrupt demands and weak legal protection as a matter of course, and thus emphasize immediate profits – or stay out of a country altogether? And do potentially corrupt figures and their clients think they can continue with business as usual, that they had better go to greater lengths to conceal their schemes, or that they can do better in the long run – not to mention staying out of jail – by playing it straight? In societies where corruption is a less pressing problem, high or improving expectations, along with the social sanctions and climate of opinion that accompanies them, arguably do as much as laws and punishments to inhibit corruption. Can fragile societies avoid the sorts of "expectations traps" (Rose and Shin 2001) discussed earlier, in which citizens and officials expect very little of each other and, by and large, get just that?

Expectations are subtle, contextual, variable across time and among individuals, and notoriously difficult to measure. We should not assume that expectations are rational or accurate, nor reduce them to cost-benefit calculations. Indeed, the illicit nature of corruption, the uncertainties and risks that accompany it, and the basic unpredictability of fragile situations mean that – initially at least – hunches, fear, and desperation may be all some people have to go on. Expectations matter in more settled situations, to be sure, but the problems of fragile societies make corruption a particularly tempting way to try to reduce uncertainties, avoid some varieties of risk, and compensate for high levels of distrust.

Expectations, and the problems they raise, are likely to differ significantly from one corruption syndrome to the next. The insecurity characteristic of Oligarchs and Clans, the notion that it is risky to challenge central domination in an Official Moguls society, and the relative predictability of corruption in Elite Cartels cases are examples. Changing expectations may also contribute to transitions from one syndrome to another: an Elite Cartels situation in which key interests decide that political defeat will not leave them in the wilderness – or dead – and that political accommodations can be made without unacceptable risks, may be en route to an Influence Markets situation. An Oligarchs-and-Clans case in which citizens begin to believe they can act effectively and safely in the political arena may be on the road to an Elite Cartels situation. On the other hand, an Official Moguls network whose principals feel power and wealth rapidly slipping away – or, members of an Elite Cartel who see collapse as imminent – might be on the verge of a slide into Oligarchs and Clans. Expectations can thus affect the strength of institutions de facto as well as *de jure*: in Zambia, for example, DiJohn (2010: 4) points to a "relatively stable and inclusive bargain among contending elites" as a force enhancing the resilience of the state over the long term. One way to avoid doing harm, therefore, is to avoid overly rapid changes that make elites or faction leaders significantly more insecure. An aggressive push for elections or hasty bureaucratic reorganization, for example, might encourage top figures who fear losing power to go into corruption overdrive, be it by way of rapacious theft (Scott 1972) or egregious steps to buy support, as in Daniel arap Moi's Kenya (Klopp 2000).

But how can we know whether, and how, expectations are changing? One way is to ask people about them in surveys, and that is worth doing. But responses to expectation questions are likely to be diffuse and open to echo-chamber influences – much like corruption perceptions – and the connections between such responses and actual behavior are speculative at best. Therefore it will also be worth studying kinds of behavior that can indirectly illuminate expectations: levels of violence; trust among citizens, as well as in government, law enforcement, the courts, banks, and other institutions; investment behavior not only at the peaks of the economy but particularly in small and medium enterprises; currency trends and capital flight; and birth and emigration rates are possible examples. Many such indicators will only become meaningful over the middle to long term, but that is more or less inevitable if we are looking at lasting changes in expectations. What they have in common is that they emphasize choices and behavior reflecting people's best guesses about the future. Behavior-based indicators of expectations are also a way to cross-check more intangible evidence, such as poll data on trust, and the trends in government performance suggested by indicators and benchmarking.

Outcomes and expectations are pressing issues in fragile and extensively corrupt settings, but they may also be particularly important in Influence Market cases. In no way are those countries immune to the bureaucratic pathologies and performance problems that ordinary indicators and benchmarks could reveal. But Influence Market corruption also includes practices that are not necessarily illegal, but still put significant strain on values of fairness, equity, and due process (see Chapter 7). Business privileges that might otherwise be seen as borderline or clearly corrupt, because of the ways they convert public resources and powers into private benefits, are often written into laws and policies. Political finance practices, lobbying, and the activities of many interest groups generally break no laws, and in many ways are integral to a vibrant democracy – but can also contribute to declining competition and openness in both politics and the economy (Johnston 2005a: Chapter 4). They are a major part of what citizens have in mind when they say leaders "don't care about people like me" or run a political process that has been corrupted by money. Many political finance practices generate large flows of publicly accessible data, but ironically one outcome has been to intensify citizens' sense that democracy has become fundamentally corrupted. Both that irony of transparency, and the ways several rounds of reforms have left citizen estrangement and pessimism largely untouched, suggest that understanding expectations is of the essence in Influence Market situations.

Table 3.1 lists some possible qualitative indicators of trends in expectations. Many are quite indirect; some may be measured via economic, political, or poll data while others will be matters of expert judgment. All, however, point to ways in which reformers can identify positive deeper developments unlikely to be captured by corruption or good-governance indices.

The indicators of expectations in Influence Markets are particularly "embedded," in the sense that they are both general indicators of the overall health of the system and are open to a variety of cyclical influences. But those diffuse sorts of issues and beliefs, just as much as more specific aspects of official honesty or venality, are at issue in Influence Market situations, as I will discuss in Chapter 7. Citizens who believe that elections and representative institutions have been fundamentally corrupted may require much more than another round of reforms enacted by those same leaders in order to decide that the system is becoming more democratic and fair. Other aspects of expectations may be measurable through citizen evaluations of services. Recent surveys of Afghanistan by The Asia Foundation, and by Integrity Watch Afghanistan (Integrity Watch Afghanistan, 2010; Asia Foundation 2012), suggest that essential work can be carried out even in difficult settings. Afghanistan is a special case because of the extensive investment outside powers have in its governance, but where major national surveys cannot be undertaken focus-group efforts and routine communication with local elites could provide useful insights.

Careful assessments of the extent of bureaucratic autonomy, perhaps through evidence on variances and irregularities in administrative functions, will be valuable; too much *or* too little autonomy can be bad, but moderating trends matched by growing public trust would be good news. Particularly strategic will be those agencies that maintain state and public–private boundaries, such as customs services, the courts, and the police; the more effective they are, the less valuable personal power and access become. A similar argument can be made about taxation: reliable policies and collections can help demonstrate the effectiveness of the state and allow citizens and business people to plan for the future. Even-handed application of tax policy may help ease mutual distrust

Table 3.1 *Qualitative indicators of positive trends in expectations and corruption*

Oligarchs and Clans
- Reduced violence, capital flight; more stable currency, tax collections
- Sustained, broad-based economic growth, civil-society activity
- Investors' focus shifts toward longer-term gains
- Public–private boundaries, property rights become clearer
- Courts, police, bureaucracy become more effective, more widely trusted
- Less under-the-table political, economic activity outside official system

Official Moguls
- *Gradual* growth in political competition, economic openness, civil society
- Power, accountability become *more public, less personal*
- Elite stratum becomes larger, less monolithic, closed, and isolated
- Less political (as opposed to policy-based) intrusion into the economy
- Property rights and a genuinely private sector become more secure
- Foreign direct investment less linked to personal sponsorship, protection at the top
- Growing reliance upon law rather than force or patronage
- Growing independence of the courts, press

Elite Cartels
- Economy, politics, banking become more open, competitive, transparent
- Meaningful alternatives compete, power changes hands, at elections
- Party, elite infiltration of bureaucracy, courts, business declines
- Parties speak for, are supported by, real segments of civil society
- Parties compete at all levels, become more than individual elites' personal followings
- Bureaucracy, media, capital markets become more autonomous
- Reform activity independent of ruling elites becomes common
- Privatizations are genuine; quasi-state sector shrinks

Influence Markets
- Trust in government, political leaders, national and local institutions increases
- Belief in fairness of political, economic, legal processes increases
- Political participation and electoral turnouts grow
- Consumer, business confidence levels show sustained increases
- Growing belief that society is "headed in the right direction," that citizen views count

over time, particularly if the taxes are seen to finance quality-of-life improvements. An analogous qualitative change in the political arena would be a growing reliance on parties and interest groups with genuine social foundations. Parties that are more than personal vehicles for elites' ambitions, and those that advocate citizens' lasting interests by political means, rather than "public-utility"-style parties created to enhance democracy as an abstract value (Van Biezen 2004), are essential for self-interested political contention, and will be less vulnerable to collective-action problems. In that same connection, the effective freedom enjoyed by opposition groups and critical segments of the press will also be worth careful monitoring. Again, halfway states may have to be tolerated: it is far better that critics be bought off than be shot.

Finally, positive economic trends are important indicators of expectations too, both in themselves and as signals that institutionalization (even if for less-than-ideal reasons) is taking root. Broad-based expansion, even if at a slow rate, can reduce the zero-sum nature of intergroup competition. Diversification of the economic base can contribute to greater pluralism in politics (Chavez 2003). Longer time horizons for economic initiatives can be a sign of improved expectations, too. Where insecurity is easing and dealing with officialdom is becoming less risky – even if predictability reflects Elite Cartel collusion rather than a wholly rational state – investors can develop a more sustained presence. Overall, the best medium-term outcomes may not be less corruption as such – how would we know? – but rather, corruption situations that are less disruptive and insecure, and more predictable and compatible with economic and social development.

Conclusion

This chapter has treated a number of complex questions at general levels in order to show the importance of fragile situations as a cautionary factor for anti-corruption reform, and make a case that we can do positive things about them. In any actual case there will be specific influences at work that may complicate the schemes offered here or create new opportunities. That is likely to be all the more true in post-conflict situations, where political and institutional problems may be compounded by fear, resentment, and bitter memories too recent to easily overcome. There will be no substitute for detailed knowledge of the society, its history and development, and the ways those deeper influences shape contemporary corruption.

At the same time, the syndromes scheme is intended to sort many of those variations into broad categories. Knowing what syndrome of corruption is predominant in a society will be key to devising appropriate reform strategies and avoiding missteps, and a useful starting point in diagnostic terms for dealing with fragility, since each syndrome points to a particular set of causes, effects, risks, and opportunities. As suggested toward the end of Chapter 2, deep democratization defines differing tasks and goals in contrasting syndrome situations. The four chapters to follow examine those contrasts and challenges more closely, considering several societies in varying degrees of detail.

Caveat lector

A word about those case-study chapters is in order. While they consider a variety of societies, they use those countries to illuminate the four syndromes and their implications – and in particular, to draw out the working meanings of deep democratization – *not* to develop detailed national action plans for corruption control, nor (as noted in Chapter 1) to provide examples from every region. While the syndromes reflect deeper and longer-term influences, the details of situations confronting reformers – economic trends, leaders and their agendas, public opinion, societies' regional and international environments, emerging scandals and other grievances, to name but a few – can change rapidly. The case studies, therefore, are aimed more at illustrating what reform and deep democratization *might* be like in given examples of the four syndromes, and how we might assess trends and progress, than at spelling out specific anti-corruption agendas reflecting all contemporary details. Similarly, they deal primarily with changes over the middle to long term, not with the sorts of one- or two-year timelines defining many anti-corruption projects.

Similarly, the case-study chapters will pay relatively little attention to what does, or does not, seem politically feasible at the moment. Any such judgment would be an educated guess, at best. Moreover, the countries in question are moving targets, and are chosen not only for their own intrinsic importance but also as examples of broader syndromes of corruption and challenges of reform. Chapter 4, for example, examines Tunisia and Egypt as prime cases of Official Mogul

Conclusion

corruption; that chapter was drafted during the aftermath of the 2012 Egyptian presidential election campaign, and revised just two years after the start of upheavals in Tunisia. Even the most ambitious revisions can never keep up with the actual pace of change in those societies. A more basic reason for not emphasizing political feasibility, however, is that deep democratization itself is aimed at laying the political and social foundations for reform – in effect, at creating new kinds of political possibilities over time. For that reason, therefore, the case studies do not ask which steps might or might not draw strong opposition – in a way, proposals that did not challenge established political interests would produce few changes – but rather explore ways of changing political circumstances to pave the way for whatever controls and reforms seem most compelling.

With those points in mind, then, we turn to Chapter 4, and to the formidable corruption – and challenges to reform – found in Official Moguls situations.

4 | *Official Moguls: power, protection ... and profits*

It is not power that corrupts but fear. Fear of losing power corrupts those who wield it and fear of the scourge of power corrupts those who are subject to it.

– Aung San Suu Kyi

Sidi Bouzid, Tunisia, December 17, 2010

The events that took place in the central Tunisian town of Sidi Bouzid in late 2010 are familiar by now. But they are worth another look, for not only did they mark the beginning of the "Jasmine Revolution" that ousted long-time President Zine El Abidene Ben Ali and trigger the "Arab Spring" uprisings; they also highlight underlying aspects of Official Moguls corruption that may not be fully appreciated. For decades in Tunisia and Egypt – the other case to be considered in this chapter – political power was tightly held at the top, institutions were weak, and both citizens and the economy were exploited by top-level figures, their families, and their favorites.

On that Friday morning 26-year-old Mohammad Bouazizi, a young fruit and vegetable seller and the sole breadwinner for his widowed mother, his uncle, and five siblings, was accosted by market inspectors and a policewoman because his vegetable cart was unlicensed (this account draws upon Abouzeid 2011; De Soto 2011). Such encounters are common, and sometimes they can be settled by paying a small fine. But in this instance, as in many others, the officer apparently was after a larger bribe. She refused Bouazizi's offer to pay the ten-dinar official fine (between six and seven US dollars, not a trivial sum for a poor vegetable

---

Great thanks to Bruce Rutherford, whose numerous comments and suggestions have added a great deal to this chapter.

seller) and instead seized some of his produce, as well as his scales – essentially, his sole piece of business capital. Then the policewoman slapped Bouazizi, spat in his face, and insulted his dead father – all in front of spectators. The young man went to local government headquarters; whether he sought to complain, get his scales back, or even to apply for a license mattered little, for no one would see him. A short time later he returned to the government offices; in front of the building he doused himself with paint thinner, which he set alight. Bouazizi was hospitalized, but died on January 4, 2011 – by which time his fellow Tunisians were in open rebellion against the regime. By January 14, Ben Ali had fled.

The shorthand version of those events and their extended consequences – that Tunisians, and then citizens in other Arab societies, rebelled in large part because of corruption – contains considerable truth (on the "Arab Spring" generally, see Lynch 2012; Noueihed and Warren 2012; Shehata 2012). But Bouazizi's case was not the first of its kind. Moreover, to focus just on the apparent extent of corruption would be to miss some important points. Unlike much corruption in many liberal democracies, the impetus in Sidi Bouzid did not come from a private party seeking to buy or rent influence, but from officials who viewed citizens as targets. They must have had a strong sense of impunity, for they did not act under cover of darkness or take Bouazizi off into a back alley. Instead, they made their demands, and indulged in direct humiliations, in front of an audience from whom they likely expected little resistance. That sense of impunity, and the fact that the abused citizen could get no help from officials, were arguably extended shadows of Ben Ali's system of power and patronage (on similar connections in Egypt, see Blaydes 2010).

Bouazizi himself was no activist or anti-corruption campaigner. He was a poor man with few prospects – despite his university education – who simply wanted to make a living. His goal was to get a permanent licensed market stall and someday buy a pickup truck to use in the produce trade. But obtaining a loan was out of the question: as De Soto (2011) points out, the young man had no collateral – not even his family's home, for which a legitimate title was impossible to get.

Indeed, Bouazizi's legitimate options were few. Finding a job commensurate with his education would have been difficult in the best of times, and would have required political connections he did not have. He had to make an off-the-books daily payment just to use a patch of ground in the marketplace; that gave him a chance to sell his produce but also exposed him to demands for more bribes. "Going legal" was out of the question:

> Bouazizi might have tried legalizing his business by establishing a small sole proprietorship. But that's easier said than done. We calculated that doing that would have required 55 administrative steps totaling 142 days and fees amounting to some $3,233 (about 12 times Bouazizi's monthly net income, not including maintenance and exit costs) (De Soto 2011).

As suggested in Chapter 3, it is likely that most of those steps, fees, and licensing requirements were created and enforced more to generate income for officials than to create a well-regulated market. Politics offered no more hope: the Ben Ali regime, as we shall see, existed primarily to enrich and protect the President, his family, and politically connected elites. The market sellers in Sidi Bouzid likely knew all too well that top-down exploitation extended, by various connections, all the way down to the neighborhood and village level.

The extortionate demands our young produce seller encountered on that day were objectionable enough in themselves. But they were only symptoms of a far more pervasive system of political hegemony, scarce economic alternatives, and very weak official and political institutions. Had no one demanded any money – indeed, if such demands somehow had ceased – Bouazizi would still have been in a desperate situation. As suggested in Chapter 1, corruption in Official Moguls societies is not a "problem" in government, but rather integral to the process of governing itself. Countless observers have urged the new regimes of the Arab world – as well as old ones still in power – to "tackle" or "root out" corruption. But that idea underestimates the ways abuses of power and wealth reflect, and perpetuate, basic patterns of participation and institutions – in this case, the weakness of both in the face of domination from above. Changes of regime were long overdue, but in both Egypt and Tunisia key elements of the old system remain entrenched.

Discussing corruption and reform in today's Tunisia and Egypt is an audacious exercise. The full story of economic, political, and human-rights abuses under the Ben Ali and Hosni Mubarak regimes may never be told. Realities in both societies change daily, even hourly: early sections of this chapter were first drafted on a day when Mubarak reportedly was pronounced clinically dead, then was described as ill but alive, and after a few hours was said to have suffered a fall in prison,

Sidi Bouzid, Tunisia, December 17, 2010 89

its medical consequences unclear. Tunisia's political transition, at a national level, got off to a relatively positive start (Stepan 2012), as the moderate Islamist Ennahda (Renaissance) Party promised openness, and a balanced relationship between religion and state, following its election victory in October 2011. More recently, however, popular discontent with the new government has grown, along with complaints that the economy is not improving. Some reports suggest police harassment of citizens – particularly, of women – has become even worse (Ben Mhenni 2012; Ghribi 2012).

Egypt, for its part, held parliamentary elections beginning in late 2011, and concluding in January 2012; two rounds of presidential voting followed in May and June of 2012. The latter culminated in victory for Muhammad Mursi, candidate of the Muslim Brotherhood, over Ahmed Shafiq, a former Air Force Senior Commander and Prime Minister under Mubarak. But the presidential campaigns were marked by controversy; an election commission dominated by figures from the old regime intervened at one point to remove ten names from the ballot. Then, even more ominously, the military seized key legislative, budgetary, and constitutional powers on the eve of the final round and the announcement of results. Mursi's victory was greeted with joy in Cairo's Tahrir Square, and with relief by many others that the Supreme Council of the Armed Forces (SCAF), supposedly only an interim authority, did not overturn Mursi's clear, if narrow, majority. When Mursi took office on June 30, 2012, it was unclear just what powers – if any – he would possess. In the months since he proved to be surprisingly aggressive in moves against the military leadership, but ineffective at reviving the economy; his presidency was also shaken in late 2012 by protests against his claims of additional powers. On July 3, 2013, he was ousted by the army.

The fog of reform

What, if anything, can reformers do in such settings? What should they refrain from doing? And how can they know whether progress is being made? In this chapter I will consider these issues in deliberately limited terms.

Egypt and Tunisia are not identical. However tempting it is to emphasize geographic and religious similarities, particularly in light of their common upheavals, they differ in social scale (Egypt's population is between nine and eleven times as large as Tunisia's, depending upon the estimates we use), economic characteristics, and historical relationships with European and Middle Eastern countries. Tunisia's Islamic heritage incorporates a variety of distinctive traditions and cosmopolitan tendencies (Stepan 2012), along with others common to the broader region, making for its own pattern of relationships among religion, law, and the state. The modern Tunisian state evolved largely as an extension of the personal and family interests of two powerful leaders – Habib Bourguiba, followed by Zine Ben Ali – while Egypt's far larger and less coherent state has a longer and more complicated history. It was not so much shaped by Mubarak or his allies as exploited by them, in its fragmentation and inefficiency, not only for enrichment but also to build support in a large and fractious society.

Rather, we consider the two countries together here because they exemplify the Official Moguls syndrome of corruption; if anything, contrasts between them help emphasize that none of the four syndromes arises in identical form everywhere it holds sway. Our central question is thus not "how can Tunisia, Egypt, and similar societies become consolidated democracies?" Desirable as such an outcome might be, it is not immediately on the cards. Too many elements of the old regimes remain; too few credible institutions and opportunities for political and economic participation are available. Trust – both in government and among citizens – is too scarce, and poverty too extensive for rapid democratic consolidation to be likely. Worse yet, a hasty dash for democracy, by too quickly threatening entrenched segments of the *ancien régime* and undermining such institutions as do exist, could invite repression, greater violence, and the profound insecurities and disruptions associated with Oligarchs and Clans. It is also worth remembering that democracy, if and when it arrives, will bring corruption problems of its own.

Equally, the central question is not "what anti-corruption controls should Egypt and Tunisia put in place?" Corruption remains a critical grievance, but as noted it was less a problem within those regimes than their reason for being – a factor propping them up during their long run. The processes by which top elites and their cronies enriched and protected themselves were sustained by formidable incentives, some (as we shall see) originating via well-meaning aid from outside. In an atmosphere of polarization and distrust, creating major new anti-corruption powers can be risky business; particularly in Egypt, such powers would likely become clubs for various factions to swing at the other. Nor, finally, will I place great emphasis on what does or does not seem politically possible in 2013, other than to assume that quick and lasting reductions in corruption across the board are unlikely at this point. Deep democratization, after all, is less about directly attacking corruption than about improving the political possibilities for checking it over the medium to long term.

As argued in Chapter 2, the most pressing challenge of deep democratization in Official Moguls cases is to increase political pluralism within a safe and open political space. By "pluralism" I do not mean a rapid transition to the elaborate universe of shifting interests driving liberal democracy. Instead, the need is to begin building countervailing forces – recall our "thought experiment" in which an absolute dictator faces no constraints – that are autonomous, rooted in society, and able to defend their interests by political means. Can Egypt, Tunisia, and other societies contending with Official Moguls open up to farmers, women, unemployed students, and owners of small and medium enterprises, for example, and can they provide political space within which they might safely contend and compete? That state of affairs need not resemble full democracy; indeed it very likely will not for some time. Meaningful civil liberties, credible courts, and law enforcement that protects citizens rather than oppressing and humiliating them may be the first priorities.

That agenda is more modest than many reform advocates may wish, but it is potentially far-reaching in terms of social depth. Pluralism and safe political and economic space are means to subsequent political changes and possible reforms, not the answer to corruption in themselves. And as Chapter 3 argues, in fragile situations such as those of today's Tunisia and Egypt deep democratization entails a long process of building trust – not only in government but among citizens – and of establishing the effectiveness and fairness of basic government functions. A final point is very important: gradualism does not mean we do nothing about corruption until circumstances are perfectly aligned. In fact, both increased pluralism and safe space will require some highly targeted and effective anti-corruption measures. But they will not be the opening shots of an assault on all corruption. Rather, they will be steps toward enabling people like Mohammad Bouazizi, who only wanted to make a living, to defend themselves by political means.

Official Moguls in action

"Official Moguls" is shorthand for corruption practiced by top figures within a hegemonic regime, or by lower-level functionaries who have reason to think they will be protected, in a setting where opposition and official institutions are weak. Official Moguls corruption may involve figures holding state powers – the top figures in a regime – but can also include political cronies, family members and other personal favorites. Unlike Influence Markets, where wealth intrudes into state functions, in the process crossing comparatively clear boundaries between the private and public sectors, here state power intrudes into the economy and society. In smaller societies the Moguls' networks may be relatively simple, but in more complex countries they can decentralize somewhat – particularly where economies are creating new opportunities more rapidly than they can be controlled by any small group (China is an example). Serious corruption is often protected by the threat of force, and thus can be particularly arbitrary and unpredictable, but between periods of crisis Official Mogul corruption is unlikely to be as chaotic or violent as that seen in Oligarch-and-Clan situations.

Political opportunities in such societies are scarce. Economic opportunities both legitimate and corrupt, be they the results of liberalization, mineral extraction, or flows of external aid and investment, are somewhat more plentiful but tend to be dominated by the politically powerful – often becoming forms of patronage and control. Official Mogul corruption thus is not a disease that threatens to bring down the system; rather, it can be the lifeblood of the system itself. Without a degree of pluralism and a safe political and economic space, opposition to corruption will be weak, and those suffering from it will have few options.

Tunisia: big stakes in a small country

Tunisia's eleven million citizens occupy a territory of about sixty-three thousand square miles in North Africa, a location that in recent decades has afforded economic access to southern Europe but which, for a longer time, exposed it to manipulation by French and Italian interests (World Factbook 2013). France took control in 1881, invading the territory and creating a protectorate; after World War II, however, nationalist movements in both Tunisia and Algeria weakened the French hold on the region. Tunisia became independent in 1956 under the leadership of Habib Bourguiba. Bourguiba's attempts to build a socialist economy met with relatively little success, and his one-party state was hardly democratic. But he did make rights for women more extensive than those elsewhere in the region, and his secular style of rule made Tunisia a moderating influence in the region, as well as an attractive partner for France and other European powers.

By 1987 the ailing Bourguiba was easily forced from power by Zine Ben Ali. A brief interlude of political decompression followed; the parliamentary elections held in 1989 were more free than any under the old regime, and Tunisia for a time had the air of a modernizing secular Arab state. By the early 1990s, however, the outlines of Ben Ali's political and economic machine, and the corrupt tactics it employed, were becoming clear. The President, his wife Leila Trabelsi, and extended family moved into the real estate, tourism, and export sectors in a big way:

A commission established in the weeks after Ben Ali's overthrow, and including public accountants and specialists in the intricacies of administrative or real estate law, examined some 5,000 complaints. The report it released in November [2011] exposed a vast system of structured corruption by which the Ben Ali in-laws and their cronies helped themselves to the best of everything: stakes in the most lucrative businesses, exemption from customs dues, choice public land. Government institutions such as tax authorities and the judiciary, even private banks, became instruments of coercion. Recalcitrant chief executives would get slapped with an audit or see their loans dry up or their authorizations revoked (Chayes 2012).

For those not deterred by administrative harassment there was always a risk of torture, either by police or by national security forces. In 2008 police forces reportedly fired on protesters, killing several; during the 2010–11 uprising the police were more widely feared than was the army (Code 2012). It was not just in Aung San Suu Kyi's Myanmar that corruption dominated through fear; that sort of climate is common to many Official Moguls cases.

In the aftermath of the uprising the new regime went after Ben Ali and Trabelsi family assets, but the sheer scale and complexity of their business empire has made for slow progress:

When it comes to dealing with internal assets, the Tunisian government has managed to confiscate hundreds of businesses, banks, insurance companies and several pieces of real estate that were controlled by the previous regime.

Many of these are in the form of conglomerates, such as Princesse Holding – a group controlled by Ben Ali's son-in-law, Sakher el-Materi – that encompasses businesses in all major sectors of the Tunisian economy, ranging from car importers to publishing companies and banks. The broad scale of the confiscations attests to just how widespread corruption was under the old regime. Nearly all major businesses were either owned outright by the former ruling family or had arrangements with them. Government ministries were often used as tools for furthering the same interests (Chayes 2012).

The family had a lavish existence, appropriating valuable antiquities for use in their various homes. Sakher el-Materi, for example, kept a massive marble "Gorgon's Mask" that he had arranged to have stolen from Algeria in 1996 (Deimling 2012). When one of the family's seaside villas was thrown open to the public after the old regime fell, visitors were stunned by the level of opulence and the scope of theft from the nation (Raghavan 2011). Belhassen Trabelsi, Ben Ali's 49-year-old brother-in-law, was accused in Tunisia of a range of abuses, and in mid 2012 agreed to return from Canada to face trial. He found the family business very profitable indeed:

According to U.S. Embassy cables leaked by the whistleblowing website WikiLeaks, Belhassen Trabelsi is "the most notorious family member" in Ben Ali's extended family. The cables refer to the entire family as a "quasi-mafia," noting that "the Trabelsis' strong-arm tactics and flagrant abuse of the system make them easy to hate." Described in the French press as a "hoodlum," Trabelsi profited from his sister's 1992 marriage, using public institutions and resources to create a Tunisian business empire that included luxury hotels, an airline, a radio station, a newspaper and two banks (Aliriza 2012; see also Tu 2012).

The biggest challenge has been repatriating family assets held abroad, totaling $15 billion by some accounts. While few foreign governments wish to appear to back the Ben Ali/Trabelsi families, cooperation has been uneven; many significant assets are held by shell companies, or under false or unknown names. In some countries Tunisian investigators must prove that assets were stolen before they can be released – not an easy task. Canadian police sources suggest that Ben Ali family members had at one time held between C$10 million and C$20 million in assets in Canada (Tu 2012).

The networks included family favorites too: a US diplomatic cable written in 2008, released by WikiLeaks in 2010, observed that

"Seemingly half of the Tunisian business community can claim a Ben Ali connection through marriage, and many of these relations are reported to have made the most of their lineage" (Thorne 2012). Whether or not that claim is an exaggeration, powerful networks of Ben Ali beneficiaries remained in the country even after the dictator and his wife fled. They constitute a powerful and well-placed interest, and they are unlikely to surrender their advantages easily. "'Our main difficulty lies with those people who profited in the old system,' says Samir Annabi, the new chief of Tunisia's National Commission against Corruption and the Misappropriation of Funds. 'They will try to defend themselves. It's a continuation of the old system'" (Chayes 2012). Indeed, there are concerns that members of the new regime will seek not to beat those old networks but to join them.

In confronting corruption, then, Tunisia is taking on much of its past, particularly the ways the state evolved and the fundamental interests it did and did not serve. So far the results are sobering; many citizens see corruption as worsening (Balleny 2012), particularly at the ground level, where police and local functionaries now have more discretion than under Ben Ali. One poll reported that three-quarters of Tunisians "do not believe that the new government succeeded in fighting corruption and bribery in its first 100 days" (Chayes 2012). The newly appointed Deputy Prime Minister for Transparency and Fighting Corruption, Abderrahman Ladgham, announced in 2012 that henceforth June 11 would be a national anti-corruption holiday, a move seen as an empty gesture by many (Joline 2012a). Not long after that, Mohamed Abbou, Minister for Administrative Reform, resigned, complaining that the Prime Minister was reneging on promises to give him enough power to act (Daraghi 2012). Some eighty-two judges were fired in mid 2012 as part of a corruption inquiry (Associated Press 2012c), as were twenty customs officers in a separate incident (Joline 2012b), but it is debatable whether that signals progress or merely confirms that corruption remains widespread.

Indeed, "corruption" in Tunisia refers not just to the economic dealings of elites, or to day-to-day demands for bribes, but rather to a nationwide, top-to-bottom system of "extractive" (Acemoglu and Robinson 2012) governance and economic practices, one backed up by violence, torture, and human-rights violations. For most citizens the real test of reform will be the openness and fairness of society as a whole, the extent to which citizens can advocate and defend their interests within a safe and fair political process, and ultimately, whether they will have a chance at a better life.

Egypt: corruption, revolution – or was it a coup?

When Hosni Mubarak took power in Egypt, days after Anwar Sadat was assassinated by military officers while reviewing a victory parade on October 6, 1981, it was unclear just how long-lived his presidency would be (on Egypt and the Mubarak era generally, see Bradley 2008; El-Mahdi 2009; Blaydes 2010; Bowker 2010; Amin 2011; Stacher 2012; Rutherford 2013). The former Air Force Commander had been Sadat's Vice President since 1975 – indeed, he was wounded by the assassins – yet was relatively unknown. Further, his position linked him to Sadat's peace treaty, and relatively open dealings, with Israel – a policy that helped spur the assassins and had caused Egypt's suspension from the Arab League. Mubarak moved quickly to consolidate power, however, reinstituting an Emergency Law first imposed during the Nasser years, strengthening the nation's domestic security apparatus and giving military officials key roles in his government. When Mubarak finally left office on February 11, 2011, in the face of mass unrest across much of the nation, he had become one of Egypt's longest-lasting leaders. By most accounts, those same years in office had also made him quite wealthy indeed (although early estimates of Mubarak's assets, initially ranging as high as US$70 billion, were almost certainly vastly overstated: see Hope 2012a).

Egypt is both one of the world's oldest societies and one of its youngest. Half of its nearly ninety million citizens are under 25 years old (World Factbook 2013). Its territory stretches from Gaza and Israel southwestward into the desert; the Nile valley is, in parts, highly fertile and extensively cultivated, but 97 percent of the country is non-arable. Over four in ten Egyptians are urbanites, with much the biggest concentration – over ten million – in and around Cairo. Many, particularly among the young, are educated, for universities are virtually free, yet unemployment is endemic. By one account 87 percent of the unemployed are between 15 and 29 years old, and university graduates are far more likely to be unemployed than are those who did not attend (Camplin 2011). The growth and investment centers in the economy – oil and minerals, large-scale agriculture, real estate – are effectively closed to most young Egyptians, and since 2011 those sectors that had created some jobs, such as tourism and manufacturing, have been in decline. That the demonstrations in early 2011 were heavily populated by unemployed young people surprised no one. The relatively extensive use of text messaging and social media (Rane and Salem 2012) captured the attention of many observers, some of whom coined terms like "the Facebook Revolution," but that aspect of the events arguably had much more to do with the uneven distribution of opportunity and deprivation in Egyptian society than with anything distinctive about social media.

Official Mogul corruption has long been both cause and effect of those inequalities. As in Tunisia, being born into the ruling family was an excellent career move, in financial terms; sons Alaa and Gamal Mubarak prospered in both the legitimate business arena and in more dubious pursuits. Both were tried, along with their father, on corruption charges in early 2012; those charges were dismissed because the statute of limitations had run out, but a second trial on charges of insider trading was launched later in the year (*Agence France Presse* 2012a; *The Telegraph* 2012). Mubarak's financial empire included military cronies, government ministers, and what one observer (Hansen 2012) has termed "a thuggish clique of businessmen and politicians" in Mubarak's National Democratic Party. Some were involved in Mubarak family dealings; many more carried out their own schemes and scams under the dictator's protective gaze.

In the wake of the uprising, Zakaria Azmi, Mubarak's one-time Chief of Staff, was convicted of corrupt activities netting an estimated $7 million (Associated Press 2012a, 2012b). The former Oil Minister, Security Chief, and Tourism Minister have all been convicted of major corruption; so too was former Trade Minister Rachid Mohammad Rachid, who has yet to be apprehended, and steel executive Ahmad Ezz, a Rachid crony (Ibid.). Indeed, presidential candidate Shafiq was himself under investigation, and fled the country (supposedly to make a pilgrimage) shortly after his electoral defeat (Ibid.; Reuters 2012).

The military had great economic clout in what has been termed "The Egyptian Republic of Retired Generals" (Abul-Magd 2012; although taken as a whole, the military is not monolithic: see Awad 2012). Ownership of businesses by military organizations or top officers has never been investigated in detail; some estimate that such holdings make 10 to 45 percent of the economy (Hansen 2012). In 2011 the military lent the Egyptian Central Bank the equivalent of US$1 billion, and apparently did so without great difficulty (Stacher, quoted in Hansen

2012). A *Sydney Morning Herald* report (McGeough 2012) underlined the generals' stake in defending the bad old ways of doing business:

Major-General Mahmoud Nasr warned that despite the dawn of democracy, there would be no civilian encroachment on the military's sprawling business empire. "We'll fight for our projects," he harangued local reporters. "We have sweated for 30 years and we won't leave them for anyone to destroy."

Remarkable stuff. It's not as though the general is talking about a few garrison tuckshops. Shrouded in official secrecy, the military is estimated to control between 15 and 40 per cent of gross domestic product through its food and drinking water, electronics and whitegoods, chemical and agricultural enterprises – even hotels and real estate.

Land, be it in rapidly growing Cairo or the country's fertile or seaside areas, was a particularly important focus of wheeling and dealing (a dynamic reinforced by the fact that real property is untaxed in Egypt). One extended scenario (Hope 2012b) involved the large and, after thirty years, still-unfinished Gezira Tower and Hotel. Developer Khaled Aly Fouda, a former government statistician, acquired the hotel site in 1968, and by the early 1980s had begun excavations for the tallest building in Egypt. He was plagued, however, by bureaucratic political obstructions that seemingly had no purpose other than allowing better-connected businessmen to intervene, and officials to demand payments. After years of frustration Hussein Salem, a Mubarak associate, offered to break through the bottlenecks; all he wanted in return was full ownership (for which he would have paid Fouda only $500,000). Fouda refused the deal, and was left with title to an empty high-rise shell. Another of Fouda's projects, a beachfront hotel and resort in the Sinai, was nearly ready to open in 1996 when the Ministry of Defense seized the land, citing "strategic interests." The ensuing political and legal wrangling lasted fifteen years until Fouda, on the eve of the Cairo uprisings, finally agreed to sell to the Ministry for only a small fraction of his overall investment. By contrast, those who played nicely with officials could often buy land at low prices and see their projects through to conclusion.

Arable farmland is equally strategic. As Abu Dhabi's *The National* (Collard 2012) reports:

[Yussef Wali, the former Egyptian agriculture minister] was convicted earlier [in 2012] and sentenced to 10 years in prison for a deal that saw thousands of hectares of public land near Luxor transfer into the hands of Hussein Salem, a

Official Moguls in action

businessman close to Mubarak. Under the terms of the deal, the land – valued at over 208 million Egyptian pounds [around US$34.3 million] ... was sold to Salem for just 8 million Egyptian pounds [about US$1.3 million].

Salem also took care to reward his patrons, including Hosni Mubarak himself, who at one point received a seaside villa.

But another factor in such deals was 1990s-era development aid from the United States and other donors intended for irrigation of new regions, opening them up to efficient farming. Perhaps not surprisingly, a significant portion of such aid money ended up benefiting top officials and military officers:

Instead of seeding the desert with the wheat and affordable produce required to feed Egyptians, most of this reclaimed land was given to connected businessmen who cultivated high-profit strawberries, guavas and mangos bound for European supermarkets ... In theory, the money earned from these cash crops would be used to buy cheaper goods (like wheat) on the international market, while at the same time being invested in projects to create jobs for Egypt's unemployed. Instead, investors built heavily mechanised mega-farms, providing few jobs and little food for the domestic market. At the same time, many allege that large international loans were used to fill coffers, rather than implement development projects (Ibid.).

For many poorer families – also saddled by the government's cuts in subsidies, unfavorable lending policies, and bans on agricultural unions (Ibid.) – there was little choice but to leave the land for the city. Meanwhile Egypt, once roughly self-sufficient in terms of food production, became one of the world's largest importers of wheat.

The extent to which development aid might have helped bankroll Official Mogul corruption remains a concern. Such aid is channeled to and through national governments, yet the ability of donors to supervise its actual uses is restricted by recipients' national sovereignty and, in the case of many lending organizations, by longstanding principles of non-interference in domestic affairs. Where regimes face few demands for accountability and official institutions are weak, aid can fuel the schemes of top figures and their clients. Corruption in aid-funded programs is by no means limited to Official Moguls situations, but the hazards in such cases would seem particularly great. Indeed, it does not take much imagination to ask whether symbolic compliance with some anti-corruption agreements – easy enough for an unchallenged regime to orchestrate – might make a particularly good smokescreen for the real corrupt action. A similar argument has been made (Landolt 2012) with respect to human-rights-oriented technical assistance; there, too, a regime might make a fine show of openness and enlightened policy in selected, relatively unstrategic, parts of politics and society, in order to divert attention from abuses elsewhere.

As in Tunisia, officials' sense of impunity extended to the everyday treatment of citizens. Police and security officials engaged in extensive torture with little fear of prosecution. Under the infamous Emergency Law as many as 100,000 Egyptians were imprisoned as political prisoners, some of them for as long as twenty years. While some citizens brought successful civil actions claiming damages for torture, for the vast majority legal recourse was out of the question. Arbitrary arrest and imprisonment without trial were systematic: al-Nadim, a human-rights group, reported in 2007 that "[t]orture is the official state policy and not only the responsibility of an officer here or there." As of mid 2012, some 300,000 citizen complaints against police had still received no attention. Until investigations can be carried out by credible jurists or a "truth commission" the full scale of abuses will never be known, but clearly such practices strongly discouraged citizens from speaking out (Olster 2012).

Another parallel to Tunisia has been the difficulty of locating and recovering stolen assets (Evripidou 2012; McGrath 2012). The wide variation in estimates of Mubarak's own wealth gives some indication of the uncertainties of that task, although there is little doubt that the former President, his family, and his cronies took significant wealth out of a society in which two of five citizens subsist on less than two dollars a day (Hansen 2012). Mubarak-era spoils are scattered around the world, held in a variety of well-hidden forms under many names. European investigators are focusing on nineteen individuals, including Mubarak relatives and close allies. The difficulties of locating the assets of Mubarak crony Hussein Salem (the real estate manipulator described above) symbolize the challenges confronting investigators:

For Egyptian authorities trying to determine the fate of what they believe are billions of dollars in ill-gotten wealth during the Mubarak era, the challenge posed by Salem is monumental: how to unravel the mostly smoke-and-mirrors financial edifice that one of Egypt's shrewdest businessman built to mask his business transactions.

Court documents obtained by *The National* show that Salem and his family presided over a business empire that stretched from France to Hong Kong and included companies and off-shore accounts in the UAE, Spain, Switzerland and Romania.

Yet Egyptian investigators examining the financial dealings of Mubarak-era political and business figures have found only meagre amounts of cash held in Salem's name in Egypt (Hope 2012c).

Canadian officials have widened the search to 140 names (McGrath 2012). As of mid 2012 a total of SF410 million (just under US$425 million) in assets had been frozen in Switzerland, along with £105 million (about US$163.5 million) in the United Kingdom, but proceedings are still required before those funds can be returned to Egypt.

Here too, investigators must rely on cooperation from other countries, which in turn can vary depending upon geopolitical factors. But many in Egypt question just how vigorously their own investigators are pursuing the connections. Some accuse the investigators of engaging in delaying tactics to allow allies of the old regime to move assets to new hiding places. Where specific steps have been taken, as with Egyptian requests for data from the United Kingdom, some suspect the local authorities are simply going through the motions – and none too rapidly at that. Such contentions are impossible to evaluate from a distance, but they give some indication of the credibility problems corruption fighters encounter.

Citizens have been routinely abused in less violent ways as well: police demands for bribes from drivers, shopkeepers, and others were, and still are, a fact of life (Husain 2012). The Mubarak regime abounded with contrived rules, regulations, and bureaucratic procedures that seemingly had little purpose other than to put the squeeze on citizens and small business operators. Under the new regime lower-level demands for bribes continue unabated, or may even have increased (Hope 2012d, 2012e). One journalist reported, in the Spring of 2012:

At a Cairo vehicle licence bureau, despondency finally gave way to despair. In the heaving crowd, which had been waiting with little to do but watch the insects creep across the walls, scuffles broke out.

The clerk behind the glass sat sipping tea, apparently unperturbed by the tumult. With no waiting list, he smiled across the crowd at the best-dressed man in the room and a woman wearing pricey sunglasses, who acknowledged his glance and pressed forward to be served first.

It is a scene that is sadly familiar to many Egyptians, who dread applying for official documents knowing they may have to spend hours, days or even weeks waiting in grubby offices to complete the paperwork that consumes their lives ...

Some people waiting for paperwork complain that low-level graft has become even worse since the uprising because of lax law enforcement.

Weary citizens list an entire vocabulary of gestures, glances and phrases to show a palm must be greased.

"I wish you a trouble-free day," "Offer me a cup of tea," and "Help me buy something nice for the kids," are often accompanied by a knowing smile. Many Egyptians refer to bribes with the euphemism "al-halawah" – "the reward"[1] (Saleh 2012).

As in Tunisia such demands, and the financial burdens they create, are bad enough. But it is in the long-term view that the full picture becomes clear. Generations of Egyptians have come of age in a society whose governing figures have systematically enriched themselves, impoverished their citizens, and closed off any and all routine avenues of recourse. They have done those things not just through bribery, graft, and greed, but also via ineffective courts, politicized police, monopolistic one-party politics, pervasive networks of personal power rather than of public authority, appeals to nationalism made more compelling by xenophobic threats and symbolism – and, of course, through the all-too-immediate threat of arrest and torture.

Thus, Egypt's plight is not just (!) a corruption problem; it is a political dilemma, as Acemoglu and Robinson make clear:

To Egyptians, the things that have held them back include an inefficient and corrupt state and a society where they cannot use their talent, ambition, ingenuity, and what education they can get. But they also recognize that the roots of these problems are political. All the economic impediments they face stem from the way political power in Egypt is exercised and monopolized by a narrow elite. This, they understand, is the first thing that has to change (Acemoglu and Robinson 2012: 2–3).

Despite the recent coup, that challenge remains. What could be done?

---

[1] I thank Bruce Rutherford for pointing out that *al-halawah* literally means "the sweet," or perhaps a "sweetener," much as small bribes are described in many other societies.

Toward pluralism and safe space

The immediate challenge in Tunisia and Egypt is not primarily to detect, punish, or prevent specific corrupt dealings, but rather to begin to change the political situation that has enabled, fed upon, and protected those abuses. "Begin to change" is a deliberate choice of words, for the needed transformations are fundamental. One is to move toward greater pluralism: more people must have a real chance to express their needs, be they in regard to corruption or any other issue, and to defend themselves and their interests. For that to become reality such interests must become active, first and foremost; moreover, they need political space that is – and is seen to be – open, free from manipulation and, above all, safe. Without such changes – without, in effect, enabling the emergence of sustained political will at the grassroots – most anti-corruption measures will lack an essential base of support. The transformation will require considerable time as well as changes in widely held perceptions and expectations. If they are accomplished we will by no means see an end to corruption; as suggested in Chapter 2 greater pluralism, and safe political and economic space, are steps toward other essential political changes. The agenda proposed here is not – by a wide margin – that of "building democracy," but rather of taking the first steps out of the political dilemma described above.

To be sure, that agenda will require focused anti-corruption and institution-building efforts, particularly with respect to the "safe" part of the political space agenda: the courts, law enforcement, and security forces must be early reform priorities, along with building accountability in those sectors. The management of development aid, and official diversions of flows of investment, should also be priorities. But while major across-the-board reform offensives are understandably attractive, particularly in light of the suffering of Tunisians and Egyptians over the past decades and the scarcity of "open moments" in their political histories (Ghani and Lockhart 2007), rushing the process of change may squander valuable opportunities and even make matters worse. Politics, particularly in Egypt, is at the moment not so much pluralizing as polarized; it is easy to imagine anti-corruption weapons becoming tools of factional conflict and reprisal. Institutions are weak: even if sound legislation were passed, could anyone effectively demand it be enforced? In a politicized judiciary, what are the odds that cases would be fully investigated and fairly tried? Similarly, while resentment of corruption became strong enough to topple dictators in both countries, ordinary citizens are still far removed from real power. Civil society – to the extent that the term is meaningful – is weak and intimidated. Too direct and rapid a push for reform may expose citizens to renewed repression and violence by those with a stake in the empires corruption built. Indeed, there is a strong risk that entrenched interests, witnessing the possible rise of challengers to the old ways of doing things, might respond by putting corruption into overdrive as uncertainties multiply. Thinking about the risks of reform and having a sense of *what not to do* – at least, not for a while – can be essential.

A related priority – one making professionalization and accountability in the courts essential – is the establishment of dependable civil liberties. That is so, clearly, for citizens. But a free, independent, and credible press can also play an essential role. After decades of political pressures and intervention, how autonomous are news outlets, and how skilled are they at investigating corruption cases rather than just indulging in a parade of personalities? Lest those questions seem to dismiss the many courageous journalists who have reported on the past years' events in North Africa, they do not; rather, they emphasize the protection such reporters and investigators will need in years to come.

In the wake of the uprisings some degree of pluralization is more or less inevitable. As in other cases where diverse and, in many ways, contradictory interests have been temporarily united by opposition to an old order, fragmentation is likely (in Tunisia it has already begun: see Ltifi 2012), and probably even desirable. With respect to Egypt and Tunisia we have seen widespread concern, particularly in the United States, over "the Islamists," but they are scarcely a monolithic movement. The Muslim Brotherhood has its factions, its ambitious business people, and divergent schools of thought about the best ways forward; the Brotherhood, in turn, does not see eye to eye on all issues with the intensely conservative Salafis. Al-Nur, the Salafi political party, showed considerable strength in the 2011–12 parliamentary elections, winning about a quarter of the seats; it was quite critical of the Brotherhood's leadership and its role in past corruption. It advocates a much more traditional style of Islamic rule, including less favorable treatment for women (for a recent overview see Rutherford 2013: 15–18; see also Brown 2011). In Tunisia, the resignation of the new government's Anti-Corruption Minister was widely reported not only as an unfortunate event for the reform cause, but as a possible sign of emerging divisions in the new regime (Daraghi 2012). In any event, we might well ask: if the old style of governing is unacceptable, and Islamic parties are to be avoided, what alternative system of authority is there to hold a new system together (an optimistic view on Islamist parties is offered by Van Dyke 2012)?

Overall, Egypt and Tunisia – despite the latter's encouraging early efforts to make peace between religion and the state (Stepan 2012) – have basic choices to make about what sorts of societies they want to be, and what a better, more broadly inclusive style of government and politics might look like. It is in no way self-evident that the best answers to those questions will follow the model of liberal democracy, but I would still suggest that the process of seeking answers must include as broad a range of groups, outlooks, and interests as possible.

Standing the political system on its head

Corruption is often described as a dread disease spreading relentlessly through a society, threatening a general collapse unless we confront it quickly and directly. Attractive as such depictions may be as a way to recruit supporters for reform, when it comes to Official Moguls corruption they can be misleading. In such cases corruption was not something undermining the system of governance; rather, it *was* the system, or at the very least it provided powerful incentives sustaining political hegemony. While the endgame in several societies during the uprisings of 2010–12 was surprisingly quick, the regimes that eventually fell had been in place for 24 (Ben Ali), 29 (Mubarak), and in the case of Libya's Muammar Gaddafi, 42 years. To be sure, official state institutions were very weak – a factor that likely hastened the fall once it had gathered momentum – but the fundamental loyalties of the old regimes were personal, reinforced by rewards for cronies and fear for the rest. Indeed, in both Egypt and Tunisia powerful interests cemented by corruption remain; the military, large segments of the bureaucracy, the courts, and a predatory political–business class will not give up their advantages easily.

The challenge now, made much more difficult by Egypt's recent coup, is to attract citizens into a safe political arena, show them they have a personal stake in reform, and persuade them that they can safely back effective leaders and administrators while putting pressure upon the incompetent and corrupt. That sort of grassroots change would stand the old top-down, patronage-driven Official Moguls system on its head, opening up processes by which meaningful demands can come from the bottom upwards, giving those in charge good reasons to be responsive and accountable.

Just as a tenacious political synergy is part of Official Mogul corruption, synergy is also an issue in the alternative scenario envisioned here. A more open political system has countless moving parts, and feedback loops are the essence of accountability. Political, legal, economic, cultural, historical, psychological, and other factors mesh in a complex yet mutually reinforcing web. It does not have a "start" button we can push, nor any set of institutions we can put in place that would guarantee success. The essence, instead, is enabling people to make sustained and effective demands for openness and accountability because they believe they stand to benefit from trends in those directions.

Openness to whom?

What sorts of participation and contention, among what sorts of groups and outlooks, do we seek? Contention among just a few large factions over relatively few issues, and particularly over issues that cannot be compromised, seems more likely to become a series of feuds than a fluid political process, particularly where material need is great and trust has historically been scarce. By contrast, large numbers of groups offering individuals multiple simultaneous identifications (political groups, yes, but also social, recreational, and cultural groups, mutual-aid societies, and so forth); groups of differing sizes and scopes (neighborhood groups, but also political parties; economic interests, but also people sharing various regional or cultural affinities); and those offering diverse rewards and incentives, not only dealing with shared problems but also offering sociability and a degree of prestige (see Chapter 8) – are a more promising alternative. Similarly, contention over issues open to compromise would be a useful counterbalance to struggles over religious doctrine, and could defuse, rather than accumulate and reinforce, antagonisms over time. Groups in several districts with a common purpose of pushing for better public utilities could differ over other issues and yet still be an effective presence.

While such ideals echo western pluralist thinking they fall well short of calling for liberal democracy. Even so, they will entail changing habits and expectations deeply ingrained during generations under the Moguls. Citizens, individually and in groups, will need to come forward – and, just because they seem to us to share a common interest does not mean they will do so. The expectation that there is no point in political participation, and the understandable apprehension that it might be dangerous, will not be dispelled overnight. The idea of trusting one's neighbors may be slow to take hold. Today's established liberal democracies often seem less than vibrant; how dare we hope for anything better in the wake of Official Moguls?

Strategic goals

There is no simple way forward, but it may be helpful to think in terms of *strategic goals* (what, beyond "less corruption," do we seek overall?); *tactical measures* (steps that can contribute to those strategic changes); *risks* (what problems we might cause while trying to do good things); and *indicators of progress* (ways to judge whether progress is being made, and to convince citizens reform is for real).

A first strategic goal, essential if we are to help change expectations, is confronting the nature of the problem. That the old regimes in Tunisia and Egypt were massively corrupt and repressive will surprise no one, but revealing – insofar as possible – the full scale of past abuses can help identify targets for reform and open some minds as regards a new regime's resolve. A full, honest, and public inquest into corruption, torture, and other abuses under the old governments will be a painful experience, to be sure. More to the point, it will be extremely difficult to do in societies where judges and bureaucracies have been politicized, banking and finance have been private games for the wealthy, and police abuses have been protected by a wall of silence. Moreover, there is a risk that general law enforcement would suffer following the shakeups and dismissals that would likely ensue, and that newly jobless police and security personnel would become a disruptive presence. In Egypt at least, the idea of a general inquest has gained little traction politically – particularly since the military *coup*. Perhaps independent commissions headed by a broadly representative group of respected figures, or a truth-and-reconciliation approach augmented by carefully designed amnesties, might make the process less threatening. Continuing to seek the return of stolen assets and prosecuting various "big fish" can be delicate issues, but some success of both sorts may be essential to win credibility for further reform. The primary emphasis should be on revealing the truth, identifying opportunities for checking future abuses, and on showing that matters are now done differently.

Carefully managing expectations is another important strategic goal. Political and reform leaders should be frank about the time and effort required to implement even the most urgent corruption controls in areas such as the courts, police, and the use of development aid. "Zero tolerance" proclamations are unlikely to be taken seriously; citizens very likely have heard similar sloganeering in the past. Merilee Grindle's notion of "good-enough governance" (Grindle 2004, 2007) may not make an inspiring slogan, but can be a helpful guide for reform since it emphasizes ability to deliver services and address poverty – key factors, as we have seen, in fragile situations. One way to raise expectations in realistic ways would be to publish evidence of government performance on a regular basis (more on that idea below). Leaders' expectations are critical too: they should be prepared for adverse consequences once inquiries and serious reforms begin to take hold. The resulting revelations may well create dire headlines and drive international perceptions downward, encouraging some to claim reform has failed. For that reason, and as a valuable if intangible reward and incentive, public recognition for successful and honest officials should accompany the bad news.

Basic civil liberties, more secure property rights, and an end to torture and police harassment will be essential to bringing new voices out into a safe political space. International evidence (Isham, Kaufmann, and Pritchett 2000) suggests that core civil liberties – to demonstrate, to criticize the government publicly, to meet and organize – are more effective than elections or liberal institutions in terms of improving the ways governments use international aid. Those changes cannot just be proclaimed; they need to be implemented, and then citizens must be allowed time to appreciate that things are changing for the better. Genuine press freedom would help make such improvement believable, although the new leadership will need to be tolerant of the increased controversy and scrutiny a free press will (and should) create. Other basic changes will depend in part upon new police and judicial leadership, as well as on autonomy and increased professionalism in both sectors. I will suggest below that citizens must play an integral role in showing that such changes are bearing fruit.

Deep democratization, more or less by definition, attacks corruption indirectly. But some anti-corruption targets should become early priorities because of their potential to facilitate pluralization and the development of safe space, and those enhancing the "stateness" of the state. In the first category corruption among the police and security forces, and within the judiciary, should be prime early targets, as noted. Training, positive rewards (which need not all be tangible) for ethical and effective individuals and workgroups, and dependable, higher pay can be useful positive incentives. Military corruption could be an equally urgent, but even more difficult, priority; depending upon the strength of civilian officials, second- and third-best options might be most prudent. Partial financial amnesties in exchange for providing evidence and resigning from the armed forces or, for former generals turned businessmen, conflict-of-interest restrictions on dealing with military bodies, could be a step forward. Unsatisfying as amnesties-with-new-rules will be, they might over time begin to fragment military economic interests. Moves against police and military corruption will require a more independent, professional, and credible judiciary, which is no small challenge in its own right.

A second anti-corruption priority should be controls that underwrite and demonstrate the "stateness" of the state. That means at least two things: a state that does the basic things it should do – maintaining order, defending society, policing its borders, and raising and spending revenue effectively – and a transition to governing via public roles, institutions, and loyalties rather than personal power and fealty. Again, the police and security forces will be critical, as may others such as the customs authorities; reorienting them, through changed incentives, training, and new leadership, away from repression toward service and protection is both challenging and essential. Taxation that is simple, understandable, predictable, perceived as equitable, and is linked to results will be a priority. Some governments post signs at highway-repair sites reading "Your Tax Dollars at Work" for precisely that last reason and, clichés though they may be, they reflect an important aspect of accountability. Unlike the Philippines where, as we shall see in Chapter 5, thousands of public facilities and improvements bear the name or initials of a prominent politician wishing to take personal credit, it would be far better to give credit to public agencies and principal commissioners who are attaining their goals.

Earlier in this chapter I suggested that there may be a lamentable synergy between Official Mogul corruption and international flows of aid, investment, and capital. To the extent that that is true such funds, from the time basic agreements are reached until the results are in place, should be a priority for financial and performance audits, the latter involving citizens wherever possible. Societies struggling to shake off the Official Moguls cannot carry that burden alone: donating and investing countries and organizations must look to their own monitoring and control procedures, and western societies must give particularly close attention to flows of illicit funds to and through their financial institutions. All are tall orders, to be sure, but those challenges also offer opportunities: in a closer-to-ideal world we might imagine agreements under which repatriation of stolen assets by affluent societies is accelerated, within the bounds of due process and common sense, in connection with detailed conditionality regarding the uses of those funds, and perhaps of aid as well.

Citizens and their roles are priorities for action too. Years of accumulated abuses brought thousands into the street, but can their participation be sustained? Mobilizing farmers, entrepreneurs, teachers, women, and other citizens to speak for themselves, in a setting where official impunity has been a long-term fact of life, is a challenge. The inevitable temptation is to concentrate on organizing purposive, reform-oriented groups – organizations seeking corruption control as a public good. But such groups will quite likely encounter collective-action problems, as noted in earlier chapters, and their promises of a better life may not be believed. Worse yet, where taking issue with the recent past is still dangerous, they may become targets for repression, chilling citizen participation in general. But citizen groups need not have explicit anti-corruption agendas nor, indeed, even be explicitly political in their goals. As I will argue in Chapter 8, those offering more diverse appeals such as social activities, awards, and recognition, and mutual-assistance schemes (Johnston and Kpundeh 2002) can help to build trust and networks that can serve many purposes. Over time their growth and autonomy can highlight progress in opening up political space, although in Tunisia and Egypt religious groups, appeals, and grassroots leaders will inevitably play a major role in any civil-society revival. Still, citizens can play a role in assessing the quality of services, encouraging participation focused upon quality-of-life issues that are also open to cooperation and compromise, and better government performance can do much to change expectations.

Judicious deregulation of many routine activities, so that citizens need not waste endless hours at government offices; performance indicators on the functions that must remain (how long it takes, and how many steps are involved, to get a license); and rewards, even if intangible, for officials who serve citizens well can help build both the appearance and reality of greater accountability. An analogous goal in the political realm is the orderly growth of well-structured political competition – parties and candidates that offer real alternatives and bid for, rather than control, citizen support. Fair electoral procedures are clearly a part of that mix. So too might be representative institutions and electoral laws – parliamentary rather than presidential, and proportional representation rather than first-past-the-post elections – that set a manageable threshold for winning at least some representation, offer a place to multiple parties and viewpoints, and create incentives to engage in coalition-building and compromise.

Over the longer term political finance arrangements will be important too, although they may require resources that are in short supply. Emphasis should be on providing resources for competitive politics rather than driving money out of the process (Johnston 2005c), and on providing incentives to parties and leaders to bring citizens into the process. Bounties for registering voters might be beneficial (but must be monitored for fraud); creating matching formulae could magnify the importance of small individual contributors too, particularly where many citizens will have a hard time contributing any money at all. Too much emphasis on transparency should be avoided, however: citizens may be reluctant to be named as donors, so opportunities for small anonymous contributions must remain. In many Official Mogul cases poverty and all-too-fresh memories of coercion may be too widespread to make political finance policies an early option, but if participation and trust do begin to grow, such policies could help build positive momentum.

Tactical measures

A variety of more specific measures may both aid the broader changes outlined above and help energize participation in political life. One promising idea already being tried in a variety of societies, as noted in Chapter 3, is "crowd-sourcing": the gathering of information on satisfaction with government performance and corruption as people experience it. To be sure, social media and related technology are vulnerable to state interference; at one point during the struggle to oust Mubarak, Egyptian authorities attempted to cut off internet access. The same technology that can mobilize large numbers of demonstrators might also be used to spread disinformation. Still, the value of demonstrating to citizens that their experiences and problems matter is difficult to overstate, as is the value of learning more about corruption as a day-to-day experience. Soliciting accounts based on citizens' own experiences is a low-threshold way to encourage them to participate – provided that they feel safe in doing so – and can identify targets for reform and benchmarks of progress.

Bureaucrats in Tunisia and Egypt were not just practitioners of corruption; they also became a powerful interest in their own right, and they have not gone away. Short of wholesale replacement of state employees – likely an unwise move – perhaps it is possible to gradually weaken bureaucratic interests in the old ways of doing things. Indicators and benchmarks of government performance could separate effective officials and agencies from others, and help guide the distribution of any new resources and incentives that become available. Resources are likely to be scarce for some time, however, so we might also consider a "weed-and-seed" strategy process, dismissing the clearly corrupt and unproductive while rolling their pay over into better compensation for the achievers (Klitgaard 1988). The goal is not to outbid corrupt interests – difficult in the best of times – but to make bureaucratic jobs valuable enough in terms of pay and status that they would be painful to lose. In that connection intangible rewards and incentives, such as recognition, higher status, and professional training, can be highly valued. Initially, at least, top officials are likely to fight such schemes, and to "game" or simply falsify any data they do produce; that is another reason to use crowd-sourced information as a reality check.

New economic opportunities will be essential both to improving citizens' quality of life and to encouraging new interests to come into politics. Longstanding difficulties in the region's economies, the wider global situation, and corruption itself all make such changes difficult to produce. Still, two ideas, one working at the grassroots and one at the top, might be of some value. First, creating or expanding micro-credit schemes and similar initiatives, as well as well-monitored aid for small and medium enterprises, could have great promise. As we have already seen, some previous aid schemes were hijacked by well-connected military figures, bureaucrats, and Mubarak protégés, with the result that small-scale farmers and many other citizens were pushed aside. Carefully monitored, well-publicized schemes to channel start-up resources to the grassroots might be a valuable initiative, particularly in light of Egyptian banks' longstanding reluctance to lend to small and medium enterprises. Some international businesses might be enlisted as reform advocates, perhaps through mutual non-corruption agreements; if confidence that flows of capital are less likely to be diverted takes hold, investments could become considerably more rewarding. Conditionality in aid policy could be linked to launching indicator-and-benchmark schemes in key sectors, and then to improved performance.

Allied with the economic ideas above are a variety of measures intended to make it difficult to conceal, or export, illicit capital and other assets. Manipulations cannot be ended completely, but banking, finance, and real estate – particularly, land dealings – could be made more "tamper-evident." Requiring real names on bank accounts; credible and more transparent rules for registering businesses and land titles, and trading in securities; domestic "know your customer" programs for banking and finance sectors, along with other anti-money-laundering initiatives; more reliable and transparent taxation; enhanced conflict-of-interest rules coupled with financial disclosure requirements (again, a change that well-placed political business people will resist, but one that might be linked to various amnesties); and improved auditing standards in both the public and private sectors would be important medium-term goals. In addition to making some corruption more difficult to carry out or conceal, they could also increase the sense that "economic space," too, is safe and more predictable.

The point of these recommendations has been to explore the reform implications of the Official Moguls syndrome of corruption, with an emphasis on ways to increase political pluralism and open up safe political and economic space. While there could be considerable synergy among the measures proposed, they need not all be put in place for any to be beneficial. It may be possible to take some steps toward greater pluralism without requiring that the system become democratic. The best judges of which measures are more and less urgent will be those most familiar with a given situation. There can be significant contrasts among Official Moguls cases; moreover, possibilities and contrasts can change rapidly in ways that cannot be anticipated here.

Notes of caution

Reform is risky as well as difficult. Official Moguls corruption is not an abstraction; rather, as Egyptians and Tunisians know all too well, it can be an extension – even part of the basis – of the power of a whole regime. Frontal assaults on corruption are thus also attacks on powerful interests; early on, the institutions and safeguards we might take for granted elsewhere will be weak. While the goal is to develop a social and political counterbalance for such dominant interests, reformers must avoid putting citizens at risk in struggles they cannot win. Another hazard is that new anti-corruption powers, and such credibility as they may have, can be taken over by one elite faction to be used against others. Corruption has been a pretext for many coups and political crackdowns around the world; if a new anti-corruption law or commission merely becomes a way to imprison leaders of opposition parties or civil society, they will have done more harm than good.

Reform plans that are overly simple or set up on too-short timelines must thus be avoided. ICAC-style commissions are a frequent suggestion, but that idea requires genuine independence, law-enforcement capacity, and major resources. If such a commission is deemed essential, it might be advisable to create it as a part, or as an outcome, of the sort of impartial truth-and-reconciliation process suggested above, and to define its mandate carefully: better to do a few things well than to proclaim an across-the-board offensive that fails. Even then, an ICAC will require continuing support, particularly as its activities begin to threaten entrenched interests. Two of the so-called "prongs" of the classic ICAC strategy – public education, and advice and training aimed at corruption prevention – should not be overlooked as early priorities. An ICAC, like other direct attacks on corruption, may take years to bear fruit, and may cause more bad news and controversy than public virtue in the early stages.

An additional problem is that many reform efforts intended to raise the risks of corruption do far more to create uncertainty. Risks, which can be estimated, and uncertainty, which cannot, are different things; the latter may both make more corruption possible and increase the incentives to engage in it. Reforms that are poorly structured, uncertain in their backing, or erratically enforced tend to undermine better measures by making the whole enterprise less credible, and by reducing demonstration effects in the eyes of both potential wrongdoers and law-abiding citizens and investors. Indeed, many forms of "middleman corruption" thrive on uncertainty itself (Oldenburg 1987; Khanna and Johnston 2007).

The final hazard is the biggest of all. Too much pressure upon Official Moguls corruption, without building a base of social support and improving institutions such as law enforcement, banking, and the courts might tip it over into the far more disruptive Oligarchs-and-Clans syndrome. There are several ways that might occur: challenges to entrenched elites that rapidly increase their insecurity, or that raise uncertainties for them without increasing the risks of corruption, can shift corruption into overdrive: corrupt figures, not knowing how much longer their opportunities will last, may decide to steal as much as they can, as fast as they can steal it. That is a possibility no matter how we proceed, but if state, legal, and political institutions have been disrupted without replacements, personal and factional ties among the Moguls may emerge as the strongest remaining institutions. That combination of high stakes, few rules or institutional limits, and prominent, aggressive contenders marks the Oligarchs-and-Clans syndrome, and makes it devastating to economic and democratic development. Overly rapid or poorly monitored influxes of aid and investment can also encourage Oligarch-and-Clan corruption by putting new stakes out on the table for the powerful and well-placed to wrestle over.

Progress indicators

A final question remains, one that is particularly compelling in light of the need to show citizens there is a point to bringing their aspirations and grievances into the political arena. How do we know whether, and where, we are making progress, and how do we know we are doing more good than harm?

Two sorts of approaches can be useful here. The first has to do with specific government functions and performance, and with citizens' roles in evaluating those dimensions. Indicators and benchmarks of bureaucratic processes and service delivery, as noted, can help identify corruption "hot spots," specifying sensible counteractions (where a particular process is markedly slow, for example, it should be streamlined), giving credit to successful managers and political leaders, and showing citizens that reform is changing things. Citizens can play an active role in many benchmarking processes, particularly with respect to the police and security forces: statistical indicators of torture are not going to become available, but citizen reports and impressions of that and other aspects of law enforcement will be valuable. "Social Audit" practices, such as those in India, are worth exploring too; there, citizens gather to discuss and evaluate the performance of public agencies, often using data provided by the agencies themselves, and to discuss the implications with public officials. Experiments in participatory budgeting have proven popular in Porto Alegre, Brazil, and elsewhere in the Americas, and could be launched in selected communities. Such participation and consultation are valuable in themselves; if they can be shown through benchmarking to help produce positive results, that should enhance both pluralism and a sense of safe space. Other kinds of data-gathering should be considered: the Public Expenditure Tracking Systems (PETS) implemented in several Latin American countries have produced encouraging results, particularly in the education sector – in itself a key service-provision area for demonstrating effectiveness and fairness (these examples of citizen participation are explored in Johnston and Apaza 2009).

A final range of indicators focuses less upon specific kinds of performance than upon changing expectations. People who trust their neighbors and expect them to support, or at least to abide by, reforms will be more likely to back such measures themselves. Business people and investors who expect that their assets will be safe and that official harassment will be the exception, not the rule, will be more effective at reviving and opening up the economy. Those who expect that corruption will be detected and punished may be less likely to indulge in it, or to tolerate it in others. Those who expect institutions to be effective may be less likely to ship their capital abroad – and so forth. As noted in Chapter 3, expectations are subtle and difficult to measure, but more indirect indications of expectations can tell us a great deal. They might include qualitative or quantitative evidence of:

- growth, greater inclusiveness, and more open competition in politics and the economy;
- a more confident, assertive, and active civil society, and – judging by surveys and trends in violence – greater trust among citizens;
- increased official responsiveness to public problems and demands; growing tendencies for that responsiveness to occur through official roles and public mechanisms, rather than through personal networks;

- reduction in the numbers, and strength, of private armies and personal elite factions in the bureaucracy, military, and security forces; a general reduction in violence and tension in society;
- a trend toward a more open elite stratum, and for bottom-up political connections driven by real social interests to coexist with top-down connections;
- less political and administrative intrusion into the economy;
- greater trust and confidence in the courts, police, judiciary, property rights, and administrative processes; and
- the rise of more independent and critical news media, and of more sophisticated reporting on corruption and reform issues.

Some of the changes in expectations underlying those sorts of changes may be open to assessment by surveys and social audits, but others will have to be inferred qualitatively by those knowing the society best. All of those sorts of trends are vulnerable to reversals – at times, ironically, because of the revelations, controversies, and stresses that will inevitably accompany real progress against corruption – but they will give us more useful feedback than any national-level corruption index scores. Trust and positive expectations will be particularly difficult to nurture in societies that have suffered from decades of abuse by Official Moguls. But they are essential if citizens are to help open up a safe political and economic space, and to advocate their own interests – not only because of generalized outrage about corruption, but because they hope to live better lives.

Conclusion

The ideas proposed here are not, in themselves, a how-to anti-corruption plan for knocking down Official Moguls, if only because such cases are by no means alike. The role and influence of Islamist movements and values in Tunisia and Egypt, for example, has no direct counterpart in China, Haiti, or Myanmar. Even other Islamic societies with Official Moguls corruption – the Emirates, for example, not to mention today's Syria – differ in critical ways, as do Moguls cases where Islamic movements are significant but not dominant (consider Nigeria, for example, or Uganda). Instead, the purpose here has been to explore what deep democratization might mean in a Moguls situation, and how we might pursue it with a strategic, as well as specifically anti-corruption, agenda in mind.

Finally, "Official Moguls" is not a synonym for extensive corruption. Societies contending with Oligarchs and Clans also get poor scores on most indices, and present some similar outward symptoms such as poverty, a weak civil society, and corrupt figures who act with a sense of impunity. But their underlying dynamics are different; deep democratization is also a longer-term goal, but the opportunities, risks, and steps to be taken differ in important ways. We turn to that syndrome of corruption, as seen in the Republic of the Philippines and elsewhere, in Chapter 5.

5 | Oligarchs and Clans: high stakes and insecurity

> If you know how rich you are, you are not rich. But me, I am not aware of the extent of my wealth. That's how rich we are.
>
> – Imelda Marcos

> We will get to the truth. That's what we're all asking for.
>
> – Corazon Aquino

Introduction: there for the taking

Oligarch-and-Clan corruption generates some of the most spectacular corruption stories we are likely to see. As a contentious, sometimes violent scramble for high stakes in a setting of very weak official institutions, it poses difficult challenges and great risks for reformers. Opportunities for political and economic gain abound, while the institutions on which many corruption controls depend – courts, law enforcement, the bureaucracy, political parties, civil societies, and levels of trust – are overmatched by powerful factions exploiting government, society, and the economy. The state usually has little autonomy with respect to oligarchs and their followings, and often little public credibility. Taxes are not reliably collected, revenues from natural resources are likely to be squandered or stolen, and public services are chronically short of resources. Even where civil society does exist, reform efforts by citizens are hobbled by repression and potential violence – not to mention the poverty and desperation that corruption helps perpetuate. Can anything be done to check this disruptive and dangerous form of corruption?

Countries confronting Influence Market and Elite Cartel corruption may have serious problems, but they also have some basis for governing – relatively strong state institutions in the first instance and, in the second, the elite political networks at the heart of Elite Cartel corruption itself. Oligarch-and-Clan cases, by contrast, lack such foundations. Superficially, it is easy to confuse those situations with Official Moguls: corruption can be spectacular, its harm pervasive, and both sorts of situations will score poorly on international rankings. But in Official Moguls situations there is little doubt who governs, while where we see Oligarch-and-Clan corruption it can be unclear whether anyone is in charge at all. Economic and political activities are poorly institutionalized, and may be most active outside official arenas and legal frameworks. Business can be highly risky; politics can be factionalized, rapacious, and fraught with repression. Personal loyalties override official duties and accountability; the situation can be rewarding in the short term, but loyalty to an oligarch is only as valuable as the rewards he can provide. Those oligarchs may have to buy supporters' loyalties again and again, necessitating constant corruption and making violence an attractive alternative means of control. Corrupt deals proliferate but lack guarantors, making them disruptive, unpredictable, and prone to violence.

Here, as in Egypt and Tunisia, corruption controls need solid social, political, and institutional foundations. But unlike Official Moguls cases, where gradually increasing pluralism is a primary goal, in Oligarch-and-Clan cases pluralism abounds, particularly in terms of multiple elite factions and families, but in a climate of insecurity dominated by powerful oligarchs. The goal is institution-building, and the first challenge is to govern – not just to improve administration and corruption control, but also to maintain "stateness," providing: revenue functions and a credible judiciary; public safety, meaningful civil liberties, and the rule of law; and orderly banking, a sound currency, and meaningful property rights, for example.

Here again, safe political and economic space is a primary strategic goal. Without it, citizens will be hard put to protect themselves and assert their interests by political means. But those efforts also need a coherent direction, lest the potential force of numbers be dissipated by the lack of a common focus. That does not mean reformers need to be of a single mind – far from it – but rather that reform activism must become a visible and reliable part of the political scene, such that bad actors will expect to face significant opposition, whistleblowers will know they will have at least some backing, and potentially reform-minded elites will have political incentives to act on those values in

Introduction: there for the taking

sustained and effective ways. As with reforms in our Official Moguls situations, opening up safe space and increasing reform activism will not, by themselves, end corruption – but they will be significant steps toward that goal, and toward deeper democratization. And again as in our previous cases, specific corruption controls will be a part of, and should be given priority based on the potential for aiding, both processes.

Anything goes

From a reform standpoint, the essence of Oligarch-and-Clan corruption is that both corrupt figures and those with a stake in checking them are insecure. In a climate of expanding but poorly institutionalized opportunities and contention, faction or family leaders build personal power bases bridging nominal public–private boundaries. Power and wealth are up for grabs and few credible rules govern the scramble. Winners often find it difficult to protect their gains; protection rackets, violence, and capital flight may be the results. Losers are vulnerable on many levels; law enforcement and the courts are ineffective at best and can become tools for grabbing power and protecting assets. This sort of corruption is not only rapacious; it is also unpredictable and a powerful force for injustice. Reform advocates and civil-society groups that might elsewhere take a stand against corruption may find it far more prudent to keep their heads down. Investors may simply go elsewhere, or seek quick profits while keeping their exit options open rather than pursuing long-term growth (Keefer 1996; Campos, Lien, and Pradhan 1999). In that sort of setting many familiar reforms are unlikely to be effective. Improved accountability and public management are urgent needs but lack institutional frameworks and political backing. Indeed, because effective enforcement mechanisms are lacking, such reforms may not so much increase the risks of corruption as create further uncertainty – ironically, intensifying the general climate of insecurity. Further liberalizing the economy in the name of reform may erase whatever boundaries remain between wealth and power while putting more assets up for grabs.

Reformers must reduce insecurity if they are to open up safe ways for citizens to protect their own interests. That means, first, strengthening institutions that serve as guarantors of safety, and of political, civil, and property rights. Trust, both in government and among citizens, is likely to be in short supply – probably for good reason – and yet if distrust is not overcome, reform is all the more likely to fall victim to collective-action problems. As for corruption itself, the middle- to long-term goal is in part to check the worst abuses, but also to shift toward less disruptive forms while building institutional frameworks capable of withstanding its effects. Insecurity must also be reduced for top officials, corrupt and otherwise, and even for the oligarchs themselves. Otherwise the dynamics driving the most egregious abuses – steal it today, because you don't know what life will be like next month – and follow-on problems like violence and capital flight are unlikely to abate. Oligarchs who feel less threatened, and who can deal with officials capable of effective action by legitimate means, will not shift immediately to legitimate enterprises; the stakes available will often be too large for that. But they may have less reason to constantly buy personal support, cultivate linkages with organized crime, and send their financial gains abroad. Over time they may come to see orderly competition, predictable policy and enforcement, secure property rights, sound currency and banking, and a reduction of violence as serving their own interests, too.

The Philippines: wealth, power, and family ties

Corruption has long been a fact of life in the Republic of the Philippines, part of a climate of dependency and insecurity that weakens democratic processes and divides popular resistance to abuses of wealth and power. All too often it is linked to electoral fraud, pervasive poverty, and violence. The Philippine experience is scarcely identical to that of all other Oligarch-and-Clan cases, but it illustrates all too well the dynamics and effects of that syndrome. It also shows the importance of strategic reforms making it possible – and safe – for citizens to develop a political voice, take economic initiatives, and insist on accountability, before specific controls will have a full chance to succeed.

High hopes and sobering realities

Over ninety million *Pinoys* and *Pinays* occupy an archipelago of more than 7,700 islands in the Western Pacific. It is a land of considerable natural resources and immense social energy. At many points it has also been a strategic location for American geopolitical interests: the US held the territory as a colonial possession following the Spanish–American war and set up the basic institutions of government. Thousands of American and allied soldiers, nurses, and civilians died there during World War II, with as many as 140,000 being captured and imprisoned by Japanese forces (Cogan 2000). Post-war development was both spurred and distorted by American strategic interests, as US funds flowed into the region and immense military bases were established at Subic Bay and Clark Airbase (both sites have since reverted to the Philippines). For many Filipinos, American backing for Ferdinand Marcos and his martial law regime is an unpleasant memory.

Outbreaks of "people power," such as the mass demonstrations that ousted Marcos in 1986 and that forced Joseph "Erap" Estrada from the presidency in 2001, put the Philippines on the world's front page from time to time. At other times, however, the country flies under the international radar, its apparent outbreaks of democratic progress often giving way to long periods during which elections are held but the people cannot effectively govern themselves. The economy has been dominated by inward-looking[1] economic elites protecting domestic fiefdoms rather than pursuing aggressive development and regional influence; as a consequence the nation has missed out on major economic opportunities. One observation has it that during periods of growth in Latin America the Republic was treated as the Asian society it is, yet during Asian boom times it might as well have been the westernmost country in South America. Over ten million Filipinos work abroad at any given time, many in appalling conditions but others well-integrated into host economies, and their remittances are a major factor in the national economy. Still, despite the country's size and connections to the English-speaking world, the Philippines remain a socially distant society for much of the world.

Oligarch-and-Clan corruption operates along the lines of extended families. It enriches well-placed patriarchs, their relatives, and followers; some become major national figures while others tend local enterprises and political enclaves. At the same time it helps keep the nation poor. International investors find policy and implementation unpredictable, lines of access to government personalized and politicized, and projects riskier and less profitable than they might be elsewhere. Citizens benefit less from public spending than they

---

[1] My thanks to Jaime Faustino for that characterization.

should: corruption impedes health service delivery and reduces use of facilities. In the public education sector it is linked to reduced test scores, lower quality and ranking of schools, and lower satisfaction with education, and to more pronounced inequalities on those dimensions (Azfar and Gurgur 2005; Lewis 2006). Corruption is integral to, if by no means the only cause of, the nation's chronic pattern of uneven, stop-and-go growth, and striking inequalities in wealth.

State and society in the Philippines are extensively intermingled at the level of personal connections and obligations, yet all too often disconnected in terms of official duties and accountability. Citizens often find it easier to deal with problems via "fixers" than to demand that agencies perform more effectively (Amorado 2007). Such operators may reduce short-term transaction costs, but also encourage perceptions of government as remote, arbitrary, and unresponsive (Khanna and Johnston 2007) – views that are often well-founded. Over the longer term such "fixers" weaken demands for better performance while adding to the sense of uncertainty. Worse yet, a seemingly helpful middleman can become an influence peddler or extortionist when the stakes are larger (Amorado 2007). It can be difficult to say exactly where private dealings and networks end and "the state" begins – and thus, to say what standards of behavior should apply.[2]

On May 10, 2010, Filipinos chose a new president. Election campaigns are always intense in the Philippines, where hyper-presidential politics places great power – legitimate and otherwise – in the hands of the winner. But that year the stakes were higher than ever. For some time there was a question as to whether the election would happen at all: President Gloria Macapagal Arroyo, who succeeded Estrada in 2001, tried numerous ploys to postpone or cancel the vote. Violence sometimes marks election campaigns too; a November 2009 ambush in Maguindanao carried out by the Ampatuan political clan killed nearly sixty people, while a grenade attack at a rally in mid April 2010 killed two more. There was also a chance that the election itself would end in failure: for the first time voting was automated, which some critics warned might make it easier to produce phony results on a large scale. In light of the way Arroyo and cronies arranged for a large majority during the 2004 vote count, such fears were not overplayed. There was

---

[2] Thanks to Steve Rood and Frederic Schaffer for their perceptive comments on these points.

a sense that the country might be at a crossroads: Arroyo was deeply unpopular, and government was seen by many as inept and responsible for much of the nation's widespread poverty.

In the end the campaign – despite Maguindanao – was comparatively peaceful, and automated voting "exceeded low expectations" (Calimbahin 2011; on the recent history of the Commission on Elections (COMELEC), see Calimbahin 2009). The winner was Liberal Party candidate Benigno "Noynoy" Aquino III, the son of Benigno "Ninoy" Aquino Jr. (assassinated in 1983 by military operatives at the Manila airport now bearing his name) and the late Corazon "Cory" Aquino, thrust into the presidency by the same 1986 wave of "people power" that ousted Ferdinand Marcos. Aquino's slogan – *Kung Walang Corrupt, Walang Mahirap* ("If no one is corrupt, no one will be poor") – put corruption problems front and center. But doubts persisted about Aquino's level of determination, as he was not particularly effective as a Senator; his mother, while deservedly revered as a human being, had not been a strong President. Halfway into President Aquino's term the jury was still out on his performance: Aquino has showed major determination in backing the impeachment and removal of Supreme Court Chief Justice Renato C. Corona (Whaley 2012a), and in the arrest of former President Arroyo – still a representative in the lower house – on charges of misusing lottery funds (earlier charges of election fraud, on which she had been detained for several weeks, were dismissed in mid 2012) (Whaley 2012b). There are some indications that the country's long-term growth prospects have been enhanced by the Aquino administration's reform efforts, along with others that their short-term economic impact has been negative in some sectors. Public opinion has been mixed: only 10 percent of those responding to a June 2011 poll said they expected "Noy" to be unsuccessful, but 68 percent said it was still "too early to tell,"[3] while a September 2012 survey found his job ratings and trust ratings were enjoying a marked rise (*Sun Star Manila* 2012). Many of the scandals that have made the headlines during President Aquino's first year

---

[3] Social Weather Stations, Second Quarter 2011 Social Weather Survey, face-to-face interviews of 1,200 adults in Metro Manila, the rest of Luzon, Visayas, and Mindanao, June 3–6, 2011. Item text: "In the long run, do you think President Noynoy Aquino will be a successful or unsuccessful President, or do you think it is too early to tell?" Sampling error margin for national results ±3%; online at www.sws.org.ph/index_pr20110627 (viewed January 14, 2013).

involve misconduct under Arroyo, but have done little to improve perceptions overall. Some critics allege that Aquino has protected corruption suspects closely allied to his campaign and administration (*Manila Standard* 2012).

The scope of the dilemma

Just how bad is the corruption situation? In 2012 regional rankings by Political and Economic Risk Consultancy (PERC), a Hong Kong risk assessment firm, made headlines in Manila by ranking the Philippines worst in the region out of sixteen countries, its score of 9.35 coming close to the lower bound of 10.0 (India had the next-worst score, at 8.75) (PERC 2012). That estimate, while subject to all the drawbacks of any such index, is broadly in line with others. You's comparison with Taiwan and South Korea (2005) concludes that the Philippines has been the most corrupt of the three since at least the early 1980s, and quite possibly since the mid 1950s. Whatever one makes of such judgments, the nation has suffered greatly from corruption. The Philippines should be another Asian economic power; while American aid and investment following independence in 1946[4] served US goals at least as much as it was intended to build the country's economy, much the same could be said about Japan, South Korea, and Taiwan, all far more successful in economic terms. The basic development issue is not just that bribes, demands for kickbacks, contract skimming, and the like have been widespread, but also that they are unpredictable (Bocchi 2008) – a fact that reflects the insecurities of the Oligarch-and-Clan syndrome.

Arroyo's presidency may have begun amid condemnations of Estrada, but it quickly became viewed as extensively corrupt in its own right. "GMA," as she is known, is credited by some with improving legal frameworks and procurement processes (Oyamada 2005). But strong evidence of election tampering during the 2004 presidential count, when Arroyo won a full term in her own right; of corruption in the customs service orchestrated by "First Gentleman" Jose Miguel ("Mike") Tuason Arroyo; of links to corruption in the telecom sector,

---

[4] The Philippines first declared independence from Spain in 1898, but the declaration never attained international acceptance. The United States finally recognized the nation's independence on July 4, 1946, although Independence Day was later changed to June 12.

and in the military; and of appointing political cronies to the *Sandiganbayan* (the Republic's national corruption court), constitutional commissions, and the sensitive position of Ombudsman[5] all fed perceptions of a pervasively corrupt administration. Evidence that 46 million pesos (around US$1.1 million) of US aid intended to fund joint military exercises had been diverted to the Arroyos and to friendly generals in 2007 has drawn considerable attention from American investigators (Reyes 2009; Oliveros 2011). Allegations against the family continued after she left office; Ignacio "Iggy" Arroyo Jr., younger brother of the former First Gentleman, continued in 2011 to claim ownership of sizeable bank deposits registered in the false name of "Jose Pidal" despite allegations that they were the proceeds of his brother's schemes. After Ignacio Aquino's death in January, 2012, the money did revert to his family (ABS-CBN 2012).

Considerable corruption takes place within large institutions. In 2011 seven Roman Catholic Bishops, all Arroyo supporters, came under fire for receiving 6.9 million pesos (around US$170,000) in funds and automobiles – Bishop Juan de Dios Pueblos, for example, requested a $39,000 four-wheel-drive SUV as a birthday present for himself – from the Philippine Charity Sweepstakes Office, a government body that distributes lottery proceeds for charitable purposes (GMA News 2011). The revelations were a matter of much interest in a poor, intensely Catholic society. *Agence France Presse* reported that:

The scandal stems from accusations that then-president Gloria Arroyo used state lottery funds to give the seven bishops 4WD vehicles and 8.38 million pesos ($196,000) in cash between 2007 and 2010 to buy their support. The cars and donations came as Arroyo faced an impeachment crisis stemming from accusations of corruption and that she rigged the 2004 presidential elections (*Agence France Presse* 2011).

In July 2011, the cars were returned, but not before several bishops were summoned before the Senate to explain their actions.

Scandals in the military have involved considerably larger sums: investigations in 2010 and 2011 revealed a *pabaon* or "send-off

[5] Since the end of Arroyo's presidency that Ombudsman, Merceditas Gutierrez, was impeached on charges of taking little or no action in response to a string of scandals in the Arroyo government (Cabacungan 2011), and resigned before facing trial in the Senate. My thanks to Cleo Calimbahin for providing useful details for this discussion.

money" system that diverted funds in amounts as large as 300 million pesos – about US$7 million – to each of several retiring Chiefs of Staff. The system was disarmingly simple, involving "conversions" of other sorts of expenditures: "If you order P10 million worth of medicine, the supplier will deliver only P5 million worth and the other P5 million will be in the form of cash but [the supplier] will sign the delivery receipt for P10 million. That's a conversion. In some cases, there [is] no delivery, ghost delivery" (ABS-CBN 2011). References to "jet-setting generals and their wives" are common. While ordinary personnel are more likely victims of corruption than perpetrators, a Pulse Asia poll ranked the military as the most corrupt national institution (Piramide 2011).

In many respects, however, the presidency and formal structures of government are just one public face of a more deeply ingrained pattern of Oligarch-and-Clan corruption revolving around the nation's powerful elite families. Those families not only surface again and again in accounts of corruption; they are also central to an understanding of wealth and power in the Philippines.

Family oligarchs and their clans

Family ties are important in Philippine life in ways that rival almost any other society (McCoy 2009). That is true from the grassroots on up to the highest levels of politics and the economy. Between eighty and two hundred and fifty powerful families have long dominated politics, the economy, and regional social structures (Hutchcroft 1991; McCoy 1993). Many hold local or regional power while others dominate national politics, the bureaucracy, and business over shorter or longer timespans (Araral 2006: 266–7). Some family oligarchs have long-standing prestige while others are *arrivistes*. High-profile anti-corruption institutions such as the Ombudsman and the Presidential Anti-Graft Commission (PAGC) are widely seen (rightly or wrongly) as serving various oligarchs and their backers. Coronel, Chua, Rimban, and Cruz, describing these "rule makers," explain that:

political dynasties have been able to use their positions to expand their land holdings or their business empires, using their preferential access to privileges from the state – loans, franchises, monopolies, tax exemptions, cheap foreign exchange, subsidies, etc. These privileges have made these families wealthy, allowing them to assemble formidable election machines that guarantee victory at the poll[s] (Coronel, Chua, Rimban, and Cruz 2004, quoted in Araral 2006: 267).

Contention among oligarchs and families at the national level often gives way to hegemony in their home areas. Sidel (1996: 63) suggests that local bosses hold "virtual monopolies over coercive and economic resources within territorially defined bailiwicks." Philippine corruption is usually less violent than that of mid 1990s Russia, but in some of those local fiefdoms there is still considerable danger – as witness the Maguindanao massacre. Private armies have been growing in number too, particularly in some of the poorest provincial areas (BBC 2010; Onishi 2010).

Oligarchic influence not only benefits specific families but also preserves and exacerbates inequalities while staving off significant social change. During the 1950s, for example, the idea of land reform and redistribution gained political ground, in substantial part as a way to counter rural guerrilla movements but also, for a time, with American backing. Powerful landed families, capitalizing upon growing anticommunist sentiment in the US, were able to block such proposals (You 2005: 22–5; see also MacIntyre 1994 and Moran 1999), solidifying major privileges over succeeding generations (You and Khagram 2005). Such inequalities account for much of the variation in corruption among Korea, Taiwan, and the Philippines because the wealthy have more reason and opportunity to corrupt, while the rest are weaker and more vulnerable (You 2005: 14). Over the longer term corruption produces greater tolerance of both inequality and the wealthy; top strata can amass influence and protect wealth by both corrupt means and official policy while redistributive pressures are weakened. In such situations countries can fall into "vicious circles of inequality and corruption" (You 2005: 14–19; You and Khagram 2005).

As in other Oligarch-and-Clan cases (Johnston 2005a: Chapter 6) corruption in the Philippines, like politics generally, is marked by contention among families and followings, and overlaps the boundaries between public and private sectors. Public agencies and policies – including law enforcement and reforms – can be colonized or even "owned" by one faction or another. Regulatory policies, often unpredictable in their enforcement and impact, frequently do more to protect particular fiefdoms than to pursue coherent goals (Bocchi 2008). The end of Ferdinand Marcos' martial law did not reduce the scope of corruption; if anything it has become more contentious and disruptive. Kang (2002), for example, observes that the nation moved from pervasive rent-seeking in the pre-Marcos era to a "predatory" style during martial law – during which Ferdinand and Imelda not only plundered the economy but steered corrupt benefits to favored families while excluding others – and on to a "laissez-faire" type of corruption since then. That today's scramble lacks the top-down orchestration of the Marcos era (Bocchi 2008: 17, at note 23) only adds to the climate of unpredictability and insecurity.

But the oligarchs of the Philippines are also distinctive in some respects. In contrast to their Russian counterparts, Philippine oligarchs for the most part lead actual families, often interwoven into alliances and wider followings, rather than factions built on patronage alone (Hutchcroft 1991; McCoy 1993; Gutierrez 1994; Hutchcroft 1998). To call someone "an oligarch" is not necessarily to allege corruption; instead, they are people heading up networks of influence, leadership, and obligation that can be put to diverse, and often quite legitimate, uses. Family oligarchs may at various times be initiators of corruption, victims of it, advocates of reform, prominent public benefactors, or all of the above.[6] Family connections may check the worst excesses of the oligarch-and-clan syndrome: Filipino extended families are exceptionally cohesive, and members have fewer alternative paths to wealth and power, as well as less temptation to look elsewhere. Philippine oligarchs may thus face less pressure to engage in constant thievery just to pay off supporters. Similarly, the head of a prominent family who advocates reform can command considerable attention and draw upon a strong supporting constituency.

The Ampatuans of Mindanao

Any number of stories could illustrate the logic of Oligarch-and-Clan corruption in the Philippines; McCoy's account (1993) of the rise, fall, and reinvention of the Lopez family as a formidable media-based combine is a fascinating saga of politics, business, and power. But few families, other than the Arroyo clan, have claimed more recent attention than the Ampatuans of Mindanao (this account draws on BBC 2010;

---

[6] My thanks to Steven Rood for his insightful comments on that and related points.

Daily Tribune 2010; *Mindanao Daily Mirror* 2010; Regalado 2010; CMFR 2013).

The Ampatuan clan came to worldwide public attention because of its alleged role in the Maguinadanao massacre of 2009, but its power and reach – indeed, what the BBC (2010) termed "the culture of impunity surrounding them" – were apparent to anyone familiar with the southern Philippines. Scrutiny of the family's affairs following the massacre revealed not only its capacity for violence but also a range of corrupt activities. Unlike some of the old-line oligarchic families, the Ampatuans only began to amass wealth and influence in the early twentieth century, and then as merchants and regional traders. Political power came during the 1970s, when Ferdinand Marcos needed a reliable ally in what is now the Autonomous Region of Muslim Mindanao (ARMM). That area, then as now, was home to a variety of separatist movements with violent tendencies of their own, as well as to some of the poorest areas in the entire country. Andal Ampatuan Sr., head of the clan, was named Mayor of Maganoy Town; later, under the first President Aquino, he became Officer-in-Charge of the surrounding area. Under President Arroyo Ampatuan became governor of Maguindanao; the clan played a major role in putting GMA over the top in the 2004 election and a son, Zaldy, became governor of ARMM. Not only were those powerful positions in their own right; they also enabled the clan to tap into substantial national funding. Other posts followed for various family members, and as of late 2009 ten of the thirty-four local governments of Maguindanao were run by family members.

The Ampatuan clan ran the region more or less as it wished. When an investigation of the use of federal funds was finally carried out in the wake of the massacre, the auditors required military escorts in order to guarantee their personal safety. Estimates of the clan's plundering of government funds run as high as PHP2 billion (about US$47 million) for 2008–9 alone; documented diversions and theft, by themselves, amounted to over PHP1 billion. Ampatuan Sr. was found to own at least twenty-seven houses, two of them described as "mansions," and ninety-one vehicles. Other family members hold substantial amounts of real estate too. More ominously, the family controlled a private army of between 600 and 4,000 men, along with enough weaponry to make it a widely feared force. Despite national policies (ineffective in many regions) against private armies, President Arroyo authorized exceptions to make it easier for the Ampatuans to organize their forces. The Maguindanao massacre, by many accounts, was carried out by Andal Ampatuan Jr., with his father's authorization, at the head of a group of 150 armed men. Subsequent investigations linked various members of the clans to a variety of killings extending back many years.

Criminal charges relating to the massacre are still under adjudication as of early 2013. As with other powerful clans, the Ampatuan family includes members engaged in legitimate business and living quiet lives. And, to be fair, few other clans – even those engaged extensively in corruption – have amassed and used firepower on the scale found in Maguindanao. But the pattern of family fealty, regional power, political connections, and corruption is one that has been seen, with many variations, for generations.

The electoral disconnection

As in other democracies contending with pervasive poverty (Sun and Johnston 2010), electoral competition has not checked corruption in the Philippines. In some ways, in fact, electoral pressures intensify it. Great hopes often accompany the election of a new president, as we have seen, and senators – elected nationwide and, therefore, often seeing themselves as future presidents – frequently portray themselves as agents of change. Yet the first President Aquino, despite her considerable popularity, could not fundamentally alter the situation. President Fidel V. Ramos (1992–8), a former military leader, did not come from an old-line family, and at times took on the oligarchs and instituted reforms with some success (Araral 2006); a common appraisal is that Ramos at least showed that the nation *could* be governed. But Ramos was quite protective of his military backers, who in a limited sense might be considered his own extended family. His successor, former film star Joseph "Erap" Estrada, was so flagrantly corrupt that a second round of "People Power" drove him from office. Yet as we shall see, a significant share of the population supported Estrada – not despite his patronage practices but because of them.

Oligarch-and-Clan corruption not only diverts resources that might otherwise aid the poor; it also weakens and divides their potential influence, in part through pervasive vote-buying. Vote-buying is a corruption problem in itself, but it is also a window on the role of ordinary citizens and the poor in the political and cultural system

(Schaffer 2002a, 2002b). It is a material exchange, in part – both an effect and a cause of poverty. But it is no simple quid pro quo. Schaffer has shown that while most who are offered money by candidates take it, only about a third of them actually sell their votes. Some go on to vote as they would otherwise have done, in effect following Manila Cardinal Jaime Sin's advice to "take the bait but not the hook." Others would have supported their political patron anyway, and still others do not vote at all. Some who resist taking money will accept food instead; others rationalize the cash as "goodwill money" (*pamigay*) rather than as direct payment for a vote (Schaffer 2002a: 24). In those senses vote-buying is no single practice, but rather involves a bundle of diverse yet overlapping motives – a way to get something out of those who govern or seek to do so, and an equalizer, however temporary, in symbolic ways (Schaffer 2002a: 14–16, 2002b).

In addition to direct payments, many political patrons sponsor "community projects such as school building, street lighting, well digging, and drainage cleaning" (Schaffer 2002a: 6). The names of projects, repeated on numerous signs and billboards as well as on facilities themselves, often spell out the initials of the politician who provided them. (One such sign near the water's edge at Manila Bay, touting the justifiably famous sunsets there, seemed to suggest the sunset itself was provided by the Mayor.) Patrons may also provide potential supporters with free medical care, scholarships, discounted funerals, and the like (Ibid.). Such projects and services can be of some value, but they are often wasteful in implementation and low in quality, serving patrons' interests before they address objective needs. Indeed, to protect their political investments patrons can go to great lengths to prevent the relocation of poor voters to areas outside their turf (Ibid.).

Those ways of doing things are not just political opportunism but also express deeper elements of political culture – in effect, a particular kind of social contract.[7] Many citizens hold a strong sense of *demokrasya* – values resting not primarily upon processes of liberal democracy, but rather upon help with personal problems. Schaffer, for example, found that many citizens in a Quezon City *barangay* (community) thought the Marcos presidency was a good example of *demokrasya*: during those years the intervention of officials and patrons made

---

[7] My thanks to Jerry Hyman for suggesting that way of thinking about political relationships in the Philippines.

it easier to arrange for lenient treatment by banks, government offices, and others whose help was needed. That immediate help often had a long-term price, be it in terms of votes, cash, or political loyalty, was less important than that it was available. Estrada, too, had his backers among the poor, and in fact his short-lived presidential candidacy in 2010 drew significant support in public opinion polls. *Demokrasya*, Schaffer argues, is linked in turn to *kalayaan*, an idea evolving out of family relationships and first attached to politics toward the end of the colonial era. *Kalayaan* conveys a sense both of freedom from cruel rulers and a kind of unity and mutual care analogous to a child's experience in a close and indulgent family (Schaffer 2009). At the same time, however, those values are reinforced by immediate, often desperate, need; for many voters the decision to accept political money has a rational basis.[8]

Those notions have obvious appeal to people for whom poverty, danger, and insecurity are facts of everyday life, and for whom government has long been remote and unresponsive. But they are not a promising model for holding officials accountable or checking abuses of power. Over the long term many Filipinos are acquiescing in their own political manipulation and dependency, an argument that in no way blames the victims but rather highlights the unsatisfactory choices they are offered. Electoral politics, while highly competitive and contentious, is driven by rivalries among oligarchs, families, and parties, not by the interests of broad constituencies nor by success at addressing their needs. The net effect is to divide and neutralize the force of unified numbers – the sole independent political resource available to most poor communities. Moreover, as I will suggest below, vote-buying intensifies a variety of collective-action problems that confront reformers everywhere.

The depth of the problem

No one should attribute all of the nation's problems to corruption, and in no way does it negate all that is good about its people. Even successful reforms would leave the country with formidable challenges. Still, corruption has helped produce, and in important ways has been sustained by systemic factors including a chronically ill economy;

---

[8] Thanks to Cleo Calimbahin for emphasizing that point.

spectacular inequalities (You 2005: 19); an ineffective, weak-but-heavy state; political processes that are contentious yet rarely decisive, save in the sense of giving one elite faction temporary advantage over others; elections and representative institutions whose dynamics are more top-downward than bottom-upward; a judiciary facing many threats to its independence and credibility; and large segments of society living in deep poverty. The causes and consequences of Oligarch-and-Clan corruption are embedded in Filipino history and society; reforms too must attack issues running far deeper than corrupt practices themselves.

As noted earlier, state and society are too closely intermingled at some levels yet oddly disengaged in other ways. Particularly during election campaigns interactions among citizens, politicians, and officials are intense, if shaped by what-have-you-done-for-me-lately expectations; but at other times officials who accomplish little are not only tolerated but left free to pursue their own schemes. The country may have fallen into an "expectations trap" (Rose and Shin 2001) in which governing elites demand relatively little of citizens *as citizens*, and citizens expect little from government's official activities. Much the same has been true in business: Bocchi (2008: 18) argues that the private sector expects low returns, in part because of a business and policy environment shaped by unpredictable corruption, and thus neither seeks nor gets investment on the scale that might seem justified. The resulting "low-capital equilibrium trap" keeps citizens poor and businesses focused on defending domestic positions rather than upon aggressive development.[9] Together, those dual traps have turned the Republic's mix of ineffective government, poverty, and weak accountability into a tenacious equilibrium (see also Mishra 2008).

Lasting reform, therefore, is not just a matter of improving administrative procedures and altering the micro-climate of risks and incentives shaping the behavior of individual officials. Indeed, anti-corruption "projects" – many reflecting the outlooks of international donors more than of Filipinos themselves – abound. In a way the country has had too many such projects, their contradictions and lack of overall impact contributing to a sense of pessimism about reform in general. No more is corruption control only a matter of new laws and higher penalties: such improvements are always worth pursuing, but

---

[9] Midway through the Noy Aquino presidency, a modest wave of economic optimism seemed to suggest that low-investment traps have begun to weaken.

domestic observers generally agree that most of the legislation the Republic needs is in place. Even "frying" some "big fish" – notably, former Chief Justice Corona, but also the arrest of GMA – will not lead, by itself, to systemic changes. Rather, reform in the Philippines is a political challenge – one of making it possible and safe for citizens to demand and reward better government for their own best interests, of encouraging them to do so, and of rewiring the political system to produce greater accountability to their needs. How such a process might work is the focus of the following section.

From *demokrasya* to a deeper democracy

Many obstacles stand between Filipinos and a political process that would enable them to put their needs at center stage (on the Republic's "democratic deficit" generally, see Hutchcroft and Rocamora 2003). One problem is electoral democracy itself: democratic systems hold no patent on corruption control – far from it – and vote-buying shows how competitive elections can encourage more of certain kinds of corruption, not less. Another is that most oligarchs have a stake in the status quo, one that some at least are all too willing to protect in violent means. Against that are arrayed the weak, fragmented forces of the have-nots. A third obstacle has to do with expectations: at one level, when it comes to corruption control Filipinos have heard it all before – yet results have been disappointing. At another level, the relationships and habits at the heart of *demokrasya* and *kalayaan* are not only deeply rooted in the nation's culture and its dynamics of poverty, but are also manifestations of the collective-action problems plaguing reform everywhere. Better government would benefit the whole nation, but is unlikely to motivate sustained reform pressure if the loss of short-term benefits – the proceeds of vote-selling or the personal help provided by patrons – is unlikely to be made up any time soon. As noted in Chapter 1, institutions could be devised to serve as guarantors: farmers or merchants could make a mutual pledge not to pay off the police, bureaucrats could pledge to refuse bribes and report offers, or voters in a *barangay* could enter into a covenant not to sell their votes and to demand, instead, that elected officials make good on past promises. But building those institutions is a collective-action problem too (Rothstein 2000, 2011; Teorell 2007).

From demokrasya *to a deeper democracy*

What goals should reformers pursue in an Oligarch-and-Clan situation? As in the Official Moguls cases in Chapter 4, it may be useful to think in terms of strategies – broader, long-term goals; tactics, or specific steps to be taken; the risks of reform; and the question of how to assess and demonstrate progress. Because opening up safe political and economic space is a strategic challenge common to both Official Moguls and Oligarch-and-Clan situations, some of the recommendations to follow will be similar to those discussed in Chapter 4. Encouraging reform activism, however, is a strategic contrast with the Moguls cases, and here we will consider some different proposals. An understanding of that syndrome may point us toward some useful goals. As in earlier sections of this book, the emphasis is not on devising a grand agenda and then building citizen support – although such processes are hardly irrelevant – but rather upon choosing anticorruption and related tactics that are most likely to enhance the ability of citizens to raise and advocate issues meaningful to them, and thereby to advance strategic goals. Some of those issues will deal directly with corruption, while others may be connected in more indirect ways. But as our discussions of collective-action problems emphasize, what those issues must have in common is that they express problems, needs, and hopes that relate directly to citizens' own interests and quality of life. Thus, we are concerned not just – or even primarily – with finding "fixes" for specific corrupt practices, but rather with enhancing citizens' and society's capacity to resist corruption. Finally, as in our other case-study chapters, I will not place much emphasis on what does or does not seem politically possible now or in the near future. Here, too, the case at hand is under study not only for its own sake, but also as an example of a broader syndrome of corruption. Political possibilities would be a guess at best, and a moving target in any event; moreover, the deep democratization approach is aimed at widening those possibilities in the long run, and would accomplish little if it did not, at some point, challenge entrenched interests.

A safe space

Maintaining a safe political and economic space requires, at a minimum, that the state demonstrate its "stateness" – that is, that it can maintain order and perform basic functions of government. Maintaining security and the rule of law, particularly in regions dominated by oligarchs, is a part of that challenge, and is essential to reducing overall insecurity. Civil liberties – generally secure for most Filipinos, if not in every locale – are integral to this goal as well. A related issue is a court system that is – and is perceived to be – accessible, fair, and expeditious (a challenge in many other countries, including some established democracies). Other ways to assert "stateness" might include more predictable tax policies and collections, along with simplification of procedures (an area in which the Republic has made progress in recent years), and easier, more transparent and less expensive ways to establish titles to property, register businesses, and the like. Other improvements aimed at reducing risks in the economy – simplified and reliable regulatory and customs functions, for example – can help alleviate some of the expectations and insecurities that leave people and businesses vulnerable to corrupt demands. (Sustained and visible improvements in customs services might have a "big-fish" effect too, given the reported high-level involvement in corruption in those agencies.)

At present anti-corruption projects proliferate while responsibility for corruption control is divided several ways. As a result the projects have little coherence or public credibility: most projects are probably worthwhile in themselves, but citizens lack a clear picture of what is being done, "project fatigue" sets in, and progress becomes difficult to publicize above the "noise." Meanwhile, integrity bodies are regarded as ineffective at their regular responsibilities. For those reasons it would be beneficial to consolidate anti-corruption responsibilities that have been scattered among the Ombudsman, PAGC, blue-ribbon bodies, and others. A new consolidated agency should have clear jurisdiction over investigatory and prosecutorial processes at all levels. It should have its own arrest and subpoena powers, and should either possess the power to prosecute cases or be able to compel prosecution upon appeal to the President. Equally important is that it be given sufficient staff and resources to follow up complaints effectively; in years past, numerous staff slots in the Ombudsman's office and other bodies have gone unfilled because of resource problems and, possibly, factional rivalries. The new consolidated agency should minimize its involvement in donor-driven anti-corruption projects, particularly in terms of commitments to administer such projects directly. The Hong Kong ICAC's history may not be directly applicable in the Philippines – a vastly larger, more complex, and logistically challenging society – but its policy of soliciting citizen complaints, and following them up *while protecting the complainants*, is worth emulation, even if it must be targeted to just a few agencies or policy sectors at the outset.

All of the reservations about ICAC-style initiatives that have been expressed earlier still apply in the case of the Philippines. Checks on a consolidated agency's power will be essential: it must respect the rights of citizens, work within the constitutional structure, and police its own staff rigorously. Great care must be taken that a new consolidated corruption-control agency not become, or be seen as, a tool used by one family or faction to persecute others, or a smokescreen concealing intensified elite wrongdoing. To that end the Republic might recruit an Eminent Persons Group (EPG) from many segments of society to advise on and oversee the consolidated agency, appoint/remove its head, and report to the public on a regular basis. A body of well-known, prestigious individuals[10] of known independence and integrity could serve as an important guarantor for reforms. (Given the pervasiveness of corruption and the continuing power of prominent families, recruiting such a group might be far from simple, but it would be worth the effort to do so.) If the new anti-corruption agency has the support of an EPG empowered to remove its leadership, that can be a major continuing endorsement. The EPG and its staff could review and comment upon anti-corruption audits and government performance data, annual reports from the President and the new anti-corruption agency, and other reform initiatives, interpreting them for the citizens at large. The EPG would not be the nation's chief anti-corruption crusaders, but rather would play the roles of honest broker and trust-builder.

The *Sandiganbayan* – the special national anti-corruption court – has been the focus of both hopes and criticism over the years. While its public credibility has improved greatly since 2009 (TAG-SWS 2012: 8), it was long understaffed and slow-moving. Cases have traditionally not been heard expeditiously, but rather have been broken up into segments and heard over periods of as long as seven years. The new anti-corruption agency, which should have oversight powers with respect to the court's operational issues (but not power to review cases), should

---

[10] Most such individuals would, in all likelihood, have notable-family backgrounds, and thus potential "baggage" of their own. However, as noted, some prominent family heads have emerged as reform leaders; President Aquino himself has several powerful family lines in his background. Selection of an EPG would be delicate business but does not seem impossible.

continue efforts to speed up the *Sandiganbayan*, in part by restricting its case load to large or high-profile cases and also by maintaining full staffing and resources. This is not just another way of urging the court to pursue only the "big fish": a *Sandiganbayan* that deals effectively with a collusive ring of middle-level officials, or attacks vote-buying in many areas, may accomplish more in terms of deterrence than a few sensational "big fish" trials.

It is important to enhance the professionalism, political independence, anti-corruption competence, and credibility of the judiciary generally, emphasizing – for the sake of both safe space and reform activism – protection of human and property rights. Filipino jurists have considerable *de jure* independence, but that must be balanced by responsibility and accountability to the constitution: India is an example of a democracy with an independent but less-than-responsible judiciary. To some extent, in the Philippines judicial politics and decision-making have been perceived as another arena for corrupt influence – an arena, ironically, lying beyond the legitimate reach of elected officials because of its formal independence.

A different, and more controversial, sort of safe-space proposal is to offer amnesties for those who have gained from corruption, tax evasion, and other activities undermining "stateness" – giving limited immunity to prosecution, and perhaps a chance to keep some portion of their illicit gains, in exchange for producing evidence. Authorities could then employ that evidence in further investigations and prosecutions. Critics point out, with some justification, that amnesties have been tried in the past, very likely too often. Corrupt figures have been able to pass up one amnesty in the hope that a better one would come along, or to give up an old scheme of corruption in favor of new ones with confidence that they too would eventually lead to amnesty. At the very least, any effective amnesty effort should await significant institutional improvements in the courts and law enforcement.

The bureaucracy includes significant numbers of individuals who object to corruption and want to oppose it, but who find it difficult and risky to act on their own.[11] Helping them build mutual-support networks, providing bonuses for good performance where possible, and

---

[11] I benefited greatly from a discussion of this issue with the late Professor Emmy Boncodin, of the National College of Public Administration and Governance, University of the Philippines, in 2009.

giving recognition, added professional status, and promotions can be valuable incentives. Providing credible whistleblower protection is also a safe-space initiative. It may be possible to separate the truly reform-minded from those who simply give lip service to the idea by closely examining government performance indicators for positive changes, or by issuing incentive-linked challenges keyed to those indicators, and then observing which officials and working groups step forward and act. For example, tax collectors who come closer to revenue targets while reducing irregularities could be singled out in positive ways. Bureaucratic resources are limited, but some important kinds of incentives to high-integrity performance – recognition, as noted, or new training opportunities and increased responsibilities – need not be costly. When corrupt officials are dismissed, their salaries should be rolled over into improved compensation for strong performers.

Perhaps the most intractable factor threatening safe political space – in the sense of a citizen's ability to express a free and unconstrained choice – is vote-buying. It is unlikely that any enacting or enforcing legislation, on its own, would be sufficient to change such practices, but stepped-up action by COMELEC – an agency that has been in place since 1940, but that has had a checkered history over many of the years since (Calimbahin 2009) – would be a positive first step. In the end the most important check on vote-buying, broadly defined, might be a change of expectations as citizens begin to judge elected officials on the quality of governmental performance and officials are given reason to think that offices will be won or lost on that basis, rather than through paying voters. Changing expectations is no simple or quick project, as noted in Chapter 3, but ideas to be discussed below regarding the public assessments of government performance would, again, be an important part of any such effort.

Reform activism

As difficult as it may be to open up safe political and economic space, have we got reason to think citizens will use that space? Here too, there are no quick fixes, but there are things that can be done – particularly if that activism is linked to problems with and improvements in the quality of citizens' lives. It is in this area that we will see reform ideas differing more clearly from those discussed above and in the context of Official Moguls. In order to build sustained public demand and support for reform, it must be clear to citizens that they stand to benefit from it in real ways. As with vote-buying, lasting positive change is as much a matter of changing expectations as it is a challenge of policy changes or civic education. To that end, several important, if long-term, steps can be taken.

First, and a general point of great importance, reform and corruption control must be designed and framed in terms of fighting poverty and improving the quality of life for citizens. Then, as discussed in Chapter 3, evidence of government performance – improved services and administrative procedures will be critical – should be gathered and published on a regular basis. That process should involve citizens and civil-society groups as much as possible, a development that is already emerging in the Philippines in some regions and policy sectors (more on this idea below). Over time, policies and allocations of resources that are seen to be fair and effective can ease distrust among citizens, and in government, create positive incentives and rewards for effective administrators and elected officials, and help minimize collective-action problems. These efforts should be part of a general push for what might be called "enhanced transparency" (Johnston and Apaza 2009) – not only making valid and useful information about government accessible, but involving citizens in gathering, assessing, and formulating responses to it.

A Citizen Advocate could be appointed within each cabinet-level public service department. Advocates would serve as a focal point for public complaints, demands, and suggestions, and by their presence would send strong signals that such citizen input is welcome and valued. Citizen Advocates could report not only to agency heads and Cabinet Secretaries, but also to the unified anti-corruption agency; the Eminent Persons Group proposed above could select them. Advocates should be given significant staffing and funding and be granted appropriate powers to maintain the anonymity of citizens filing complaints. Where complaints involve apparent corruption the advocates would be required to report not only to the anti-corruption agency, but also to complainants about the outcomes of investigations. The Citizen Advocates should report to the public on an annual basis, summarizing the flow of citizen complaints, and recommending improvements as needed.

Political finance policy should be devised to encourage bottom-up participation and well-structured competition among parties with broad and legitimate social bases. Possible steps toward those goals might include generous and creative matching formulae for small contributions to parties, rather than to candidates; protection, including anonymity if desired, for citizens making small donations; providing funds for parties that demonstrate a genuine social base by obtaining large numbers of small contributions in several sections of the country; and free time on commercial as well as on state-owned broadcast channels for parties and candidates demonstrating a genuine social base. Here the key idea is to use political finance rules and resources not to drive money out of election campaigns, but rather to encourage broad-based, open, and competitive politics in which candidates have reasons to speak for genuine social constituencies (a more detailed argument on that point appears in Johnston 2005c). That sort of competition could add political force to virtually every proposal in this chapter.

Another possible step toward more socially rooted political competition might be to return to the former practice of electing senators from districts. At present they are elected nationally to six-year terms, with half the Senate chosen every three years; perhaps not surprisingly, many see themselves as potential presidents, rather than as advocates of local and regional interests. To be effective, however, this proposal should be coupled not only with indicators of government performance, but also with an end to lump-sum budgeting in sectors such as public works. Recent practices have made it difficult, from an administrative standpoint, to link legislation and appropriations to actual projects and results, as well as to scrutinize the use of public resources; from a political standpoint, a budgetary process that links appropriations and spending to specific outcomes would make it easier for citizen groups, the press, and opposition candidates to hold senators and others to their promises regarding public spending in their regions.

A top priority, in terms of citizen support for reform and positive changes in expectations, is to launch, refine, and sustain an anti-corruption curriculum in the schools. Hong Kong's nearly forty-year effort at anti-corruption education, coupled with effective policies for protecting and giving follow-up information to citizen complainants, has paid major dividends in terms of public resistance to corruption and willingness to file reports (Chan 2005). The key is starting early in the schooling process, weaving anti-corruption themes – cultural and anti-poverty themes, as well as official roles and civic values – through multiple aspects of the curriculum, and then sustaining the effort throughout a student's schooling and for subsequent waves of students. To be sure, the Philippines is a far larger and more geographically scattered society compared to Hong Kong, and education in a democracy serves a wider range of purposes and constituencies; for guidance it might well be worth watching similar efforts in other full-scale democracies.

Risks of reform: what not to do

While the human consequences of corruption demand forthright action, it is important to remember that we can do the wrong things for the best of reasons, and that not everything called a "reform" is a good idea in a given setting. Some of the precautions we might offer to reformers in the Philippines will be familiar from the discussion of Tunisia and Egypt, and apply elsewhere too. First, depending too much upon an anti-corruption "champion" may well turn out to be self-defeating. Even if such a leader were to emerge, enhancing the anti-corruption capacity of society as a whole, and citizens' ability to defend their own interests by political means, are the primary goals. A relapse might be likely when that leader hands over power to others, particularly in a hyper-presidential system such as that of the Philippines. If such a handover does *not* happen – if anti-corruption becomes the pretext for a semi-permanent claim on power – many of the purposes of reform will have been defeated. "Strong-hand" scenarios for reform, whether they take the form of rule-by-decree, martial law, or military coups, have a dismal track record, and in fact have all too often been pretexts for seizing, and cashing in on, power.

Second, "frying a big fish" *might* open the door to more sustainable reforms by demonstrating top-level commitment, but is unlikely by itself to produce fundamental changes. Deterrent effects will likely be short-lived, and may only encourage bad actors to do a better job of covering their tracks – or, to intensify intimidation. Further, a fish fry will not make citizens any more able to demand and reward accountable government. High-profile trials and convictions may also be seen – and indeed, might *be* – just another round in the long-term contention among powerful factions. In areas where oligarchs dominate through violence, the fry-a-big-fish approach might be an unavoidable necessity: if a president is determined to fry a fish, perhaps it should be of the

Ampatuan variety. Quite apart from the risks of violent revenge, however, such a move would have political costs: taking down a major regional oligarch could well antagonize a number of other factions, along with voters who might have come to expect protection or petty benefits as a part of an oligarch's domination.

The consolidated anti-corruption agency proposed above, like specific anti-corruption projects, could become a weapon for rival oligarchs; some critics might say that happened, in the past, with the Office of the Ombudsman and the PAGC. Even if that is not literally true, such perceptions are important lessons in the importance, and difficulty, of maintaining the credibility of corruption controls. The Eminent Persons Group suggested earlier must, therefore, have genuine independence and credibility, and be able to depend upon presidential support. Similarly, aggressive privatization and deregulation can turn into a feast for the oligarchs if sound legal and financial infrastructure – courts, equity markets, property rights, banking, and taxation, for example – is lacking.

Civil-society-based reforms have a natural appeal, but care must be taken to avoid placing citizens at risk. Also essential is to ensure that citizens, and NGO leaders in particular, understand government and corruption problems well enough to enable them to know what to do. Initiatives closely linked to citizens' own interests will have better chances of surviving and succeeding. A final precaution will make many reformers quite uncomfortable, but given the entrenched power of Oligarchs and Clans, it is important: be very cautious about reform initiatives that rapidly increase the insecurity of the oligarchs. Doing so may encourage them to go into corruption overdrive, as noted in earlier chapters, or to intensify the intimidation tactics at which some are already far too skilled. Directly attacking their economic and political empires, or attempting to confiscate their gains, may be to pick a fight that cannot be won. Too much political competition too soon, particularly if not structured by open and accountable parties, may likewise heighten insecurity and encourage more vote-buying and electoral fraud. It is better to turn up the heat gradually, bringing more competitors into more open political and economic arenas, for example, or using indicators of government performance to show that the scope for corruption is being squeezed out of important public functions and agencies.

None of that is to suggest that we tolerate oligarchical power and abuses for the long run. It does, however, suggest that gradually reducing the scope for the worst abuses and increasing legitimate economic and political alternatives are more promising than high-profile, but ultimately futile, frontal assaults. Hyper-presidential politics, the personalized nature of the major political forces, and the weak state of civil society may mean that a political and economic détente may have to be worked out at the elite level first. Indeed, though the idea is even more controversial, tolerating some forms of elite collusion might be a workable backdoor path toward an Elite Cartels situation as oligarchs, facing more competitors and autonomous grassroots political forces, make common cause to defend themselves. While far from optimal, and far from free of abuses by the wealthy and powerful, cases such as South Korea and Botswana (Johnston 2005a: Chapter 5) suggest that Elite Cartels might be less insecure and violent, more predictable, and therefore more conducive to sustained economic development and rising standards of living, than Oligarchs and Clans. Tolerating some kinds of corruption while fighting others will draw many objections, and rightly so. But it is worth remembering that Oligarch-and-Clan corruption in the Philippines thrives upon the unpredictability and insecurity that have done so much to keep the nation poor and its democratic processes weak. The nation's political, administrative, and social institutions have only limited scope for dealing with additional stress, even if it is induced by reform. It may be better, in the long run, to move toward a somewhat more open and predictable system without pushing the current oligarchs into a corner.

Demonstrating progress

Convincing evidence of progress against corruption is essential, over time, if any of the strategies proposed here are to gather sustained support. What the public will see as positive evidence is a complex question; some symbolic changes may be as important, at least in the short term, as anything else. One of President Aquino's more popular and visible first-year moves was to put limits on the use of "wang-wangs" – sirens on official cars (Office of the President 2011; Hamm 2012). Not only had many citizens resented how officials of even fairly modest status moved noisily about Metro Manila, stopping traffic and cruising through signals, such practices had become a symbol of elite privilege generally. Given the security risks prominent people might face now, as they sit in traffic along with everyone else, perhaps that move should not be seen as purely symbolic.

Over time, however, government must not only become more fair, responsive, and effective; it must be *seen* to be doing so. Leaders who contribute to such changes should be able to take political credit for doing so, while those who are less successful must be called to account. For the reasons outlined in Chapter 3, international corruption rankings lack the detail, validity, precision, and responsiveness to change that we need to track the progress of reform, but other approaches are possible. They include gathering and publishing indicators of government performance on a regular basis, benchmarking them as explained in Chapter 3. Such a scheme could be launched by choosing one or two sectors with direct impact on the quality of life – such as the Department of Education, and the Bureau of Internal Revenue or other taxation bodies – in order to demonstrate improved performance (or lack of it) in very detailed ways. That sort of evidence, in turn, can be used to reward the work of effective administrators, as well as allowing elected officials to take credit for positive trends. Whether such political credit might or might not strike a policy analyst as fully deserved is less important than the notion that those seeking electoral support begin to put specific and demonstrable improvements in government high on the agenda. The consolidated anti-corruption agency could use the data as part of regular performance-and-integrity reviews of key agencies and service sectors, involving citizens and social organizations in those reviews.

The indicator-and-benchmark process was discussed in more detail in Chapter 3; for now it is enough to point out that these processes offer citizens the opportunity to evaluate how well services are being provided, targets are being met, and improvements are being implemented – a critical aspect of building accountability, and – over time – of shifting the focus of official–citizen dealings from personal favors to public performance. Further, data and benchmarks allow us to locate, and estimate the scale of, specific vulnerabilities to corruption, and point to the sorts of countermeasures that are called for – again, as discussed in Chapter 3. Moreover, improved data can send important signals that the scope for and profitability of corruption are being reduced. While data-gathering, benchmarking, and publication of results on the scales proposed are no small undertaking, and may well encounter significant resistance from officials and their private clients, they offer a chance to build accountability and reward effective leaders and managers at all levels.

A variety of such data-gathering activities are underway already in the Philippines at the initiative of various non-governmental organizations. Groups like Road Watch[12] and Procurement Watch[13] are becoming more common, and have at times been able to demonstrate the local effects of poor – or improved – government performance in ways that engage citizens' own interests. Efforts by Procurement Watch to back procurement reform legislation are outlined by Pimentel (2005). One promising data-gathering initiative is the Performance Governance System (PGS), launched in 2004 by the Institute for Solidarity in Asia (ISA) in conjunction with the Center for International Private Enterprise in Washington, DC. PGS involves community consultative processes, through which performance goals are defined and a locally appropriate "scorecard" is agreed upon, as well as data-gathering. While the process is typically initiated in a community with ISA support and advice the goal is to have PGS become integral to routine local governance, and to be supported by local support and "ownership" (see Morrell 2010). While these, and other similar data-gathering processes, are not aimed at presenting comprehensive assessments of corruption vulnerabilities over time, the principle of gathering government performance data for public analysis, discussion, and subsequent reform efforts has gained considerable standing in recent years. Expanding such efforts and giving them top-level backing can be an effective way to build citizen support for reform.

Regular lifestyle-and-asset disclosures, and conflict-of-interest reviews, for important elected and appointed officials would not so much build general citizen activism as enhance a more general culture of accountability – but could also become a focus of citizen action if they showed results that were clearly out of line. These assessments should be conducted before an individual takes office, at regular intervals during tenure of office, and at the point the individual leaves public service or moves to another public position. While disclosures should not be so odious as to drive good people out of public service, they should also be sufficiently rigorous and detailed to provide meaningful information to the press and the public. Top leadership should portray disclosure

---

[12] See www.transparencyreporting.net/index.php?option=com_content&view=article&id=70:road-and-bridge-watch&catid=53&Itemid=77 (viewed January 14, 2013).

[13] See www.procurementwatch.org.ph/ (viewed January 14, 2013).

requirements as opportunities to demonstrate integrity, not an intrusion upon private affairs or a paralyzing threat of legal problems. A key issue in the Philippines is how far to extend such disclosures along family lines: who, exactly, really owned the "Jose Pidal" funds allegedly belonging to "Mike" Arroyo – or to his late brother? Similarly, "Erap" Estrada had multiple families, not all of which were subject to any disclosure requirements. Aggressive regulations requiring assets to be registered in the names of their actual owners aided South Korea's drive for corruption control and could be beneficial in the Philippines too, although there are legitimate fears that such disclosures might target owners for extortion and kidnapping and create added incentives for capital flight. Setting those apprehensions to rest is a part of the general need to reduce insecurity and enhance the rule of law.

Finally, a variety of other kinds of evidence could help us understand expectations among citizens, business people, investors, and possible participants in corruption. They include, but are not limited to, evidence on trends in violence, vote-buying, capital flight, currency fluctuations; tax collection; foreign domestic investment (particularly that aiming at longer-term gains); the actual and perceived security of property rights; and size and activity of private armies. Some such indicators – for example, currency fluctuations – are readily available already, but could be looked at in new ways; others, such as reliable evidence on vote-buying and private armies, might well be difficult to find and verify. Even those that cannot be measured with decimal-point precision could give us useful indications of trends in the insecurity that is so central to Oligarch-and-Clan corruption, and in the credibility and effectiveness of government.

Conclusion

None of the proposals above, by themselves or collectively, offer any sort of guarantee that corruption in the Philippines will be significantly reduced. The idea, instead, is to move toward politics and government that give citizens real opportunities to protect themselves politically against abuses of power, and to plan for the future and act on those ideas, and that encourage them to feel relatively secure about doing so. Changed expectations are also critical to minimizing collective-action problems. While such challenges cannot ever be completely avoided, Ostrom (1998) argued that the pursuit of shared goals can still produce "better-than-rational" results; perhaps our goal is to change expectations in such a way as to encourage people to think that what is not strictly rational today might be worth a try based on plausible future rewards.

The most important changed expectations of all have to do with poverty reduction. If people trying to cope with poverty, or to improve their lot, have reason to think that there are safe and legitimate alternatives to corruption, if venal officials begin to rethink the idea that poor people can be bought off and exploited with impunity, and if official policy and institutions are demonstrably and *fairly* pursuing better standards of living, then actively supporting corruption controls and forgoing current corrupt benefits may seem less daunting or futile. Those are, to be sure, all extremely large "ifs." But Oyamada (2005) has made strong arguments that the overall ineffectiveness of government has been one of the biggest obstacles to building effective and credible anti-corruption strategies. Poverty reduction will not cut into corruption across the board, either on grounds of material incentives or improved expectations – note the ways, discussed above, in which vote-buying is not only a material quid pro quo. But it seems safe to say that without visible and sustained progress against the nation's entrenched poverty problems, reforms of any sort are unlikely to achieve lasting success.

The path toward those goals will not be smooth or direct. It may be that as popular demands for better and more responsive government gain force, today's oligarchs and their clans will make common cause to stave off change. That sort of situation is far from optimal, but as noted would resemble an Elite Cartels situation that is likely to be less violent, more predictable, and more favorable for economic development (Johnston 2005a: Chapter 5) – a variation on the "good-enough governance" theme. Even then, however, the challenge remains of escaping the "expectations trap" that has served individual politicians and elites so well, and the nation as a whole so badly – and to forge a new kind of social contract, one driven from the grassroots upward rather than by the interests of oligarchs and their factions. As suggested in earlier chapters, such changes have taken place in other societies, many of them suffering from significant corruption problems of their own. Such developments have not originated in grand anti-corruption campaigns, but rather in far more comprehensive (if, admittedly, usually unplanned) "deep democratization" processes that directly engage, and visibly serve, the interests of people and groups in society.

6 | *Elite Cartels: hanging on with a little help from my friends*

Robo para la corona.
(I steal for the Crown.)
— Jose Luis Manzano, Argentine Minister of the Interior, 1989

Argentina: potential and paradox

Few large developing countries would seem as well-positioned for sustained democratic and economic development as Argentina, yet few swing so sharply between breakthrough and near-collapse. At the beginning of the twentieth century Argentina was one of the world's wealthiest countries, but entered a long decline (on political aspects of that process see Waisman 1987). At the start of the twenty-first it experienced a spectacular economic crisis, devastating citizens' savings and incomes, and precipitating a series of brief and unsuccessful presidencies. That happened despite almost two decades of democratic politics, at least judging by formal institutional criteria, and a dozen years' economic reforms based on the most fashionable neoliberal ideas. A decade hence Argentina has done much to revive its economy, and electoral politics remains firmly in place. Yet its future is hard to predict.

Through it all corruption has been a constant feature. For generations Argentina has experienced entrenched Elite Cartel corruption (an excellent historical and contemporary analysis can be found in Guillan Montero 2011). To a remarkable extent Elite Cartels have withstood, even capitalized upon, democratization and other systemic reforms, such as transparency measures, regional and international agreements, and above all market-oriented neoliberal reforms (Manzetti 2009). The

---

This chapter has greatly benefited, in ways both general and specific, from the comments and suggestions of Aranzazu Guillan Montero and Luigi Manzetti. Great thanks to both.

result has been networks of collusive elite interests and informal institutions strong and flexible enough to stave off complete collapse – and also, to resist reform.

So much to gain, for better or worse

South America's second-largest nation became independent in 1816, wrote its first constitution in 1853, and rapidly became a regional economic power. It is a big place, reaching from sub-tropical and desert areas in the north to the Antarctic in the south (its claim to a wedge of Antarctica itself is recognized by few other countries), and from the South Atlantic on the east to the Andes on the west. There are large regions of rich farmland, and significant mineral resources. The population of around 42 million is largely European in extraction.

Economically and socially Argentina presents the profile of a successful middle- or upper-middle-income country: the annual GDP per capita, at $17,700 (this and the following are 2011 statistics: World Factbook 2013), is slightly higher than that of Chile, and well above that of any other country in Latin America. Ninety-two percent of the population is urban, with greater Buenos Aires much the largest city at about 13 million residents; life expectancy is 77 years and literacy rates exceed 97 percent. The constitution was patterned broadly after those of the United States and Chile: Argentina is a federal republic (twenty-three provinces plus Buenos Aires, an autonomous city) with a presidential/separation-of-powers structure. The president and members of the bicameral legislature are chosen by direct election – unlike the United States, through a party list system of proportional representation – and the judiciary is a formally coequal branch with significant powers of oversight and review.

But Argentina's problems run deep. Economic growth leveled off in the decade following World War I; a long decline followed, interrupted only sporadically by periods of revival, from the 1930s onwards (Manzetti 2009: 143ff). Both drawing political impetus from that trend, and adding to it, were frequent periods of authoritarianism until 1983. From 1946 through 1955, when he was ousted by the military, the redoubtable Juan Domingo Perón presided over the politically conservative but redistribution-oriented populism to which he gave his name. *Peronismo* (also called *Justicialismo*, in the sense of "social justice") modernized some sectors of the economy through

Argentina: potential and paradox 153

extensive state intervention and protectionism, but also aided the rise of powerful vested economic interests – not least, the military itself (Brömmelhörster and Paes 2003: Chapter 2; Manzetti 2009: 143). Its corresponding political movement – not quite a party organization, but more of a diverse and shifting social as well as political formation – has proven remarkably tenacious, not least because of its organizational adaptability (McGuire 1997) and lack of constraining internal rules and structure (Levitsky 2003). Perón did not invent elite collusion, but his policies created strong incentives sustaining it; ever since, various combinations of those interests have remained powerful, and much of the past thirty years' electoral politics has been a factional fight over who can claim the Perón legacy. Informal, collusive "arrangements" have been crucial to the continuing force of Elite Cartel corruption, as we shall see.

The economic meltdown that finally came in December 2001 was a culmination of factors ranging from political misrule to chronically weak institutions to the debatable wisdom of the neoliberal agenda itself. Ineffective governance, mounting debt, and the end of the Convertibility Plan that had pegged the peso to the US dollar led to a currency collapse, a run on banks, massive demonstrations, and political upheaval (Evans 2003). But the crisis was also an end point for a strategy of governance and reform. Privatization, deregulation, and trimming back the state's economic role have often been advocated not only as a recipe for development, but also as anti-corruption strategies: get government, its distorting influence, and above all its grasping bureaucrats out of the economic loop, the argument runs, and officials will no longer have powers to put out for rent. Several sectors of the economy did need less political interference, and in fact the first few years of neoliberalism seemed a resounding economic success. But in a setting of weak official institutions and accountability, and pervasive elite collusion, privatization did not so much reduce corruption as put new riches up for grabs.

The economic crash that followed 2001 was painful: GDP for 2001 dropped by nearly 4.5 percent over the previous year, and for 2002 was down by almost 11 percent from 2001 (Trading Economics 2013). But it was also short-lived, as Argentina enjoyed another boom beginning around 2003 and led by rising prices of agricultural exports. Growth slowed in 2007, but rebounded again; the GDP grew by an estimated 8.9 percent in 2011 (World Factbook 2013). As in the past, however, the distribution of growth has been strikingly uneven, and current unemployment rates are estimated at over 20 percent (Ibid.). Corruption continues apace; in fact elite collusion remains one of Argentina's strongest de facto institutions (Lauth 2000; Helmke and Levitsky 2004; Darden 2008; Guillan Montero 2011: 125).

In this chapter I will explore the Argentine case both in itself and as an example of the wider Elite Cartels syndrome of corruption. As in the previous case-study chapters the goal is not to develop an anti-corruption "action plan," but rather to explore what deep democratization might mean, require, and accomplish in an Elite Cartels setting. Again as before, I have not paid close attention to what might seem politically marketable as of early 2013; any such judgment would be subject to rapid change, and could well differ from other Elite Cartel cases. More to the point, deep democratization itself is intended to open up political possibilities over the middle to long term. That point is particularly important for Elite Cartel corruption; while the coercion backing Official Moguls and the insecurities of Oligarch-and-Clan situations are not completely absent in Argentina, corruption there depends upon official impunity that has political roots. Without deep political change it is unlikely that corruption control will make much progress.

Elite Cartels in Argentina

Elite Cartel corruption derives its strength from extended networks of elites sharing political influence and corrupt benefits among themselves while staving off, or pre-empting, political and economic challengers (Johnston 2005a: Chapter 5). Cartels may include party leaders, media owners, military officers and business people, ethnic and communal leaders, political officials, and bureaucrats in networks extending across public–private boundaries, agencies and sectors of the economy, and levels of government. Much corruption is controlled from above and underwrites the durability of those networks. Jose Luis Manzano, quoted at the outset, stole "for the Crown" because he was not concerned solely with his own enrichment; he also provided political and economic benefit for his superiors, and for the broader elite network that gave him power. In turn, he could expect protection from above so long as he continued to serve that informal institution (Guillan Montero 2011: 475–9). Argentina's elites, like American machine politicians of old, have to win elections from time to time. But that need not be difficult: ineffective legislative and judicial oversight, extensive intervention (legal and otherwise) in the economy, politicized policy and implementation, and mutual "colonization" among business, politicians, and the bureaucracy offer the leadership a deep pool of patronage rewards and relatively few constraints.

Far from being chaotic or threatening impending collapse, Elite Cartel corruption normally sustains informal institutions, codes of behavior, and sanctions that, for better and worse, are among the strongest in the nation's governance (Guillan Montero 2011: Chapter 8). It underwrites a degree of de facto political stability and predictability, if not necessarily legality, thus partially and selectively compensating for moderately weak official institutions. International investors may find such situations tolerable or even attractive, compared to Official Moguls or Oligarch-and-Clan situations; several societies with Elite Cartels (Italy, Botswana, South Korea, and Argentina itself) have experienced times of economic success. But elite collusion also undermines accountability and weakens political competition. The result, over many years, has been a developmental trap – a system of rule just effective enough to give key elites a stake in the status quo, yet which delays the growth of open competition in politics and the economy, and keeps civil society vulnerable.

The face of Argentine corruption

Somewhat like Ben Ali in Tunisia and Mubarak in Egypt, Argentina's top leaders can act with impunity, but it is an impunity built more upon political foundations than on fear and coercion. Weak institutions and politicized administration help finance the networks preserving political power; oversight and demands for accountability are weak. Argentina has held regular elections since 1983, but even though elites have often governed the country badly, extensive collusion among them, and the dependence of much of the citizenry upon patronage and favors dispensed through (mostly Peronist) political networks, mean that electoral outcomes have more to do with elites' success at tending to their followings than with any success at governing the nation. As a consequence, they usually have little incentive to improve the quality of government.

Elite Cartel corruption can thrive behind a façade of political competition. From the standpoint of maintaining elite support, the ideal situation is to face just enough competition to make the threat of defeat – and of losing corrupt rewards – believable. Further down the hierarchy, exposing a certain number of miscreants to punishment is an object lesson to those who might embarrass the regime. When they are needed, there are more direct ways to maintain control: while Argentina's "Dirty War" era of 1976–83 (Marchak and Marchak 1999) lies well behind it, Guillan Montero (2011: 499–500) notes that some whistleblowers still die suspicious deaths. An Argentine journalist described the ways corruption cases were handled under Néstor Kirchner: "[I]f there is corruption, hide it; if it cannot be hidden, [ensure] that no one can prove it. If it is public and can be proved, then the public official involved must leave office, not for being dishonest but for being a bungler" (Ibid.: 476). There is no way of knowing the full extent of corruption, particularly because so much takes place at high levels. Citizens, in fact, seem to experience somewhat less of it in daily life than do many of their neighbors in the region (Santoro 2006; Guillan Montero 2011: 11).

An extensive overlap of commercial and official elites and their interests began to emerge even before independence (this discussion draws upon Manzetti 2009; Blake and Kohen 2010). Mutually beneficial deals were common; at times, for example, government would build public projects or launch economic initiatives, turning them over to private owners once they were in full swing. Dubious nationalizations, foreign exchange manipulation, and favoritism were frequent. Politically connected bidders and vendors could count on extensive government business, often at inflated prices and with few competitors, so long as they paid for such privileges. The military governments that were common between 1930 and 1983 could do more or less as they pleased; over time the military became a major economic and business interest in fields such as steel, petrochemicals and arms production. That those enterprises were never very efficient (Brömmelhörster and Paes 2003: 27) did not keep them from being profitable for well-placed figures both in and out of uniform.

In late 1983 Raúl Alfonsín became the first elected president of the contemporary democratic era. Alfonsín headed the *Unión Cívica Radical* (Radical Civic Union, or UCR), the main opposition to the Peronist *Partido Justicialista* (Justicialist Party, or PJ). His administration, while far from completely clean, was likely the most honest of the current era (Guillan Montero 2011: 17). It was during Carlos Menem's presidency (1989–99) that abuses moved into high gear (this discussion draws upon Manzetti 2009; Blake and Kohen 2010; Guillan Montero 2011). Menem, of the PJ, took office in the midst of an economic crisis; despite having campaigned on traditional policies of extensive state intervention in the economy, redistribution, and generous benefits and subsidies, he quickly became the most aggressive neoliberal reformer in the region (that change and its political consequences are analyzed by Stokes 1999). Menem likely had few alternatives: existing policies had hit the wall, and the global policy consensus was shifting toward the claimed virtues of open markets. With the enthusiastic backing of international policymakers Menem quickly launched several major privatizations. Early results were promising: for about three years Argentina seemed finally to have put economic doldrums behind it. Behind the scenes, however, cronyism moved to the top of Menem's agenda.

Even under the best circumstances privatization and deregulation would have conferred very large advantages upon small numbers of people. In Argentina's climate of presidential dominance, weak legislative and judicial constraints, and politicized administration – a situation that superficially sped "reform" but gutted oversight (Manzetti 2009: 153–71) – the new economics fueled unprecedented corruption. In late 1990, for example, the American meat-packer Swift complained that in exchange for fast-tracking taxation and customs treatment of a planned investment it had encountered extensive demands for bribes by figures including Menem's brother-in-law. Menem at first dismissed reports of that "Swiftgate" scandal by a noted investigative reporter as the work of "journalistic criminals," but ultimately a close personal advisor had to step down and a cabinet reshuffle ensued. The privatization of Aerolíneas Argentinas allegedly involved US$80 million in bribes paid by Spain's Iberia Airlines. Telephone company ENTEL was supposedly divided into two competing private entities but, thanks to friendly officials, became two parallel monopolies controlling different areas. Privatizations of major toll roads, and of state broadcasting facilities and the airwave rights that went with them, took place on suspiciously favorable terms. Correo Argentino, the postal service, nearly fell into the hands of "mafia-like" bidders (Ibid.: 172, 176–7) but for some last-minute media revelations; after several years in private hands the service was later renationalized.

Privatization allowed well-connected business people to acquire major public assets at bargain prices and then – as the ENTEL case suggests – to run them on privileged terms. Top political figures profited too: no one knows the full scale of Menem's take, although some claims range as high as US$15 billion (Casey 2012). The nation, by contrast, got far less for its assets than it should have received, and there was little lasting benefit to the economy. Collusion and uncompetitive practices flourished while few private owners followed through on their promises of investment and improved service (this discussion draws upon Manzetti 2009: Chapter 4). Networks of politicians and business people grew even less accountable because they now did more business in the private sector, yet retained top-level protection. Many privatizations took place out of the public view; direct sales of assets via closed-door negotiations, rather than through open bidding, became common. Such public bidding as did occur frequently involved falsification of data, manipulation of privileged information, and a variety of service-after-the-sale favors from friendly officials. Thanks to compliant judges "[p]roperty rights became whatever Menem wanted them to be, depending on the circumstances of the moment" (Ibid.: 159). The situation sent strong signals to other investors that they had better make "arrangements" of their own, and to legislators and regulators that efforts at serious oversight meant directly challenging some of the most powerful people in the Republic.

Privatization was not the only aspect of market reform that energized corruption. The 1991 Convertibility Plan pegging the peso at par with the US dollar created incentives for foreign exchange manipulations that took advantage of differences between the peso's official and market value. Lower taxes and tariffs were part of the neoliberal playbook, but also could be traded for illicit payments, as seen in the Swiftgate case. Price differences between domestic goods and the imports with which they increasingly competed encouraged customs fraud. Money laundering became more profitable, both for those involved and for officials willing to look the other way. Corruption continued as well in procurement and public contracting; IBM and Siemens were among the firms implicated in dubious bidding processes and "sweetheart" contracting. Menem's advisors and cabinet members were the focus of numerous corruption allegations, and the President himself was involved in multiple cases when he left office in 1999.

Collusion was extensive in the political realm as well. In 2000 Fernando de la Rúa, Menem's successor who came to office at the head of a UCR-dominated coalition, sought passage of labor reforms. Needing support in the Senate, de la Rúa advisors, including his intelligence chief and closest personal friend, engaged in vote-buying from both major parties (BBC 2000; *New York Times* 2000; Blake and Kohen 2010: 29–30). Judges stripped eleven senators of their immunity from prosecution in order to investigate the affair – although journalists questioned the lead judge's personal links to Menem – and leaders of both parties were forced out. Payments and favors for legislators had long been common: on several occasions the Menem government, faced with opposition boycotts of roll calls, placed stand-ins at legislators' desks to cast their votes (Manzetti 2009: 155). But de la Rúa had taken office pledging to end Menem's abuses, and had a reputation for personal honesty. That, and the cross-party nature of the venality, made the Senate scandal particularly disruptive. In late 2000 his Vice President resigned in protest over administration inaction; the UCR suffered major losses in the 2001 elections, and rumors spread that the President and much of the cabinet were on the payroll of international economic interests. While the economic crisis at the end of 2001 had many causes, such perceptions no doubt weakened de la Rúa's ability to mount a credible response. By late December, 2001, he resigned.

Néstor Kirchner, elected President on a PJ ticket in 2003, took a variety of public steps aimed at curbing corruption (Ibid.: Chapter 4), but by most assessments change was uneven. Patronage within Kirchner's personal following continued, as did investigations targeting former Menem allies. In the name of undoing an episode in which Menem had added five allies to the Supreme Court, Kirchner dismissed four of those members and saw a fifth resign in protest; he then re-filled the positions with backers of his own (Ibid.: 151). On the other hand, Kirchner is credited by some analysts (Levitsky and Murillo 2008: 21) with significantly improving the quality of the judiciary in the course of that and subsequent changes. The clearest evidence of the adaptability of Elite Cartel corruption, however, has come since 2003, when Kirchner began the long process of reversing Menem's market reforms; despite that about-face, corruption did not change in any fundamental way. When Roberto Lavagna, the Economy Minister, reported in 2005 that bidding on major contracts was routinely rigged, Kirchner forced him from office. In many ways Néstor Kirchner's presidency was a continuation of Menem-style politics by somewhat different means:

By 2007 the Argentine government was rocked by a stream of corruption scandals, forcing out of office high-profile officials, including Lavagna's successor ... Rather than taking the opportunity to reassert its role, Congress (where Kirchner's backers had a comfortable majority in both houses) reformed the criminal law code to make corruption crimes more difficult to prosecute and allowed hundreds of pending trials to be dismissed. In short, while a "conservative" Menem had made great strides to destroy political accountability, the "left-leaning" Kirchner was finishing the job (Manzetti 2009: 193).

Kirchner extended his protection to fewer top officials than did Menem, but his methods were more direct. A "Peronist leader" observed that "one of the great differences between Menem and Kirchner is that, while Menem had friendly judges to save his friends, Kirchner has friendly judges to put his enemies in jail" (quoted in Guillan Montero 2011: 477).

Néstor Kirchner left office in 2007; by then he was plagued by health problems, although his bigger problem was insufficient support for a second term. He did, however, arrange to be succeeded by his wife, Cristina Fernandez de Kirchner. She was re-elected in 2011 at the head of an electoral sweep by her *Frente para la Victoria* (Front for Victory) faction of the PJ (Calvo and Murillo 2012). A year into her first term it emerged that a "drugs mafia" had

manipulated legal drugs to sell them to unions' welfare benefits providers in order to exact resources from the public health system. Some of the pharmacy owners involved had been major donors of Cristina Kirchner's political campaign, while the public official responsible for overseeing the health insurance system had been the "cashier" of the campaign (Guillan Montero 2011: 132; on other scandals in 2007 see Blake and Kohen 2010: 48).

Patronage and clientelism are as central to the Kirchner style as they have been for other Peronist leaders. One example is the 30,000-member *La Cámpora* youth organization (*Christian Science Monitor* 2012), which provides its followers with a variety of benefits and modest trappings of status. Similarly, public pension programs offer a continuing stream of jobs and political rewards to backers in the provinces (Morss and Rust 2012). The government continues to distribute many social benefits through its client organizations – a powerful system of patronage and cooptation in a society where many depend on those benefits (Villalón 2007).

Most recently, a major scandal has enfolded Amado Boudou, Kirchner's Vice President. Boudou has been accused of influence peddling, embezzlement, and money laundering, among other things, for diverting currency-printing contracts to a politically friendly firm with no prior experience of doing such work. Financing has involved a shell company known as The Old Fund, which investigators claim is actually a political slush fund operated by Boudou and his cronies. Boudou has been accused of being a silent partner in the printing firm, and of orchestrating a network of executives as front men for his business dealings with the government. He defends his intervention on behalf of the printing firm as the sort of help politicians routinely offer struggling businesses, and claims the support of Argentina's top tax official, the central bank, and president of the national mint. For critics, however, that last point exemplifies the high-level networks that have been an Argentine tradition. President Kirchner has expressed support for Boudou, leading to allegations of a cover-up. In August of 2012 her government pushed a public takeover of the printing firm through the legislature; the move was portrayed as an effort to get to the bottom of the scandal, but also replaced the judge investigating the case with members of the Kirchner cabinet, including the president of the mint (*Washington Post* 2012).

Costs and consequences

While the full costs of Argentine corruption will never be known, one estimate, for the period 1980 through 2006, put the total at US$10 billion (Guillan Montero 2011: 468). Another suggests that Menem-era kickbacks – during the time of supposedly corruption-inhibiting market reforms – amounted to between US$3.2 billion and US$6 billion (Manzetti 2000). Those figures refer only to the political and administrative side of corrupt dealings; on the business side, the value of underpriced assets, unearned profits, weak business competition and public oversight, corruptly obtained tax and customs breaks, and the promised investments that were never made remain unknown. Business people willing to hand over bribes and kickbacks totaling billions, however, must have expected to recover those expenditures, and then some, in the newly privatized economy, and the fact that such practices continued for years suggests that they must have been right. Corruption costs, in many years, roughly equaled the national education budget, and were several times the national budget for health services (Guillan Montero 2011: 23). Perhaps most tragic for a nation trying to raise its standard of living, PricewaterhouseCoopers has estimated that during the 1990s foreign direct investment lost by Argentina because of poor transparency totaled US$18.7 billion (cited in Manzetti 2009: 175–6).

Equally important, if less quantifiable, have been the costs of reduced competition and openness in politics, and lost accountability in policy-making and administration. While the presidency and legislative majorities have changed hands several times since 1983, real party competition, as opposed to factional varieties, is very weak – an issue to be discussed below. Since Menem's time presidents have often marginalized the legislature and judiciary and circumvented administrative oversight (Manzetti 2009: 165–71). Thus, corruption has not only yielded immense profits for individuals, but has also solidified a style of rule that has served the country poorly. It has done so through networks of top elites sharing a stake in corrupt gains, and via patronage extending downward through many official agencies (Ibid.: 180–7) and outward into society – weakening accountability and coopting, or chilling out, dissent.

The tenacity of Elite Cartels

The most striking thing about Argentine corruption, in many respects, is not its extent, cost, or colorful techniques and cast of characters, but its *adaptability*. Elite Cartels persist, and opposition has been ineffective, because of the powerful political and economic elites they bring together. Moreover, both beneficiaries and those who suffer from corruption expect it to continue (with respect to vote-buying, for example, see Stokes 2005: 317–18). Corruption has persisted despite, and at times because of, both formal institutions and the public policies which have often proposed as remedies. Argentina has regular, competitive elections. Its news media are regarded as partially free (Freedom House 2012); moves by the current Kirchner administration have raised concerns, but the press has often been critical of misrule. Its constitution provides for extensive separation of powers, as does its federal structure. Transparency in government is relatively strong by regional standards (Stechina 2008), although that derives more from the activities of journalists than from legally mandated access to information. Menem's market-oriented reforms were more aggressive than any others in the western hemisphere; after they were partially rolled back beginning in 2003, however, not much changed about corruption. Whatever the nation's policies and institutional alignments, however, real power resides in the elite networks that dominate and exploit them.

Elite Cartel corruption, more than other syndromes, illustrates the difference between "democratization" in a formal institutional sense and deep democratization – the ability of citizens to resist corruption by political means, as outlined in earlier chapters. Argentine citizens can vote, own property, and criticize the regime, but they have few alternatives to playing on elites' terms in politics and the economy, and little recourse in the wake of abuses. Passive resistance to corruption, or avoiding contacts with officials, may be of some value, and fits in with the general pattern of extensive high-level deal-making coupled with more limited corruption in citizens' daily lives. But directly challenging elites is widely seen as futile, and at times dangerous. Nine out of ten adults say they are "not very" or "not at all interested" in politics (Turner and Carballo 2010: 281); while popular commitment to democracy as a system remains strong, trust in the courts and (even more) political parties, bureaucrats, the legislature, and trade unions has plummeted (Ibid.: 274).

Similarly, it is not that there has been no popular resistance or contention; during the 1990s several grassroots movements publicly took issue with Buenos Aires and the provincial bosses (Liikala 2002; Villalón 2007; Auyero, Lapegna, and Poma 2009; Lapegna 2012), and massive street demonstrations beginning in late 2001 helped bring a series of short-lived presidencies to early conclusions. Those movements, however – like the large demonstrations of 2012, it appears (Pachter 2012) – lacked the organizational or institutional means to make demands in ways elites could not ignore. Many organizations were neutralized by injections of centrally orchestrated patronage.

Argentina also has anti-corruption laws on the books, some of them reflecting regional and international commitments. Enforcement is weak and inconsistent, however, with judges and prosecutors facing strong pressures to halt inquiries, ignore evidence, or impose token punishments. A few lesser figures are charged, convicted, and punished – enough to remind potential challengers, dissidents, and ingrates to stay in line – but not enough to constitute a serious anti-corruption effort (Guillan Montero 2011: 475–500).

Elections without mandates

Why have three decades of regular, competitive elections not enabled Argentine citizens to oust the corrupt and reward those who govern well? The answers begin with the nature of political competition, electoral laws and voting arrangements, relations between national and provincial political leaders, and the implications of extended networks of patronage.

Outcomes of elections are a serious matter, if only because they affect control over strategic powers and critical assets, but they have not systematically reflected the views and interests of real social constituencies: even when the presidency or legislative majorities change hands, most election "mandates" have not redirected policy. Menem's presidency led to dramatic changes in economic policy, as we have seen, but those new directions were never presented to voters as an electoral choice. After the 2001 economic meltdown the UCR became a weak political force, at times receiving vote shares in the single digits; as a result, electoral competition has taken place primarily between factions of the PJ. That competition is real enough, from the standpoint of those directly involved, but it has more to do with who can lay claim to the still-formidable symbolism and heritage of *Peronismo* than with mobilizing popular constituencies behind policy alternatives.[1] Indeed, PJ presidents have pursued a wide variety of goals.

Competing factions are organized and rewards distributed from the top downwards, although, as we shall see, provincial leaders play key roles too. Loyalties, particularly among legislators, are primarily to the patrons who put them in office, not to constituents. Factional rivalry is arguably all the more bitter because of the strong symbolic appeal of *Peronismo*, and may take on an all-or-nothing nature: unlike leaders of competing parties, who can expect their bases of support to remain from one election to the next, leaders of losing factions might find it difficult to stay viable after an electoral defeat. Joseph Stiglitz argues, with respect to economic competition, that "When competition is very restricted, the real effect of competition is often waste, as the competitors fight over who gets to exploit the consumer" (Stiglitz 2012: 112). Argentina's electoral competition is effectively restricted to elites from

---

[1] Argentina is hardly alone in that regard; as we shall see in Chapter 7, one recurring problem in Influence Market cases is political competition that can be more apparent than real, more symbolic than substantive.

major factions, and entry by any new competitors is difficult for reasons ranging from the electoral system to top-level monopolies over patronage. The competition is not over mobilizing a social base by addressing their needs and aspirations, but rather over who can most effectively exploit voters in order to control lucrative state and political power. Without competing policy agendas support must be generated by other means. Stokes (2005: 325), for example, shows that vote-buying is more common when competing parties or factions are ideologically similar. Recently the PJ has consolidated, to some extent, behind the Kirchners' Front for Victory faction, but that only extends a highly personalized, top-down political style. There has been only a modest parallel recovery in UCR's strength as an opposition party.

That style of competition reflects the workings of the electoral system too. The national legislature is chosen via closed-party-list proportional representation: a party's nominees are presented to voters en bloc, on lists frequently drawn up by provincial governors, with voters denied the chance to split tickets or express preferences among a party's candidates. Seats are awarded based on the distribution of votes among various parties' lists; party leaders, not voters, decide the order in which candidates are seated from each list. Particularly under presidential systems, which encourage a winner-take-all approach to competition rather than coalition-building, the closed-list system has been linked to high levels of apparent corruption (Persson, Tabellini, and Trebbi 2003; Kunicová and Rose-Ackerman 2005; Chang and Golden 2007; Manzetti 2009: 26).

Thus senators and deputies owe their places on the party list, their votes, and ultimately their seats to governors and other party leaders (Manzetti 2009: 152–8; Blake and Kohen 2010: 33–4), not to particular groups of voters, locations (four members are elected for each constituency), or policies for which they can claim ownership. In part because of informal non-competition arrangements between political parties and factions, many governors face little competition within their bailiwicks: ten out of twenty-three provinces, excluding Buenos Aires, were held by the same party from 1983 through 2003, eight of them by Peronist governors (Levitsky and Murillo 2005; Blake and Kohen 2010: 41). In the resulting "microclimates of impunity" (Blake and Kohen 2010: 41; see also Guillan Montero 2011: 128) most legislators are judged by how well they facilitate deals between provincial and national elites. When their party holds the presidency as well, legislative careers become a balancing act between the wishes of the local bosses and the national executive, whose initiatives they are generally expected to ratify without much critical examination – and it is worth noting that those local and national agendas can conflict. In that sort of climate, developing a personal political base, specializing in substantive policy, or overseeing the executive are nearly impossible; indeed, only about 30 percent of the senators and deputies are even listed for a second term (Levitsky and Murillo 2005; Manzetti 2009: 152–3; Blake and Kohen 2010: 33–4).

Santiso (2008: 46 *et passim*) argues that ineffective audit functions, for example, are fundamentally a political failing. Legislators seldom confront the executive; when they do, it is often as a ploy in bargaining over other issues. It is unusual for oversight powers to be used effectively for their own sake (Guillan Montero 2011: 240–2, 377). Committees are numerous yet weak; both individual legislators and committees receive poor staff and analytical support (Ibid., 376–7). The incentives, over a one-term legislative career, to get along by going along are compelling, and if one can make money in the process, so much the better. The complex accommodations among levels of political power are one more way Elite Cartels differ from domination by Official Moguls, while the durability of the informal elite networks sets them apart from the chaos and insecurity of Oligarchs and Clans.

Voters theoretically cast a secret ballot, but in practice their choices are subject to considerable pressure and manipulation. The ballot itself is not compiled by a central authority and presented to voters at polling stations; instead, most are printed and distributed by the parties themselves and, not surprisingly, present only that party's list. A common tactic is to give voters a ride to the polls on election day, give them their ballots while in the car, and then make sure they cast the "right" ballot (Stokes 2005; Blake and Kohen 2010: 32). Backing up such practices are more pervasive social controls: through family networks, personal contacts, local hearsay and voters' own reputations, party functionaries have a sound idea of who has backed the ticket and thus who will, and will not, be entitled to various kinds of help once the election is over:

> It is ... hard for voters to dissemble before people they've known all their lives: as one grassroots party organizer in Argentina explained, "you know if a neighbor voted against your party if he can't look you in the eye on election day" (Stokes 2005: 317).

Petty patronage – often meager, yet desperately needed – comes at a political price (Cleary and Stokes 2006; Lapegna 2012), further weakening the influence of voters. Federally financed social benefits are critically important to provincial governments as well as to poor people: funding for such benefits can amount to 70 percent of provincial budgets and, as Manzetti (2009: 181–5) reports, much discretionary spending by presidents flows into patronage practices described, in some peripheral provinces, as "lurid" (Cleary and Stokes 2006: 67–9). Within the administrative apparatus patronage is both a powerful way to keep bureaucrats and party operatives in line and a major drain on scarce resources. In a recent year "bonuses" and back-hand pension benefits channeled to employees in social security agencies came at an estimated cost of US$50 million. During the 1990s an estimated ten thousand illegal pensions were handed out, often to PJ backers in poor communities. The national Medicare system has likewise suffered; losses from fraud and patronage have been estimated as high as $2.2 billion annually (Manzetti 2009: 186–7). Distribution of some benefits is frequently delegated to community, labor, and farmers' organizations, pacifying those groups and potential dissidents in the process: any show of political unreliability will send the benefits, and the credit for distributing them, elsewhere. Like the legislators, such groups' political situations are complicated to begin with: one farmers' organization, for example, found itself actively backing the PJ at the national level while opposing it in its province (Lapegna 2012: 14). Yet where official functions and channels are unlikely to produce results, dealing with a patron, on the patron's terms, becomes a citizen's only choice. Those opportunities for control mean that upper-level and provincial leaders have a positive disincentive to improve the quality of administration and services.

Freeing up the markets, revving up the corruption

As with electoral competition, Elite Cartel corruption managed not only to survive, but indeed to thrive in the liberalized economy launched in the early 1990s. Rolling back the scope of government was advocated by many as a way to get at the roots of corruption, rent-seeking, and economic inefficiencies, but in many ways the Menem years were a bonanza for well-placed, ambitious business people and their political allies.

In fact privatization may have an unfortunately close fit with Elite Cartels. In Chapter 4 I suggested that foreign aid and investment proved particularly vulnerable to predatory leaders and generals in Egypt and Tunisia. Elite Cartels, where they dominate a country's governance, enjoy considerable impunity. But unlike the Moguls their clout is not unilateral: political hegemony ordinarily involves mutually beneficial alliances with business, rather than broad-based repression and personally seizing assets and enterprises. The latter practices are far from unknown in Argentina, but elites there operate in a more fluid setting: they face multi-party elections, popular and press criticism, and at least nominal scrutiny and oversight by the legislature, courts, and administrative agencies. Privatization thus was an effective way to cloak high-level deal-making in a guise of legality – indeed, of reform. In the early 1990s a sense that the nation had reached an economic crossroads hastened the process domestically, while the often-uncritical backing of liberalizers in Washington and elsewhere gave it ideological cover. Privatization could easily be proclaimed a success in terms of macro-indicators – an initial wave of growth, for example, and a 75 percent decline in the size of the federal workforce (Manzetti 2009: 180) – while less defensible details could be hidden away, and critics bought off or intimidated. Once privatized, an enterprise might still have many political connections yet be even less subject to public scrutiny than before. Market reforms may have been an initial success in statistical terms, but if anything they enriched and extended the impunity of the business–political networks Teichman (2002) describes as "powerful holding companies."

To live up to the claims advocates make on its behalf, privatization requires strong, orderly markets with sound rules and property rights, relatively easy entry, and transparent practices and symmetries of information, among other foundations (Stiglitz 2012: Chapter 2). Similarly, privatization and healthy markets require credible oversight, both for redistributing assets and maintaining honest practices thereafter. Generations of political intervention made many such guarantees illusory in Argentina, and Menem weakened them still further; what remained were the elite business–political alliances that had been there all along. A legislative commission on privatization was established, but it was politicized and ineffective (Manzetti 2009: 155). Early in his term Menem packed the highest court with his backers, who proceeded to become advocates of executive policies; similarly, audit and control agencies were weakened via patronage (Santiso 2008; Manzetti 2009: 159–61). Ironically, some of the clearest evidence of political manipulation of the economy can be seen over the past decade, in the relative ease with which the Kirchners have rolled back important aspects of the market revolution. Renationalization, after all, can provide just as many sweetheart deals as privatization did. Argentina taught the world important lessons about the ways markets depend on strong, accountable government, but in terms of corruption, a disastrous boom-and-bust cycle, and the impunity with which market reforms were exploited, the Argentine people paid an immense price.

Similarly, international and regional anti-corruption commitments imposed few real restraints. A code of public ethics was promulgated, for example, and Argentina signed on to the Inter-American Convention against Corruption, but neither was seriously enforced. International pressures on Argentina were overwhelmingly for privatization at a breakneck pace, not for careful implementation of anti-corruption policies. Indeed, during the 1990s Argentina could point to privatization itself as an anti-corruption initiative, if only in its broad outlines. Meanwhile anti-corruption compacts would be implemented by political figures who had a substantial stake in corruption, and through many of the same agencies they had undercut and intimidated. Formal transparency measures, ironically, may have made some shady deals even easier to carry out: data on market reforms were made accessible, but in forms, at times, and in manners of the government's choosing. Some disclosures of corruption have had more to do with factional rivalries than with transparency for its own sake, as some political operators find scandalous information useful in gaining advantages over others (Balán 2011). Bona fide efforts to get citizens and third-party guarantors involved in oversight were few and far between, by contrast (on the distinction between simply making data available and practicing genuine openness see Johnston and Apaza 2009). There resulted a variety of transparency rituals that probably did more to demonstrate the scope of elites' impunity, and thus the risks involved in directly challenging them, than to create accountability (Stechina 2008; for similar points about Brazil see Norlin 2003).

The rewards of collusion

This chapter can only point out a few characteristics of Argentine corruption. Still, the profile of an Elite Cartel case, and the contrasts between it and other syndromes, are clear. Networks of politicians, business people, and their clients have taken advantage of chronic institutional weakness, and have resisted competitive pressures in both politics and an ostensibly liberalized economy, through collusion and political hegemony – enriching themselves in the process. Violence has scarcely been absent, but the resulting Elite Cartels have ruled more through political impunity than by the sorts of coercion seen in Official Moguls cases. Uncertainties and insecurity are a fact of life for many citizens and smaller enterprises, as are the deprivations that accompany that state of affairs; all of that has increased dependence upon the benefits elites choose to distribute. But those insecurities have in many ways been orchestrated by the top leadership, rather than reflecting the fundamental disintegration seen in the worst Oligarchs-and-Clans cases. For both better and worse, collusive networks and the informal institutions and norms they create (Guillan Montero 2011) both intensify insecurities and enable elites to capitalize upon them.

The sources and sustaining framework of Elite Cartel corruption in Argentina are thus more clearly political than those we have seen in our other cases. Changing the situation for the better – indeed, changing it at all – is fundamentally a political task. But using an elite-dominated political process to challenge those elites' interests is difficult work. At the grassroots Argentina possesses considerably more pluralism than do Egypt and Tunisia, but many social interests are neutralized or bought off more than they are effectively mobilized. In important respects they still lack open, safe political space. It is unlikely that the political–business alliances and their ways of doing things could suddenly be swept aside, and in any case, this could disrupt the lives of poor and working people most of all. It may be that we must work with "useful stalemates" in which citizens acquire enough political resources and autonomy to resist egregious elite exploitation, while some elites decide that more open and accountable conduct is a workable way forward. What might such a process look like, and what specific changes should be early priorities?

In search of accountability and real competition

Argentina illustrates, with considerable clarity, an argument offered in Chapter 1: rather than developing an anti-corruption master plan and then trying to build citizen support for it – a strategy vulnerable to collective-action problems, low levels of trust, and poor expectations – we might be better off making early priorities of those anti-corruption measures most likely to strengthen citizen influence and autonomy.

Reformers often call for "political will," but Argentina suffers no shortage of that. The problem is that political will is oriented far too much toward serving the interests of top-level political and business networks while far too little originates at the grassroots. I suggested in Chapter 2 that deep democratization, in Elite Cartel situations, is a matter not only of encouraging reform activism but also of creating safe political and economic space. Reform activism refers here to enabling and encouraging citizens to advocate and defend their own interests, autonomously and effectively, within the political system. "Autonomously and effectively" are key points: Argentina has a considerable history of activism, one that enjoyed a revival from 1992 onwards (Villalón 2007). But the autonomy of many citizen groups has been compromised by patronage that Lapegna quite rightly calls "de-mobilizing" (Lapegna 2012). Moreover, citizen initiatives have had to compete with political movements orchestrated from above. *Peronismo*, with its associated labor unions and other groups, is a classic example, but so is today's *La Cámpora* youth organization, thirty-thousand strong, controlled by President Kirchner (*Christian Science Monitor* 2012). Those influences, along with intimidation and violence, weak guarantees of rights, and stark social inequalities have rendered many grassroots movements ineffective and vulnerable to patronage-based control.

Safe space is equally problematical: while the dark days of Argentina's "Dirty War" are well in the past, whistleblowers and other critics have faced retaliation, as we have seen. Opposition legislators have seen outsiders occupy their desks and cast their votes on major legislation. Voters are subject to the sorts of pressures described above, and their votes are neither wholly free nor secret. Would-be entrepreneurs confront a range of well-entrenched, politically protected owners and enterprises, and cannot depend upon the courts or regulatory agencies to maintain fair play. Among the top priorities, then, for strengthening citizen voices is to enable them to cast a truly free and secret ballot offering real choices; enjoy sound property rights (for those owning anything at all) and fair economic treatment; and demand better government and a higher quality of life.

Anti-corruption measures have an important place in that scenario, but as a means of aiding political transformation, rather than as ends in themselves. Without a stronger citizen voice and enhanced accountability even the best reforms will likely fail or – as Argentines have seen too often – be turned to corrupt elites' advantage. The scope of change envisioned here inevitably suggests a long-term process, but gradualism may be necessary for other reasons too. An abrupt weakening in elite networks or surge in political competition may intensify corruption by making elites more insecure. Pushed to an extreme, that trend could break Elite Cartels into warring factions; the collapse of longstanding "arrangements," coupled with already-weak official institutions, could lead to Oligarch-and-Clan corruption. Alternatively, a dominant leader with business and military backing might seize control – quite possibly in the name of controlling corruption – not only ending electoral democracy but also creating new Official Moguls.

Reform will require a series of openly competitive elections, alternations of power via genuine popular mandates, steps toward economic openness, and lasting improvements in government and economic performance that are visible in citizens' daily lives, to change expectations. But if citizens can reward effective government and punish the most corrupt over time, accountability may become rewarding and disincentives to collusion can be created. Acting through the political system and the legitimate economy, rather than turning to the politically costly protection of patrons, might become more attractive. Turner and Carballo (2010), drawing upon Lipset (1963), argue that effective and responsive government can pay large long-term dividends:

> [I]ncreasing government transparency can, over the long run, build higher levels of confidence in public institutions ... Programmes that build fairness and equity, such as those that help citizens to gain a good education and to find meaningful, well-remunerated work, build confidence in the system as well as a sense of personal security. Most importantly, perhaps, legitimacy will build over time if economic prosperity can be maintained and hard work rewarded, if leaders can anticipate and avoid crises like those of the past and if groups can refrain from withdrawing their support for leadership when a new crisis threatens. These goals may seem a tall order, especially given the experience of Argentina with political legitimacy over the past hundred years, but they remain the most critically important objectives for the hundred years to come (Turner and Carballo 2010: 282).

The steps proposed below will neither guarantee such changes nor end all corruption. Many citizens – who, after all, have amassed considerable skill at dealing with remote and complex government agencies – will continue to prefer the personal and accessible help of "fixers" and patrons to undertaking longer and more uncertain political journeys. The Kirchner presidencies also suggest that for many leaders a combination of confrontational style and patronage-based demobilization remains more useful than more open, conciliatory approaches. Still, a consistent, reliable, even boring government that visibly succeeds at doing basic things well would seem a necessary, if not sufficient, target for reform. Leaders who do such things need not be charismatic – it might be better if they were not – but they could build trust and persuade citizens that there is a real point to politics and government.

Safe political and economic space

The ability to advocate one's own interests freely and without fear is an essential part of any such scenario. Ending reprisals, threats, and subtler pressures against whistleblowers, witnesses, journalists, and voters will require improved judicial and bureaucratic as well as legislative oversight. Encouraging and protecting more active and independent civil-society groups – not just reform groups but associations of virtually any sort – can build social capital and organizational skills, enhance social trust, and foster a sense of efficacy. Argentines are known for their strong family ties and extensive socializing (Turner and Carballo 2010: 281–2); perhaps strong, autonomous social forces can be built on that foundation as trust increases.

Those groups, and the electorate generally, will need to resist manipulation from above more effectively. At present *Peronismo*, in its various manifestations, is not only a political outlook but also, in some ways, a shared identity (Ostiguy 2009) linking elites to the people – primarily on the elites' terms, of course. Attempts to build a stronger civil society that are portrayed as a clean break from the Peronist past are unlikely to be widely credible; they would not only mobilize elite opposition, but would also require many citizens to give up benefits that, even though they come via "demobilizing" patronage, may be urgently needed. Opening up alternatives to Peronist groups, on the other hand, would be more effective, particularly if linked to improvements in government services and quality of life rather than just serving the personal agendas of political patrons, as has been the case with most "parties" that have emerged since the crisis of 2001. They should offer – perhaps even begin with – opportunities to socialize, gain recognition within local communities, build mutual trust, and pool resources to deal with common problems.

A second key way in which elites have controlled the populace and neutralized critics has been via patronage and vote-buying. As we have seen, some social welfare agencies have turned their payrolls into patronage networks, and distribution of some benefits (such as *planes trabajar*, publicly financed part-time work) has been delegated to local groups. Some of those groups were the extensions of existing political factions, but others were emerging social movements and protest groups. Either way, patronage is a process of political control via the age-old practice of rewarding friends while excluding enemies. Many of the emerging, potentially critical, groups were neutralized and lost their autonomous initiative (Villalón 2007: 150; on clientelism in the region see Hilgers 2012).

For those reasons, high-priority anti-corruption measures would include strict monitoring of agency payrolls, ending the process of turning citizen groups into extensions of an already-politicized national bureaucracy, and ensuring that aid flows to those who need and qualify for it, independently of political loyalties. Both are more easily said than done, and old expectations may be slow to change. Cutting off or formalizing access to benefits that once could be had from a local party operative will be painful business. More autonomous legislators, from the standpoint both of oversight and of having genuine local support, will thus be essential. A system of independent inspectors general for social service agencies, given powers of investigation and prosecution and required to report publicly on a regular basis, would also be a positive step, as would stepped-up data-sharing and cross-checking of recipient lists across agencies and levels of government. Because much patronage flows through the channels of provincial governments, scrutiny of provincial agencies will be needed as well; for that same reason, advocates of these proposals should expect to encounter passive and active resistance.

Other aspects of safe space include more secure civil liberties and human rights. Here, independent legislators with real incentives to engage in oversight and investigations could play a major role in improving the functions of the police, judiciary, and security institutions.

Reform activism: strengthening citizens' voices

Reform activism might have an explicit anti-corruption focus at times, but must include enhanced ability to act with autonomy on a wider range of problems and grievances, too. Either way, a political system genuinely oriented toward accountability to the public, and driven by real competition for citizens' support, can be both the means, and one of the ends, of reform activism. We might begin by building a more transparent, participatory, and competition-oriented political finance system, and by making voters' choices freer by offering a truly secret ballot and counting the votes honestly. An independent Elections Authority would be a good first step. Argentina, and other nations, could do far worse than study Mexico's *Instituto Federal Electoral* (IFE),[2] which continues to be one of Mexico's most trusted national institutions (Morris 2010: 147–9). Such an authority, given top-flight independent leadership, sufficient resources to conduct balloting across the country, and the power to investigate possible violations, bring legal charges, and conduct prosecutions, could reduce the pressures and intimidation experienced by some voters. It should produce an Australian ballot listing all recognized candidates from all parties for all offices, publicize it widely in advance, yet make it available to voters only when they present themselves at the polls – where their privacy must be protected. Polling hours and locations must be widely published and then maintained in practice. Recognized parties should be able to place a designated, publicly identified poll watcher in each voting location,[3] but their activities should be carefully specified and supervised by the authority. The same should apply to party operatives and other campaigners within a certain distance from the polling place,

---

[2] General background on IFE can be found at www.ife.org.mx/portal/site/ifev2 (viewed January 22, 2013).

[3] It is tempting to propose the same privileges for reform-oriented non-governmental organizations, but problems can arise with respect to distinguishing bona fide reform groups from those that are there to influence or intimidate voters. In the United States, for example, a self-appointed group called "True the Vote" (see www.truethevote.org/, viewed January 22, 2013) has sent teams of observers to numerous polling places in the name of checking what they claim is frequent voter fraud. Critics, however, charge the group with focusing excessively on poorer and minority-group areas more likely to turn out a large Democratic vote, and some voters have complained that the group's mostly white poll watchers in those locations are intimidating and a form of harassment (Vincens and Khan 2012).

to prevent those figures from accompanying voters into the polls. Powers to investigate and prosecute intimidation practices, as well as the "softer" but still potent ways of steering voter choices described above, should be nationwide.

Counting the ballots, and compiling and proclaiming results, are particularly open to abuse, and therefore need careful oversight by the authority as well as scrutiny by the parties' observers. While those processes must be efficient, great care should be taken with any moves to automate them. While we can envision electronic voting schemes that would work well under ideal conditions, in practice they may be prone to politically contrived "breakdowns," and could even offer one-stop shopping to anyone able to compromise a handful of electoral officials: why go to the expense of stealing ten thousand votes when you can bribe one or two technicians?

Legislators indebted to provincial governors who, in turn, often face little real electoral competition, have little or no incentive to press for accountability. Electing a portion – half, or at least a third – of the deputies and senators on a single-member district format, preferably with a run-off between the top two vote-getters should no majority emerge in the first round, and allowing candidates to place themselves on the ballot by obtaining signatures or significant numbers of small contributions, could encourage locally rooted candidates with an incentive to help their constituents. Like any reform idea this one brings its own risks, such as fraud in qualifying for the ballot and the conversion of those local benefits into personal patronage. The Elections Authority would need to monitor fraud; a local focus is not altogether a bad thing if combined with, and perhaps counterbalancing, a working level of party discipline. Electing no more than half of each body in such a fashion should, however, keep district electorates large enough that outright vote-buying would be expensive, particularly if a majority is required to win. The advent of compulsory primary elections in 2011 makes such an idea more feasible. Legislators who build their own political bases could develop longer careers, specialize in local and regional issues, and develop the political standing necessary to exercise real oversight over executive and judicial conduct.

Political finance arrangements could also serve these goals. As we have seen, even when elections are closely fought nationwide (which has not been the case recently) there is much less competition within many of the provinces. Requiring a demonstrated base of small contributors or valid signatures to qualify for the ballot, matching small individual contributions – perhaps at a significant multiple – with public funds, and rewarding parties for fielding candidates in many provinces could enhance competition.[4] Requiring parties to register well before the primary election, and then restricting public funding in both primary and general-election rounds to those declared parties and their candidates, could increase the value of running under an opposition banner; indeed, the 2011 primary may have begun to draw some support back to the opposition UCR (Calvo and Murillo 2012: 149). One drawback of the 2011 primary at the presidential level was that each faction presented only one candidate (Ibid.); linking early funding to demonstrated popular support might bring forth more candidates within each party. A choice among three credible primary candidates might reduce the monopoly influence of top-level personalities, although offering ten or eleven candidates might well leave dominant personalities facing fragmented opposition, or produce nominees with no real mandates.

In general, political finance policies should encourage socially rooted competition and the generation of genuine popular support, rather than driving money out of the political process (Johnston 2005c). Any public funding must be generous enough to be meaningful; setting spending and contribution limits too low will make circumventions the norm. Above a certain contribution level, fast and easily accessible public disclosure of contributions and spending is a good thing, but individuals contributing less than some lower limit should have the option of confidentiality, lest fear of reprisals by employers or local political operatives keep them from participating at all. Those small donations should be matched at particularly generous levels. To succeed, all of these schemes would require careful implementation by a genuinely autonomous Elections Authority.

Can reform advocacy and citizen participation be sustained outside of episodes of major scandal? That issue must be addressed at both the individual level and in terms of the broader system. The former will be a

---

[4] While we might otherwise consider bounties for the parties based on registering citizens to vote, in Argentina voting is compulsory between the ages of 18 and 70. Linking such funds to actually getting the voters to the polls would create incentives to continue the same "persuasion" practices reformers should be trying to inhibit.

focus of Chapter 8, where we discuss the diverse incentives and appeals needed to sustain any organization or movement. The latter, social level – one that includes both political and economic factors – has been the focus of an intriguing analysis by Chavez (2003). She compares two neighboring Argentine provinces, San Luis and Mendoza, showing how strengthening party competition can build support for the rule of law. In Mendoza checks and balances, and judicial autonomy, are relatively strong, and governors respect restraints on their power, as a result of the province's vigorous electoral competition.

Chavez pushes the analysis deeper, however, arguing that the dispersal of economic interests is essential to genuinely competitive politics. As I suggested in Chapter 2, contention among social interests is as important as contention between them and those in power. Considerable political energy can develop as people realize that where many interests and ideas contend, they not only have the opportunity, but also the responsibility, to stand up for themselves. The perceived fairness of competition is critical – an issue to be raised below, as regards accountability, and in Chapter 7 (see also Stiglitz 2012: Chapter 4). While we should never ignore ideas, symbolic appeals, and intangible interests as political motivators, material interests can not only encourage political contention and competition, but also set the stage for new political settlements:

Socioeconomic complexity increases the likelihood of disputes that help create countervailing power centers. Because economic disputes require a referee to adjudicate them peacefully, they create pressure for the rule of law. Schubert contrasts the nomadic Cheyenne Indians of the nineteenth century and the pre-World War II Barotse farmers of Northern Rhodesia. Unlike the roving Indians, whose need for an arbiter was minimal, frequent property disputes among the Barotse farmers led to a demand for a legal system. In their cross-cultural study of fifty-one societies, Schwartz and Miller found that those with the least developed legal institutions were the "simplest" with the lowest degree of economic specialization. The "mediationless" societies had no need to institutionalize mechanisms of dispute settlement. The authors attribute the absence of mediation to a lack of substantial property. "There is much evidence to support the hypothesis that property provides something to quarrel about." In Europe the introduction of powerful new economic actors set the stage for the rule of law. Tocqueville reflects on how democracy advanced as asset ownership expanded from a small group of landholders to include the clergy and eventually the "commoners" (Chavez

2003: 430; see also Schubert 1974: 14–25; Schwartz and Miller 1964: 165; and de Tocqueville 1994: 4–5).

Securing property rights, improving the performance of regulatory agencies – both procedurally, and in terms of the legislation they are charged with implementing – and guaranteeing open entry and fair play in markets would be steps in a similar direction. Where appropriate, titles could be conferred upon those who have effectively held property for a long time but have not been able to establish ownership (De Soto 1989; for critiques see Barros 2010). Attempting to challenge entrenched interests just in the name of reform as a public good has collective-action problems, as noted, but real dispersal of economic resources could draw lasting support. Such changes will not be simple; Argentina's recent economic revival was driven primarily by agriculture, and does not seem to have spurred diversification. But once in place, such diversity of interests can become a dynamic force for the rule of law and accountability.

Accountability among elites

A stronger voice will have limited impact unless elites become more accountable. One dimension of accountability is vertical: representatives indebted to those who placed them on the ballot will serve political bosses and themselves, not citizens. Competition among elites' personal factions, rather than among parties with real social roots, will do more to enable exploitation than accountability. Another dimension is horizontal accountability: judges with little independence, or who are merely advocates for policies emanating from the *Casa Rosada*, are unlikely to give citizens a fair hearing. Bureaucracies colonized by political and business interests, neutralized by shaky mandates and payrolls converted to patronage, and accustomed to concealing what they do rather than acting transparently, will be poor guarantors of fair play.

Another priority, therefore, is to strengthen the separation of powers, judicial functions, legislative oversight, and basic linkages of democratic representation. In principle, Argentine legislators have opportunities to check the executive, or to create agencies that do so, but as we have seen they are more likely to facilitate "arrangements" between Buenos Aires and provincial governors. Can Argentina weaken the governors' positions by disbursing significant intergovernmental revenues in the form of block grants or dedicated revenue streams, defined by statute rather than negotiated with the President? With the aid of independent judges and inspectors general, directing revenues to predefined services and functions by local or provincial agencies could undercut both the sorts of "arrangements" noted above and the practice of distributing many benefits through local political cronies. At present the legalities and realities of intergovernmental finance diverge considerably, and in changing ways; significant funding simply eludes federal controls once it has been devolved to the provincial level (Guillan Montero 2011: 447). Well-supervised block grants, however, might check abuses, as would tracking the provision of designated services through the sorts of indicators and benchmarks outlined in Chapter 3. Performance data could both signal whether funds are being effectively used and give successful political leaders the opportunity to claim credit for better government.

Other familiar anti-corruption measures might also contribute to accountability. Frequent, credible financial disclosure requirements for national and provincial elected officials and top administrators, and for political parties and lobbying groups, are not panaceas, but could make collusive arrangements more evident. Disclosure rules would require strong leadership and institutional support – perhaps from the Elections Authority or a similar body – and would also benefit from an enhanced judiciary. Much the same is true of Freedom of Information legislation that, among other benefits, might make policy-making and implementation more tamper-evident. These measures would be aided considerably by strong guarantees of press freedom.

Given the tenacity of government–business collusion, transparency in the private sector is of equal importance. Financial markets, ownership of assets, and corporate governance should be targets for enhanced transparency – if not immediately because of the weakness of official institutions, certainly over time as accountability demands gather strength. Such reforms could aid the diffusion of economic interests by persuading investors to see Argentina in a more favorable light. Renationalization schemes such as the recent state takeover of Yacimientos Petrolíferos Fiscales (YPF) oil (Romero 2012), and any further privatizations, should be particular targets for scrutiny, however, lest schemers see such moves as a way to cash in before transparency becomes truly bothersome.

The bigger picture

The goal, ultimately, is to encourage political convergence around mutually acceptable political settlements – ultimately, around rules and institutions – that draw support because they work. Is that hope realistic? We might hope for a high-profile "renovator" or the emergence of some unprecedented coalition (Chapter 2) leading the way to stronger institutions that produce better quality of life. Those idealistic scenarios are not wholly implausible; Acemoglu and Robinson's account (2012: chapters 7, 10, 11) of the rise of "inclusive" institutions in England and elsewhere give some reasons for optimism.

Perhaps more likely, however, is a less triumphant scenario of useful stalemates. Rather than triumphing over corrupt elites, a wide range of groups might reach a rough political parity with them, and among themselves – a situation in which their demands cannot necessarily prevail, but also cannot usually be ignored. Orderly rules, perhaps emerging as informal norms and only later becoming institutionalized, might well become preferable to continued tension and uncertainty. After all, many of Argentina's de facto institutions are informal arrangements among the relative few with a place at the political table (Guillan Montero 2011: Chapter 8). More inclusive processes of negotiation and mutual adjustment could lead to more widely acceptable ways of governing. Those now excluded would acquire a stake in a system offering fair play, and those in charge could build lasting support by governing well. Even elites viewing such developments as threats might, in time, conclude that with better government they can become richer than before, and maintain high social and political standing, without the uncertainties and risks of the old order. For both, the reasoning might be: I cannot dominate you, and I will not let you dominate me, but contention and uncertainty are costly and difficult to live with. We might as well agree on some basic rules as to how things will be run. I will not get all I want, and neither will you; we'll be watching each other to make sure we follow through. Reiterated over time such interactions – however grudging they might be at the outset – can foster trust in place of tension (Axelrod 1984). Even very specific settlements with modest initial implications could encourage wider acceptance of institutions and their value. Conversely, a major concern about Influence Market corruption is that growing inequality might undermine such shared interests – a topic for Chapter 7.

Horizontal accountability – the extent to which institutions, leaders, and political interests are answerable to each other (see, inter alia, O'Donnell 1999) – is critical as well. Strong presidents have circumvented the separation of powers in numerous ways: since constitutional amendments in 1994 envisioned as restraining the presidency, for example, Menem and successors have frequently used emergency decrees (*decretos de necessidad y urgencia*, or DNUs) to get their way, and legislators were unwilling to stop them (Manzetti 2009: 168–85). At times when the executive and legislature have been controlled by different parties or factions, some oversight has occurred, but more often legislators have used those functions as bargaining chips with the executive (Guillan Montero 2011: 445–7, 474–500). Changing that state of affairs is a political as well as constitutional challenge. Some of our earlier suggestions, to the extent that they succeed in increasing competition among socially rooted parties, may help improve legislative and judicial functions.

More specific changes, however, are worth considering. Enhanced, well-enforced conflict-of-interest rules for elected and appointed officials could inhibit collusion, particularly if they extend to deals made via family members or other personal associates. "Well-enforced" is a key phrase, however, as previous codes have lost effectiveness through nonenforcement. To make such provisions workable, banking secrecy and other forms of financial opacity must also be addressed: requiring assets to be held in the real names of their owners, and similar disclosure of who actually operates businesses and public–private partnerships, can help courts and legislators determine just whom they are overseeing and what risks are created by their holdings. The 2012 scandal surrounding Vice President Amado Boudou, featuring murky manipulations of "The Old Fund," reflects such complications:

Corporate secrecy laws make it difficult to determine who owns what in Argentina, but the newspapers *Clarín*, *La Nación* and *Perfil* followed The Old Fund money to a complex web of other shell companies, overseas holdings and *prestanombres* – people who "lend their names" for a small fee to create fraudulent incorporation papers (Associated Press 2012d).

Enhanced transparency in lending and securities markets would also be useful; improved scrutiny of companies' capital sources and indebtedness could reveal interlocking structures of investment and debt within some Elite Cartels. Stronger anti-trust policies could encourage easier entry into markets, a proliferation of contending interests, and a stronger sense of fair play.

A more transparent economy might inhibit abuses in several ways. While much corruption seemingly reduces risk, uncertainty, and transaction costs when compared to weak institutions, it might become less attractive as better alternatives emerge. All such changes would make it more difficult for small groups to dominate politics and markets. Improved public procurement and contracting processes backed by a system of indicators and benchmarks could make collusion more risky. Mexico is one of several countries to conduct many procurement processes online in real time.[5] With World Bank assistance Argentina has embarked on its own initiative[6] for automated, transparent, and socially inclusive procurement practices, but enhancements in technical capacity and commitment to police informal alternative channels of procurement are needed too. If such processes were open to international competitors on a fair basis, Argentina might reduce its losses of inward investment due to corruption, and attract competitors willing to compete on grounds of efficiency and innovation.

Professionalization and independence of the judiciary are key elements of horizontal accountability as well (this discussion draws upon Guillan Montero 2011: chapters 7, 8). Despite a system that ostensibly assigns cases to judges on a random basis, jurists have been able to angle for lucrative and politically useful cases via political connections (Ibid.: 478), while parties to cases may go shopping for friendly judges. Where the parties involved are not well-connected or are unlikely to generate major bribes, such is less likely, but in other instances judges turn cases into political bargaining chips, or opportunities to negotiate pre-trial settlements for a price. Relatively few cases involving high-profile parties ever come to trial. Independent monitoring of case assignments and disposition, clearance rates, judicial backlogs, amounts of time involved in handling cases, and the frequency of negotiated settlements by various judges could improve judicial functions. Enhancing the role of bar associations in reviewing judicial nominations – a change that would also require a less politicized Judicial Council, the body

---

[5] An overview of Mexico's Compranet system can be found at https://compranet.funcionpuhttpblica.gob.mx/web/login.html(viewed January 22, 2013).
[6] See www.argentinacompra.gov.ar/prod/onc/sitio/Paginas/Contenido/FrontEnd/index2.asp (viewed January 22, 2013).

responsible for appointing, disciplining, and dismissing judges – might also support accountability. These proposals will encounter significant opposition: accountability, genuine political competition, and an autonomous electorate are among the things Elite Cartels work hard to pre-empt. Moreover, some of them may bring corruption risks of their own. But changes are possible: Mexico's IFE – a success in many ways, even given controversies about its actions during the 2006 and 2012 presidential elections – would have seemed a remote possibility in the mid 1980s; Colombia moved to an Australian ballot in 1991 (Brusco, Nazareno, and Stokes 2004: 79).

Conclusion: the new Argentina – one more time

If elections, separation of powers, and economic liberalization have not greatly restrained Argentina's Elite Cartels, we should not expect to track the progress of reform simply by enumerating the controls that are put in place, or by tracking corruption index scores. The best-conceived reforms are unlikely to change international perceptions, and rankings that draw upon them, for some time to come, and in the interim may actually make such index scores worse.

Success can still be visible, however, if we look in the right places. Indicators of government effectiveness and the quality of services at all levels will be useful. Special attention should be given to local government: according to Weitz-Shapiro (2008), local corruption can have a particularly negative effect upon citizens' satisfaction with, and trust in, the democratic system. Waisbord (2004) makes a similar point in observing that scandals directly affecting the quality of life do the most to mobilize popular response among Argentines, particularly in an overall climate of "scandal fatigue." As in the Philippines (see chapter 5), reformers must relentlessly link corruption control to poverty reduction, and to the quality and security of everyday life, and be prepared to show measurable effects in terms of government services and performance. If citizens can see that social benefits are reaching their communities more effectively, and are being allocated fairly rather than as political rewards, the value of their political choices and the importance of watching representatives carefully may become more apparent. Similarly, we may wish to look for evidence that more parties are fielding candidates in more parts of the country, that party and business infiltration of the bureaucracy and judiciary is on the

Conclusion: the new Argentina – one more time

decline, and that more reform activity is originating from the grassroots. When legislators begin to serve longer careers, develop political bases of their own, specialize in policy and oversight functions, and take credit for visible improvements in their communities, we may be seeing an emerging political basis for a more effective accountability.

Nothing proposed here will be "the answer" to Elite Cartel corruption in any place where it is entrenched. The ideas are offered, instead, as ways to help citizens demand that answers be sought, and to reward leaders who find them. We are discussing not just the creation of anti-corruption controls, but rather the transformation of a political system into one capable of creating and sustaining reforms we might not even envision. That will involve changing habits and expectations of long standing – not just those guiding relationships among collusive elites, and among their potential critics and competitors, but also those that have led so many citizens to conclude that effective government concerned with their well-being is not a real option. Even if positive trends should appear, they may seem subtle and only indirectly linked to reform. Indeed, they may well come disguised as political controversy and friction. In time, however, Argentines can govern themselves more effectively, and in so doing, unleash their nation's immense potential.

7 Influence Market corruption: wealth and power versus justice

> Yes, as through this world I've wandered
> I've seen lots of funny men;
> Some will rob you with a six-gun,
> And some with a fountain pen.
>
> – Woody Guthrie

Introduction: pervasive, yet elusive

Compared to the egregious abuses of Official Moguls and the toxic mix of insecurity and violence linked to Oligarchs and Clans, it is tempting to view Influence Markets as a lesser concern. Most societies in this category are successful market democracies. Influence Market corruption does not devastate whole governments and economies, nor does it negate the rule of law; indeed, as we shall see, some of its key processes are rooted in the law itself. Cases of outright corruption are generally seen as exceptions to the norm, and reformers have access to legal frameworks, information, and political rights that their counterparts in many other societies can only wish for. Corruption controls devised in Influence Market societies are often offered to other societies as strategies to emulate.

Yet Influence Market corruption is in some respects the most worrisome syndrome of all. First, it is *elusive*: it can be difficult to say just which practices are corrupt, which merely have unfortunate consequences, and which are the skillful exploitation of legitimate opportunities. Despite the relatively solid and legitimate legal frameworks in such societies it can be unclear what is or is not a public role, resource, or concern. Some of the activities that will concern us in this chapter are praised as contributing to the vitality of society, and enjoy extensive political and normative "cover" thanks to the market values that

Introduction: pervasive, yet elusive

increasingly rule such societies (Sandel 2012). Yet those activities exacerbate real injustices, do significant harm to society at large, and at times convert public policy into a maze of private advantages.

We have defined corruption not in terms of a clear set of boundaries, but rather as a dilemma common to all societies: that of evolving limits on the ways people pursue, use, and exchange wealth and power. In succeeding chapters I have emphasized citizens' ability to take part in shaping those boundaries as the essence of deep democratization. That concern may seem misplaced with respect to established democracies, but some of the most worrisome Influence Market activities and outcomes arise within strong institutions, and under the protection of legally enacted policies, rather than in defiance of them. In that and in other ways more developed societies may, ironically, also have more developed forms of corruption (McCullum 2005). The rapid growth in inequalities of income and wealth occurring in many market societies, for example, are celebrated by many as evidence of economic openness and the just rewards of effort and risk-taking. Inequality by itself is not corruption; neither, in itself, is wealth. Those points should be kept front and center in the discussions to come. But if portions of both reflect rent-seeking in the private sector (Stiglitz 2012: chapters 2, 3) that is underwritten and protected by public policy and resources, then those practices and their social consequences raise questions of corruption. Do such connections qualify as *abuses* of public power and resources, and do they justify demands for accountability to the public? More to the point, do people raising such issues have any real options within a political and policy system already shaped by the interests of the wealthy? Those are corruption issues in the sense proposed in Chapter 1 – questions of where boundaries should be drawn and interests should be restrained, and of who should have a say in the matter.

International dimensions of Influence Market corruption are of equal concern. Corruption controls found in market democracies dominate reform agendas despite the fact that they are often the outcomes of longstanding political contention, rather than being what helped check the problem to begin with. Reforms appropriate for affluent, well-institutionalized market democracies – privatization, for example – may be irrelevant or even harmful when deployed against contrasting syndromes. But a more basic issue is the way Influence Market corruption tends to reach out from its "home" societies into others, aided again by the force of market values and the interests holding a stake in them. Corruption in the developing world cannot be blamed solely on rich countries, but their contribution to the problem is frequently overlooked. Banks in the west often hold the assets, and protect the interests and identities, of corrupt operators in poor societies. Some corporations based in industrialized countries – even those that generally play by the rules at home – still bribe officials elsewhere, often with the implicit protection of their home governments. Indeed, we may well be witnessing the emergence of regional and global elites – Janine Wedel's (2009) memorable term for them is "flexians" – who move back and forth across public–private boundaries, serve many and often conflicting interests, and seemingly operate everywhere while not being accountable anywhere. If drawing fundamental boundaries around market power and its political influence is difficult in well-institutionalized democracies, what – if anything – can be done at the global level?

At the beginning of this book I proposed a developmental ideal: political systems and markets that are not only free, open, and competitive, but are also institutionalized in ways that check their excesses and uphold fair play. Many market democracies honor such values, and see them as justifying a range of political and economic outcomes. But the realities of those societies often fall well short of that ideal, particularly in terms of citizens' ability to participate in effective ways. That ideal should be kept clearly in mind, for on the markets side of the ledger, the discussion to come might easily be misunderstood as objecting to the sorts of rewards a free and open market ought to provide for effort, innovation, and risk-taking. But that is not my argument. Because the boundaries of Influence Market corruption are unclear, many of its practices are defended as acceptable – even desirable. But Influence Market corruption *reduces* openness, *restricts* opportunities, is aimed at *avoiding* risks and keeping competitors at bay, and yields disproportionate, *unearned* rewards. The losers, often, are other businesses – perhaps the more nimble and innovative among them – as well as citizens in general, who must make do with an economy that is less open, adaptable, and productive than it would otherwise be.

On the political side, similar points can be made. An open democratic system derives its energy and, in no small part, its legitimacy from the ability of citizens and groups to advocate their own interests. Wealth per se should disqualify no one from a full and fair opportunity to speak his piece. But neither should the lack of wealth, and citizens in many market democracies see wealth and privilege as undermining democratic values and processes (Pharr and Putnam 2000), even where laws are not usually being broken. Influence Market corruption raises questions of freedom, fairness, and justice that are subtle and controversial, and that democratic political systems find difficult to address. Those questions challenge us to look beyond process-oriented justifications of advanced polities and economies, and to consider older ideas such as a system's capacity to command loyalty (Dobel 1978). They highlight Warren's (2004) notion that corruption in a democracy is best understood as "duplicitous exclusion." Societies in the Influence Markets category have considerable deep democratization work to do.

No two Influence Market cases are identical. In this chapter Australia, France, and the United States will illustrate the normative complexities, slippery domestic politics, and global reach of the Influence Markets syndrome. We conclude with thoughts on the difficulties of democratic accountability, both domestically and on a global scale where the uses and abuses of power, for most people, are simply out of reach. That discussion will focus mostly on the United States, a case that exemplifies Influence Markets and their consequences with considerable clarity (Hacker and Pierson 2010; Stiglitz 2012), but I will also consider ways in which those processes and consequences are more widespread.

Three affluent democracies: Australia, France, the United States

Influence Market cases feature market economies that are well integrated into the global system and generally have sound legal frameworks, formally competitive electoral systems, and numerous opportunities for private interests to seek influence through political intermediaries. Those interests – mostly, but not only, businesses – usually seek influence over specific decisions made within institutions strong enough to implement them effectively. Access and influence thus become marketable commodities. The political operators – parties, in some democracies, and well-connected individuals everywhere – need money to succeed in a competitive electoral system, to augment their reputations for being influential, and sometimes to underwrite less honorable activities. Influence-dealing is hardly the only form of corruption in these societies: familiar variations on bribery and extortion

Table 7.1 *Scores on major governance indices*

	1996 (rank)	2000	2004	2008	2011 (rank)
World Bank Institute:					
Control of corruption					
Australia	1.89 (14/184)	1.96	2.10	2.07	2.16 (8/212)
France	1.26 (30/184)	1.36	1.34	1.38	1.51 (20/212)
United States	1.57 (18/184)	1.66	1.86	1.42	1.25 (31/212)
World Bank Institute:					
Voice/accountability					
Australia	1.46 (17/200)	1.51	1.52	1.39	1.43 (12/215)
France	1.31 (24/200)	1.16	1.44	1.31	1.20 (26/215)
United States	1.36 (20/200)	1.34	1.31	1.12	1.13 (32/215)
TI: CPI					2012 (rank)
Australia	8.60 (10/54)	8.3	8.8	8.7	85 (7/174)
France	6.96 (19/54)	6.7	7.1	6.9	71 (22/174)
United States	7.66 (15/54)	7.8	7.5	7.3	73 (19/174)

Sources: http://info.worldbank.org/governance/wgi/pdf/wgidataset.xlsx; http://cpi.transparency.org/cpi2012/ (both sites viewed February 3, 2013). (For 2012, CPI scores are points out of a maximum of 100.)

occur as well, particularly at lower levels. But it is what makes the Influence Markets syndrome distinctive, and such a pressing concern.

No one will ever know the full extent of corruption in Australia, France, or the United States, but they are widely regarded as well-governed. Table 7.1 presents their scores, over a series of years, on three widely publicized governance rankings: the World Bank's "control of corruption" and "voice and accountability" indicators, and Transparency International's Corruption Perceptions Index (CPI). For all three indicators, high scores are positive results.

None of the indicators above is a valid measure of corruption per se; all rest heavily or entirely on perceptions. For the CPI, results cannot be compared over time. But they suffice to make the point that Australia, France, and the United States have been perceived as well-governed for many years. US scores on corruption control, and on voice and accountability, have deteriorated somewhat over time, but none of the three is seen as experiencing a systemic corruption crisis. A look behind the overall scores, however, shows that all three have their corruption difficulties.

Australia: dockworkers, the police, and state politics

Anyone judging Australia solely by the scores in Table 7.1 might be surprised at how prominently corruption issues feature in domestic news and political life. While a 2012 survey (McAllister, Pietsch, and Graycar 2012: 5) found that under 1 percent of respondents reported that they or a family member had "often experienced corruption in the past five years," 43 percent said that corruption in Australia was on the rise. Another 41 percent said corruption has remained at the same levels. Respondents saw the news media, unions, and political parties as the nation's most corrupt institutions, while the armed services, civil servants, and police (the latter once viewed as seriously corrupt, as we shall see) were perceived as least corrupt. Since the 1970s a number of cases have made big news – often, in connection with state politics. Australia's six state governments, like their counterparts in the United States, make important decisions and spend significant sums. In several, politics is a bare-knuckles affair featuring strong personalities, close connections between political parties and major interests, and pitched competition among those broad political formations (on Australian corruption generally, see Grabosky and Larmour 2000; Perry 2001; Hindess 2004).

During the 1970s, for example, concern grew about the power of the Federated Ship Painters and Dockers Union in Melbourne's Victoria docklands (Williams 1986, 1991; Perry 2001: 90–2). The criminal records and numerous aliases of many union officials, links to organized crime and police corruption, and union involvement in devising and then covering up a variety of "bottom-of-the-harbour" enterprises – so named because their records had a way of conveniently vanishing – led to the formation of the Costigan Commission (1980–4), whose investigation eventually reached far beyond Victoria harbor. The Commission was launched by Prime Minister Malcolm Fraser's Liberal Party federal government, which initially was quite happy to link the competing Australian Labor Party (ALP) to unsavory people and doings. But it turned in time to corporate activities too, much to the displeasure of the Liberals. At one point the Commission trained its sights on media mogul Kerry Packer, whose newspaper had urged the creation of the Commission, on suspicion of gambling and organized crime connections. Packer challenged the allegations and no formal charges were made against him – an outcome that for some illustrated the ability of wealthy and powerful individuals to elude the law. Eventually the Costigan investigations became sufficiently embarrassing to both major parties that by consensus its activities were ended in 1984. Only some of the issues it dealt with qualified as public-sector corruption in a formal sense, and yet the inquiry did much to put abuses of power high on the national agenda.

The northeastern state of Queensland, and the political empire of its long-time Premier Johannes "Sir Joh" Bjelke-Petersen, were the focus of the Fitzgerald Inquiry in 1987–9 (Williams 1991; Perry 2001: 92–4). Bjelke-Petersen, who served as Premier from 1968–87, had long been controversial. His rule at the head of the conservative National Party was marked by allegations of police brutality and violations of civil liberties, as well as by more diffuse suspicions of corruption. A 1987 documentary by the Australian Broadcasting Corporation finally brought the latter issues to a head. Evidence of extensive police corruption in the state, featuring links between top police officials and brothel owners, became national news. The program aired, as it happened, while Sir Joh was out of the state pursuing his national political ambitions, and in his absence the Deputy Premier launched an inquiry under the leadership of Judge Gerald Edward (Tony) Fitzgerald. Unlike the Costigan Commission, which actively pursued wrongdoers, Fitzgerald focused on systemic problems for prosecutors and legislators to remedy. Still, the state's Police Commissioner was convicted and sent to jail, as were two Queensland government ministers and lower-level officials. In December, 1987, Bjelke-Petersen retired from political life, but a sense of significant corruption problems lingered. As Williams (1991: 92) sums up, "In essence, Fitzgerald believed that the legitimacy of government in Queensland was called into question by an allegedly unfair electoral system which maintained a government in power for a quarter of a century with only minority support." Single-party dominance at the state level, and the increasing expenses of party politics generally, have been running themes in several Australian corruption cases (Perry 2001: 86–9, 111–12).

"West Australia Inc." was what many called "the interacting and often interlocking power alliances surround[ing] government" (O'Brien 1988) in that state in the 1980s (see also Grabosky and Larmour 2000; Perry 2001: 94–7). Timber, mining, and other extractive businesses were influential there, thanks to its remoteness as well as to its resources, but by the mid 1980s networks of political, business, academic, and

Three affluent democracies: Australia, France, the United States 193

other "chancers" (O'Brien 1988: 4) were trading in influence and access, amassing significant wealth in the process. A private foundation and Rothwells Bank served as umbrella organizations; generous state buyouts of a bank and a mining company, and a history of large business-related commissions, raised the stakes of the influence market considerably. For one buyout commissions were large enough to finance the purchase of a Perth-based television network. A state effort to aid the petrochemical industry channeled contracts to a little-known, but well-connected, Hong Kong construction company with no experience on such projects. When the ALP government of Premier Brian Burke left office, several of his associates became directors of Rothwells – a move some saw as "exit bonuses" for their loyalty. Later, West Australia experienced a number of corruption cases involving police, in some cases linked to organized crime; deals involving property developers and political parties are controversial too. In late 2012 the head of the state's Corruption and Crime Commission complained that despite the extensive powers of his office, political constraints and gaps in the law keep make it difficult for him to pursue private figures – including Burke himself – and public officials alike (WAtoday 2012). That commission, in turn, has been criticized by the WA Police Union as "ineffective," and as having generally "lost its way" (WAtoday 2012).

Recent cases continue to feature state-level parties, politicians, and business interests. Victoria has recently established its own state Independent Broad-Based Anti-Corruption Commission (*The Australian* 2012a). In 2008, for example, the New South Wales Independent Commission Against Corruption (ICAC) – launched in 1989 by the state government, in part because of widespread sentiment that NSW would be a prime focus for state-level corruption – investigated ALP ties to developers, hotel and resort operators, and club owners. Cozy relations had been in place for some time: between 1998 and 2008 NSW Labor received an estimated AUS$13.2 million (at the time, US$12.6 million) from developers (Phillips 2008). A 2012 ICAC inquiry found similar abuses by forty-one individuals in, or dealing with, fourteen local governments (Bajkowski 2012). Leaders in the Health Services Union have been accused of abusing their union positions and exploiting their leverage within Medicare, the nation's public health system (Horowitz 2012). While many allegations of state and local corruption focus on ALP governments and party officials, an effort in South Australia to create an independent watchdog was reportedly blocked by the Liberal Party (*The Australian* 2012b).

Indeed, one difficulty in arriving at an assessment of corruption in Australia is the intense nature of party contention. Corruption stories in some news outlets have a strong partisan flavor and – as with the Costigan Commission – virtually every major state-level inquiry or commission has been portrayed as an attempt by one party or another to smear its opposition. Australia exemplifies a phenomenon in many Influence Market societies: the same political competition that one hopes might check abuses, or at least allow voters to toss the scoundrels out, also creates a cloud of allegations that can be difficult to evaluate. Indeed, the increasing power of global markets to constrain domestic policy options may make corruption allegations an increasingly tempting – if very poor – substitute for party competition on policy issues. It can be difficult, in many democracies, to distinguish among aggressive political hardball, "revelations" driven by partisan motives, and outright abuses of funds, networks, and power. In many of those societies, political competition at the national level does not carry over to lower jurisdictions; it is entirely possible to see a local arm of a competitive national party ruling with impunity, or being marginalized (again with impunity), at lower levels. A more optimistic view, however, might be that intense party competition makes it more likely that corruption problems will at least come to light. Even if competition-driven revelations mean that roughly ten out of every five significant cases of corruption will make headlines, it could be that Australia *seems* "A Very Wicked Place" – Perry's (2001) subtitle, but also a remark dating from 1839 – and yet is well-governed on the whole. The 71 percent expressing satisfaction with Australian democracy in 2012 (McAllister, Pietsch, and Graycar 2012: 7) might well agree, as might most observers around the world.

France: the many corridors of power

France is clearly a democracy, but one of a particularly centralized and elite-oriented sort. Its powerful presidency and bureaucracy link, in various ways depending upon the party in power, to the *Grandes Écoles* (the prestigious institutions that train most of the country's top officials and many in the business class as well), business networks, and elites in other sectors to produce decision-making and policy implementation more coordinated and top-down in nature than that of many other liberal democracies. Power does change hands as a result of elections, and citizens do matter. The rule of law, and property rights, are secure, and some corruption controls are broadly effective. At the same time, however, France may suffer the defects of its virtues: electoral competition intensifies elite demand for funding, engaging networks strong and organized enough to turn some major businesses into paymasters for contending parties and factions.

In the 1970s and 1980s a number of scandals illuminated some of those high-level dealings. One of the more entertaining was the "sniffer plane" episode, in which sophisticated fraudsters and their political contacts persuaded the government to spend the equivalent of US$50 million on a specially equipped airplane that supposedly could, by sampling the surrounding air, locate remote deposits of petroleum (*New York Times* 1984). The case was part of a larger pattern of government agencies' appropriating and spending significant sums outside of official systems of control. Such was the case with *Carrefour du Développement*, a voluntary association with close ties to the Ministry of Cooperation (dealing with Africa and former French colonial regions) and segments of the Socialist Party. After the Socialists' defeat in the 1986 elections, investigations revealed dubious financial dealings involving the outgoing Minister of Cooperation, Christian Nucci. Appropriations officially totaling FF50 million (around US$7.2 million) – but likely adding up to much more – had been routed through *Carrefour* and a similar organization, *La Promotion Française*. Some had financed a French–African summit conference that ran wildly over budget; others went to purchase a luxurious armored car for President François Mitterrand and a castle for Yves Chalier, Nucci's *chef du cabinet*. Chalier fled to South America with significant amounts of cash. Other funds flowed into a series of falsely documented contracts and purchases benefiting lower-level operatives, found their way back into the Socialist Party's hands, or vanished (Becquart-Leclercq 1989: 191–8).

Former President Jacques Chirac was a polished and successful national politician, but during his time as Mayor of Paris – 1977–95, during which he also served as Prime Minister from 1986 to 1988 – some referred to him as "the shark." Allegations of voter fraud, of bankrolling jobs for his RPR (*Rassemblement pour la République*, or "Rally for the Republic") party via the city payroll, and of kickbacks from public housing construction contracts were frequent during his mayoralty. Suspicions of similar diversions from school construction in the *Île-de-France* region also pointed to Chirac, among others; some of those funds reportedly flowed to the RPR but smaller shares also reached the Socialists. Also implicated were Alain Juppé, one-time Prime Minister and RPR Secretary General; Jean Tiberi, Chirac's successor as Mayor; and Tiberi's wife Xavière. Businessman Jean-Claude Mery was responsible for extracting business funding for the RPR; a videotape discovered after Mery's death in 1999 contained detailed descriptions of the kickbacks, including one payment of FF5 million to Chirac – through an intermediary, but in the Mayor's presence. Chirac moved directly to the presidency in 1995, acquiring immunity from prosecution as a result, but after he left office in 2007 controversy heated up again. Suffering a variety of ailments, and retaining the high status of his former office, Chirac did not attend the ensuing trial, testify, or give depositions. In 2011 he was given a two-year suspended sentence for embezzlement (Schofield 2011; Vinocur 2011).

Police in Marseille made corruption news in late 2012. Twelve members of the BAC (*Brigade Anti-Criminalité*), responsible for the tough northern districts of the city, have been indicted, and another eighteen suspended, on charges that include organized extortion and drug-dealing. The investigation began when a cache of drugs, money, and watches was found above a false ceiling in Brigade headquarters. Reports have surfaced regarding the lavish lifestyles of some BAC officers, and of others' expectations that restaurateurs would routinely provide free meals. Top officials may have been notified of the abuses as long ago as 2009, but did not act. Some local observers believe corrupt police are responsible for a number of recent murders, although those suspicions have yet to be investigated. The Marseille episode is France's worst police corruption scandal in many years (*Agence France Presse* 2012b; Samuel 2012a).

Former President Nicolas Sarkozy has been under investigation since he left office in May 2012, in part for activities that show how rivalries among elites nominally on the same side of the political spectrum can drive corruption. In 1995 Sarkozy, an up-and-coming center-right politician, served as manager and chief fundraiser for Edouard Balladur's unsuccessful presidential campaign at the head of the UPM (*Union pour un Mouvement Populaire*) party. That put him at odds with Chirac – Balladur and Chirac were competitors in the first round of that year's election – a rivalry that has become more bitter over the years. Sarkozy allegedly turned French arms deals, including the sale of submarines to Pakistan, into a funding conduit for Balladur's campaign. *L'Affaire Karachi*, as the episode became known, turned tragic a few years later when Pakistani suicide bombers attacked a bus in Karachi, killing eleven French naval engineers – allegedly in retaliation for the embarrassment corruption revelations caused top Pakistani military figures. Nicolas Bazire, a close Sarkozy associate, was indicted in late 2012 for handling arms-related "retro-commissions" funneled to the campaign. More recently, Sarkozy has been reported to have given special tax treatment to Liliane Bettencourt, heiress to the L'Oréal fortune, in exchange for her bankrolling Sarkozy's 2007 presidential campaign, and as having "exonerated" the Aga Khan from all French tax obligations. Precisely what benefits, if any, flowed to Sarkozy from the latter move have yet to be determined (*Agence France Presse* 2012c; P. Allen 2012; Berthelsen 2012).

United States: the pot keeps simmering

Corruption is a continuing concern in the United States, despite the nation's leadership role in global reform efforts. Rightly or wrongly many Americans see governments at several levels as undermined by corruption. Formal corruption controls are well-developed – the US was the first country to attempt to control international bribery by its home corporations – but social and political controls may be weaker than they appear (Johnston 2012). Electoral competition, in particular, is more apparent than real: the 2012 presidential campaign was fought mostly in seven to ten states, out of fifty, and in many years only about a dozen races for seats in the 435-member House of Representatives are decided by a 2 percent margin or less (Liptak 2012).

The Watergate scandal of the 1970s marked a turning point in terms of trust in political leaders, and encouraged journalists and reformers to seek out corruption. In its sources and consequences Watergate was a unique chain of events, but among its most important consequences was the bundle of new and revised campaign finance rules that followed over the next several years. A full description of those reforms is beyond the scope of this discussion (for details see FEC 2012); but it is striking that a system in which the overwhelming majority of political funding is raised, spent, and reported within the law still seems corrupted in the eyes of large majorities. A 2011 national opinion poll,[1] for example, found that 86 percent agreed with the statement "Elected officials in Washington are mostly influenced by the pressure they receive on issues from major campaign contributors"; in 1977 the same statement drew agreement from 77 percent. Similarly, the 2011 sampling found 67 percent agreement with the statement "Elections are generally for sale to the candidate who can raise the most money"; the corresponding figure for 1997 was 59 percent. Agreement with both statements varied little across income, education, and other demographic categories. Whatever the true extent of American corruption might be, a great many citizens see the political process as significantly distorted by the influence of wealth. Whether viewed in terms of Dobel's (1978) argument that corruption is the failure of a system to command the loyalty of citizens, or in the context of contention over the proper uses of, and connections between, wealth and power, that is a significant corruption issue.

The generally favorable scores given the US on global corruption indices mask a wide variety of state and local cases, as well as revealing blind spots in the indices themselves. In the late 1980s, for example, two-thirds of Oklahoma's County Commissioners were convicted on charges of diverting public works resources and crews to improve private property – typically their own, and their supporters', driveways and occasionally swimming pools (Holloway with Meyers 1993). Such practices had been a norm of sorts within the friends-and-neighbors culture of Oklahoma county politics; indeed, the earliest charges caused some to wonder what was wrong with such practices. Louisiana's colorful state politics has long been shaped by influence-trading, patronage, and contracting fraud (Applebome and Alford 2005). Massachusetts has a lamentable reputation for chronic corruption, not only in Boston city politics (Beatty 2000) but also in public works projects such as the massive "Big Dig" that rebuilt Boston's highways and tunnels (Smith 2006). Popular Connecticut Governor John Rowland was jailed after revelations that he had pressured state

---

[1] CNN Poll: "Interviews with 1,015 adult Americans conducted by telephone by Opinion Research Corporation on June 3–7, 2011. The margin of sampling error for results based on the total sample is plus or minus 3 percentage points. The sample includes 911 interviews among landline respondents and 104 interviews among cell phone respondents." Online at http://i2.cdn.turner.com/cnn/2011/images/06/12/new.poll.pdf (viewed January 29, 2013).

contractors into major cash gifts and financing home improvements (Yardley 2004). The most notorious recent state-level case arose in Illinois in late 2008, when then-Governor Rod Blagojevich allegedly tried to sell a US Senate seat being vacated by President-elect Barack Obama (and, therefore, to be filled by a Blagojevich appointee) to the highest bidder. Blagojevich was impeached and removed from office, and in 2011 was convicted on seventeen felony charges in federal court. He received a fourteen-year prison sentence, giving Illinois the dubious distinction of having had two successive governors, and four of the seven elected since the 1960s, imprisoned (Coen and Chase 2012).

The federal level has had its share of corruption problems too. Contracting and procurement for post-war peacekeeping and reconstruction in Iraq were points of particular vulnerability: Blackwater, a shadowy international security services firm since renamed Academi, was widely regarded as a prime offender (Mazzetti 2010), but numerous businesses and political figures – American, Iraqi, and international – also found places at the trough. We will never know the full scope of resources lost to corruption in Iraq; outgoing Secretary of State Condoleezza Rice stated in 2008 that no US funds had been stolen, but other estimates run as high as US$6 billion (Khanna 2008). The Office of Special Inspector General for Iraq Reconstruction (SIGIR) concluded that overall the effort had been a failure (SIGIR 2009; see especially chapters 20, 21), but noted that fraud was a less serious problem than waste of resources.

Rightly or wrongly, many Americans regard lobbying and corruption as near-synonyms. There is a clear difference – lobbying is, after all, a constitutionally protected form of free speech – yet since 2003 many have seen Jack Abramoff as symbolizing both. Abramoff allegedly misrepresented his activities to Indian-tribe clients, who had paid him millions of dollars in lobbying fees only to see much of that money diverted to personal and political uses, and very little by way of effective advocacy. Abramoff's network was broad and deep, including domestic and international clients and reaching upward to include powerful figures such as Representative Tom DeLay of Texas, who enjoyed golfing trips abroad and other considerations at Abramoff's expense. In 2006 Abramoff pleaded guilty on three counts of fraud and corruption, and in 2008 was convicted on a series of influence-dealing charges; he was sentenced to six years in federal prison but was released in 2010 (*New York Times* 2010; Abramoff 2011). In 2005 DeLay resigned his

House seat and party leadership position following his indictment on federal money-laundering charges; he was convicted of illegal campaign-funding practices in a Texas state court in 2011 (Smith 2011). As of late 2012 that case was still under appeal (Hennessy-Fiske 2012).

A final set of examples illustrates ambiguities inherent in many Influence Market dealings. The shadowy financial practices, extremely large executive bonuses, and predatory lending processes that contributed to the economic crash of 2008 took place mostly in the private sector, but at times involved government or quasi-public entities too. In 2011 the Federal Housing Finance Agency sued seventeen major banks over losses incurred when they allegedly dumped "sour" home loans onto the Federal Home Loan Mortgage Corporation ("Freddie Mac") and the Federal National Mortgage Association ("Fannie Mae"), two federally backed corporations bailed out with public funds in 2008 and still government-controlled. In late 2012 New York federal prosecutors accused the Bank of America of generating large numbers of unsustainable home loans through its Countrywide Financial mortgage-lending unit, then dumping the resulting securities onto Fannie and Freddie – a publicly subsidized escape from large losses (Protess 2012). Those cases highlight the increasingly permeable boundaries between public and private sectors in Influence Market societies. Blurred public–private distinctions and the spread of "market values" erode important principles (Sandel 2012) such as prudent banking practices. The crash and its aftermath highlighted the difficulty of holding private parties accountable for extracting what amount to publicly subsidized rents within major sectors of the private economy. The sheer complexity of highly developed economies, and the general public approval and weak government scrutiny enjoyed by economic players, make it hard to say what is or is not corrupt in modern markets, and to arouse concern over practices that, were they carried out in the public sector, would surely be seen as corrupt.

Influence Markets go global

Influence Markets, increasingly, respect no international boundaries. The attractions, force, and normative standing of market values, backed up by the economic and political clout of many Influence Market societies, extend such corruption into many other parts of the world.

Table 7.2 *Transparency International "Bribe Payers Index" scores, selected years*

BPI	1999 (rank)	2002	2006	2008	2011 (rank)
Australia	8.1 (2/19)	8.5	7.59	8.5	8.5 (6/28)
France	5.2 (13/19)	5.5	6.50	8.1	8.0 (11/28)
United States	6.2 (9/19)	5.3	7.22	8.1	8.1 (10/28)

Source: http://archive.transparency.org/policy_research/surveys_indices/bpi (viewed February 3, 2013).

Transparency International publishes a "Bribe Payers Index" (BPI), launched partially in response to complaints from developing countries. Big-ticket corruption in such countries, critics claimed, frequently has connections abroad. The CPI, by implicitly treating such cases as problems within the countries where they occur, thus gives northern and western societies something of a pass. The shortcomings of the CPI make it difficult to say just how such dealings affect poor countries' scores, but seeing corruption *in* the developing world solely as a problem *of* the developing world is to miss much of what is going on. The BPI is even less a measure of corruption than the CPI; essentially, it is an international opinion poll asking "senior business executives" in thirty nations which countries' home corporations are most likely to offer or pay bribes. Still, results for our three cases are interesting; in Table 7.2 higher scores indicate that a country is seen as more effective at checking international bribery.

Australia scores quite well on the BPI for most years; its 2002 ranking was best among the twenty-one countries then included, although by 2011 (the most recent year available) its reputation had apparently slipped somewhat. (The Netherlands topped the 2011 survey at 8.8, while China and Russia brought up the rear at 6.5 and 6.1 respectively.) The United States and France received middling judgments, with the French scores suggesting some sustained improvement in perceptions. Just what these scores mean is conjectural, but international dimensions of corruption – particularly that involving Influence Market sources – are a major concern.

Technology and the increasing scale of corporate activities contribute to the globalization of corruption: people, goods, and money move around the world with astonishing speed, while the jurisdictions, technical reach, and political interests of national governments make control difficult. In the developing world multinational corporations are often far more powerful, better organized, and more nimble than the national governments nominally in charge. Paralleling those trends is the rise of a free-floating class of international fixers and facilitators and "flexians" (Wedel 2009) who move quickly across international and public–private boundaries, "flexing" rules, roles, and procedures to suit numerous interests. Wedel makes the resulting accountability problems clear:

Today's premier influencers deftly elude ... judgment. Pursuing their coincidences of interest, they weave new institutional forms of power and influence, in which official and private power and influence are interdependent and even reinforce each other ... Flexians take these coincidences of interest to the nth degree. When an individual serves in interdependent roles, and is in the public eye promoting policy prescriptions, *and* when fundamental questions lack straight answers – Who is he? Who funds him? For whom does he work? Where, ultimately, does his allegiance lie? – we have likely encountered a flexian (Wedel 2009: 4–5).

Businesses are scarcely the sole drivers of international Influence Markets. National governments are in the mix too, cutting deals of their own and serving as guarantors for others. Sometimes governments clear the way for their "home" corporate entities, deploying influence and resources to encourage exports and not worrying about how businesses make the deals. A classic case is the United Kingdom's reluctance to enforce the law and honor treaty commitments by prosecuting British Aerospace for its dealings in Saudi Arabia (for an impressive documentary and source documents, see PBS 2009). Two banknote-printing firms owned by the Reserve Bank of Australia have allegedly bribed a range of Malaysian government officials while seeking contracts to switch Malaysian currency over to complex new plastic banknotes (Baker and McKenzie 2012; McKenzie 2012; *Sydney Morning Herald* 2012).

In other cases the role of states and politicians is more complex. France's Elf-Aquitaine oil conglomerate, now known as Total, was involved in extensive bribery in Equatorial Guinea during the 1990s, with repercussions extending into the current century (Heilbrunn 2005). Elf was long partially state-owned (during which time it put up some of the cash for the "sniffer plane"), giving the national treasury a direct stake in its international success. More to the point, it served as "paymaster" for center-right politicians including Jacques Chirac and the RPR. Elf's activities, legal and otherwise, reached deep into elite networks, the *Grandes Écoles*, state contractors and other corporate interests, the bureaucracy, and the judiciary. By 2003,

> corruption in France had become so common that many members of the political elite, irrespective of party, were under investigation ... The Elf scandal attained such proportions because an informal group of dishonest people used networks to conceal corrupt acts, apparently without fear of punishment. These networks formed a crucial element of Franco-African policy and linked officials at Elf to various African leaders in oil-exporting states. What made the Elf scandals unusual was that a group of individuals connected to Elf used a tradition of political networks in French policy circles to nest a secretive network that enabled them to embezzle huge sums of money and pay off potential whistleblowers. Political networks in France involve "nodes" of distinguished members of social and economic networks, the boundaries of which overlap and blur. Hence policymakers are active in numerous networks whose practices are embedded in social and economic interactions. The Elf scandals involved patterns of behavior that protected dishonest individuals from detection. Participants in the nested network embezzled money with little fear of punishment and therefore had few incentives to behave honestly (Heilbrunn 2005: 277–8).

Unlike Elite Cartel networks that help maintain the dominance of a political–business class, the French scandals have been driven by intense political competition, as we saw in the case of Nicolas Sarkozy and the presidential campaign of Edouard Balladur against Jacques Chirac (Samuel 2012b) and in the connections between the Socialists and *Carrefour du Développement*. Moreover, competing elite networks in France and other Influence Market countries capitalize upon, and to some extent protect themselves within, a strong state and strong institutions, rather than filling their gaps as we have seen in Argentina.

The United States' role in international corruption issues is complex in its own way. The US was the first nation to legislate against international bribery: the Foreign Corrupt Practices Act (15 U.S.C. § 78dd-1, *et seq.*) of 1977 (FCPA) uses accounting requirements for firms listed on American stock exchanges to ban bribery of foreign officials. FCPA, however, came only after revelations of bribery by American firms, including payments by Lockheed Aircraft in Japan to support sales of its aircraft (Pae 2008). Investigations by the Securities and Exchange Commission (SEC) found that "in the mid-1970s" US$300 million in "questionable or illegal payments" had been made by nearly four hundred US companies doing business abroad.[2] FCPA led to some prosecutions, but as of the turn of the century fewer than sixty charges had been filed. Since about 2007, however, FCPA – now viewed as an essential weapon against illicit international deals of many sorts – was deployed more aggressively: corporate cases have averaged 14 a year since 2007, compared to an annual average of 2.8 over the previous five years, and charges against individuals increased from an average of 6 per year to 23.6 (Shearman and Sterling 2012: 1, 3). Since 2007 businesses have paid over US$4 billion in FCPA fines (Surowiecki 2012a), and some US firms have begun to review their own operations pre-emptively in order to minimize FCPA exposure (Turner 2012). Even at that, however, critics note that unlike the United Kingdom's Bribery Act, FCPA still allows "facilitating payments" – payments to encourage officials to do their existing duties – without sharply defining what they are (Murphy 2011: Chapter IX), and that FCPA enforcement has at times been less aggressive against American firms than those based elsewhere. The largest recent settlements have involved French, Japanese, and German corporations whose activities fall under American jurisdiction in part because of their listings on the New York Stock Exchange (Wayne 2012). In any event, FCPA has scarcely ended corruption abroad by American firms; in 2012 Walmart, for example, was under investigation for bribing government officials in Mexico (Surowiecki 2012a), Brazil, China, and India (D'Innocenzo 2012).

One of the most important extended effects of FCPA was the negotiation and ratification of the OECD Anti-Bribery Treaty. The Treaty, under which thirty-four developed nations agreed to ban international bribery by their "home" corporations, entered into force in 1999 (OECD 2012). The US provided much of the impetus behind the treaty, in part because of complaints from its corporations that they faced limitations their competitors did not. FCPA was amended to conform to the Convention, and the US was an early ratifier. The Convention is

---

[2] Cited in "Foreign Corrupt Practices Act: Antibribery Provisions," United States Department of Justice, p. 2. Online at www.justice.gov/criminal/fraud/fcpa/docs/lay-persons-guide.pdf (viewed January 29, 2013).

potentially an effective weapon, applying as it does to the OECD's economically developed members and several other observer nations, but there too enforcement has been uneven: the UK, as noted, resisted taking action against bribery by British Aerospace. More recently OECD evaluators have criticized both France (Carnegy 2012) and Australia (Beck 2012) for weak enforcement. Even when the Treaty has been enforced, as in the case of US actions against British Aerospace and Siemens (PBS 2009), critics have seen the penalties as modest and enforcement as belated.

Much international corruption involves encounters between Influence Market interests and counterparts in societies experiencing quite different corruption syndromes. Those dealings are hardly one-sided, however: for every western business seeking to buy influence in a poorer society there are eager sellers, and others demanding payments from businesses. If anything, being an Official Mogul or, to an only somewhat lesser extent, an oligarch backed by a clan, can make it easier to make deals with influence-seekers. Profits amassed by both sides frequently pass through western countries; Oligarchs and Moguls find the secure banks and markets of Influence Market societies quite attractive, and for too long (a situation that has only recently begun to change) those institutions have been willing to do business on a no-questions-asked basis.

Tricky business: can we rein in the Influence Marketeers?

Whatever the full scope of Influence Market corruption, it is tempting to conclude that remedies are at hand. Influence Market corruption tends to focus on established democracies, after all, with competitive politics, sound legal and representative institutions, free and competitive news media in most cases, and comparatively strong civil societies. Particularly if our hope is that critics of corruption and those who suffer from it can mobilize politically to protect their interests, we might be forgiven for thinking that Influence Market corruption is the easiest syndrome to contain. But it is not always obvious what is corrupt and corrupting in such cases, and it can be particularly difficult to mobilize effective opposition, domestically or internationally. Indeed, its practitioners may enjoy a surprising degree of impunity while opponents can find the very processes of democracy stacked against them. As suggested at the beginning of this chapter, Influence Market corruption can be both pervasive and frustratingly elusive.

Subtleties: what is corrupt about Influence Markets?

The United States, Australia, and France definitely experience garden-variety bribery, extortion, and official theft, but many of the issues that concern their citizens most do not involve lawbreaking. Often they originate in processes that are desirable (lobbying and free political expression, or the use of personal networks and contacts) and routine arrangements that are widely supported (an active private economy with only limited roles for government). They contribute to a buoyant economy and reward innovation and personal initiative – or so we are usually told – and thus challenging them means taking on a powerful, if in some respects passive, consensus. But sometimes those activities are pushed to a point where they clash with diffuse, but widely shared, democratic ideas and conceptions of fairness.

Let us consider some closely related examples of those issues, and the questions of fairness, accountability, and trust they raise. One is the growth in inequalities of wealth and income, and the wider consequences of those trends; another is the role of money in politics; and a third broad family of issues can be termed "institutional corruption."[3] All revolve around practices that are largely legal. Are they really public concerns, or just results of the individual actions and liberties well-governed societies are supposed to protect? Do they really amount to *corruption* – and who decides? The United States provides our examples, but the underlying issues are on the agenda in many other Influence Market societies.

Consider the following American situations:

- In 2003, a major airline in the United States, seeking to avert imminent bankruptcy, secured substantial "give-back" concessions regarding pay and work rules from its flight attendants, pilots, and other employees. Not long afterwards, a large number of managers

---

[3] My thanks to Lawrence Lessig for his provocative thoughts on that concept. "Institutional Corruption" was the title and topic of a conference co-organized by Professor Lessig, Professor Mahzarin Banaji, and me at Harvard Law School early in 2012.

and executives received large bonuses (*Seattle Post-Intelligencer* 2006).
- Late that same year the US Congress enacted the Medicare Prescription Drug, Improvement, and Modernization Act,[4] popularly known as Medicare Part D, covering at least a portion of the costs of prescription drugs for most senior citizens. Among its many provisions the complex legislation made drugs produced outside the United States ineligible for coverage, and prohibited the federal government from negotiating price concessions from US drug producers. As a result of those provisions, drugs purchased under the legislation cost almost half again as much as those bought by the Medicaid system (Krugman 2012).
- Under legislation enacted in 1872 and still in effect, certain mining corporations in the United States may lease federal lands – keeping all minerals produced, and paying no royalties – for five dollars per acre (Surowiecki 2012b).
- Considerable concern exists over possible health risks from Bisphenol-A (BPA), a chemical widely used in the US for making soft plastic products like infants' pacifiers. Dozens of scientific studies have examined the risks of BPA exposure. Among 163 studies funded by government through independent institutions, 85 percent found significant harm stemming from BPA exposure. Of the thirteen studies funded by the BPA industry itself, none found evidence of harm (Lessig 2011: 22–6).
- The six heirs to the fortune amassed by a discount-store founder collectively possess wealth equal to all assets of the bottom 30 percent of the American population, or of the bottom 41.5 percent of all American households (Hsu 2012).

The situations above illustrate the accumulation of large – even extraordinary – gains by very few people, and the devolution of significant costs, risks, disadvantages, or forgone benefits upon far larger but less powerful segments of the population. Company owners and managers, pharmaceutical manufacturers, and six people who were unusually wise in their choice of ancestors have all done well. Just as striking as the inequalities involved is the fact that no laws are being broken in any of the above scenarios; indeed, in several cases the benefits in

---

[4] 117 Stat. 2066; Public Law 108–73, December 8, 2003.

question are provided, or protected, by the law itself. Some of these examples – notably, the medical research into Bisphenol-A – also share a critical, if less widely discussed dimension: they involve roles and powers that, while located in the private sector, are matters of public trust, their credibility resting on notions of service and accountability to others.

None of these scenarios fit well with mainstream definitions of corruption. Some may well see them as the inevitable outcomes of the ways our economy and public policy are organized: that's the way "the free market" works. Still others will see much to celebrate: those with the largest stake in a business, like those who have gone furthest to voice their political viewpoints, ought to reap the largest rewards, and the discount magnate should be able to pass his fortune on to his descendants. Clearly we gain nothing by applying the term "corruption" to every policy or outcome we happen not to like. But in many of these cases private interests have used political influence to obtain unfair, excessive, or unearned advantages. While the gains are overwhelmingly private, influence over *public* policy, and within public institutions, helped create and protect them.

Those activities, policies, and decisions have important public consequences, imposing significant costs on others who, for various reasons, had little to say about them. That the political processes involved have generally been legal, and that the advantages won have often been created through and protected by law, does not make a key question go away: just what is "unfair," "excessive," or "unearned," and – again – who gets to decide? Those are political questions, over which opinions can and will legitimately differ, and they admit of no simple answers. But from the perspective of corruption as a systemic dilemma – as an issue of contention over the acceptable sources and uses of wealth and power – those political questions are precisely the point. The laws, norms, and policies behind such strikingly unequal results are difficult to challenge, particularly from within a political system already profoundly shaped by wealth and the interests of those who possess it.

That system, its economy, and its outcomes will often be described as natural, even desirable, or at least more or less inevitable features of the landscape. Many speak of "the free market" as though it were a singular natural phenomenon – as an impartial distributor of gains and losses changeable only at our collective peril, rather than as an aggregation of human choices and political decisions (Stiglitz 2012:

chapters 1–4). But "free markets" thrive on strong public institutions and political intervention. Laws and law enforcement, courts and solid property rights, and sound banks and currency are among those institutions; a wide range of subsidies, tax breaks, and rules for fair competition are some key interventions. Those are all political outcomes of a political process, directly or indirectly. Even among Influence Market cases there are significant contrasts in the ways markets operate, and in the rules and restraints applied to them.

Stiglitz (Ibid.; see also Hacker and Pierson 2010; Frank 2011) argues that in the United States much wealth is derived from private-sector rents created and protected by the law, such as the non-competitive drug purchase program or minimal land-use fees paid by some mining companies. Rent-seeking in the public sector is often at the heart of corruption. When it takes place in the private sector, even in formerly-public contexts such as privatized industries, rent-seeking is generally viewed in more tolerant ways – and, by no means are all private-sector rents objectionable. But the sorts of rents and consequences that concern us here often capitalize upon the strength of public institutions in Influence Market societies. Reduced tax rates for the wealthy and the heirs to large fortunes are not rents, but neither are they a "natural" or necessary feature of free markets. Deregulation of industries, and friendly (non-)enforcement of the rules that do exist, are likewise politically conferred advantages – frequently mirrored by disadvantages for citizens and consumers. In other instances (consider, again, the drug-purchasing process) businesses seek new laws and regulations because they reduce competition. To be sure, laws are broken at times: consider the pending charges, noted earlier, against banks that dumped junk mortgages onto federally controlled housing finance agencies. But in the aftermath of the 2008 financial crisis numerous banks that had engaged in predatory lending practices received public bailouts and resumed large executive bonuses while suffering few penalties.

The inequalities of wealth and income that result, in part, from favorable policies may be politically unpopular, but are they really a public matter? To a surprising extent, the answer is yes. Levine, Frank, and Dijk (2010), for example, have found that in American counties where income inequalities have expanded most rapidly, divorce rates are higher and declarations of bankruptcy are more common, even when other causal factors are taken into account. Higher divorce rates likely have consequences for the lives of children and their performance in school (political figures advocating "family values" certainly point to divorce rates as a public issue). More frequent divorces and bankruptcy declarations can undermine the stability of neighborhoods while increasing the demand for a variety of public services and assistance. High-inequality counties also tend to experience higher levels of residential mobility, in part reflecting the divorce and bankruptcy trends already noted, and their residents tend to have significantly longer commuting distances – a trend with energy and environmental implications. Frank further notes that voters in counties where inequality is growing fastest are somewhat less likely to support public infrastructure expenditures (Frank 2010). Lynch, Smith, Kaplan, and House (2000) point to adverse effects of inequality on mortality rates and other health indicators – a consequence with policy and budgetary implications, as well as for community well-being. The United States currently confronts daunting levels of public debt, a long-term problem that could make public services and improvements benefiting large segments of the population unaffordable; few would attribute debt levels solely to inequality, but political resistance to tax and spending changes that might narrow the gap is often particularly strong among the wealthy and their political defenders. Meanwhile, debts require interest payments; while much of the public sees the debts as owed to "the Chinese," domestic banks and bondholders profit from public debt too. Whether public debt helps shift wealth up the scale, via interest payments financed out of tax revenues and through forgone services and public improvements, is a complex question. But the fact that such is rarely a matter of public debate – after all, "the Chinese" make a more attractive target – reflects, once again, the political and normative standing attached to wealth. Perhaps the most sobering large-scale effects have been noted by Stiglitz, who contends that large inequalities are now holding back economic recovery in the United States (Stiglitz 2013) and, presumably, in some other market societies as well.

Democratic institutions ought to make it possible to challenge such boundaries and advantages – in effect, to engage in the political contention that would define, provisionally at least, what is and is not acceptable about inequalities and the policies entrenching them. But as a practical matter, do political and administrative processes shaped by Influence Markets leave room for that debate? The question brings us back to the issue of money in politics. Anyone challenging current policies, and the political standing of wealth itself, must do so through a political and regulatory system, and over normative and cultural terrain, already strongly influenced by wealth. Stiglitz (2012) asks whether the United States has a political system mired in a vicious circle – one in which inequalities of wealth so sharply skew the financing of campaigns that election results further skew policy toward further inequalities. Campaign finance laws are written by incumbents, after all, few of whom wish to endanger their own seats or antagonize contributors. Incumbents are not necessarily bad people; most actively dislike the demands of fund raising, and even the most ethical will correctly point out that to do good things they must get re-elected. But in a system that already affords them considerable advantages, and in which changes introduce uncertainties that create incentives to raise more money, those already in office are unlikely to be interested in a fundamental revision of the role of private money in campaigns. To those dynamics one might add wealth-based differentials in the ability to deploy lobbyists and make use of the courts, and a popular culture that celebrates wealth, privilege, and celebrity even as inequalities mount.

Dependence upon private contributions arguably leaves neither of the two major American parties disposed to address serious inequality (on Congress, see Carville and Greenberg 2012: Chapter 9). The question is not so much (as many citizens assume) that contributors simply buy roll-call votes and specific decisions; more often it is a matter of keeping issues *off* the agenda (a classic argument is Bachrach and Baratz 1962). Hacker and Pierson (2010) argue that "drift" – policy inaction in the face of gradual changes that add to the advantages of the wealthy – is one of the key ways in which well-entrenched interests protect their positions. Few citizens are aware of the mining concessions mentioned earlier; meanwhile the five-dollar charge, whether or not it was ever a reasonable price for exploiting an acre of public land, is a giveaway today. Close links between wealthy interests and policymakers – even just similar worldviews shaped by wealth – illustrate Warren's (2004) argument that corruption in a democracy essentially amounts to "duplicitous exclusion." Critics will find other entrenched values and opinions in their way too, including attitudes toward government "interference" with business and distaste for anything portrayed as threatening jobs. Such views are scarcely without merit; but in an Influence Market setting, are there any opportunities for contention over such issues?

I suggested earlier that one of the most worrisome aspects of Influence Market corruption is the way it tends to spread from its "home" societies to other parts of the world. Corruption of all sorts can cross borders and operate on an international scale, but our Official Moguls and Elite Cartels syndromes depend heavily upon the exploitation of state and political power in specific countries, while the Oligarchs-and-Clans variety allows "big men" and their followers to capitalize upon the institutional weaknesses and opportunities in particular agencies and places. Influence Markets, by contrast, are less tied to a particular state; indeed, the rise of Wedel's "flexians," and of an increasingly free-floating international business elite, illustrate their global reach. Those elites can manipulate or hide behind state authority, but their activities and networks are increasingly transnational. We might ask whether they can be held accountable anywhere. We might even worry about the rule of law: if workable rules and accountability derive, in various ways, from "useful stalemates" – I cannot dominate you, and you cannot dominate me, but we might agree on some workable rules in order to reduce contention and uncertainty – what happens if wealthy and powerful interests conclude that they can go it alone?

The difficulties of demanding accountability and maintaining limits in that broader arena are compounded many times over. The argument that sweetheart business deals create jobs is all the more compelling when it is linked to exports: if creating aerospace jobs at home involves corruption in some far-off country, who worries about that? Under-the-table deals are the norm at those levels, we can tell ourselves, and aren't those societies corrupt already? Meanwhile, if we do not make deals, other nations are all too happy to jump in. Recent treaties and international conventions explicitly rule out many such defenses and rationalizations, but actually enforcing those norms upon sovereign states, and upon political leaders facing economically anxious voters, is difficult at best.

Influence Market corruption – seemingly the least worrisome and most extensively controlled of our four syndromes – thus begins to look like one of the more challenging varieties. A pessimist might conclude that affluent democracies and the global economic systems they dominate are not so much controlling corruption, but rather making much of it unnecessary via wealth-friendly policies and processes. Does the anti-corruption effort ultimately lead to a world in which government – the last hope, for many citizens, for protection, fair treatment, and justice –

becomes primarily the security guard protecting the rich? If, as suggested in Chapter 2, prolonged deep democratization might move a wide range of societies in the general direction of Influence Markets, are we merely rallying the forces of reform in order to march them over a cliff?

Dilemmas of reform

In some respects the key challenge for Influence Market reformers is not what to do about clearly corrupt activities, but rather whether those societies can accommodate the contentious politics of deciding what is corrupt in the first place. Can citizens wishing to change the ways public policies create private-sector rents be politically effective? Can abuses of public trust for private gain, such as dubious research or uses of professional authority to defend profitable, yet possibly harmful, products, or, dumping predatory loans onto publicly funded agencies once they become liabilities, be curbed, particularly since many take place within the law, in the private sector, and in obscure corners of institutions and processes? Those are political questions, just as the process of checking abuses of wealth and power has always been. It is ironic that affluent and successful democracies might be such unfavorable settings for addressing them.

As argued in Chapter 2, the key tasks of deep democratization in an Influence Markets setting are enhancing reform activism and maintaining accountability. With respect to the former, an essential step forward is to recognize that Influence Market societies do have corruption problems, that they are systemic rather than just the work of a few bad actors, that they have real social costs, and that serious corruption is not just something "out there" in the rest of the world. That may seem an odd suggestion for countries where reform groups abound, majorities see political money as debasing democracy, and scandals still periodically arise. But the sort of awareness I have in mind focuses not just upon institutional improvements, but rather upon power, fairness, and accountability, in its broader senses, within a democratic system. Influence Market corruption does not hobble whole economies. But as powerful interests entrench their advantages in policies that are often poorly understood, and within private organizations and processes often portrayed as serving the public, politics and the economy become less open, less competitive, less adaptable in the face of change – and less fair. For all their outward success, the politics and economies of the Influence Market world – for it is increasingly a borderless system – fall well short of the open, fair, and competitive political and economic ideals proposed at the beginning of this book.

Awareness of that sort requires more than hauling bad actors into court and preventing past abuses. The challenge is for reformers to connect corruption as a fundamental problem to citizens' concerns about living standards, personal and family security, their children's futures, and their places in democratic life – as argued in earlier chapters, to link reform to citizens' own needs and interests rather than approaching it as a public good. Reform becomes a matter of demanding accountability in the name of fairness. "Fairness" is a debatable notion – but is the system even open and responsive to that debate? The most promising way to begin is not to propose massive change – an idea that people may well see as adding to their risks and uncertainties, and that is unlikely to be taken seriously anyway. Rather, it is to start with immediate interests and needs, building awareness of how current political and economic arrangements intensify those issues. In an ironic sense, the challenge is not so much to recruit citizens to the cause of reform, but rather to focus reform efforts upon things citizens have known all along.

That raises the second deep democratization task – maintaining accountability. In most Influence Market cases the formal linkages of accountability (elections, representative bodies and their oversight functions, courts and the rule of law, and the like) are in place, yet real accountability remains elusive. Intensifying pressure for accountability upon private roles and institutions that capitalize upon public trust requires making democratic politics work, and opening up similar opportunities in the economic realm. Here there are more specific possibilities – again, not worrying greatly about political feasibility for the moment. Consider, for example, using political finance policies to encourage competition (Johnston 2005c), rather than primarily to control money or drive it out of politics (on the paradoxical effects of contribution limits see Nichols 2011). Creative systems for matching small individual contributions – doubling, tripling, or quadrupling them – could amplify grassroots voices and increase the incentive to develop broad-based support for parties and campaigns. So might offering a public-funding-only "Fair Elections" option to candidates who demonstrate a base of support by raising a certain number of small contributions, as has been done in some American states and cities (Democracy Matters 2012). Lessig (2011: 265) notes that such arrangements, where they have been given a trial, have made for more competitive elections. But he also notes two frequent objections – total amounts to be spent under Fair Elections-style funding are set arbitrarily in advance, and for some citizens the idea of having even small amounts of "their" money flow to candidates they dislike is repugnant. As a solution Lessig has proposed "The Grant and Franklin Project," a scheme under which the first fifty dollars of each citizen's taxes are converted into a "democracy voucher" given to candidate(s) of the citizen's choosing. If no such allocation is made, the funds are directed to the voter's party, or toward the costs of running elections and educating voters. Each citizen is free to add to his or her voucher allocations in an amount of up to one hundred dollars; as with Fair Elections, candidates accepting funding through the Project could spend *only* those funds. The resulting system would reflect citizen choices, and would put an overall cap on spending – but a cap set by our choices, not an a priori bureaucratic limit (Lessig 2011: chapters 16–21, and especially pp. 265–72). With any such scheme the possible range of variations is nearly infinite.

Those ideas would be partial remedies at best: in any system we can imagine, wealthy and well-organized interests will remain powerful, quite apart from the ways in which election campaigns are financed, and the problem of supposedly "independent" expenditures on advertising and other campaign activities would remain. But perceptions matter, particularly with respect to popular confidence and trust. The logic here is not that individual citizens "reclaim" the political finance process – it was never theirs – but rather that they see themselves as having a place at the table, and the system as more inclusive (Acemoglu and Robinson 2012). Similarly, making significant resources readily available to challengers, and to smaller and new parties, might present new political choices. Citizens of many democracies, promised new beginnings in campaign after campaign yet seeing little connection between their votes and what follows, might see new choices as more worthwhile. Political–finance policies by themselves cannot bring about that sort of change; equally important will be long-term public information and persuasion, and parties and candidates with good reasons to put new options out on the table. But a foundation of organized popular groups can also help improve participation and the quality of democratic life regarding many issues, not just corruption; encouraging the rise or revival of such groups will be a main concern in Chapter 8.

A related idea would be to consider filling at least some legislative seats at both the federal and state levels through proportional representation (PR) instead of the current "first-past-the-post," single-round plurality elections. The idea is to give social interests that are sizeable, yet not rooted in any one place – women, working people, environmentalists, groups sharing an ideological outlook or policy convictions – a somewhat better chance to win representation. At present many legislators' districts are uncompetitive and dominated by specific business and financial interests (Hertzberg 2004: 495–507). PR comes in many forms, and careful consideration as to the most desirable variations would be required. Further, some aspects of the American constitutional system – notably the Senate, whose members represent whole states – would not fit a PR framework, although substantial alterations to that strikingly unrepresentative body (Dahl 2003: chapters 2, 6, 7) might be in order as well. The goal of any changes should be greater openness to diverse viewpoints, checking the dominance of specific economic interests within some districts, and more competition overall.[5] That sort of reformed legislative branch might also have more incentive to inhibit regulatory capture, whereby an industry so dominates the relevant regulatory agencies that they become advocates for it, rather than for broader public concerns. A significant PR contingent within each party might also encourage party leaders to take more disciplined, yet more broadly representative, stands on national issues, checking the current tendency toward stalemate unless the issues fragment into "something for my district and contributors, something for yours." Electoral laws offer no guarantees on those scores, and any beneficial effects are likely to be incremental. But the presence of some legislators elected by broader social constituencies might counterbalance those who, because they represent places rather than people, are closely linked to specific economic sectors, and

---

[5] In Chapter 6 I proposed adding first-past-the-post seats in Argentina to bring more local interests into the legislative process. The point common to both arguments is not that PR or single-round-plurality elections are in themselves strikingly more suited to checking corruption, but rather that a mix of the two systems might offer some advantages. Under any system we might choose, political commitment to exercise oversight functions – and sustained political incentives to do so – will be critical.

check the influence marketeers who at present benefit so extensively from the institutional culture of petty compromise, obstructionism, and drift.

Such changes are unlikely to spark a vast pro-reform popular movement; in some respects, it would be just as well if they did not, for anti-corruption crusades are difficult to sustain and keep focused. But if they do foster a political environment in which more citizens believe they can voice their own views and defend their own interests effectively, and in which political elites see good reasons to take such demands seriously lest real competitors do it for them, the promises of democracy might become more credible. The decisions and policies that result will be flawed, imperfect, and at times unwise – just as they are now – but it could be that they will reflect a wider range of needs and wishes, not just those of the few.

Economic policies can produce greater fairness and inclusion too (for a general discussion see Stiglitz 2012: Chapter 10). Anti-trust agencies can do more to inhibit excessive concentrations of economic power, and regulatory bodies can be kept more independent of the economic sectors they oversee. Aggressive policies inhibiting predatory lending, increasing transparency in banking and securities, reining in extremely high pay and bonuses at one extreme, and providing livable minimum wages and meaningful workplace health and safety regulations at the other, might counteract some of the worst inequalities. Scrutiny of the public policy privileges afforded various segments of business, particularly as regards their use of public resources and government contracting, would be a tedious and contentious process, yet is essential if only because of the obscure benefits such a process could bring to light. Changes in taxation – here, admittedly, we venture into the very heart of the political minefield – could ease some of the starkest contrasts in wealth and income. In the United States, such an overhaul might reverse trends that are turning personal income taxes into taxes on work while favoring income from investments and inherited wealth. Labor policies less hostile to unionization could both address economic inequalities, over time, and restore a political and organizational base for segments of the workforce.

All of the proposals above are open to strong objections, many of them made in good faith, and all should be vigorously debated. The goal is not to abolish inequality across the board or to engineer particular outcomes, but to seek greater openness and fairness under the law – to enable citizens to challenge, by democratic means, current relationships between wealth and power as well as the outcomes those connections produce and protect. In the economic arena, the idea is emphatically not to challenge open and vigorous markets that reward innovation, productivity – and hard work. It is, instead, to support such markets by confronting entrenched practices and privileges that close off competition and monopolize rewards, impose costs on possible innovators and market entrants, and make the economy less nimble. It may be said that such ideas are not so much an attack on corruption as an attempt to change basic structures of privilege and exclusion. Given the complexities and subtleties of Influence Markets, however, that is exactly the point.

How will we know whether progress is being made? Corruption indices will give us little feedback, for they miss key aspects of Influence Market corruption. Broader political participation, by contrast, would be very good news, as would be more competitive elections and outcomes: where incumbents (even the many who mean well) are virtually assured of re-election, accountability and openness suffer. An easing of recent trends toward exaggerated economic inequality – to be sure, an immense structural and technological challenge – would be essential too. Greater levels of political trust (within reason – blind faith serves no democratic purpose); of inclusiveness in political debate and policy-making, particularly in a "dynamic center" where real negotiation and compromise are possible; and of public optimism could also point indirectly to greater accountability. A prolonged decline in the large numbers who say their leaders "don't care about people like me," and that policies are primarily shaped by the influence of political contributors, would be a positive trend. Such perceptions are diffuse and reflect myriad influences, but they are not just arbitrary or produced by mass media. They reflect deep-rooted misgivings among citizens about their place in their own societies, and their expectations about their own lives.

With respect to the international side of Influence Market corruption, there are even fewer recommendations to be made. So many of the dealings in that realm are likely to be secret, or only poorly understood, and so many take place at bewildering speed across increasingly permeable borders, that mechanisms of real accountability are difficult to imagine. Economic competition among countries, and the domestic political pressures it creates, increases the temptation to look the other way when international corruption seems likely to create jobs. Still, while more accountable democratic governments are not guaranteed to honor anti-corruption commitments – indeed, accountability might *encourage* tolerance of international bribery in the name of more jobs – it is unlikely that remote and unresponsive officials, particularly those in thrall to specific economic interests, will honor such commitments at all. Much has been made, in that connection, about the possibilities of "global civil society," a realm including some dedicated anti-corruption organizations. But will the intangible yet still critical aspects of a real civil society – a working level of trust and a sense of shared values – emerge to complement organized efforts? Will that occur among liberal democracies whose own civil societies are none too robust (Putnam 2000), and extend to places where civil society is weak, divided, or intimidated? Getting to such a state of affairs would be a fine development, but it is an immense challenge.

There is little in the foregoing that is new or particularly satisfying. We are dealing, as noted at the start of the chapter, with a pervasive yet elusive syndrome of corruption – one whose outlines are hard to define and whose sustaining processes are often seen as acceptable, inevitable, or even laudable. Ultimately the recommendations in this discussion aim less at attacking corrupt deeds and more at addressing entrenched advantages and imbalances of power. That is a tall order. But those challenges are encountered, in differing ways, by people attacking every syndrome of corruption. How such efforts can be sustained, from day to day and year to year, is among the topics of our next, and final, chapter.

8 | Staying power: building and sustaining citizen engagement

I can't tell just how many of these movements I've seen started in New York during my forty years in politics, but I can tell you how many have lasted more than a few years – none ... They were mornin' glories – looked lovely in the mornin' and withered up in a short time, while the regular machines went on flourishin' forever, like fine old oaks.

– George Washington Plunkitt

Keeping up the pressure

One day not long after the turn of the twentieth century George Washington Plunkitt, former New York State Senator and a Sachem of Tammany Hall, sat on the bootblack stand in the New York County Courthouse and delivered that assessment of reformers (Riordon 1963: 21). Deep democratization and strong political foundations for reform require citizen participation, but Plunkitt's observations remain all too true, even in a time of heightened consciousness about corruption. Collective-action problems; material need, and often the prospect of losing even petty corrupt benefits; low levels of trust among citizens, in government, and in reformers themselves; threats and intimidation by the powerful; and the sheer amount of effort and sacrifice involved in checking corruption all make citizen involvement in reform difficult to sustain. The scenario can be depressingly familiar: anti-corruption

---

This chapter draws upon Johnston and Kpundeh 2002; that analysis was expanded and elaborated in Johnston 2009b, and in my background paper for the 2008 UNDP *Asia-Pacific Human Development Report* (UNDP 2008). Sincere thanks to Sahr Kpundeh, and to Elena Borsatti, her UNDP-Colombo team, and several anonymous reviewers for their valuable advice and suggestions.

efforts debut with great fanfare and high-minded appeals, attract an initial surge of citizen and news media interest, and then gradually descend into apathy, division, or cynicism. The last several years have featured numerous examples of citizen action against corruption that drew widespread support at first, yet gradually ebbed: consider Anna Hazare's series of hunger strikes in India, in 2011 and 2012, and his initially huge mass movement that dwindled in size and enthusiasm as time went by (*Guardian* 2012). Greater pluralism and safe political space – or more focused anti-corruption activism and demands for accountability – mean little without strong and sustained citizen involvement. How can an active citizen presence be sustained?

It ought to be easy to mobilize citizens behind reform. As argued in earlier chapters, corruption tends to benefit the "haves" at the expense of the "have-nots" while undercutting accountability, political choices, civil liberties, property rights, and the rule of law. But for every Tian an Men Square or Arab Spring there are numerous other cases in which corruption is widely resented yet only weakly and sporadically opposed. In societies coping with Official Mogul or Oligarch-and-Clan corruption, actively supporting reform can be risky business – a matter of challenging the powerful over the very activities that maintain their wealth and privilege. In either case, but particularly in Oligarch-and-Clan situations where corrupt figures face considerable uncertainty and risks of their own, reformers may be met with repression and violence. In other settings the issue may be a lack of organizational vehicles – political parties, interest groups, a strong and autonomous civil society – with which to turn resentment into influence. In Elite Cartel cases, formal democratic processes may offer electoral choices more apparent than real, with political competition compromised by behind-the-scenes collusion. Reformers in Influence Market societies enjoy advantages and guarantees that are weak or absent in many other places, but even there the diffuse limits around the prerogatives of wealth, the ways official policy can confer unearned benefits and weaken competition, gaps between what citizens regard as corrupting and what the law defines as corrupt, and official complacency, connivance, or "drift" (Hacker and Pierson 2010) can make the battle for reform seem like shadow boxing. Virtually everywhere, imbalances in the ways corruption's costs and benefits are distributed – the former often being widely shared, long-term, and even intangible, and the latter being material, concentrated, and frequently immediate – usually makes the incentive for any one citizen to fight corruption on any one day surprisingly weak, while for bad actors the reasons to defend their advantages can be compelling.

Much in the foregoing chapters has emphasized the need for open, strong, accountable institutions. We have suggested ways to build support for such institutions, even in fragile situations, and to show citizens how well, or poorly, those institutions are performing. But as for participation – the other pillar of the syndromes analysis – can citizens find their voice, and sustain it long enough to have an impact? The question has no simple answer. One important approach has already been discussed in Chapter 3: building trust among citizens and in government, and demonstrating the effects of reform, via gathering, benchmarking, and publishing indicators of government performance, involving citizens in that process, and in determining responses to what the indicators tell us, as much as possible. This concluding chapter, however, considers another aspect of building sustained citizen support for reform. It begins with a discussion of social organizations as a foundation for deep democratization. Those organizations, individually or in coalitions, are unlikely to bring serious corruption problems to an early end, but they are essential for citizens who seek to defend their own interests politically, and to ensure that power and influence are used in accountable ways.

Sustained political involvement of any sort requires incentives and rewards. Groups pursuing only public goods or moral projects are unlikely to last; those offering individual benefits are much more durable, even if their wider and long-term effects upon citizens' well-being is negative. Plunkitt knew full well that Tammany's strength rested on the fact that it offered real benefits – or, at least, the hope of one day getting them – to backers at all levels. For the machine's army of voters and political foot soldiers there were petty gifts and benefits; even though they came at great long-term cost, via lost political choices and autonomy, many took that bait, and some had little choice. For the organization's core and top leadership, politics was not a cause but a way to make a living – at the top of the organization, a very nice living indeed. Reformers, by contrast, are generally not out to distribute patronage, and lack the resources to do so even if they were to try. But they, too, can connect to enduring personal motivations, particularly if we appreciate the many forms such appeals can take. As we shall see, a repertoire of diverse incentives and appeals is essential.

What's in it for me? Incentives sustaining organizations

Even in a democracy it is no simple thing to turn resentment of abuses of wealth and power into lasting influence. Building organizations is one way to win such influence, and societies where corruption is moderate frequently have civil societies rich in voluntary groups of many sorts. Few of them were founded to fight corruption, however, and most have little to do with politics and government at all. Yet by building mutual trust, affirming shared interests and values, extending face-to-face social networks, teaching organizational skills, and creating a collective resource people can draw upon in time of need – which is to say, by accumulating social capital (Putnam 2000) – organizations become a resource useful in addressing all manner of issues and problems.

Organizations are by no means the only important component of what we broadly call "civil society": intangibles ranging from mutual trust to a sense of common destiny are critical parts of the mix. They are not even the only visible manifestations of social capital: informal circles of acquaintances, or extended family networks, are valuable too, and in repressive and post-dictatorial regimes may be the strongest components of civil society to be found. But organizations are useful in diverse ways. In Influence Market settings a citizen upset by machinations at City Hall can appeal to friends and acquaintances, even in social and service organizations that officially avoid political involvement. In Elite Cartel cases such organizations might have access to, or be able to negotiate with, well-placed political figures, or carve out a niche of autonomy, over time taking advantage of growing opportunities for participation. In Oligarch-and-Clan or Official Mogul situations social organizations, even where they must keep a low profile, can be a source of mutual aid and offer some degree of strength and security through numbers. Even where direct action against corruption may be unwise or impossible, organizations can offer benefits individuals or households might find it difficult to provide on their own. But what – particularly where poverty, insecurity, and distrust are pervasive – might those benefits be, and can we combine and extend them in ways that might encourage more, and stronger, organizational networks?

Finding sustaining incentives

James Q. Wilson's enduring book *Political Organizations* (1973: see especially 33–51) considers the incentives that motivate participation in a variety of organizations. Wilson, challenging Olson (1965) and others who argued that because of collective-action problems people simply will not organize under most circumstances, observed that groups *do* form and persist, and that people act out of diverse motives rather than just by cost-benefit calculation. Similarly, Ostrom (1998) has shown that a fuller understanding of reasons for cooperation shows us that it can persist and succeed even in situations that appear quite unfavorable.

Successful groups, Wilson argued, offer members various combinations of four types of incentives:

Material incentives: rewards of tangible value, such as money, goods, or jobs.

Purposive incentives: the accomplishment of a significant goal – often, the stated purpose of the organization. Members of a group that succeeds in eradicating a disease or saving an endangered species may create a benefit available to all, but active supporters still derive special satisfaction from contributing to that goal.

Specific solidary incentives: "intangible rewards arising out of the act of associating that can be given to, or withheld from, specific individuals. Indeed, their value usually depends on the fact that some persons are excluded from their enjoyment" (Wilson 1973: 33–4). They include offices, honors, and recognition ranging from "employee of the month" awards to seeing one's own name over the door of the group's headquarters.

Collective solidary incentives: "intangible rewards created by the act of associating that must be enjoyed by a group if they are to be enjoyed by anyone" (Ibid.: 34), but which are still restricted to the group itself. These include, for example, sociability, fellowship, and sometimes prestige and exclusivity.

Wilson's material incentives may be exclusive or individual (Ibid.: 36–7). Exclusive material incentives are available to all members, but only to members; mutual-aid schemes created among urban immigrants are examples, as are the discounts on travel or insurance offered by fraternal and professional groups, or Automobile Association road and travel services. Individual material incentives are given to some members, withheld from others, and are never offered to outsiders: patronage jobs are a classic example, but below I will also discuss an idea for "corruption insurance" benefits for members of reform groups who opt into specific schemes.

Among purposive appeals, Wilson identifies goal-oriented, ideological, and redemptive categories (Ibid.: 46–7). The first include specific accomplishments or changes (e.g., cleaner neighborhood parks), while the second involve comprehensive critiques of society and seek sweeping change (e.g. the Occupy movement). A redemptive group aims not only to change society but also "to change its members by requiring them to exemplify in their own lives the new order" (Ibid.: 47). Some religious sects might fit this category. It is tempting to think of anti-corruption groups as redemptive, and as noted an anti-corruption organization will likely have to ask its supporters to forgo some benefits. But in most instances they should not pursue redemption, if only because redemptive appeals tend to wear thin fairly quickly and require even greater sacrifices by supporters than do more pragmatic reform approaches. Many such groups keep their distance from the societies they seek to redeem, rather than building a broad base for action, and others fall prey to internal disputes over the precise nature of redemption itself.

The most obvious incentives for an anti-corruption organization would seem to be purposive – better government and politics – and indeed many civil-society reform efforts begin with those appeals. But for collective-action reasons groups trading *only* in purposive appeals will find it difficult to sustain themselves.[1] Other incentives can be problematical too. Particularly where corruption or conflict has devastated an economy, reformers will have few material resources with which to sustain themselves, much less to offer as backup to purposive appeals. The targets of reform, by contrast, will often be well-fixed. For citizens worried about survival, purposive appeals, particularly when they are long-term in nature, will often lack credibility; even petty material enticements of corruption, or just the hope of crumbs from the High Table, will be all too tempting.

---

[1] Over a decade ago I was involved in an aid-funded effort to build "anti-corruption clubs" in a major former Soviet satellite country, a wonderful learning opportunity as well as an applied lesson in collective-action problems. After a very positive initial response most of the activity faded away once the external funding came to an end. The members were not lazy, timid, venal, or stupid; rather, they faced all-too-immediate challenges of daily survival, for which purposive incentives by themselves were not immediately relevant.

Multiple incentives and appeals

More successful groups, whatever their agendas, tend to use diverse, overlapping incentives aimed at multiple constituencies and engaging individuals on several levels. Fraternal groups, for example, may offer discounted insurance and a variety of forms of recognition in addition to collective benefits such as social activities and the prestige of membership. Indeed, the more segments of society a group seeks to mobilize, the more varied its appeals and incentives must become. Specific solidary incentives (Ibid., 208–10) can be crucial in this regard: offices, honors, and citations, and exclusive access to information can reward supporters. Collective solidary incentives, such as social activities, prestige, and a sense of mutual support, are also valuable. Such appeals – notably, prestige – require an "audience" (Ibid.: 40): "Corruption Fighter of the Year" awards, for example, are worth little if broader publics do not hear about them. Safe political and economic space, relatively free news media, and a measure of civil liberties within a functioning state are thus essential to making some incentives effective.

Compared to corrupt political networks, anti-corruption groups are less likely to possess extensive individual material incentives, and if they are available at all they may create internal contention. But the group can still provide exclusive material incentives – things of real value, even if created through its own efforts, that are available to members only. The immigrant mutual-aid groups noted above were funded by tiny contributions from poor people, yet provided valuable aid. An anti-corruption organization might establish a "corruption insurance" scheme in which members (a group of vendors for government procurement, for example, or stallholders in a marketplace) make mutually binding pacts not to pay bribes and kickbacks, perhaps reducing pressures coming from low-level officials. They might pool information on avoiding corrupt demands or seeking recourse or, through regular small assessments, build up a fund to indemnify members for losses incurred by refusing to pay up. The value of such pledges, and access to information and funds (not to mention the risk of forfeiting one's own contributions), would depend upon faithful compliance, as well as upon one's standing in the group – a collective solidary incentive in its own right.

What might a diverse incentive system look like, and to whom would it appeal? Table 8.1 offers some general ideas.

Of the various incentives shown in the table, the exclusive material (corruption insurance, for example) and specific solidary (access to data banks) will be least familiar in terms of reform. They can, however, attract the backing of small to medium businesses and investors – precisely those to whom a group must turn for material resources. Given the uncertainties that can surround corruption, information, even if just based on pooled experience, can be valuable. Assessments of corruption risks and agency performance (see Chapter 3) could be assembled by, and offered to, active backers. Ethics training programs, advice on auditing and compliance requirements and internal control systems, and knowledge of best practices elsewhere are similar examples. Recognition can be an inexpensive and surprisingly effective motivator; except where doing so would expose recipients to danger, organization leaders should spare no efforts in giving awards, citations, and favorable publicity to key backers and anti-corruption "champions" in and outside of government. The latter might be one way to build bridges to ambivalent or initially hostile political figures and administrators. Such efforts not only reward key individuals, but also remind citizens that when it comes to resisting corruption, they are not alone. Of course, some care is in order to ensure that those being recognized do not turn out to have something to hide.

Collective solidary incentives – sociability, prestige – may seem an afterthought, or even a luxury, but in fact they can be essential. The Hong Kong ICAC – an official anti-corruption agency, to be sure, but also a pioneer in using diverse appeals to build citizen participation and support – has long engaged in highly regarded public education campaigns with a component of fun and social activity, particularly for young people.[2] For journalists, honest contractors, and individual officials with an interest in better government, an essential degree of security can flow from formal and informal association with others: those practicing intimidation may think twice if they know critics are backed by a larger group. Conversely, organization members tempted by offers of money for silence, for example, have something important to lose if

---

[2] See, as current examples, the website for the ICAC "iTeenCamp" at www.iteencamp.icac.hk/tc/index.aspx, and that of the ICAC Clubs aimed at an older audience (www.icac.org.hk/en/community_relations_department/icacc/index.html) (both sites viewed February 1, 2013). The clubs for adults offer numerous awards and forms of recognition in addition to more purposive activities.

Table 8.1 *Varieties of incentives and target constituencies*

	Material				Purposive
	Exclusive	Individual*	Specific solidary	Collective solidary	Goal-oriented**
"Corruption insurance"		Benefits from an improved economy	Data, information banks: – on corrupt agencies, officials – on best practices – on honest officials, sources of help	Prestige, improved image Enhanced autonomy for opposition leaders, civil-society organizations, press	Reform as a public good Better governance; a more orderly and prosperous society
Vulnerability, risk assessments for specific sectors		Security via better police, legal services, stronger property rights	Research products	Sociability, fellowship, mutual encouragement	Greater fairness in politics, the economy; improved social trust, morale
Advice on prevention, control		More reliable public services and utilities	Rewards, recognition	A reputation for honesty and non-payment of bribes	Stronger, more predictable public, private institutions
Legal services		Improved public facilities	Reduced insecurity, isolation, vulnerability		Enhanced rule of law

Target constituencies for each type of incentive

Small firms, domestic entrepreneurs, investors	Individual citizens; civil society; small to medium businesses	NGOs and Professional staff, researchers in organization Benefactors, primary supporters Anti-corruption "champions"	Mass membership Journalists NGO leaders Government elites and reform-minded officials	Mass membership NGOs, journalists Aid/lending partners Democracy advocates, opposition groups Business, entrepreneurs

* While these benefits are not restricted to members only, they are of individual material value.
** Ideological and redemptive sub-types of purposes not recommended.
Source: revised from Johnston and Kpundeh 2002; based on Wilson 1973.

they are found out – membership of a prestigious and visible support group, and access to its other benefits.

Putting organizations to work

Once anti-corruption groups are established and have reached a critical mass, what are they supposed to do? Tactical choices – which sorts of controls and forms of transparency to advocate, and what sorts of government performance data to gather – are many and heavily dependent upon context. As a first approximation, however, it might be useful to consider what anti-corruption organizations can – and cannot – do.

First of all, anti-corruption organizations cannot function as a *deus ex machina*: that is, they cannot simply be inserted into a society and expected to solve its problems. In addition to the sustaining incentives discussed above, which must include more than just a purposive agenda, they need the legitimacy and credibility that only success can earn – even if only on a small scale at the outset. "Attacking the worst first," absent a particularly compelling crisis, is often an unpromising way to earn credibility. It may be better, for a time, to "pick the low-hanging fruit" in order to show that what the organization *does* do is likely to be effective. (The risk there, of course, is that relatively easy actions will become ritualized and will dominate the group's agenda, holding back its development over the longer term.)

Second, an organization cannot seek "civic" or reform goals exclusively. As earlier discussions of collective-action problems, and of incentives, suggest, anti-corruption organizations must engage the real needs and immediate interests of people. An entirely "civic," or public-goods-oriented, agenda will encounter "free-rider" problems. Many of the most useful organizations, particularly in an Official Moguls case where opportunities are beginning to open up, or in an Oligarchs-and-Clans setting, might have little or nothing overtly to do with corruption, reform, or political life. Their value, instead, would lie in the provision of other beneficial outcomes: broader and deeper networks, added social capital and organizational skills, greater levels of trust, and a reduced sense of isolation. Over time those resources can aid the activities of other, more reform-oriented groups. Ordinarily, the group should not become an investigative body or whistleblower, although it might well offer protection to the latter. Similarly, the organization should resist any temptation to become a certification body conferring anti-corruption "seals of approval"; the short-term publicity might be tempting, but such activities create large risks and offer few long-term rewards.

Finally, anti-corruption organizations should not be expected to produce quick results. As suggested above, their benefits often accrue and diffuse over time and through seemingly unrelated activities. Moreover, the basic roots of corruption have usually been in place for a long time and reflect fundamental trends and imbalances in political and economic development. Where that is the case both reform, and the broader agenda of deep democratization, can require equally basic changes. Putting the challenge that way makes it clear why a one- or two-year reform agenda is unlikely to produce much sustained progress. At the same time – an issue to be discussed below – while laying down the foundations for accountability may take a long time, once the corruption situation begins to change it can change rapidly as new expectations arise and older ones shift. That is when organizations must be ready to act, if only by helping members and backers understand and act upon the opportunities opening up to them, and groups with a record of appealing to a variety of constituencies with diverse incentives – not least, a degree of safety in numbers – are likely to be more effective in such situations.

On the other hand, there are many useful things organizations *can* do for corruption control. First, they can build citizen awareness of corruption as a shared and, often, systemic problem. Further – and particularly important in fragile situations – organizations can build mutual trust through repeated positive interactions, and reinforce shared values and expectations as well. That sort of benefit is reciprocal: as trust and shared frameworks of values become stronger, it will be easier to build organizations, and to overcome the collective-action problems that plague reform. Active, open, and legitimate groups can teach organizational skills, as citizens learn new ways to cooperate and organize activities, and find out which appeals and incentives "work" in their communities. They can hasten the emergence of local leaders with skills, credible personal reputations, and rooted social networks. Citizens of established democracies often take such assets for granted: most citizens of such societies understand the idea of autonomous organizations, how a meeting is run, and so forth. But in undemocratic or newly democratizing societies the basic idea of self-organizing autonomous groups may well be unfamiliar, and basic skills and leadership are often in short supply. Over time there may also be benefits flowing from "demonstration effects": if a reform group provides its own examples of honest, accountable leadership, it is showing what better governance might look like, and raising citizen expectations of how they ought to be treated by leaders. Finally, as suggested by some of the collective incentives discussed above, solid organizations can help spread the risks, uncertainties, and costs of fighting corruption more widely and evenly. Moreover, they are ways to link citizens to sources of external, even international support. An active and legitimate anti-corruption group offers one way to "get noticed," and over time may acquire international affiliations.

Once an organization has been launched, autonomy becomes a basic issue. What sort of relationship should it have with the regime – fighting from the opposition corner, or cooperating? Can it avoid being "played" and used by the powerful? To some extent the answer depends upon the political options available: where political and administrative leaders are hostile to reform, cooperation may be impossible, and an anti-corruption group can be forced into an opposition role, or even put at considerable risk. Particularly in Official Moguls or Oligarch-and-Clan situations, group leaders may have to play a waiting game, learning and working the social networks and educating possible supporters, but being very selective about important initiatives until the political climate improves. In more democratic circumstances strategy can still be complex: an unrelieved adversarial stance will be counterproductive or dangerous while too little independence will undermine credibility – particularly if political allies are found to be compromised.

Cautionary notes

At times we speak of organizations as though they were the sum total of a strong civil society, and of civil society as though it were a good-governance wonder drug. But organizations themselves can be vulnerable, and difficult to establish and sustain, particularly in Official Moguls and Oligarch-and-Clan situations. A strong civil society is much more than just a collection of organizations; often it is an *outcome* of the greater participation and demand for the sorts of institutions that help control corruption in more basic ways.

Making matters even more complex is the fact that organizations with possible connections to reform come in a bewildering variety.

Putting organizations to work 233

Numerous Non-Governmental Organizations (NGOs), such as Transparency International or Global Integrity,[3] are primarily aimed at corruption issues, while others like The Asia Foundation[4] do anti-corruption work as part of a wider repertoire of priorities. Another family of NGOs focuses on technical or institutional aspects of governance and reform; examples include the International Foundation for Electoral Systems (IFES),[5] or the Asia Network for Free Elections,[6] based in Bangkok. Yet another type of organization, such as Amnesty International,[7] deals with human-rights issues that are critical to the rights and guarantees needed if opposition to corruption is to flourish. Even within the context of a single corruption syndrome, there is no single template for an ideal organization.

Genuine socially rooted organizations must also deal with competitors, imitators, and impostors, sometimes sponsored and manipulated from above in order to divide or buy off opponents of corruption. Some are "briefcase organizations" consisting of one person, and perhaps a few clients, that exist as much to collect funding as to take action. Still other suspect groups are backed by political movements; indeed, some terror-related groups have masqueraded as socially concerned NGOs, raising funds through a mix of voluntary appeals, demands, threats, and violence. During the past decade, for example, Sri Lanka's Liberation Tigers of Tamil Eelam (LTTE, or "Tamil Tigers") amassed substantial influence in some British, Canadian, and Australian Tamil temples, at times under the guise of the British Tamil Association (BTA) or, in Canada, the World Tamil Movement and the Federation of Associations of Canadian Tamils. Initially, Temple members were asked for periodic contributions, but pressure quickly mounted for regular automatic bank transfers; in Toronto such demands ran to C$5,000 per family and up and, in the case of businesses, as high as C$100,000. Those funds were used for, among other things, illicit weapons purchases under the guise of charitable and social-improvement activities. LTTE support groups also allegedly engaged in passport forgery and trafficking in drugs and human beings.

---

[3] Online at www.globalintegrity.org/ (viewed February 1, 2013).
[4] Online at http://asiafoundation.org/ (viewed February 1, 2013).
[5] Online at www.ifes.org/ (viewed February 1, 2013).
[6] Online at www.anfrel.org/ (viewed February 1, 2013).
[7] Online at www.amnesty.org/ (viewed February 1, 2013).

Still other groups have been termed GONGOs (Government-sponsored NGOs) by Moisés Naím (Naím 2007). They appeal to civil society yet take their sponsorship and agendas from above:

> Gongos are government-sponsored nongovernmental organizations. Behind this contradictory and almost laughable tongue twister lies an important and growing global trend that deserves more scrutiny: governments funding and controlling nongovernmental organizations (NGOs), often stealthily. Some gongos are benign, others irrelevant. But many ... are dangerous. Some act as the thuggish arm of repressive governments. Others use the practices of democracy to subtly undermine democracy at home. Abroad, the gongos of repressive regimes lobby the United Nations and other international institutions, often posing as representatives of citizen groups with lofty aims when, in fact, they are nothing but agents of the governments that fund them. Some governments embed their gongos deep in the societies of other countries and use them to advance their interests abroad (Naím 2007: 96).

As Naím points out, there is no litmus test telling us which groups are and are not genuine charitable, good-government, or human-rights organizations. Instead we must look closely at what they do, how they do it, and whether and how they build real citizen support – in short, at their incentive systems: for example, does a group possess, or is it actively building, a real base among the poor, women, and minority groups?

Ultimately the goal of any organization-based strategy should be to contribute – using diverse incentives and appeals, to be sure – to deep democratization. Whether that means adding pluralism to the political arena, seeking and protecting safe political and economic space, engaging in sustained reform activism, or maintaining demands for accountability, the test of an organization's value will be whether it helps citizens develop the capacity, and willingness, to advocate their interests and defend themselves by political means. A very wide range of organizations can contribute to those goals – even, and in some unfavorable settings, especially those with non-reform and non-political agendas and appeals. Like most other recommendations in this book, organization-building may well be most effective in contributing to corruption control when it is an indirect and long-term effort proceeding on many fronts, and drawing its energy from citizens' own interests, grievances, and aspirations. Organizations are, in the long run, only means to the end of enabling citizens to demand, get, and reward government that is effective, open, fair, and honest – or, to put the matter another way, to participate in democratizing their societies in profound and lasting ways.

Conclusion: why *another* book about corruption?

In this book I have tried to use a generation's research and experience – my own, to some extent, but with far greater debts to others – to mount a distinctive and integrated argument about future directions for reform. The general purpose has not been to argue that the many bright, dedicated, and often courageous people leading the fight for reform have been completely wrong – far from it – but rather that there are ways we can make their efforts far more effective. They entail, among other things, an awareness of how past corruption problems in a number of societies have been brought under control, and a fuller appreciation of the roles to be played by self-interest and politics in any successful reform effort.

The geographical focus of this book has differed from that of *Syndromes of Corruption* (Johnston 2005a), its predecessor. Where the earlier volume considered three cases for each syndrome and thus was able to encompass a fairly wide range of countries and regions, this analysis has taken up fewer countries in somewhat greater depth. While that approach still enabled me to take up the Middle East (Tunisia and Egypt), Oceania (Australia), and South America (Argentina), in addition to Europe, North America, and Southeast Asia (stretching the latter category to include the Philippines), other regions have of necessity not received such direct discussion. The basic comparative focus, however, has been on the four syndromes of corruption, not primarily on regions as such; if the syndromes analysis has any validity it casts some doubt on the utility of theorizing about, say, "African" or "Asian" corruption as any sort of distinctive, unified phenomenon. Thus the countries discussed in this book are treated as examples of broader syndromes, with the hope that the underlying framework can extend the discussion to other societies with similar corruption problems.

Another contrast is that this book has had more of a United States emphasis than the earlier volume, even though that book included a short US case study too. I hope the result is not an impression of parochialism; rather, it is intended to highlight two important points. One is that, as noted at the outset, we cannot treat serious corruption as a problem "out there" in the developing world, nor can we overlook the role of developed societies in the corrupt dealings that take place in those emerging societies. In no way does that imply that wealthy countries are wholly to blame for corruption in, say, Nigeria, Thailand, or Colombia. But they are not blameless either, a fact that must be kept in mind when we compare scores on corruption indices that seem to suggest that the causes of corruption lie entirely within the places where it is perceived. Second, to the extent that our analysis of Influence Markets – and of what they suggest about current and future trends in democracy, fairness, and equality – is on the right track, the United States becomes an essential case for scrutiny. It is hardly identical to all other market democracies, and neither its corruption issues nor its reform tactics always map well onto other societies. But wherever markets, politics, and ordinary citizens are headed in this globalizing and liberalizing world, the United States seems to be getting there fastest.

I have also tried to contribute to anti-corruption thinking in six more specific ways. They include, first, the question of how corruption problems and reform challenges differ in contrasting settings. If, as I argue, it is unsatisfying and potentially misleading to rank the world's countries on a single more-versus-less dimension of corruption, what sorts of categories might be more useful? I have used *Syndromes of Corruption* as a point of departure, and have tried to explore the key challenges confronting reformers based on what those syndromes suggest. That scheme is far from perfect; among other things, more needs to be known about how contrasting syndromes may coexist within different regions, economic sectors, or levels of a given society. Nor are the four categories themselves the last word about how corruption might vary. But if, after another several years, people are talking about six different categories and syndromes, only two of which correspond to those employed here, we will still have taken important steps away from the view that the only major contrast among corruption in Denmark, Japan, Argentina, and Uganda is a difference in amounts.

A second prime concern has been how reforms should be sequenced – what to do earlier, what to delay until later on, and what good ideas from other countries should not be tried at all. While the syndromes themselves are not a developmental sequence, the steps of deep democratization can be seen as steps in a consistent direction, and they do suggest things to be done and avoided under particular circumstances.

Conclusion: *why* another *book about corruption?*

The sequencing offered in and among these chapters is of strategies – what should we be doing to advance deep democratization – not, primarily, of specific control tactics or remedies. The selection of the latter is a decision, often delicate yet urgent, to be made in particular circumstances by those who know the society best, and even in two societies within the same syndrome those choices will likely vary. In order to consider cases as examples of broader corruption syndromes, I have afforded myself the great luxury of not worrying about political possibilities. For those who must convert strategy into tactics in specific situations, however, "the art of the possible" will be of the essence.

In that connection, too, we should note that the pace of change may be very slow in some phases, yet quite fast in others. The emphasis in much of the discussion here has been upon patience and gradualism – as well as on indirect, roundabout causal sequences – in building the foundations for reform. But when the corruption situation begins to change, it can do so very quickly. Expectations are revised, new incentives become available and old ones are distributed and understood in new ways, and corrupt dealings – which are envisioned, in the syndromes theory itself, as responses to particular combinations of opportunities and constraints – can alter rapidly. Sometimes that rapid change is for the worse, as in Russia after the fall of the old Communist regime: there, an Official Moguls situation turned very rapidly into Oligarchs and Clans. But Rothstein's (2007) account of rapid reform in nineteenth-century Sweden, or perhaps a close look at the pace and sources of more recent changes in South Korea and Indonesia, suggest that positive trends too can move relatively quickly. If that is true, would-be reformers must be ready to act, and will benefit from understanding the deeper influences shaping both corruption and reform activities.

A third primary theme has been the risks of reform. As suggested, good ideas from one place might squander scarce reform opportunities, or do actual harm, elsewhere. Without even a rough sense of sequencing, the inevitable temptation is to bombard corruption problems with good ideas in no particular order. But what, short of "less corruption" – impossible to measure directly in any event – are we trying to do, and might some "best practices" undermine that mission? Might we, in the name of trying to help good people, be putting them at serious risk? Is there a danger that by changing too much, too fast, we could push one undesirable syndrome of corruption over the edge into something worse – as happened, arguably, in parts of Mexico between the mid 1980s and now? This book has emphasized caution and forbearance; the risk, of course, is of moving so slowly that key opportunities are missed. But it is an equally great misconception to think that good intentions and good ideas will necessarily produce good results, particularly when the social realities of the societies in question differ sharply from those where many mainstream reform ideas originate.

Fragile situations and societies – a fourth concern – are particularly relevant to those notes of caution. Corruption problems are frequently worst where institutions, social trust and cohesion, and economic prospects are weakest. Often they are serious *because of* such systemic fragility. Reform itself is a stress – it involves new relations between leaders and followers while disrupting old ones, new expectations at both levels, and, all too often, a need to forgo benefits flowing (or anticipated) from the very corrupt figures and practices we are hoping to check. Fragile and post-conflict societies, more or less by definition, are ill-suited to additional stress. In Chapter 3 I have offered some ways to build up greater tolerance for such stress, notably through demonstrably better government performance even if only in one or two policy sectors, and by building trust among people as well as between them and government. Those recommendations may easily be misunderstood as suggestions that we do nothing about corruption until social and institutional factors are perfectly aligned, but such is not the case. Some tightly targeted anti-corruption initiatives will be required in order to produce those improved government services, and stronger norms of accountability will be equally essential if we are to be able to document that things are changing. The key, again, is to think in terms of strategy – fundamentally, what do we need to do to help a society resist corruption? – rather than seizing immediately upon specific corrupt practices and favorite anti-corruption tactics. Equally, we must always remember that, particularly in fragile and post-conflict situations, we can do great harm by our efforts to do good.

A fifth theme might, again, seem like an argument for tolerating corruption, but is not: it is the value of "halfway" situations. Elite Cartel corruption, for example, is scarcely a good thing in itself, but it can be far preferable to continuing exploitation by Official Moguls or the insecurities, disruptions, and violence produced by Oligarchs and Clans. As cases like South Korea and Botswana (Johnston 2005a: Chapter 5) suggest, the de facto stability of Elite Cartels may encourage

Conclusion: *why* another *book about corruption?*

economic growth and, over time, allow for the growth of stronger political oppositions and civil societies. Elite Cartels are not a desirable "end point" – neither, for that matter, are Influence Markets as we now experience them – but perhaps they are a useful way station, a place where reformers and their societies can take a breather of sorts. Understanding those sorts of possibilities can help us recognize opportunities that one-dimensional, more-versus-less-corruption rankings can easily obscure.

A final contribution this book is intended to offer is a workable way to address the measurement problem, indirectly, to be sure. Thus I have put considerable emphasis upon indicators and benchmarks of government performance. They do not measure corruption itself, but can tell us a great deal, in a detailed way, about its past effects and the current incentives sustaining it – and therefore, about vulnerabilities in specific places, agencies, functions, or even budget lines of governments. Better yet, they can also offer evidence that can be compared, and thus can reveal trends, over time, and in many cases point to what we need to be doing and where we need to do it. If City A issues licenses too slowly, or if agency B pays too much for concrete, those are functions to be examined and improved. Doing so can produce government that is demonstrably more effective, and even more fair. Indicators and benchmarks can also send signals to bad actors that the scope for and profitability of corruption are being squeezed out of particular agencies and processes, and provide effective agency managers and political leaders with ways to take credit for their efforts. Indicators and benchmarks are not magical; partly because they can identify agencies and managers at fault, and partly because they may seem intrusive, or disruptive of a comfortable status quo, they will encounter resistance and be open to "gaming" or outright falsification. But where the scheme is pursued and sustained it can build citizen trust and involvement in better government efforts: indeed, often the best source of evidence on the quality of services and facilities might come from citizens themselves. At the very least, the idea can give anti-corruption groups a stronger sense of where they stand, what they need to do, and whether they are having any effects – essential feedback that most of today's approaches to measuring corruption cannot give us.

In the end, none of these ideas will be of much value unless they are understood and pursued in the context of what I have called deep democratization. That does not mean "building democracy" in the sense of holding elections or installing a particular array of national institutions. After all, liberal democracies have distinctive corruption problems of their own. It is more a matter of making institutions more inclusive (Acemoglu and Robinson 2012), leaders more accountable, and citizens more effective in shaping how they are governed, and in delineating ways in which wealth and power may and not be pursued, used, and exchanged. It is ultimately a quest for the fairness, accountability, and justice that human beings deserve but are far too often denied. Those are, after all, the reasons why we worry about corruption in the first place, and their fundamental nature is why the struggle against it will never be finished. There is much we can do, by way of institutional improvements, to take meaningful steps toward that goal. But the primary argument of this book remains that social and political foundations for those changes are essential, and thus that corruption will continue – indeed, may well be the norm – until those with a stake in ending it are able to oppose it in ways that cannot be ignored.

APPENDIX

Recognizing the syndromes of corruption

Corruption in its context

The value of thinking about contrasting syndromes of corruption is to frame a key question of reform: what underlying processes and problems shape a society's corruption problems, and how should those circumstances figure into reform scenarios? When it comes to grappling with such questions in real societies, combinations of participation and institutions are no more than useful simplifications; various examples of a given syndrome will not look exactly alike. Participation and institutions do not determine every detail of a country's corruption situation; key personalities and groups, events, popular responses, and the ever-present law of unintended consequences will all modify the impact of deeper influences. International factors can also be critical. Moreover, real societies – particularly larger and more diverse ones – may experience more than one syndrome of corruption in different levels, economic sectors, or segments of society. Still, the syndromes scheme can be a useful step beyond one-dimensional corruption indices, and can help us sort out important similarities and contrasts in the predominant forms of corruption countries experience.

While it is tempting to classify corruption cases in terms of immediate techniques – bribery, extortion, judicial corruption, violence – those sorts of characteristics do not tell us much about deeper influences on corruption and reform, and do not take us very far in terms of distinguishing among various societies' corruption problems. Even if they did, we lack comprehensive evidence as to how often, or where, a country experiences a given corruption technique. The value of examining broader and deeper influences is that we can compare

This appendix was produced, in part, with United States Government support; its judgments and conclusions do not necessarily reflect the opinions or policies of its research sponsors.

such factors across societies or over time with a useful degree of accuracy. The initial syndromes analysis (Johnston 2005a) relied on a series of country-level indicators and case studies to establish and test the four basic categories, but in examining a given society those who know it well can use a number of other kinds of knowledge to make similar judgments. Indeed, one critical common element among the various approaches to be discussed below is that there is no substitute for extensive local knowledge. Moreover, applying that knowledge to the four syndrome categories should not be a matter of trying to "get the right answer"; instead, the hope is that the syndromes lend depth and insight to what knowledgeable observers have already seen.

Fundamentally, the four syndromes are distinguished from one another by deeper factors that shape the stakes, opportunities, and constraints of various kinds of wealth- and power-seeking activities, and the connections among them. As suggested in Chapter 1, the balance between wealth and power opportunities will influence whether official clout is likely to be used for self-enrichment, or wealth is deployed in pursuit of influence and power. The strength of institutions – social, political, and economic as well as those of the state – will influence the sorts of stakes on offer, and the rules (if any, in a de facto sense) that constrain contending parties. From those factors derive a variety of related characteristics of corruption syndromes, such as the extent and sources of insecurity, the balance of power between corrupt operators and those who would regulate them or challenge them politically, and the resources, opportunities, and basic challenges shaping the reform agenda.

Table A.1 offers a general breakdown of how those contrasts may be visible on a day-to-day basis. It characterizes each syndrome by typical participants, stakes, techniques, and targets of corruption, and concludes with the sorts of corruption vulnerabilities associated with each. Some vulnerabilities may arise in more than one syndrome: electoral corruption, for example, may be common in both Influence Markets and Elite Cartel situations, although it would be likely to involve contrasting participants and agendas. As suggested above, working backwards from corrupt practices to causal factors without considering deeper influences can yield confusion.

Here too, the outlines of each syndrome are approximations; the goal is to look at "middle-level" patterns – who seeks what, from

Appendix

whom, by what means, in what sort of climate of opportunities and constraints. The contrasts among various syndromes will not be complete; police and customs corruption, or electoral fraud, might be found in any society. Still, the comparisons sketched out in Table A.1 can bring out important contrasts that can be obscured by personalities and conflicts, the fog of news reports, or public controversy.

Applying the scheme to specific societies

When it comes to putting the syndromes scheme to use in actual situations, we should remember that it refers to types of corruption problems, and not necessarily to types of systems or regimes, or to perceived seriousness of corruption. Two neighboring countries, similar in many respects, could still have contrasting syndromes of corruption: consider, in this regard, Japan's Influence Markets as a contrast to Korea's Elite Cartels (Johnston 2005a: chapters 4, 5). Similarly, countries with similar corruption problems might well differ in many details: the Oligarch-and-Clan problems of Russia and the Philippines are examples. Large, diverse, or divided societies might experience contrasting syndromes across various regions, economic sectors, or levels of government. For example, Influence Markets are the predominant form of American corruption, yet schemes and alignments typical of Elite Cartels can be found in numerous state and local governments. Given their origins in contrasting fundamental characteristics and trends of participation and institutions, however, the syndromes are unlikely to "blend" into hybrid mixes: political monopoly by top-level family Moguls might be a fact of life in one region of a country, for example, while contending oligarchs disrupt the life of another, but the two are not likely to coexist in a single place. In classifying corruption problems it will always be tempting to "split the difference" or try to combine syndromes in order to make as many facts as possible "fit." But we should do so only with great caution. If we see signs of more than one syndrome, it will likely be more useful to look for dominance in different parts of the system than to try to treat all aspects as simultaneous characteristics of the system as a whole.

What sorts of details might be particularly revealing? Table A.2 identifies some symptoms of deeper systemic influences and links them to varieties of cases. It will not necessarily describe any one society

Table A.1 *Recognizing corruption syndromes in practice*

Syndrome	Who?	Seeking what?	How?	Likely sectors	Related symptoms
Influence Markets	Private interests: businesses, lobby groups Politicians, lobbyists Bureaucrats	Bureaucratic and political access Influence over very specific decisions Money	Political contributions; personal gifts; bribes Trading in access, influence	Government: anywhere access to bureaucrats, elected officials, is valuable	Private-sector rent-seeking Intensified inequality Regulatory capture Policy "drift" with respect to wealth
Elite Cartels	Colluding elites: political, bureaucratic, business, military, etc., facing growing political, economic competition Politically "connected" wealth interests	To preserve status quo To fend off rising competitors To solidify elite networks Mutual enrichment	Political collusion, sharing corrupt $$ Politicizing bureaucracy, networking private interests Large payments, kickbacks	Electoral politics State/parastatal sectors Public contracting, procurement Privatizations and nationalizations Communications media	Electoral competition a façade for collusion Parties, elite factions colonize courts, bureaucracy Weak legislative oversight

Oligarchs and Clans	"Big Men": personal followings in government, courts, police, business Organized crime	Rapid, major gains in wealth and power Protecting those gains from state, competitors Predictability in business, government	Large-scale theft, fraud, patronage abuses; bribery of judges and police, bureaucrats Phony privatizations Violence	Liberalizing economic sectors; energy, natural resources Trading in state assets; banking, currency, money laundering Security services (formal and illicit)	Pervasive insecurity, unpredictability Sense that no one can govern Protection rackets Capital flight, economic disruption, weak property rights
Official Moguls	Monopolistic leadership (dictator, juntas) Inner circle (family, personal favorites)	Major gains in wealth To exploit, maintain dominance To tap into capital, aid flows Economic opportunities as elite political rewards	Official theft of public, private assets Misappropriation of investment, aid Phony privatizations Patronage	Investment, aid; public works, contracting, procurement Extractive industries Landownership	Extensive repression, torture, intimidation Top state, military figures are also major entrepreneurs Top-level nepotism, domination of media

Table A.2 *Examples of corruption syndromes*

Influence Markets

- Most Influence Market societies are relatively settled market democracies.
- Political and economic arenas are generally open and competitive, although participants may seek hegemonic advantages; institutions sustaining and restraining participation are strong and legitimate, even when they are controversial; rule of law is solid.
- Private interests buy, and some politicians, officials, and other third parties deal in, influence – usually over *specific* decisions (obtaining a contract, modifying a regulation); the strength of public agencies makes influence within them valuable.
- Many corruption issues involve ambiguous, legal, or even desirable activities (political contributions, lobbying and advocacy, networking) that are pushed to excess and threaten other values, and may take place primarily in the private sector.

Examples:

- Industry seeking tax changes contributes to campaigns; some of the money is used to "sweeten" bureaucrats, some vanishes.
- Pharmaceutical firm provides grants, gives cruises to doctors participating in research or clinical trials for new drugs.
- Local legislator, via spouse's investments, holds a major stake in land to be opened up by a new mass transit line.

Elite Cartels

- Many societies in this category are new or reforming democracies; de facto predictability based on elite collusion, more than on formal institutions, can aid economic development.
- Networks of elites engage in collusion, sharing corrupt takings while staving off rising political and economic competition.
- Bureaucracies, courts, military, media, and emerging civil society are often colonized by elite networks.
- Competition among political parties is more apparent than real; party leaders share corrupt benefits and rig election results; many parties are extended personal followings of specific elites, lacking a real base in society.

Examples:

- Military procurement contracts are skimmed by a general; proceeds shared with friendly politicos, bureaucrats, PM's sister, church leaders, media owner.

Appendix 247

Table A.2 (cont.)

- Leaders of parties in the governing coalition secretly divide up the patronage and kickbacks flowing from high-speed rail projects and neutralize opposition leaders with payoffs
- Officers in a semi-secret fraternal organization dominate key cabinet ministries, police, investigative agencies, and banks, diverting funds to themselves and lending to favored business people at below-market interest rates.

Oligarchs and Clans

- In Oligarch-and-Clan cases political and economic opportunities are rapidly opening up, yet institutions are very weak. Many are post-conflict or post-dictatorial societies; mutual trust and official credibility are low, and the day-to-day authority of government may be in question in some areas. Unlike Official Moguls, it can be unclear whether anyone is actually in charge.
- Civil societies tend to be weak, as do public–private boundaries; elections may be routine, but the most important competition is outside the system, among oligarchs and their followings; their influence may penetrate both government and the economy.
- In a setting of insecurity, unpredictability, and weak institutions, oligarchs and followers contend in disorderly ways within both public and private sectors, often using violence to enforce contracts, collect debts, and protect assets.
- Corruption extensively disrupts economy and investment; rule of law and property rights are very weak, and confronting corruption can be risky; formal democratic procedures offer little by way of accountability.

Examples:

- Entrepreneur's "personally owned" judge issues seizure order against competitor; order is enforced with police and mafia help.
- A patriarch, family members, and followers dominate the Ministry of Industry, enriching themselves and family businesses.
- Arms traffickers dominate the police, law enforcement, and border-control agencies in one region of a country.

Official Moguls

- Official Moguls cases are undemocratic; often a dictator or small inner circle rules, with few if any challengers. While their economies have typically opened up somewhat, they are poor, strikingly unequal societies; economic

Table A.2 *(cont.)*

opportunities are often monopolized by the regime, and used as patronage for figures personally connected to those in charge.
- Top figures engage in corruption with impunity; unlike Oligarchs and Clans, there is little or no doubt as to who is in charge.
- Opposition groups are weak, compromised, clandestine, or non-existent; "civil society" and the rule of law may have little day-to-day meaning; the regime silences critics through intimidation or torture.
- Official powers, roles, duties, and loyalties are less important than personal ones, and often protect corrupt schemes.

Examples:

– State bank and customs officials engage in import–export fraud using bank resources, backed by dictator's protection.
– Dictator, facing no competing forces, allocates land and major business monopolies among family members and generals.
– Ruling junta members tap into flows of aid and investment.

---

perfectly, but does give some indication of how the aspects of corruption we commonly witness can point to underlying influences.

In sorting out these cases, it is useful to keep some general political scenarios in mind. Influence Market cases are usually democratic and market-oriented in most respects, and yet both arenas may be dominated, or competition hampered, by the influence of wealthy and powerful private interests. Many such societies get favorable corruption-index rankings, but it could be that relatively little overt bribery takes place because wealthy people and groups find it easy to influence decisions by perfectly legal means. They are also more likely to be home to the instigators of international corruption, and to corrupt assets from all over the world, than to be extensively infiltrated by corrupt influence from without (drug gangs, however, may be increasingly important exceptions). In Elite Cartel cases top political, economic, bureaucratic, media, and other figures are fighting a rear-guard action against rising political and economic competition; they maintain strategic unity by sharing corrupt benefits. In Oligarch-and-Clan cases, everything is on the table at once, institutions and restraints are weak, and powerful individuals, families, or faction leaders contend over large stakes in a disorderly and sometimes violent manner. In Official Moguls corruption there is, as noted above, little doubt as to who is in charge; regime leadership dominates corrupt and legitimate economic opportunities, with their power being personal rather than official or political. "Public space" is scarce or non-existent, and both opposition to corruption and contention among its practitioners are generally not significant.

A "forced-choice" approach

A final approach to identifying syndromes is to answer a few deliberately simplified choices about participation and institutions. This method returns us to more of a "macro" level, in the sense that the choices have to do with underlying influences on corruption in entire societies, regions, or sectors. But because of the questions involved, it is simplest of all. Particularly given its forced-choice design, results from this approach should be judged in the context of any of the other classification methods we have discussed.

The basic approach is simple, and involves answering three questions:

1. Politically, is this case an established democracy; a new or reforming democracy now, or recently, undergoing significant liberalization; or undemocratic?
2. Economically, does this case have established, legitimate markets and general affluence; new or reforming markets and moderate affluence; or liberalizing markets with considerable poverty and inequality?
3. Overall, are political, economic, and social institutions strong and legitimate; only moderately strong, or reforming; or weak and lacking in credibility?

Now, track your answers using Figure A.1.

The questions above and the diagram below in effect present the basic relationships in Table A.1 as answers to the simplified questions. The arrows do not imply causality, but rather lead us from one answer to the next, toward a classification. Figure A.1 does not offer, nor do the syndromes exhaust, all possible combinations of answers. That is because in practice, the state and pace of democratization and economic liberalization, and the quality of institutions, tend to co-vary in broadly observable combinations, as verified with data and discussed in more detail in the original analysis (Johnston 2005a: Chapter 3).

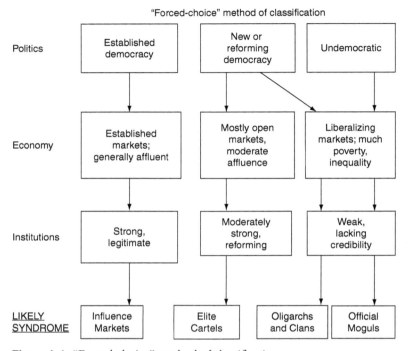

Figure A.1 "Forced-choice" method of classification

The forced-choice format uses approximations that will at times fit awkwardly, at best, with what we know about a given society; but again, it is only meant to suggest the ways participation and institutions seem to shape a society's corruption problems. It also provides a useful reminder of the deep roots each syndrome has, and may link more ephemeral details – the role of key personalities, for example, or techniques such as bribery versus nepotism versus procurement fraud – to more fundamental influences. As always, detailed knowledge of a society is never trumped by the syndromes scheme, which is intended to help us interpret what we do know.

An online[1] variation on the forced-choice scheme takes the form of a short questionnaire. It poses questions about political, economic, and

---

[1] For details, please see http://goo.gl/Ak4Ae.

Appendix 251

institutional aspects of a society, asking for agreement or disagreement with statements such as:

- In recent years economic opportunities have expanded in this society
- Property rights are not secure for most citizens
- Corruption in this society is often linked to violence

and then processes answers in such a way as to arrive at proposed syndrome classifications. The basic method is to use judgments about a society that are qualitative, yet not likely to be wholly subjective, and to capitalize upon respondents' knowledge of local realities. This questionnaire is under continuing revision, and classification results – which are reported directly to the respondent – are used only to improve the questionnaire itself, not for my own substantive research.

In the end it is possible that a given society or region simply will not fit, whatever method we choose. It may be, for example, that a given case simply does not have enough known corruption to be classified in any useful way – Singapore is often proposed as such an example – that not enough is known about actual cases, or that whatever the realities of corruption they are overridden by violence, state failure, or other sorts of crises. Further, despite the clear clustering of attributes found in the basic 2005 statistical analysis (and replicated in more recent years), we cannot wholly rule out novel combinations of our basic attributes, particularly as time passes and "hybrid" cases such as liberal–authoritarian regimes continue to develop. There is no point in forcing cases into a particular syndrome simply for the sake of neatness, and it may well be that divergent results, and the discussions they might produce, will help us improve this or any other system of categories. If we know enough about a case and its corruption to be certain that it does not fit anywhere in the scheme, we might look closely at differing regions or sectors. And if that approach still produces a muddle, then the odds are good that by then we will have a sense of *why* the case does not fit, and of what causal factors and attributes of corruption set that case apart from others. That, by itself, is still useful knowledge – an advance over a single index score or impressionistic claims about amounts of corruption.

References

Abouzeid, Rania. 2011. "Bouazizi: The Man Who Set Himself and Tunisia on Fire." *Time*, January 21. Online at www.time.com/time/magazine/article/0,9171,2044723,00.html (viewed July 13, 2012).

Abramoff, Jack. 2011. *Capitol Punishment: The Hard Truth about Washington Corruption from America's Most Notorious Lobbyist*. Washington, DC: WND Books.

ABS-CBN. 2011. "A Closer Look at 'Pabaon' System for AFP Chiefs." *ABS-CBN News.com*, January 27. Online at www.abs-cbnnews.com/-depth/01/27/11/closer-look-pabaon-system-afp-chiefs (viewed April 22, 2011).

―――. 2012. "Iggy's Family Can Claim 'Jose Pidal' Account." ABS-CBN News, February 1. Online at www.abs-cbnnews.com/-depth/02/01/12/iggys-family-can-claim-jose-pidal-account (viewed January 10, 2013).

Abul-Magd, Zeinab. 2012. "The Egyptian Republic of Retired Generals." ForeignPolicy.com, May 8. Online at http://mideast.foreignpolicy.com/posts/2012/05/08/the_egyptian_republic_of_retired_generals (viewed February 5, 2013).

Acemoglu, Daron and James A. Robinson. 2012. *Why Nations Fail*. New York: Random House/Crown Business.

Agence France Presse. 2011. "Philippine Bishops Apologise Amid Donation Scandal." *Agence France Presse*, July 10. Online at www.google.com/hostednews/afp/article/ALeqM5gTwTbLHEl5xIpfOV2FUhVv-ruWDQ?docId=CNG.bd10cf61cddde29382a1b8858bdea472.931 (viewed January 10, 2013).

―――. 2012a. "Mubarak Sons on Trial Again for Corruption." *Dawn.com*, July 9. Online at http://dawn.com/2012/07/09/mubarak-sons-on-trial-again-for-corruption/ (viewed February 5, 2013).

―――. 2012b. "Marseille Police Corruption Scandal Deepens, 30 Suspended." (October 8). Online at www.google.com/hostednews/afp/article/ALeqM5jbIXiEdV8-Bx1wMOvPrqeWcg-Aaw?docId=CNG.39915a6a5a91b6c0bee8979e6671dc1c.31 (viewed December 13, 2012).

2012c. "Sarkozy Aide Charged in 'Karachi' Corruption Scandal." *Dawn. com*, October 29. Online at http://dawn.com/2012/10/29/sarkozy-aide-charged-in-karachi-corruption-scandal/ (viewed December 13, 2012).

Aliriza, Fadil. 2012. "The Godfathers of Tunis." *Foreign Policy*, May 25. Online at www.foreignpolicy.com/articles/2012/05/25/the_godfathers_of_tunis (viewed February 5, 2013).

Allen, Douglas W. 2012. *The Institutional Revolution: Measurement and the Economic Emergence of the Modern World*. University of Chicago Press.

Allen, Peter. 2012. "Sarkozy 'Exonerated' Billionaire Aga Khan from Paying Tax, Corruption Inquiry Hears." *The Mail Online*, October 25. Online at www.dailymail.co.uk/news/article-2223084/Sarkozy-exonerated-billionaire-Aga-Khan-paying-tax-corruption-inquiry-hears.html (viewed December 13, 2012).

Amin, Galal A. 2011. *Egypt in the Era of Hosni Mubarak: 1981–2011*. New York: American University in Cairo Press.

Amorado, Ronnie V. 2007. *Fixing Society: The Inside World of Fixers in the Philippines*. Davao City: Research and Publication Office, Ateneo de Davao University.

Andersson, Staffan and Paul M. Heywood. 2008. "The Politics of Perception: Use and Abuse of Transparency International's Approach to Measuring Corruption." *Political Studies* 57:4, 746–67.

Anechiarico, Frank and James B. Jacobs. 1996. *The Pursuit of Absolute Integrity*. University of Chicago Press.

Applebome, Peter and Jeremy Alford. 2005. "History of Corruption in Louisiana Stirs Fears That Aid Will Go Astray." *New York Times*, October 1. Online at www.nytimes.com/2005/10/01/national/nationalspecial/01corrupt.html?pagewanted=all (viewed December 13, 2012).

Apter, David E. 1971. *Choice and the Politics of Allocation: A Developmental Theory*. New Haven: Yale University Press.

Araral, Eduardo K. 2006. "The Political Economy of Policy Reform in the Philippines: 1992–1998." *Journal of Policy Reform* 9:4, 261–74.

Arnold, Peri E. 2003. "Democracy and Corruption in the 19th Century United States: Parties, 'Spoils' and Political Participation," in Seppo Tiihonen (ed.), *The History of Corruption in Central Government/L'histoire de la corruption au niveau du pouvoir central*. Amsterdam: IOS Press, pp. 197–210.

Ashton, Robert. 1956. "Revenue Farming under the Early Stuarts." *Economic History Review* 8:3, 310–22.

Asia Foundation, The. 2012. "Afghanistan in 2012: A Survey of the Afghan People." Online at http://asiafoundation.org/country/afghanistan/2012-poll.php (viewed January 2, 2013).

Åslund, Anders, Sergei Guriev, and Andrew C. Kuchins (eds.). 2010. *Russia After the Global Economic Crisis*. Washington, DC: Institute for International Economics.

Associated Press. 2012a. "Close Mubarak Aide Jailed for Corruption." *The Guardian*, May 27. Online at www.guardian.co.uk/world/feedarticle/10260698 (viewed February 5, 2013).

2012b. "Egypt Mubarak-Era Minister Jailed for Corruption." *Seattle Times*, July 13. Online at http://seattletimes.nwsource.com/html/nationworld/2016242401_apmlegypt.html (viewed February 5, 2013).

2012c. "Tunisia's Judges Strike after 82 Colleagues Fired for Corruption." *Tunisia Daily*, May 31. Online at http://mobile.nytimes.com/2012/05/30/world/africa/tunisia-judges-strike-to-protest-firings.htm (viewed February 5, 2013).

2012d. "Scandal Grows around Argentine Vice President." *Seattle Post-Intelligencer*, June 2. Online at www.seattlepi.com/news/article/Scandal-grows-around-Argentine-vice-president-3604253.php (viewed September 16, 2012).

Australian, The. 2012a. "Baillieu Unfazed by Corruption Vacancies." *The Australian*, October 30. Online at www.theaustralian.com.au/news/breaking-news/baillieu-unfazed-by-corruption-vacancies/story-fn3dxiwe-1226506776149 (viewed December 12, 2012).

2012b. "SA Parliament Stalls Corruption Bill." *The Australian*, October 15. Online at www.theaustralian.com.au/news/breaking-news/sa-parliament-stalls-corruption-bill/story-fn3dxiwe-1226496249345 (viewed December 12, 2012).

Auyero, Javier, Pablo Lapegna, and Fernanda Page Poma. 2009. "Patronage Politics and Contentious Collective Action: A Recursive Relationship." *Latin American Politics and Society* 51:3, 1–32.

Awad, Marwa. 2012. "Special Report: In Egypt's Military, a March for Change." Reuters.com, April 10. Online at www.reuters.com/article/2012/04/10/us-egypt-army-idUSBRE8390IV20120410 (viewed February 5, 2013).

Axelrod, Robert. 1984. *The Evolution of Cooperation*. New York: Basic Books.

Azfar, Omar and Tugrul Gurgur. 2005. "Does Corruption Affect Health and Education Outcomes in the Philippines?" Online at http://ssrn.com/abstract=723702 (viewed February 5, 2013).

Bachrach, Peter and Morton S. Baratz. 1962. "Two Faces of Power". *American Political Science Review* 56:4, 947–52.

Bajkowski, Julian. 2012. "New Corruption Scandal Hits 14 NSW Councils." *Government News*, October 29. Online at www.governmentnews.com.

au/2012/10/29/article/New-corruption-scandal-hits-14-NSW-councils/NLXXJEMMGB (viewed December 12, 2012).

Baker, Richard and Nick McKenzie. 2012. "McCrann's RBA Defence Falls Flat." *Sydney Morning Herald*, September 26. Online at www.smh.com.au/opinion/political-news/mccranns-rba-defence-falls-flat-20120926-26kag.html (viewed December 13, 2012).

Balán, Manuel. 2011. "Competition by Denunciation: The Political Dynamics of Corruption Scandals in Argentina and Chile." *Comparative Politics* 43:4, 459–78.

Balleny, Luke. 2012. "Could Corruption be Worse in Tunisia, Egypt after Arab Spring?" Reuters, March 20. Online at http://blogs.reuters.com/the-human-impact/2012/03/20/could-corruption-be-worse-in-tunisia-egypt-after-arab-spring/ (viewed February 5, 2013).

Barro, Robert J. 1999. "Determinants of Democracy." *Journal of Political Economy* 107:6, Part 2, S158–83.

Barros, D. Benjamin (ed.). 2010. *Hernando de Soto and Property in a Market Economy*. Farnham, Surrey: Ashgate.

Barry, Brian. 1995. *Justice as Impartiality*. Oxford University Press.

BBC News. 2000. "Argentine Press Eyes Corruption Scandal." BBC News, September 3. Online at http://news.bbc.co.uk/2/hi/world/monitoring/908846.stm (viewed February 5, 2013).

2010. "The Rise of the Ampatuan Clan in the Philippines." BBC News Asia-Pacific, September 7. Online at www.bbc.co.uk/news/world-asia-pacific-11139653 (viewed January 10, 2013).

Beatty, Jack. 2000. *The Rascal King: The Life and Times of James Michael Curley, 1874–1958*. Cambridge, MA: Da Capo Press.

Beck, Maris. 2012. "OECD Blasts Australia over Foreign Bribery Cases." *Sydney Morning Herald*, October 27. Online at www.smh.com.au/national/oecd-blasts-australia-over-foreign-bribery-cases-20121026-28b8c.html (viewed December 13, 2012).

Becquart-Lerclercq, Jeanne. 1989. "Paradoxes of French Corruption: A French View," in Arnold J. Heidenheimer, Michael Johnston, and Victor T. Levine (eds.), *Political Corruption: A Handbook*. New Brunswick, NJ: Transaction Publishers, Selection 13, pp. 191–210.

Ben Mhenni, Leena. 2012. "Tunisia: Corruption and Nepotism Like in the Past." AnsaMed.info, April 24. Online at www.ansamed.info/ansamed/en/news/nations/tunisia/2012/04/24/Tunisia-Corruption-nepotism-like-the-past-blogger_6767546.html (viewed February 5, 2013).

Bentley, Arthur F. 1908. *The Process of Government*. University of Chicago Press.

Berthelsen, John. 2012. "France Goes Slow on Bribery Reform." *Asia Sentinel*, October 23. Online at www.asiasentinel.com/index.php?Itemid=229&id=4922&option=com_content&task=view (viewed December 13, 2012).

Birdsall, Nancy. 2007. "Do No Harm: Aid, Weak Institutions and the Missing Middle in Africa." *Development Policy Review* 25:5, 575–98.

Blake, C. H. and S. L. Kohen. 2010. "Argentina: The Dawn of a New Era or Business as Usual?" in Morris, Stephen D. and Charles H. Blake, *Corruption and Politics in Latin America: National and Regional Dynamics*. Boulder, CO: Lynne Rienner Publishers, Chapter 2, pp. 29–53.

Blaydes, Lisa. 2010. *Elections and Distributive Politics in Mubarak's Egypt*. New York: Cambridge University Press.

Bocchi, Alessandro Magnoli. 2008. "Rising Growth, Declining Investment: The Puzzle of the Philippines." Washington, DC: The World Bank, East Asia and Pacific Region, Policy Research Working Paper 4472 (January). Online at https://docs.google.com/a/colgate.edu/viewer?url=http://www.hks.harvard.edu/fs/drodrik/Growth%2520diagnostics%2520papers/World%2520Bank_Philipines%2520WPS4472.pdf (viewed February 5, 2013).

Bowker, Robert. 2010. *Egypt and the Politics of Change in the Arab Middle East*. Cheltenham: Edward Elgar.

Bradley, John R. 2008. *Inside Egypt: The Land of the Pharaohs on the Brink of a Revolution*. New York: Palgrave Macmillan.

Brömmelhörster, Jörn and Wolf-Christian Paes. 2003. *The Military as an Economic Actor: Soldiers in Business*. New York: Palgrave Macmillan.

Brown, Jonathan. 2011. "Salafis and Sufis in Egypt." *The Carnegie Papers* (December). Washington, DC: Carnegie Endowment for International Peace. Online at http://carnegieendowment.org/2011/12/20/salafis-and-sufis-in-egypt/8kfk (viewed January 7, 2013).

Brunnschweiler, Christa N. and Erwin H. Bulteb. 2008. "The Resource Curse Revisited and Revised: A Tale of Paradoxes and Red Herrings." *Journal of Environmental Economics and Management* 55:3, 248–64.

Brusco, Valeria, Marcelo Nazareno, and Susan C. Stokes. 2004. "Vote Buying in Argentina." *Latin American Research Review* 39:2, 66–88.

Bukovansky, Mlada. 2006. "The Hollowness of Anti-Corruption Discourse." *Review of International Political Economy* 13:2, 181–209.

Burundi Leadership Training Program (BLTP). 2012. Web page at www.facebook.com/pages/Burundi-Leadership-Training-Program-BLTP/152348634776894 (viewed February 5, 2013).

Cabacungan, Gil C. 2011. "Opposition Lawmaker Sees Long Impeachment Trial." *Inquirer.net*, April 4. Online at http://newsinfo.inquirer.net/inquirerheadlines/nation/view/20110404-329225/Opposition-lawmaker-sees-long-impeachment-trial (viewed February 5, 2013).

Calimbahin, Cleo. 2009. *An Institution Reformed and Deformed: The Commission on Elections from Aquino to Arroyo*. Tokyo: Japan External Trade Organization.
  2011. "Exceeding (Low) Expectations: Autonomy, Bureaucratic Integrity, and Capacity in the 2010 Elections." *Philippine Political Science Journal* 32:55, 103–26.
Calvo, Ernesto and M. Victoria Murillo. 2012. "Argentina: The Persistence of Peronism." *Journal of Democracy* 23:2, 148–61.
Camplin, Troy. 2011. "Egypt's Revolution and Higher Education." *Pope Center for Higher Education Policy, Commentary*, February 6. Online at www.popecenter.org/commentaries/article.html?id=2474 (viewed February 5, 2013).
Campos, J. Edgardo, Donald Lien, and Sanjay Pradhan. 1999. "The Impact of Corruption on Investment: Predictability Matters." *World Development* 27:6, 1059–67.
Carnegy, Hugh. 2012. "OECD Hits out at France over Bribery." *Financial Times*, October 23. Online at www.ft.com/intl/cms/s/0/b86cee54-1ce7-11e2-a17f-00144feabdc0.html#axzz2Exk0E0pk (viewed December 13, 2012).
Caro, Robert A. 1974. *The Power Broker: Robert Moses and the Fall of New York*. New York: Alfred A. Knopf.
Carville, James and Stan Greenberg. 2012. *It's the Middle Class, Stupid!* New York: Blue Rider Press/Penguin.
Casey, Doug. 2012. "Argentina and Today's Evita." Casey Daily Dispatch, April 25. Online at www.caseyresearch.com/cdd/doug-casey-argentina-and-todays-evita (viewed February 5, 2013).
Chan, Jenny C. Y. 2005. "Language, Culture, and Reform in Hong Kong," in Michael Johnston (ed.), *Civil Society and Corruption: Mobilizing for Reform*. Lanham, MD: University Press of America.
Chang, Eric and Miriam Golden. "Electoral Systems, District Magnitude, and Corruption." *British Journal of Political Science* 37(1): 115–37.
Chavez, Rebecca Bill. 2003. "The Construction of the Rule of Law in Argentina: A Tale of Two Provinces." *Comparative Politics* 35:4, 417–37.
Chayes, Sarah. 2012. "Corruption is Still Tunisia's Challenge." *Los Angeles Times*, June 10. Online at www.latimes.com/news/opinion/commentary/la-oe-chayes-tunisia-corruption-20120610,0,6550179.story (viewed February 5, 2013).
Christian Science Monitor. 2012. "The Argentine President's Secret Weapon? A Super-Charged Youth Movement". Csmonitor.com, July 16. Online at www.csmonitor.com/layout/set/print/content/view/print/534944 (viewed February 5, 2013).

Clausen, Bianca, Aart Kraay, and Zsolt Nyiri. 2009. "Corruption and Confidence in Public Institutions: Evidence from a Global Survey." World Bank Policy Research Department Working Paper No. 5157. Online at http://papers.ssrn.com/sol3/papers.cfm?abstract_id=1527367 (viewed February 5, 2013).

Cleary, Matthew B. and Susan C. Stokes. 2006. *Democracy and the Culture of Skepticism: Political Trust in Argentina and Mexico*. New York: Russell Sage Foundation.

CMFR (Center for Media Freedom and Responsibility). 2013. "Ampatuan Massacre Trial Update: Justice Delayed." *CMFR Ampatuan Trial Watch*, January 11. Online at www.cmfr-phil.org/ampatuanwatch/ (viewed January 11, 2013).

Code, Bill. 2012. "Tunisia's Jobless Demand Action." *SBS World News* (Australia), April 26. Online at www.sbs.com.au/news/article/1645455/Blog-Tunisias-jobless-demand-action (viewed February 5, 2013).

Coen, Jeff and John Chase. 2012. *Golden: How Rod Blagojevich Talked Himself Out of the Governor's Office and Into Prison*. Chicago Review Press.

Cogan, Frances B. 2000. *Captured: The Internment of American Civilians in the Philippines, 1941–1945*. Athens: University of Georgia Press.

Collard, Rebecca. 2012. "'Crony Capitalism' Undermines Egyptian Food Security." *The National* (Abu Dhabi), April 28. Online at www.thenational.ae/arts-culture/crony-capitalism-undermines-egyptian-food-security (viewed February 5, 2013).

Coronel, Sheila S., Yvonne T. Chua, Luz Rimban, and Boomba B. Cruz. 2004. *The Rule Makers: How the Wealthy and Well-Born Dominate Congress*. Quezon City: Philippine Center for Investigative Journalism.

Coser, Lewis A. 1977. *Masters of Sociological Thought: Ideas in Historical and Social Context*, 2nd edn. New York: Harcourt Brace Jovanovich College Publishers.

Curnow, Ross. 2003. "What's Past is Prologue: Administrative Corruption in Australia," in Seppo Tiihonen (ed.), *The History of Corruption in Central Government/L'histoire de la corruption au niveau du pouvoir central*. Amsterdam: IOS Press, pp. 37–64.

Curry, Jane L. and Doris Göedl. 2012. "Why 'Together We Are Strong' Does Not Work." *Communist and Post-Communist Studies* 45:1–2, 1–12.

Dahl, Robert A. 2003. *How Democratic is the American Constitution?* 2nd edn. New Haven: Yale University Press.

Daily Tribune. 2010. "Ampatuans Charged with Money Laundering." *Daily Tribune*, November 5. Online at www.tribuneonline.org/headlines/20101105hed1.html (viewed August 3, 2011).

Daraghi, Bourzou. 2012. "Tunisia's Anti-Corruption Minister Quits." *Financial Times*, July 1. Online at www.ft.com/intl/cms/s/0/aefe72e2-c388-11e1-ad80-00144feabdc0.html#axzz20FiF17kF (viewed February 5, 2013; requires free registration).

Darden, Keith. 2008. "The Integrity of Corrupt States: Graft as an Informal State Institution." *Politics and Society* 36:1, 35–59.

Deimling, Kate. 2012. "Former Tunisian Dictator's Son-in-Law Accused of Looting 700-Pound 'Gorgon's Mask' Sculpture from Algeria." *Blouin ArtInfo*, May 30. Online at www.artinfo.com/news/story/806427/former-tunisian-dictators-son-in-law-accused-of-looting-700-pound-gorgons-mask-sculpture-from-algeria (viewed February 5, 2013).

Delhey, Jan and Kenneth Newton. 2005. "Predicting Cross-National Levels of Social Trust: Global Pattern or Nordic Exceptionalism?" *European Sociological Review* 21:4, 311–27.

Democracy Matters. 2012. "About the Bill" (Fair Elections proposal). Online at www.fairelectionsnow.org/about-bill (viewed December 14, 2012).

De Soto, Hernando. 1989. *The Other Path*. Cambridge, MN: Harper & Row.
  2011. "The Real Mohamed Bouazizi." *Foreign Policy*, December 16. Online at www.foreignpolicy.com/articles/2011/12/16/the_real_mohamed_bouazizi (viewed February 3, 2013).

de Sousa, Luis, Peter Larmour, and Barry Hindess. 2009. *Governments, NGOS and Anti-Corruption: The New Integrity Warriors*. New York: Routledge.

DFID (Department for International Development). 2009. "Building Peaceful States and Societies: A DFID Practice Paper." London: DFID. Online at www.dfid.gov.uk/Documents/publications1/governance/Building-peaceful-states-and-societies.pdf (viewed February 5, 2013).

Diamond, Larry J. and Marc F. Plattner (eds.). 1994. *Nationalism, Ethnic Conflict and Democracy*. Baltimore: Johns Hopkins University Press.

Dietz, Simon, Eric Neumayer, and Indra de Soysa. 2007. "Corruption, the Resource Curse and Genuine Saving." *Environment and Development Economics* 12, 33–53. Online at www.environmental-expert.com/Files%5C5253%5Carticles%5C14330%5Cart2.pdf (viewed February 5, 2013).

DiJohn, Jonathan. 2010. "State Resilience against the Odds: An Analytical Narrative on the Construction and Maintenance of Policital [sic] Order in Zambia Since 1960." Working Paper No. 75. London School of Economics, Destin Development Studies Institute. Online at http://mercury.ethz.ch/serviceengine/Files/ISN/117444/ipublicationdocument_singledocument/18ac245a-1d5e-4b06-907a-5670f3275ef4/en/WP75.2.pdf (viewed February 5, 2013).

Dincer, Oguzhan C., Christopher J. Ellis, and Glen R. Waddell. 2010. "Corruption, Decentralization and Yardstick Competition." *Economics of Governance* 11:3, 269–94. Online at http://link.springer.

com/article/10.1007%2Fs10101-009-0067-x?LI=true (viewed February 5, 2013).

D'Innocenzo, Anne. 2012. "Walmart Earnings Q3 2012: Retailer Probing Violations of Anti-Bribery Act In Brazil, China, India." *Huffington Post*, November 15. Online at www.huffingtonpost.com/2012/11/15/walmart-earnings-q3-2012_n_2138423.html (viewed December 13, 2012).

Dix, Sarah, Karen Hussmann, and Grant Walton. 2012. "Risks of Corruption to State Legitimacy and Stability in Fragile Situations." U4 Anti-Corruption Resource Centre and Tiri, prepared for UK Department for International Development (DFID) Research Department (February 21). Online at www.u4.no/publications/risks-of-corruption-to-state-legitimacy-and-stability-in-fragile-situations/ (viewed January 2, 2013).

Dobel, J. Patrick. 1978. "The Corruption of a State." *American Political Science Review* 72:3, 958–73.

Doig, Alan. 1984. *Corruption and Misconduct in Contemporary British Politics*. Harmondsworth: Penguin.

Drew, Katherine Fischer. 2004. *Magna Carta*. Westport, CT: Greenwood Press.

Dworkin, Ronald. 1977. *Taking Rights Seriously*. London: Duckworth.

Edelman, Murray. 1985. *The Symbolic Uses of Politics*. Champaign, IL: University of Illinois Press.

El-Mahdi, Rabab. 2009. *Egypt: The Moment of Change*. London: Zed Books.

Espinal, Rosario, Jonathan Hartlyn, and Jana Morgan Kelly. 2006. "Performance Still Matters: Explaining Trust in Government in the Dominican Republic" *Comparative Political Studies* 39:2, 200–23.

Evans, Leslie. 2003. "The Crisis in Argentina." UCLA International Institute (April 4). Online at www.international.ucla.edu/article.asp?parentid=3566 (viewed February 5, 2013).

Evripidou, Stefanos. 2012. "Searching for Mubarak's Millions in Cyprus." *Cyprus Mail*, June 10. Online at http://m.cyprus-mail.com/cyprus/searching-mubarak-s-millions-cyprus/20120610 (viewed February 5, 2013).

FEC (United States Federal Election Commission). 2012. "Federal Campaign Finance Laws." Online at www.fec.gov/law/feca/feca.shtml (viewed December 13, 2012).

Financial Times. 2008. "UK 'Unlawfully' Scrapped BAE Probe." FT.com, April 11. Online at http://us.ft.com/ftgateway/superpage.ft?news_id=fto041120080448538287 (viewed April 15, 2008).

Fischer, Martina and Beatrix Schmelzle. 2009. "Building Peace in the Absence of States: Challenging the Discourse on State Failure." Berlin: Berghof

Research Center for Constructive Conflict Management. Berghof Handbook for Conflict Transformation Dialogue Series Issue No. 8. Online at https://docs.google.com/a/colgate.edu/viewer?url=http://www.berghof-handbook.net/documents/publications/dialogue8_failing states_complete.pdf?LANG%3D (viewed January 2, 2013).

Forbes. 2007. "OECD Says UK's Dropping of BAE-Saudi Corruption Probe Symptom of Wider Problem." Forbes.com, March 14. Reprinted online at www.abcmoney.co.uk/news/14200739400.htm (viewed February 5, 2013).

Frank, Robert H. 2010. "Income Inequality: Too Big to Ignore." New York Times, October 16. Online at www.nytimes.com/2010/10/17/business/17view.html?_r=1&adxnnl=1&adxnnlx=1355429631-DgfCLYPgAu KwZftbuoLY/w (viewed December 13, 2012).

———. 2011. *The Darwin Economy: Liberty, Competition, and the Common Good.* Princeton University Press.

Freedom House. 2012. "Freedom of the Press 2012" (Argentina). Online at www.freedomhouse.org/report/freedom-press/2012/argentina (viewed January 23, 2013).

Freeland, Chrystia. 2000. *Sale of the Century: Russia's Wild Ride from Communism to Capitalism.* New York: Crown Business.

Friedrich, Carl J. 1974. *Limited Government: A Comparison.* Englewood Cliffs, NJ: Prentice Hall.

Frisk Jensen, M. 2008. "Korruption og Embedsetik: Dansk Embedsmænds Korruption i Perioden 1800 til 1886." Aalborg, Denmark: Aalborg University dissertation.

Fund for Peace. 2013. "The Failed States Index 2012." (In conjunction with *Foreign Policy*.) Online at www.foreignpolicy.com/failed_states_index_2012_interactive (viewed January 3, 2013)

Gerring, John and Strom C. Thacker. 2005. "Do Neoliberal Policies Deter Political Corruption?" *International Organization* 59:1, 233–54.

Ghani, Ashraf and Clare Lockhart. 2007. "Writing the History of the Future: Securing Stability through Peace Agreements." *Journal of Intervention and Statebuilding* 1:3, 275–306.

Ghribi, Asma. 2012. "Tunisian Women with Foreign Men Illegally Targeted by Police." Ramadan.com, June 11. Online at www.ramadan.com/news/tunisian-women-with-foreign-men-illegally-targeted-by-police.html (viewed February 5, 2013).

GMA News. 2011. "Facing Growing Scandal, Bishops to Return SUVs." GMA News, July 7. Online at www.gmanetwork.com/news/story/225635/news/nation/facing-growing-scandal-bishops-to-return-suvs (viewed January 10, 2013).

Golden, Miriam A. and Lucio Picci. 2005. "Proposal for a New Measure of Corruption, Illustrated with Italian Data." *Economics & Politics* 17:1, 37–75.

Goldman, Marshall I. 2003. *The Piratization of Russia: Russian Reform Goes Awry*. New York: Routledge.

Goodin, Robert E. 2004. "Democracy, Justice, and Impartiality," in K. Dowding, R. E. Goodin, and C. Pateman (eds.), *Justice and Democracy*. Cambridge and New York: Cambridge University Press, Chapter 6, pp. 97–111.

Grabosky, Peter and Peter Larmour. 2000. "Public Sector Corruption and its Control." Australian Institute of Criminology, *Trends and Issues in Crime and Criminal Justice*, Report number 143. Online at www.aic.gov.au/documents/5/4/2/%7B542945A1-12F3-4834-9072-FDAF963F6E84%7Dti143.pdf (viewed December 12, 2012).

Grindle, Merilee S. 2004. "Good Enough Governance: Poverty Reduction and Reform in Developing Countries." *Governance* 17:4, 525–48.

  2007. "'Good Enough Governance' Revisited." *Development Policy Review* 25:5, 533–74.

Guardian, The. 2012. "Anna Hazare Begins Latest Hunger Strike Despite Dwindling Support for Campaign." The Guardian, July 29. Online at www.guardian.co.uk/world/2012/jul/29/india-anna-hazare-hunger-strikes (viewed January 31, 2013).

Guardian Unlimited. 2008. "The BAE Files." Online at www.guardian.co.uk/baefiles/0,,2086493,00.html (viewed February 4, 2013).

Guillan Montero, Aranzazu. 2011. "As If: The Fiction of Executive Accountability and the Persistence of Corruption Networks in Weakly Institutionalized Presidential Systems. Argentina (1989–2007)." PhD thesis, Georgetown University.

Gutierrez, Eric U. 1994. *The Ties That Bind: A Guide to Family, Business, and Other Interests in the Ninth House of Representatives*. Pasig: Philippine Center for Investigative Journalism, Institute for Popular Democracy.

Hacker, Jacob and Paul Pierson. 2010. *Winner-Take-All Politics: How Washington Made the Rich Richer – and Turned Its Back on the Middle Class*. New York: Simon and Schuster.

Hamm, Catherine. 2012. "Manila: The No Wang-Wang Airport." *Los Angeles Times*, October 5. Online at www.latimes.com/travel/deals/la-trb-manila-the-no-wangwang-airport-20121005,0,1378557.photogallery (viewed January 14, 2013).

Hansen, Suzy. 2012. "The Economic Vision of Egypt's Muslim Brotherhood Millionaires." *Businessweek.com*, April 19. Online at www.

businessweek.com/articles/2012-04-19/the-economic-vision-of-egypts-muslim-brotherhood-millionaires (viewed February 5, 2013).

Heidenheimer, Arnold J. 1970. "The Context of Analysis," in Arnold J. Heidenheimer (ed.), *Political Corruption: Readings in Comparative Analysis*. New Brunswick, NJ: Transaction Books, pp. 3–28.

2002. "Introduction to Part I," in Arnold J. Heidenheimer and Michael Johnston (eds.), *Political Corruption: Concepts and Contexts*, 3rd edn. New Brunswick, NJ: Transaction Publishers, pp. 3–14.

Heilbrunn, John R. 2005. "Oil and Water? Elite Politicians and Corruption in France." *Comparative Politics* 37:3, 277–96

Helmke, Gretchen and Steven Levitsky (eds.). 2004. "Informal Institutions and Comparative Politics: A Research Agenda." *Perspectives on Politics* 2:4, 725–40.

Hennessy-Fiske, Molly. 2012. "Tom DeLay Attorney Asks Texas Judges to Overturn Conviction." *Los Angeles Times*, October 10. Online at http://articles.latimes.com/2012/oct/10/nation/la-na-nn-tom-delay-texas-conviction-20121010 (viewed December 13, 2012).

Hertzberg, Hendrik. 2004. *Politics: Observations and Arguments*. New York: Penguin.

Hilgers, Tina (ed.). 2012. *Clientelism in Everyday Latin American Politics*. New York: Palgrave Macmillan.

Hindess, Barry. 2004. "Corruption and Democracy in Australia." Democratic Audit of Australia, Report number 3. Australian National University. Online at http://democratic.audit.anu.edu.au/papers/focused_audits/200408_hindess_corruption.pdf (viewed December 12, 2012).

Hirst, Derek. 1986. *Authority and Conflict: England, 1603–1658*. Cambridge, MA: Harvard University Press.

Hoffman, David E. 2002. *The Oligarchs: Wealth and Power in the New Russia*. New York: Public Affairs.

Hofstadter, Richard. 1955. *The Age of Reform: From Bryan to FDR*. New York: Alfred A. Knopf.

Holloway, Harry with Frank S. Meyers. 1993. *Bad Times for Good Ol' Boys: The Oklahoma County Commissioner Scandal*. Norman, OK: University of Oklahoma Press.

Hood, Christopher. 2006. "Gaming in Targetworld: The Targets Approach to Managing British Public Services." *Public Administration Review* 66:4, 515–21.

Hope, Bradley. 2012a. "Mubarak Family Worth Hundreds of Millions, Not Billions, Investigators Say." *The National* (Abu Dhabi), October 23. Online at www.thenational.ae/news/world/africa/mubarak-family-worth-hundreds-of-millions-not-billions-investigators-say#ixzz2AK1yK3Y8 (viewed January 7, 2013).

2012b. "A Towering Reminder of Egypt's Corrupt Decades." *The National* (Abu Dhabi), May 20. Online at www.thenational.ae/news/world/a-towering-reminder-of-egypts-corrupt-decades (viewed February 5, 2013).

2012c. "Mubarak's Friend and Tycoon Hussein Salem Tests Egypt's Investigators." *The National* (Abu Dhabi), October 24. Online at www.thenational.ae/news/world/middle-east/mubaraks-friend-and-tycoon-hussein-salem-tests-egypts-investigators#ixzz2AK2DORTe (viewed January 7, 2013).

2012d. "Mubarak's Egypt, Where Everything Was for Sale." *The National* (Abu Dhabi), October 25. Online at www.thenational.ae/news/world/africa/mubaraks-egypt-where-everything-was-for-sale (viewed January 7, 2013).

2012e. "Want Something Done? Get Your Hand in Your Pocket and Offer a Bribe." *The National* (Abu Dhabi), October 25. Online at www.thenational.ae/news/world/middle-east/want-something-done-get-your-hand-in-your-pocket-and-offer-a-bribe#ixzz2HJB5BAMN (viewed January 9, 2013).

Horowitz, Carl. 2012. "Australian Health Services Union President Resigns Following Revelations of Corruption." *National Legal and Policy Center*, September 12. Online at http://nlpc.org/print/4137 (viewed December 12, 2012).

House of Commons, United Kingdom; Nolan Committee. 1995. "Standards in Public Life, First Report of the Committee on Standards in Public Life." (Command document 2850 - I). London: Her Majesty's Stationery Office.

House of Lords, United Kingdom. 2008. "Opinions of the Lords of Appeal for Judgment in the Cause: R. (on the application of Corner House Research and others) (Respondents) v Director of the Serious Fraud Office (Appellant) (Criminal Appeal from Her Majesty's High Court of Justice)." Session 2007–8, [2008] UKHL 60, on appeal from [2008] EWHC 246 (Admin); July 30. (Text of the Law Lords' decision affirming the Serious Fraud Office decision to halt investigations into dealings between British Aerospace and the government of Saudi Arabia.) Available online at www.controlbae.org/jr/Lords_judgment.pdf (viewed February 5, 2013).

Hsu, Tiffany. 2012. "Wal-Mart Heirs Worth as Much as Bottom 41.5% of American Families." *Los Angeles Times* (July 18). Online at http://articles.latimes.com/2012/jul/18/business/la-fi-mo-walmart-heirs-20120718 (viewed December 13, 2012).

Huntington, Samuel P. 1968. *Political Order in Changing Societies*. New Haven: Yale University Press.

Hurstfield, J. 1973. *Freedom, Corruption and Government in Elizabethan England*. Cambridge, MA: Harvard University Press.

Husain, Ed. 2012. "Where Are We Heading in Egypt?" Council on Foreign Relations, May 24. Online at http://blogs.cfr.org/husain/2012/05/24/where-are-we-heading-in-egypt/ (viewed February 5, 2013).

Hutchcroft, Paul D. 1991. "Oligarchs and Cronies in the Philippine State: The Politics of Patrimonial Plunder." *World Politics* 43:3, 414–50.

1998. *Booty Capitalism: The Politics of Banking in the Philippines*. Ithaca, NY: Cornell University Press.

and Joel Rocamora. 2003. "Strong Demands and Weak Institutions: The Origins and Evolution of the Democratic Deficit in the Philippines." *Journal of East Asian Studies* 3: 259, 292.

Integrity Watch Afghanistan. 2010. *Afghan Perceptions and Experiences of Corruption: A National Survey 2010*. Online at www.iwaweb.org/corruptionSurvey2010/NationalCorruption2010.html (viewed January 2, 2013).

Isham, Jonathan, Daniel Kaufmann, and Lant Pritchett. 2000. "Civil Liberties, Democracy, and the Performance of Government Projects." *World Bank Economic Review* 11:2, 219–42.

Johnston, Michael. 1998. "What Can Be Done About Entrenched Corruption?" in Boris Pleskovic and Joseph E. Stiglitz (eds.), *Annual World Bank Conference on Development Economics 1997*. Washington, DC: The World Bank, pp. 149–80.

2005a. *Syndromes of Corruption: Wealth, Power, and Democracy*. Cambridge and New York: Cambridge University Press.

2005b. "Keeping the Answers, Changing the Questions: Corruption Definitions Revisited," in Ulrich von Alemann (ed.), *Dimensionen politischer Korruption: Beiträge zum Stand der internationalen Forschung*. Politische Vierteljahresschrift Sonderheft 35/2005. Wiesbaden: Verlag für Sozialwissenschaften, pp. 61–76.

2005c. "Political Finance Policy, Parties, and Democratic Development." Washington, DC: National Democratic Institute for International Affairs, 2005. Online at www.ndi.org/files/1949_polpart_johnston_110105.pdf (viewed February 5, 2013).

2009a. "Components of Integrity: Data and Benchmarks for Tracking Trends in Government." Paris: Organization for Economic Cooperation and Development (OECD). Online at www.oecd.org/officialdocuments/displaydocumentpdf?cote=GOV/PGC/GF%282009%292&doclanguage=en (viewed January 18, 2013).

2009b. "Civil Society Organisations, Corruption and Human Development: An Asia-Pacific Perspective," in Anuradha K. Rajivan and Ramesh Gampat (eds.), *Perspectives on Corruption and Human Development* (vol. II). New Delhi: Macmillan, Chapter 22, pp. 905–59.

2010. "Assessing Vulnerabilities to Corruption: Indicators and Benchmarks of Government Performance." *Public Integrity* 12:2, 125–42.

2012. "Corruption Control in the United States: Law, Values, and the Political Foundations of Reform." *International Review of Administrative Sciences* 78:2, 329–45.

and Carmen Apaza. 2009. "Beyond Transparency," analytical paper for project entitled *Agenda sobre la Estatalidad para la Democracia en América Latina*. Secretariat for Political Affairs, Organization of American States, Washington, DC.

and Sahr J. Kpundeh. 2002. "Building a Clean Machine: Anti-Corruption Coalitions and Sustainable Reforms." World Bank Institute Working Paper number 37208 (December).

Joline, Courtney. 2012a. "Anti-Corruption Fight Gets a Holiday in Its Honor – But Is It Enough?" *TunisiaLive.net*, (June 8). Online at http://tunisie-news.info/english/11226-anti-corruption-fight-gets-a-holiday-in-its-honor-but-is-it-enough-tunisia-live (viewed February 5, 2013).

2012b. "20 Tunisian Customs Officers Dismissed Amidst Corruption Reform." *TunisiaLive.net*, June 9. Online at www.ramadan.com/news/20-tunisian-customs-officers-dismissed-amidst-corruption-reform.html (viewed February 5, 2013).

Jordan, Grant. 1998. "Towards Regulation in the UK: From 'General Good Sense' to 'Formalised Rules.'" *Parliamentary Affairs* 51:4, 524–37.

Kang, David C. 2002. *Crony Capitalism: Corruption and Development in South Korea and the Philippines*. Cambridge and New York: Cambridge University Press.

Keefer, Philip. 1996. "Protection against a Capricious State: French Investment and Spanish Railroads, 1845–1875." *Journal of Economic History* 56:1, 170–92.

Kerkhoff, Toon. 2012. "Hidden Morals, Explicit Scandals: Public Values and Political Corruption in the Netherlands (1748–1813)." PhD thesis, University of Leiden.

Kernaghan, Kenneth. 2003. "Corruption and Public Service in Canada: Conceptual and Practical Dimensions," in Seppo Tiihonen (ed.), *The History of Corruption in Central Government/L'histoire de la corruption au niveau du pouvoir central*. Amsterdam: IOS Press, pp. 83–98.

Kerr, K. Austin. 1980. "Organizing for Reform: The Anti-Saloon League and Innovation in Politics." *American Quarterly* 32:1, 37–53.

Kettle, Martin. 2007. "Don't Romanticise Putney." *The Guardian*, October 31. Online at www.guardian.co.uk/commentisfree/2007/oct/31/dontromanticiseputney (viewed December 27, 2012).

Khanna, Jyoti and Michael Johnston. 2007. "India's Middlemen: Connecting by Corrupting?" *Crime, Law, and Social Change* 48: 3–5, 151–68.

Khanna, Satyam. 2008. "Rice: 'No American Money' was Lost in Iraq." *Thinkprogress.com*, December 16. Online at http://thinkprogress.org/politics/2008/12/16/33794/rice-corruption-iraq/?mobile=nc (viewed December 13, 2012).

Klitgaard, Robert. 1988. *Controlling Corruption*. Berkeley, CA: University of California Press.

Klopp, Jacqueline M. 2000. "Pilfering the Public: The Problem of Land Grabbing in Contemporary Kenya." *Africa Today* 47:1, 7–26.

2002. "Can Moral Ethnicity Trump Political Tribalism? The Struggle for Land and Nation in Kenya." *African Studies* 61:2, 269–94.

Krugman, Paul. 2012. "Medicaid on the Ballot." *New York Times*, October 28. Online at www.nytimes.com/2012/10/29/opinion/krugman-medicaid-on-the-ballot.html?_r=0 (viewed February 5, 2013).

Kunicová, Jana and Susan Rose-Ackerman. 2005. "Electoral Rules and Constitutional Structures as Constraints on Corruption." *British Journal of Political Science* 35: 573–606.

Kurer, Oskar. 2005. "Corruption: An Alternative Approach to its Definition and Measurement." *Political Studies* 53:1, 222–39.

Landolt, Laura K. 2012. "Supporting Dictatorship and Promoting Human Rights? UN Technical Assistance to Egypt." *Journal of Intervention and Statebuilding* 6:2, 145–66.

Lapegna, Pablo. 2012. "Social Movements and Patronage Politics in Argentina: Towards a Relational Understanding of Processes of Demobilization." Paper presented at the Annual Meeting of the American Sociological Association. Denver, CO, August 17–20.

Larraín B., Felipe and José Tavares. 2004. "Does Foreign Direct Investment Decrease Corruption?" *Cuadernos de Economica* 41: 217–30.

Lauth, Hans-Joachim. 2000. "Informal Institutions and Democracy." *Democratization* 7:4, 21–50.

Ledeneva, Alena V. 2006. *How Russia Really Works: The Informal Practices that Shaped Post-Soviet Politics and Business*. Ithaca: Cornell University Press.

Leite, Carlos and Jens Weidmann. 1999. "Does Mother Nature Corrupt? Natural Resources, Corruption, and Economic Growth." Working Paper of the International Monetary Fund (July). Online at https://docs.google.com/a/colgate.edu/viewer?url=http://www.imf.org/external/pubs/ft/wp/1999/wp9985.pdf (viewed February 5, 2013).

Lessig, Lawrence. 2011. *Republic, Lost: How Money Corrupts Congress – and a Plan to Stop It*. New York: Twelve Books.

Levine, Adam Seth, Robert H. Frank, and Oege Dijk. 2010. "Expenditure Cascades." Online SSRN: http://dx.doi.org/10.2139/ssrn.1690612 (viewed December 13, 2012).

Levitsky, Steven. 2003. *Transforming Labor-Based Parties in Latin America: Argentine Peronism in Comparative Perspective*. New York: Cambridge University Press.

and María Victoria Murillo (eds.). 2005. *Argentine Democracy: The Politics of Institutional Weakness*. State College, PA: Pennsylvania State University Press.

2008. "Argentina: From Kirchner to Kirchner." *Journal of Democracy* 19:3, 16–30.

Lewis, Maureen. 2006. "Governance and Corruption in Public Health Care Systems." Center for Global Development Working Paper No. 78. Online: http://ssrn.com/abstract=984046 (viewed February 5, 2013).

Liddle, R. William. 1985. "Soeharto's Indonesia: Personal Rule and Political Institutions." *Pacific Affairs* 58:1, 68–90.

1996. "Indonesia's Democratic Past and Future." *Comparative Politics* 24:4, 443–62.

Liikala, Anne Beard. 2002. "Grassroots Civil Groups: The Potential and Limits of Democratic Change in Argentina's Interior Provinces." *Cambridge Review of International Affairs* 15:3, 515–30.

Lineberry, Robert L. and Edmund P. Fowler. 1967. "Reformism and Public Policies in American Cities." *American Political Science Review* 61: 3, 701–16.

Lipset, Seymour M. 1963. *Political Man: The Social Bases of Politics*. New York: Anchor Books.

Liptak, Adam. 2012. "The Vanishing Battleground." *New York Times*, November 3. Online at www.nytimes.com/2012/11/04/sunday-review/the-vanishing-electoral-battleground.html?_r=0 (viewed December 13, 2012).

Lock, Geoffrey. 1989. "The 1689 Bill of Rights." *Political Studies* 37:4, 540–61.

Lowi, Theodore J. 1968. "Gosnell's Chicago Revisited Via Lindsay's New York." Foreword to Harold F. Gosnell, *Machine Politics: Chicago Model*, 2nd edn. University of Chicago Press.

Ltifi, Afifa. 2012. "Tunisia's Second Largest Democratic Party Divides." *TunisiaLive*, May 17. Online at http://en.lemag.ma/Tunisia-s-Second-Largest-Democratic-Party-Divides_a1490.html (viewed February 5, 2013).

Lynch, John W., George Davey Smith, George A. Kaplan, and James S. House. 2000. "Income Inequality and Mortality: Importance to Health of Individual Income, Psychosocial Environment, or Material

Conditions." *BMJ* (formerly *British Medical Journal*) 320, 1200–4. Online at www.bmj.com/content/320/7243/1200 (viewed December 13, 2012).

Lynch, Marc. 2012. *The Arab Uprising: The Unfinished Revolutions of the New Middle East*. Perseus Books Group.

MacIntyre, Andrew. 1994. "Business, Government and Development: Northeast and Southeast Asian Comparisons," in Andrew MacIntyre (ed.), *Business and Government in Industrializing Asia*. St. Leonards, Australia: Allen & Unwin.

Manila Standard. 2012. "Aquino's 'Shadow Cabinet' Keeps Dark Secrets." *Manila Standard*, September 20. Online at http://manilastandardtoday.com/2012/09/20/aquinos-shadow-cabinet-keeps-dark-secrets/ (viewed January 10, 2013).

Manning, Nick, Dirk-Jan Kraan, and Jana Malinska (OECD GOV). 2006. "How and Why Should Government Activity Be Measured in 'Government at a Glance'?" Online at http://search.oecd.org/officialdocuments/displaydocumentpdf/?doclanguage=en&cote=gov/pgc(2006)10/ann1 (viewed February 5, 2013).

Manzetti, Luigi. 2000. "Keeping Accounts: A Case Study of Civic Initiatives and Campaign Finance Oversight in Argentina." College Park, MD: IRIS Working Paper 248, University of Maryland. Online at www.iris.umd.edu/Reader.aspx?TYPE=FORMAL_PUBLICATION&ID=4f66af44-0246-4fd4-9df9–72a4f01f3ce5 (viewed February 5, 2013).

2009. *Neoliberalism, Accountability, and Reform Failures in Emerging Markets: Eastern Europe, Russia, Argentina, and Chile in Comparative Perspective*. University Park, PA: Pennsylvania State University Press.

Marchak, M. Patricia and William Marchak. 1999. *God's Assassins: State Terrorism in Argentina in the 1970s*. Montreal: McGill-Queen's University Press.

Margolies, Amy. 2009. "Peacebuilding and Anti-Corruption: Room for Collaboration?" *New Routes* 14:3, 34–7.

Marquette, Heather. 2012. "Building Integrity in Fragile Contexts." University of Birmingham, International Development Department Policy Brief No. 02/12 (March). Online at www.birmingham.ac.uk/schools/government-society/departments/international-development/news/2012/03/building-integrity-in-fragile-contexts.aspx (viewed January 2, 2013).

Mazzetti, Mark. 2010. "2 Ex-Workers Accuse Blackwater Security Company of Defrauding the U.S. for Years." *New York Times*, February 10. Online at www.nytimes.com/2010/02/11/us/11suit.html (viewed December 13, 2012).

McAllister, Ian, Juliet Pietsch, and Adam Graycar. 2012. "Perceptions of Corruption and Ethical Conduct." (Australian National University Poll.) Research School of Social Sciences, ANU College of Arts and Social Sciences. Report No. 13 (October). Online at https://docs.google.com/a/colgate.edu/viewer?url=http://politicsir.cass.anu.edu.au/sites/default/files/2012-10-26_ANUpoll_ethics_corruption.pdf.pdf (viewed December 12, 2012).

McCoy, Alfred W. 1993. "Rent-Seeking Families and the Philippine State: A History of the Lopez Family," in Alfred W. McCoy (ed.), *An Anarchy of Families: State and Family in the Philippines*, Madison, WI: University of Wisconsin, Center for Southeast Asian Studies, in cooperation with Ateneo de Manila University Press.

(ed). 2009. *An Anarchy of Families: State and Family in the Philippines*. Madison: University of Wisconsin Press.

McCullum, Hugh. 2005. "Africa Underdeveloped in the Corruption Field Too." NewsfromAfrica.org, October 4. Online at www.newsfromafrica.org/newsfromafrica/articles/art_10483.html (viewed December 12, 2012).

McGeough, Paul. 2012. "Authoritarian Habits Prove Hard to Break." *Sydney Morning Herald*, April 8. Online at www.smh.com.au/opinion/politics/authoritarian-habits-prove-hard-to-break-20120407-1wi1m.html (viewed February 5, 2013).

McGrath, Cam. 2012. "Egypt: Mubarak Still Has His Billions." AllAfrica.com, May 8. Online at http://allafrica.com/stories/201205080105.html (viewed February 5, 2013).

McGuire, James W. 1997. *Peronism Without Perón: Unions, Parties, and Democracy in Argentina*. Stanford University Press.

McKechnie, Alastair. 2009. "Drawing on Experience: Transforming Fragile States into Effective Ones." Development Outreach series (October). Washington, DC: The World Bank. Online at https://docs.google.com/viewer?url=http%3A%2F%2Fsiteresources.worldbank.org%2FWBI%2FResources%2F213798-1253552326261%2Fdo-oct09-mckechnie.pdf (viewed January 2, 2013)

McKenzie, Nick. 2012. "More Questions over RBA Role in Corruption Scandal." *ABC News*, September 12. Online at www.abc.net.au/news/2012-09-11/more-questions-over-rba-role-in-corruption-scandal/4255344 (viewed December 13, 2012).

Merton, Robert K. 1957. *Social Theory and Social Structure*. New York: Free Press.

Middle East Online. 2013. "Islamists Strengthen Position in Latest Egypt Cabinet Reshuffle." *Middle East Online*, January 7. Online at www.middle-east-online.com/english/?id=56319 (viewed January 8, 2013).

Mindanao Daily Mirror. 2010. "Ampatuans Rapped for Plunder." DailyMirror.com, January 17. Online at www.dailymirror.ph/Jan*2011/Jan172011/front1.html (viewed July 30, 2011).

Mishler, William and Richard Rose. 2005. "What are the Political Consequences of Trust? A Test of Cultural and Institutional Theories in Russia." *Comparative Political Studies* 38:9, 1050–78.

Mishra, Ajit. 2008. "Persistence of Corruption: Some Theoretical Perspectives." *World Development* 34:2, 349–58.

Moran, Jon. 1999. "Patterns of Corruption and Development in East Asia." *Third World Quarterly* 20:3, 569.

Morrell, John. 2010. "The Performance Governance System in the Philippines: Building the Capacity of Local Institutions." Washington, DC: Center for International Private Enterprise (April 30). Online at www.cipe.org/sites/default/files/publication-docs/043010.pdf (viewed January 14, 2013).

Morris, Stephen D. 2010. "Mexico: Corruption and Change," in Stephen D. Morris and Charles H. Blake, *Corruption and Politics in Latin America: National and Regional Dynamics*. Boulder, CO: Lynne Rienner, Chapter 6, pp. 137–63.

Morss, Elliott R. and Richard Rust. 2012. "What is Kirchner Doing in Argentina?" *Global Economic Intersection*, April 26. Online at http://econintersect.com/wordpress?p=21431 (viewed February 5, 2013).

Mungiu-Pippidi, Alina. 2006. "Corruption: Diagnosis and Treatment." *Journal of Democracy* 17:3, 86–99.

Murphy, Aaron G. 2011. *Foreign Corrupt Practices Act: A Practical Resource for Managers and Executives*. Hoboken, NJ: Wiley.

Murshid, Navine. 2013. *The Politics of Refugees in South Asia*. New York: Routledge.

Naím, Moisés. 2007. "What is a Gongo? How Government-Sponsored Groups Masquerade as Civil Society." *Foreign Policy* 160, 96–95.

New York Times. 1984. "Foes Blame Giscard For Sniffer Plane Scheme." Nytimes.com, November 21. Online at www.nytimes.com/1984/11/22/world/around-the-world-foes-blame-giscard-for-sniffer-plane-scheme.html (viewed December 12, 2012).

  2000. "Spreading Bribery Scandal Shakes Argentina's Senate." Nytimes.com, September 19. Online at www.nytimes.com/2000/09/19/world/19ARGE.html (viewed June 27, 2013).

  2008. "States' Data Obscure How Few Finish High School." Nytimes.com, March 21. Online at www.nytimes.com/2008/03/20/education/20graduation.html?em&ex=1206244800&en=41ef2372a3728605&ei=5087%0A (viewed September 5, 2008).

2010. "Times Topics: Jack Abramoff" (includes archive of news stories). Nytimes.com, June 24. Online at http://topics.nytimes.com/top/reference/timestopics/people/a/jack_abramoff/index.html (viewed December 13, 2012).

Nichols, Philip M. 2011. "The Perverse Effect of Campaign Contribution Limits: Reducing the Allowable Amounts Increases the Likelihood of Corruption in the Federal Legislature." *American Business Law Journal* 48:1, 77–118.

Norlin, Kara Elizabeth. 2003. "Political Corruption: Theory and Evidence from the Brazilian Experience." PhD thesis, University of Illinois at Urbana-Champaign.

Noueihed, Lin and Alex Warren. 2012. *The Battle for the Arab Spring: Revolution, Counter-Revolution and the Making of a New Era*. New Haven: Yale University Press.

Nye, Joseph. 1967. "Corruption and Political Development: A Cost-Benefit Analysis." *American Political Science Review* 61:2, 417–27

O'Brien, Amanda. 2007. "Corruption Watchdog 'Muzzled.'" *The Australian*, October 31. Online at www.theaustralian.com.au/news/nation/corruption-watchdog-muzzled/story-e6frg6pf-1111114762745 (viewed December 12, 2012).

O'Brien, Patrick. 1988. "West Australia Inc.: A State of Corruption." *Quadrant* 32:11, 4–18.

O'Donnell, Guillermo. 1999. "Horizontal Accountability in New Democracies," in Andreas Schedler, Larry Diamond, and Marc F. Plattner (eds.), *The Self-Restraining State: Power and Accountability in New Democracies*. Boulder, CO: Lynne Rienner, Chapter 3, pp. 29–51.

OECD (Organization for Economic Cooperation and Development). 2008. "Tax Treatment of Bribes." Online at www.oecd.org/topic/0,3373,en_2649_34551_1_1_1_1_37447,00.html (viewed February 4, 2013).

2012. "Anti-Bribery Convention." Online at www.oecd.org/daf/briberyininternationalbusiness/anti-briberyconvention/ (viewed December 13, 2012).

Office of the President, Republic of the Philippines. 2011. "Aquino Vows to End Culture of 'Wang-Wang.'" July 25. Online at 'www.news.pcoo.gov.ph/archives2011/jul25.htm#'wang-wan (viewed January 14, 2013).

Okrent, Daniel. 2010. *Last Call: The Rise and Fall of Prohibition*. New York: Scribner.

Oldenburg, Philip. 1987. "Middlemen in Third-World Corruption: Implications of an Indian Case." *World Politics* 39:4, 508–35.

O'Leary, Cornelius. 1962. *The Elimination of Corrupt Practices in British Elections, 1968–1911*. Oxford: Clarendon Press.

Oliveros, Benjie. 2011. "Stamping Out Corruption in the AFP and the Government." Butallat.com, February 11. Online at http://bulatlat.com/main/2011/02/11/benjie-oliveros-stamping-out-corruption-in-the-afp-and-the-government/ (viewed January 10, 2013).

Olken, Benjamin A. 2005. "Monitoring Corruption: Evidence from a Field Experiment in Indonesia." NBER Working Paper No. W11753. Online at www.nber.org/papers/w11753 (viewed February 5, 2013).

Olson, Mancur. 1965. *The Logic of Collective Action*. Cambridge, MA: Harvard University Press.

Olster, Marjorie. 2012. "Victims of Egypt's Old Regime Still Await Justice." Associated Press/Salon.com, June 3. Online at www.salon.com/2012/06/03/victims_of_egypts_old_regime_still_await_justice/ (viewed February 5, 2013).

Onishi, Norimitsu. 2010. "Filipino Politicians Wield Private Armies, Despite Ban." *New York Times*, February 23. Online at www.nytimes.com/2010/02/21/world/asia/21phils.html (viewed January 10, 2013).

Ostiguy, Pierre. 2009. "Argentina's Double Political Spectrum: Party System, Political Identities, and Strategies, 1944–2007." Working Paper No. 362, Helen Kellogg Institute for International Studies, Notre Dame University (October). Online at http://kellogg.nd.edu/publications/workingpapers/WPS/361.pdf (viewed January 23, 2013).

Ostrom, Elinor. 1990. *Governing the Commons: The Evolution of Institutions for Collective Action*. New York: Cambridge University Press.

—— 1998. "A Behavioral Approach to the Rational Choice Theory of Collective Action." *American Political Science Review* 92:1, 1–22.

Oyamada, Eiji. 2005. "President Gloria Macapagal-Arroyo's Anti-Corruption Strategy in the Philippines: An Evaluation." *Asian Journal of Political Science* 13:1, 81–107.

Pachter, Damian. 2012. "Argentina Protests 2012: Anti-Government Protesters Flood Streets in Hundreds of Thousands." *Huffington Post*, November 9. Online at www.huffingtonpost.com/2012/11/09/argentina-protests-buenos-aires-protesters-flood-streets_n_2102528.html (viewed January 18, 2013).

Pae, Peter. 2008. "Ex-Lockheed Chief Told of Paying Bribes." *Los Angeles Times*, December 21. Online at http://articles.latimes.com/2008/dec/21/local/me-kotchian21 (viewed December 13, 2013).

Papyrakis, Elissaios and Reyer Gerlagh. 2004. "The Resource Curse Hypothesis and its Transmission Channels." Working Paper: Institute for Environmental Studies, Vrije Universiteit Amsterdam: Online at http://papers.ssrn.com/sol3/papers.cfm?abstract_id=603062 (viewed February 5, 2013).

PBS (Public Broadcasting Service). 2009. "Black Money." Online at www.pbs.org/wgbh/pages/frontline/blackmoney/ (viewed December 13, 2012).
Peck, Linda Levy. 1990. *Court Patronage and Corruption in Early Stuart England*. Boston: Unwin Hyman.
PERC (Political and Economic Risk Consultancy, Ltd.). 2012. "The Web of Corruption in Asia." Hong Kong: PERC (March 21). Online at www.asiarisk.com/subscribe/exsum1.pdf (viewed January 10, 2013).
Perry, Peter John. 2001. *Political Corruption in Australia: A Very Wicked Place?* Aldershot: Ashgate.
Persson, Torsten, Guido Tabellini, and Francesco Trebbi. 2003. "Electoral Rules and Corruption." *Journal of the European Economic Association* 1:4 (June), 958–89.
Pharr, Susan J., and Robert D. Putnam. 2000. *Disaffected Democracies*. Princeton University Press.
Phillips, Richard. 2008. "Australia: NSW Labor Embroiled in Corruption Scandal." World Socialist Web Site, March 7. Online at www.wsws.org/articles/2008/mar2008/iemm-m07.shtml (viewed December 12, 2012).
Philp, Mark. 1997. "Defining Political Corruption," in Paul Heywood (ed.), *Political Corruption*. Oxford: Blackwell, pp. 20–46.
  2001. "Access, Accountability and Authority: Corruption and the Democratic Process." *Crime, Law and Social Change* 36:4: 357–77.
  2002. "Conceptualizing Political Corruption," in Arnold J. Heidenheimer and Michael Johnston (eds.), *Political Corruption: Concepts and Contexts*, 3rd edn. New Brunswick, NJ: Transaction Publishers.
Pimentel, Maria Kristina Villanueva. 2005. "Procurement Watch, Inc.: The Role of Civil Society in Public Procurement Reforms in the Philippines," in Khi V. Thai, Armando Araujo, Rosalyn Y. Carter, Guy Callender, David Drabkin, Rick Grimm, Kirsten Jensen, Robert E. Lloyd, Cliff McCue, and Jan Telgen (eds.), *Challenges in Public Procurement: An International Perspective*. Boca Raton, FL: PrAcademics Press, Chapter 3, pp. 37–47.
Piramide, Aven. 2011. "The Armed Forces, Most Corrupt?" Philippine Star.com, April 14. Online at www.philstar.com/Article.aspx?articleId=676247&publicationSubCategoryId=109 (viewed April 22, 2011).
Politkovskaya, Anna. 2007. *A Russian Diary: A Journalist's Final Account of Life, Corruption, and Death in Putin's Russia*, translated by Arch Tait. New York: Random House.
Protess, Ben. 2012. "U.S. Accuses Bank of America of a 'Brazen' Mortgage Fraud." *New York Times*, October 24. Online at http://dealbook.nytimes.com/2012/10/24/federal-prosecutors-sue-bank-of-america-over-mortgage-program/ (viewed February 5, 2013).

"Publius" (Alexander Hamilton, James Madison, and John Jay). 1987. *The Federalist Papers*, edited by Isaac Kramnick. Harmondsworth and New York: Penguin.

Putnam, Robert D. 2000. *Bowling Alone: The Collapse and Revival of American Community*. New York: Simon and Schuster.

Quimpo, Nathan G. 2009. "The Philippines: Predatory Regime, Growing Authoritarian Features." *Pacific Review* 22: 3, 335–53.

Raghavan, Sudarsan. 2011. "In Tunisia, Luxurious Lifestyles of a Corrupt Government." *Washington Post* Foreign Service, January 28. Online at www.washingtonpost.com/wp-dyn/content/article/2011/01/28/AR2011012801921.html (viewed February 5, 2013).

Rane, Halim and Sumra Salem. 2012. "Social Media, Social Movements and the Diffusion of Ideas in the Arab Uprisings." *Journal of International Communications* 18:1, 97–111.

Regalado, Edith. 2010. "Audit Shows Ampatuans Amassed P2B in 1 Year." ABS-CBNnews.com, December 27. Online at www.abs-cbnnews.com/nation/12/27/10/audit-shows-ampatuans-amassed-p2-b-1-year (viewed June 27, 2013).

Rehren, Alfredo. 2004. "Politics and Corruption in Chile: The Underside of Chilean Democracy." *ReVista: Harvard Review of Latin America* (Spring).

Reinikka, Ritva and Jakob Svensson. 2003. "Survey Techniques to Measure and Explain Corruption." World Bank Policy Research Working Paper No. 3071. Online at http://papers.ssrn.com/sol3/papers.cfm?abstract_id=636433 (viewed February 5, 2013).

2006. "Using Micro-Surveys to Measure and Explain Corruption." *World Development* 34:2, 359–70. Online at http://ideas.repec.org/a/eee/wdevel/v34y2006i2p359-370.html (viewed February 5, 2013).

Reuters. 2012. "Ex-Candidate, under Graft Probe, Quits Egypt." Reuters.com, June 26. Online at www.reuters.com/article/2012/06/26/us-egypt-shafik-idUSBRE85P0M020120626 (viewed February 5, 2013).

Reyes, Bobby. 2009. "Why the Arroyo Family and Its Rasputins Will Meet General Noriega's Fate." Mabuhay Radio, May 18. Online at www.mabuhayradio.com/philippine-presidency/why-the-arroyo-family-and-its-rasputins-will-meet-general-noriega-s-fate (viewed January 10, 2013).

Riordon, William L. 1963. *Plunkitt of Tammany Hall*. New York: Dutton.

Roberts, Clayton. 1980. *The Growth of Responsible Government in Stuart England*. Cambridge University Press.

Robertson-Snape, Fiona. 1999. "Corruption, Collusion, and Nepotism in Indonesia." *Third World Quarterly* 20:3, 589–602.

Romero, Simon. 2012. "Move on Oil Company Draws Praise in Argentina, Where Growth Continues." Nytimes.com, April 26. Online at www.

nytimes.com/2012/04/27/world/americas/ypf-nationalization-draws-praise-in-argentina.html?pagewanted=all&_moc.semityn.www (viewed February 5, 2013).

Rose, Richard and Doh Chull Shin. 2001. "Democratization Backwards: The Problem of Third-Wave Democracies." *British Journal of Political Science* 31:2, 331–54.

Rose-Ackerman, S. 1999. *Corruption and Government: Causes, Consequences, and Reform.* Cambridge University Press.

Rothstein, Bo. 1998. "State Building and Capitalism: The Rise of the Swedish Bureaucracy." *Scandinavian Political Studies* 21:2, 149–171.

2000. "Trust, Social Dilemmas and Collective Memories." *Journal of Theoretical Politics* 12:4, 477–503.

2007. "Anti-Corruption: A Big Bang Theory." Göteborg University, Quality of Government Institute, Working Paper 2007:3. Online at www.sahlgrenska.gu.se/digitalAssets/1350/1350652_2007_3_rothstein.pdf (viewed February 5, 2013).

2011. *The Quality of Government: The Political Economy of Corruption, Social Trust and Inequality in an International Comparative Perspective.* University of Chicago Press.

and Dietlind Stolle. 2008. "The State and Social Capital: An Institutional Theory of Generalized Trust." *Comparative Politics* 40:4, 441–67.

and Eric M. Uslaner. 2005. "All for All: Equality, Corruption, and Social Trust." *World Politics* 58:1, 41–72.

Rubin, Irene S. 1998. *Class, Tax, and Power: Municipal Budgeting in the United States.* Washington, DC: CQ Press.

Rubinstein, W. D. 1983. "The End of 'Old Corruption' in Britain 1780–1860." *Past and Present* 101, 55–86.

Rustow, Dankwart A. 1970. "Transitions to Democracy: Toward a Dynamic Model." *Comparative Politics* 2:3, 337–63.

Rutherford, Bruce K. 2013. *Egypt after Mubarak: Liberalism, Islam, and Democracy in the Arab World,* revised edition. Princeton University Press.

Sachs, J. and A. M. Warner. 2001. "The Curse of Natural Resources." *European Economic Review* 45(4–6), 827–38.

Saleh, Yasmine. 2012. "Hopes for a New Egypt Marred by Pervasive Corruption." Reuters, April 25. Online at http://uk.reuters.com/article/2012/04/25/uk-egypt-corruption-idUKBRE83O0VR20120425 (viewed February 5, 2013).

Sampford, Charles, Arthur Shacklock, Carmel Connors, and Fredrik Galtung (eds.). 2006. *Measuring Corruption.* Aldershot: Ashgate.

Sampson, Steven. 2005. "Integrity Warriors: Global Morality and the Anti-Corruption Movement in the Balkans," in Dieter Haller and Chris Shore (eds.), *Corruption: Anthropological Perspectives*. London and Ann Arbor, MI: Pluto Press Ltd., pp. 103–30.

Samuel, Henry. 2012a. "Marseille Police: Crime, Corruption and Cover-Up at the Highest Level." *The Telegraph*, October 12. Online at www.telegraph.co.uk/news/worldnews/europe/france/9605614/Marseille-police-crime-corruption-and-cover-up-at-the-highest-level.html (viewed December 13, 2012).

2012b. "Nicolas Sarkozy Faces Questioning in Raft of Investigations as Immunity Ends." *The Telegraph*, May 9. Online at www.telegraph.co.uk/news/worldnews/nicolas-sarkozy/9255097/Nicolas-Sarkozy-faces-questioning-in-raft-of-investigations-as-immunity-ends.html (viewed December 13, 2012).

Sandel, Michael J. 2012. *What Money Can't Buy: The Moral Limits of Markets*. New York: Farrar, Strauss, and Giroux.

Sandholtz, Wayne and William Koetzle. 2000. "Accounting for Corruption: Economic Structure, Democracy, and Trade Source." *International Studies Quarterly* 44:1, 31–50.

Santiso, Carlos. 2008. "Eyes Wide Shut? Reforming and Defusing Checks and Balances in Argentina." *Public Administration and Development* 28:1, 67–84.

Santoro, Daniel. 2006. "Global Integrity Report" (Argentina). Washington, DC: Global Integrity.

Schaffer, Frederic C. 2002a. "Disciplinary Reactions: Alienation and the Reform of Vote Buying in the Philippines." Paper presented at a conference on "Trading Political Rights: The Comparative Politics of Vote Buying," Cambridge, MA (August 26–7). Online at http://web.mit.edu/CIS/pdf/Schaffer%20-%20Disciplinary%20Reactions.pdf (viewed February 5, 2013).

2002b. "What is Vote Buying?" Paper presented at a conference on "Trading Political Rights: The Comparative Politics of Vote Buying", Cambridge, MA (August 26–7). Online at www.gsdrc.org/docs/open/PO14.pdf (viewed February 5, 2013).

2009. "Translating 'Democracy': Why It Doesn't Always Mean What We Think It Does, and Why That Matters." Paper presented at a conference on "Varieties of Democracy," Wesleyan University, Middletown, CT, May 1, 2.

Schattschneider, E. E. 1960. *The Semi-Sovereign People: A Realist's View of Democracy in America*. New York: Holt, Rinehart and Winston.

Schofield, Hugh. 2011. "Chirac-Villepin Allegations Revive Sleazy Memories." BBC News Europe, September 12. Online at www.bbc.co.uk/news/world-europe-14886113 (viewed December 12, 2012).

Schubert, Glendon. 1974. *Judicial Policy Making*. Glenview, IL: Scott Foresman.

Schwartz, Richard D. and James C. Miller. 1964. "Legal Evolution and Societal Complexity." *American Journal of Sociology* 70:2, 159–69.

Scott, James C. 1972. *Comparative Political Corruption*. Englewood Cliffs, NJ: Prentice Hall.

Seattle Post-Intelligencer. 2006. "Manager Bonuses Rankle American Airlines Pilots." Seattlepi.com, March 6. Online at www.seattlepi.com/business/article/Manager-bonuses-rankle-American-Airlines-pilots-1197670.php (viewed December 13, 2012).

Shaxson, Nicholas. 2007. "Oil, Corruption and the Resource Curse." *International Affairs* 83: 6, 1123–40.

Shearman and Sterling. 2012. "FCPA Digest: Cases and Review Releases Relating to Bribes to Foreign Officials under the Foreign Corrupt Practices Act of 1977." Washington, DC: Shearman and Sterling LLP. Online at www.shearman.com/files/Publication/bb1a7bff-ad52-4cf9-88b9-9d99e001dd5f/Presentation/PublicationAttachment/590a9fc7-26 17-41fc-9aef-04727f927e07/FCPA-Digest-Jan2012.pdf (viewed January 29, 2013).

Shefter, Martin. 1976. "The Emergence of the Political Machine: An Alternative View," in Willis D. Hawley (ed.), *Theoretical Perspectives on Urban Politics*. Englewood Cliffs, NJ: Prentice Hall.

Shehata, Samer S. (ed.). 2012. *Islamist Politics in the Middle East: Movements and Change*. London: Routledge.

Sidel, John. 1996. "Siam and Its Twin? Democratisation and Bossism in Contemporary Thailand and the Philippines." *IDS Bulletin* 27:2, 56–63.

SIGIR (Special Inspector General for Iraq Reconstruction). 2009. *Hard Lessons: The Iraq Reconstruction Experience*. Washington, DC: US Government Printing Office. Online at www.sigir.mil/publications/hardLessons.html (viewed December 13, 2012).

Smith, Michael W. 2006. "The Road to Hell: The Corruption and Malfeasance of Boston's 'Big Dig'." *International Journal of Interdisciplinary Social Sciences* 3:3, 193–202.

Smith, R. Jeffrey. 2011. "Tom DeLay, Former U.S. House Leader, Sentenced to 3 Years in Prison." *Washington Post*, January 10. Online at www.washingtonpost.com/wp-dyn/content/article/2011/01/10/AR2011011000557.html (viewed December 13, 2012).

Stacher, Joshua. 2012. *Adaptable Autocrats: Regime Power in Egypt and Syria*. Stanford University Press.

Stave, Bruce (ed.). 1972. *Urban Bosses, Machines and Progressive Reform*, Lexington MA: D.C. Heath.

Stechina, Viviana. 2008. "Conditions for Corruption. Institutions, Executive Power, and Privatization in Argentina and Chile in the 1900s." PhD thesis, Department of Government, Uppsala University.
Stepan, Alfred. 2012. "Tunisia's Transition and the Twin Tolerations." *Journal of Democracy* 23:2, 89–103.
Stiglitz, Joseph E. 2012. *The Price of Inequality: How Today's Divided Society Endangers Our Future.* New York: W.W. Norton.
  2013. "Inequality is Holding Back the Recovery." *New York Times*, January 19. Online at http://opinionator.blogs.nytimes.com/2013/01/19/inequality-is-holding-back-the-recovery/ (viewed January 24, 2013).
Stokes, Susan. 1999. "What Do Policy Switches Tell Us about Democracy?" in Bernard Manin, Adam Przeworski, and Susan C. Stokes (eds.), *Democracy, Accountability, and Representation.* Cambridge and New York: Cambridge University Press, Chapter 3, pp. 98–130.
  2005. "Perverse Accountability: A Formal Model of Machine Politics with Evidence from Argentina." *American Political Science Review* 99:3, 315–25.
Strömberg, Håka. 2000. *Allmän Förvaltningsrätt.* Malmö: Liber.
Summers, Mark W. 1993. *The Era of Good Stealings.* New York: Oxford University Press.
Sun Yan and Michael Johnston. 2010. "Does Democracy Check Corruption? Insights from China and India." *Comparative Politics* 42:2, 1–19.
Sun Star Manila. 2012. "Poll: Aquino's Trust, Performance Ratings Up." Sun Star Manila, September 19. Online at www.sunstar.com.ph/manila/local-news/2012/09/19/poll-aquinos-trust-performance-ratings-243753 (viewed January 10, 2013).
Surowiecki, James. 2012a. "Invisible Hand, Greased Palm." *The New Yorker*, May 14. Online at www.newyorker.com/talk/financial/2012/05/14/120514ta_talk_surowiecki (viewed December 13, 2012).
  2012b. "Corporate Welfare Queens." *The New Yorker*, October 8. Online at www.newyorker.com/talk/financial/2012/10/08/121008ta_talk_surowiecki (viewed December 13, 2012).
Swart, Koenrad W. 1949. *Sale of Offices in the Seventeenth Century.* The Hague: Martinus Nijhoff, pp. 112–27.
Sydney Morning Herald. 2012. "New Documents on RBA Banknote Corruption." *Sydney Morning Herald*, September 12. Online at http://news.smh.com.au/breaking-news-national/new-documents-on-rba-banknote-corruption-20120912-25r28.html (viewed December 13, 2012).
TAG-SWS (Transparent and Accountable Government/Social Weather Stations). 2012. "The TAG 2012 SWS Surveys on Corruption." Quezon City: Social Weather Stations. Online at http://cancham.com.

ph/wp-content/uploads/2012/10/TAG-2012-23Octrev2.pdf (viewed January 13, 2013).

Teichman, Judith. 2002. "Private Sector Power and Market Reform: Exploring the Domestic Origins of Argentina's Meltdown and Mexico's Policy Failures." *Third World Quarterly* 23:3, 491–512.

Telegraph, The. 2012. "Egypt: Protesters Vent Anger after Hosni Mubarak's Sons Are Acquitted." *The Telegraph*, June 2. Online at www.telegraph.co.uk/news/worldnews/africaandindianocean/egypt/9307635/Egypt-Protesters-vent-anger-after-Hosni-Mubaraks-sons-are-acquitted.html (viewed February 5, 2013).

Teorell, J. 2007. "Corruption as an Institution: Rethinking the Nature and Origins of the Grabbing Hand." Gothenburg: The Quality of Government Institute, University of Gothenburg, Working Paper 2007:5. Online at www.qog.pol.gu.se/digitalAssets/1350/1350653_2007_5_teorell.pdf (viewed February 5, 2013).

Theobald, Robin. 1990. *Corruption, Development, and Underdevelopment*. Durham, NC: Duke University Press.

Thompson, Dennis F. 1993. "Mediated Corruption: The Case of the Keating Five." *American Political Science Review* 87:2, 369–81.

　1995. *Ethics in Congress: From Individual to Institutional Corruption*. Washington, DC: Brookings.

　2005. *Restoring Responsibility: Ethics in Government, Business, and Healthcare*. New York: Cambridge University Press.

Thorne, John. 2012. "In Tunisia's Sentencing of a Dictator, a Model for Bringing Justice?" *Christian Science Monitor*, June 14. Online at www.csmonitor.com/World/Middle-East/2012/0614/In-Tunisia-s-sentencing-of-a-dictator-a-model-for-bringing-justice (viewed February 5, 2013).

Thucydides. 1954. *History of the Peloponnesian War*, translated by Rex Warner. London: Penguin.

Tiihonen, Paula. 2003. "Good Governance and Corruption in Finland," in Seppo Tiihonen (ed.), *The History of Corruption in Central Government/L'histoire de la corruption au niveau du pouvoir central*. Amsterdam: IOS Press, pp. 99–118.

de Tocqueville, Alexis. 1994. *Democracy in America* (vol. I), edited by Alan Ryan and Henry Reeve. New York: Alfred A. Knopf.

Trading Economics. 2013. "Argentina GDP Growth Rate." Online at www.tradingeconomics.com/argentina/gdp-growth (viewed January 16, 2013).

Treisman, Daniel. 2000. "The Causes of Corruption: A Cross-National Study." *Journal of Public Economics* 76:3, 399–457.

Tu Thanh Ha. 2012. "Tunisian Fugitive Ready to Face Trial at Home." *The Globe and Mail*, May 8. Online at http://m.theglobeandmail.com/news/

world/tunisian-fugitive-ready-to-face-trial-at-home/article4105454/?service=mobile (viewed February 5, 2013).

Turner, Frederick C. and Marita Carballo. 2010. "Cycles of Legitimacy and Delegitimation Across Regimes in Argentina, 1900–2008." *International Social Science Journal* 60:2, 273–83.

Turner, Kris. 2012. "Owens-Illinois Launches Internal Probe for Possible Bribery." *Toledo Blade*, October 30. Online at www.toledoblade.com/business/2012/10/30/Owens-Illinois-launches-internal-probe-for-possible-bribery.html (viewed December 13, 2012).

UNDP (United Nations Development Program). 2008. *Tackling Corruption, Transforming Lives: Accelerating Human Development in Asia and the Pacific*. New Delhi: Macmillan.

United Nations. Department of Economic and Social Affairs. 2010. *Reconstructing Public Administration after Conflict: Challenges, Practices, and Lessons Learned*. New York: United Nations.

Uslaner, Eric M. 2004. "Trust and Corruption," in Johann Graf Lambsdorf, Markus Taube, and Matthias Schramm (eds.), *Corruption and the New Institutional Economics*. London: Routledge.

Van Biezen, Ingrid. 2004. "Political Parties as Public Utilities." *Party Politics* 10:6, 701–22.

van der Meer, Frits M. and Jos C. N. Raadschelders. 2003. "Maladministration in the Netherlands in the 19th and 20th Centuries," in Seppo Tiihonen (ed.), *The History of Corruption in Central Government/L'histoire de la corruption au niveau du pouvoir central*. Amsterdam: IOS Press, pp. 179–96.

Van Dyke, Matthew. 2012. "Why Islamists Winning Elections Is Good for Democracy and the War on Terrorism." *Huffington Post*, April 3. Online at www.huffingtonpost.com/matthew-vandyke/why-islamists-winning-ele_b_1398261.html (viewed February 5, 2013).

Van Klaveren, Jacob. 2002. "Corruption as a Historical Phenomenon," in Arnold J. Heidenheimer and Michael Johnston (eds.), *Political Corruption: Concepts and Contexts*, 3rd edn. New Brunswick, NJ: Transaction Publishers, Selection 5, pp. 83–94.

Varese, Federico. 2001. *The Russian Mafia: Private Protection in a New Market Economy*. Oxford University Press.

Vatikiotis, Michael R. J. 1998. *Indonesian Politics under Suharto: The Rise and Fall of the New Order*. London: Routledge.

Villalón, Roberta. 2007. "Corruption and Legacies of Contention: Argentina's Social Movements, 1993–2006." *Latin American Perspectives* 34:2, 139–56.

Vincens, A. J. and Natasha Khan. 2012. "Election Observers Proliferate at Polls," *Washington Post* (August 24). Online at www.washingtonpost.

com/politics/election-observers-proliferate-at-polls/2012/08/24/1452 c3ba-ed4f-11e1-a80b-9f898562d010_story.html (viewed February 6, 2013)

Vinocur, Nick. 2011. "Chirac, Villepin Deny Took Millions in Africa Cash." Reuters.com, September 12. Online at www.reuters.com/article/2011/09/12/us-france-graft-idUSTRE78B4DA20110912 (viewed December 12, 2012).

Waisbord, Silvio R. 2004. "Scandals, Media, and Citizenship in Contemporary Argentina." *American Behavioral Scientist* 47:8, 1072–98.

Waisman, Carlos H. 1987. *Reversal of Economic Development in Argentina: Postwar Counterrevolutionary Policies and their Structural Consequences*. Princeton University Press.

Warner, Carolyn M. 2007. *The Best System Money Can Buy: Corruption in the European Union*. Ithaca, NY: Cornell University Press.

Warren, Mark. 2004. "What Does Corruption Mean in a Democracy?" *American Journal of Political Science* 48:2, 328–43.

Washington Post, 2012. "Argentina Prepares Seizure of Currency Printer after Tax Chief Joins Vice President in Scandal." *Washington Post*, August 7.

WAtoday. 2012. "WA Police Union Slams 'Ineffective' CCC." WAtoday.com.au, September 26. Online at www.watoday.com.au/wa-news/police-union-slams-ineffective-ccc-20120926-26kyi.html (viewed December 12, 2012).

Wayne, Leslie. 2012. "Foreign Firms Most Affected by a U.S. Law Barring Bribes." Nytimes.com, September 3. Online at www.nytimes.com/2012/09/04/business/global/bribery-settlements-under-us-law-are-mostly-with-foreign-countries.html?pagewanted=all (viewed December 13, 2012).

Wedel, Janine R. 2009. *Shadow Elite: How the World's New Power Brokers Undermine Democracy, Government, and the Free Market*. New York: Basic Books.

Weitz-Shapiro, Rebecca. 2008. "The Local Connection: Local Government Performance and Satisfaction with Democracy in Argentina." *Comparative Political Studies* 41:3, 285–308.

Whaley, Floyd. 2012a. "Philippine Chief Justice Removed Over Omission in Report on Assets." Nytimes.com, May 29. Online at www.nytimes.com/2012/05/30/world/asia/philippines-chief-justice-removed-over-finances.html?_r=0 (viewed January 10, 2013).

2012b. "Philippines Ex-President is Arrested in Hospital on New Charges." Nytimes.com, October 4. Online at www.nytimes.com/2012/10/05/world/asia/philippines-ex-president-arrested-in-hospital-on-new-charges.html (viewed January 10, 2013).

White, Andrew D. 1890. "The Government of American Cities." *The Forum*, 357–72.
Williams, Robert. 1986. "Crime and Corruption in Australia." *Corruption and Reform* 1:2, 101–13; also in Robert Williams, Jonathan Moran, and Rachel Flanary (eds.), *Corruption in the Developed World*. Cheltenham: Edward Elgar, 2000, pp. 499–511.
  1991. "Investigating Corruption, Implementing Reform: The Australian Case." *Australian Studies* 6, 86–96; also in Robert Williams, Jonathan Moran, and Rachel Flanary (eds.), *Corruption in the Developed World*. Cheltenham: Edward Elgar, 2000, pp. 512–22.
Wilson, James Q. 1973. *Political Organizations*. New York: Basic Books.
Wolpe, Howard and Steve McDonald. 2006. "Training Leaders for Peace." *Journal of Democracy* 17:1, 132–8.
  2008. "Democracy and Peace-Building: Re-thinking the Conventional Wisdom." *The Round Table* 97: 394, 137–145.
Wolpe, Howard, with Steve Mcdonald, Eugene Nindorera, Elizabeth McClintock, Alain Lempereur, Fabien Nsengimana, Nicole Rumeau and Alli Blair. 2004. "Rebuilding Peace and State Capacity in War-Torn Burundi." *The Round Table* 93: 375, 457–67.
Wood, Elisabeth Jean. 2001. "An Insurgent Path to Democracy: Popular Mobilization, Economic Interests, and Regime Transition in South Africa and El Salvador." *Comparative Political Studies* 34:8, 862–88.
Woodrow Wilson Center International Center for Scholars. 2012. "The Burundi Leadership Training Program." Online at www.wilsoncenter.org/the-burundi-leadership-training-program (viewed February 5, 2013).
World Factbook (US Central Intelligence Agency). 2013. "The World Factbook." Online at www.cia.gov/library/publications/the-world-factbook/ (viewed January 17, 2013).
Yardley, William. 2004. "Connecticut's Governor Steps Down: Overview; Under Pressure, Rowland Resigns Governor's Post." Nytimes.com, June 22. Online at www.nytimes.com/2004/06/22/nyregion/connecticut-s-governor-steps-down-overview-under-pressure-rowland-resigns.html (viewed December 13, 2012).
You Jong-sung. 2005. "Embedded Autonomy or Crony Capitalism? Explaining Corruption in South Korea, Relative to Taiwan and the Philippines, Focusing on the Role of Land Reform and Industrial Policy." Presented at the Annual Meeting of the American Political Science Association, Washington, DC (September). Online at http://irps.ucsd.edu/assets/003/5292.pdf (viewed February 5, 2013).
  and Sanjeev Khagram. 2005. "A Comparative Study of Inequality and Corruption." *American Sociological Review* 70, 136–57.

Zhu Boliang. 2009. "Economic Integration and Corruption: The Case of China." Paper prepared for the annual conference of International Political Economy Society, College Station, TX, November 13–14. Online at https://ncgg.princeton.edu/IPES/2009/papers/F120_paper2.pdf (viewed February 5, 2013).

Zuern, Elke. 2006. "The Contentious Poor: Marginalization in an Era of Constitutional Democracy," translated by E. Zuern. (Originally published as "La pauvreté en débat. Marginalité et démocratie constitutionnelle en Afrique du Sud." *Politique africaine* 103, 27–45.)

2011. *The Politics of Necessity: Community Organizing and Democracy in South Africa.* Madison: University of Wisconsin Press.

Index

Abbou, Mohamed 95
Abramoff, Jack 199–200
abuse of power 9
accountability, horizontal 179–80, 182
Acemoglu, Daron
  on Egypt 102
  on extractive governments/
    institutions 64–5
  on inclusive institutions 9, 181
  on politics/political reforms 36, 44,
    45, 46
activism, reform
  in Argentina 171, 175–7
  and deep democratization 234–5,
    236–7, 239–40
  goals of 234–5
  in Influence Market corruption
    societies 213–14
  in Philippines 141–4
  success of 235
  tasks of 230–2
advocates, citizen 142
L'Affaire Karachi (French corruption
  scandal) 196–7
Afghanistan
  surveys of citizen expectations in 81
  trust in 65–6
Aga Khan, French tax exempt status of
  197
agencies against corruption (ICACs) 61
  in Australia 193–4
  drawbacks of 114
  in Hong Kong 61, 227
  in Philippines 138–9, 145
agency resources, comparisons of 73
agreements
  anti-bribery 204–5
  political contention leading to 44–7
Alfonsín, Raúl 156–7

Aliriza, Fadil 94
Allen, Peter 197
amnesties for corrupt officials 140
Ampatuan, Andal Jr. 132
Ampatuan, Andal Sr. 131
Ampatuan, Zaldy 131
Ampatuan clan (Philippines) 130–2
Anti-Bribery Treaty (OECD, 1999)
  204–5
anti-corruption activism *see* reform
  activism
anti-corruption agencies (ICACs) 61
  in Australia 193–4
  drawbacks of 114
  in Hong Kong 61, 227
  in Philippines 138–9, 145
anti-corruption education 143–4
anti-corruption movement xii
  accomplishments of 1, 9–10
  in United States 39–43
  see also reform activism
anti-corruption reforms xii–xiii, 3, 30
  citizen participation in 220–2
  incentives for 225, 226–30
  conventional, drawbacks of 53–4
  and deep democratization 234–5,
    236–7, 239–40
  and fragility 60–2, 83–4, 238
  goals of 62, 107–11, 121–2, 238–9
  historical 29–30
  risks of 114–15, 144–6, 237–8
  socio-political foundations of 3,
    34–5
  success of 2, 14, 15–16, 115–16, 237
    building trust 14–15, 62–3
    and collective-action challenges 15
    and poverty reduction 150, 184–5
    and syndromes of corruption 53,
      54–5, 84, 236

285

anti-corruption reforms (cont.)
  citizen participation/civil society
      role 145, 221–2, 223
    see also Elite Cartel corruption;
      Influence Market corruption;
      Official Mogul corruption;
      Oligarch-and-Clan corruption
  uncertainty created by 114–15
  see also individual countries; reform
    activism
anti-machine reformers (United States)
    39–43
Aquino, Benigno 'Noynoy' III 125–6
Aquino, Corazon 119, 132
Arab Spring
  in Egypt 89, 101–2
  start of 86–8
  in Tunisia 88–9
Argentina 151, 152
  anti-corruption reforms in 154, 169,
    170–3
    accountability among elites
      179–80, 182
    and economic/political reforms
      173, 175–6, 178–9
    success of 181–5
  civil society in 173–4
  corruption in 151–2, 154–61, 169–70
    adaptability of 162–3
    costs of 161–2
  economy in
    crisis 153–4
    reform of 157–8, 167–9, 178–9
    role of military in 156
  patronage systems in 167, 171
    needs for ending of 174
  politics/elections in 155, 158–9,
    164–6, 171, 177–8
    needs for reform of 173, 175–6
  presidents
    Alfonsín 156–7
    de la Rúa 158–9
    Kirchners 156, 159–61, 169, 173
    Menem 157, 168–9
    Peron 152–3
Arroyo, Gloria Macapagal 124–5, 126–7
Arroyo, Ignacio "Iggy" 127
Aung San Suu Kyi 86
Australia
  corruption in 190, 191–4, 201

ICACs in 193–4
political competition in 194
autocracy 31–2
autonomy, of anti-corruption
    organizations 232
Azmi, Zakaria 97

Balladur, Edouard 196–7
basic services provision, and quality of
    government 63–6
Bazire, Nicolas 197
Ben Ali regime (Tunisia) 86–8, 93–5
benchmarks, of government
    performance 71–6
benefits
  of corruption 10–11
  social, in Argentina
Bettencourt, Liliane 197
Bjelke-Petersen, Johannes ("Sir Joh")
    192
Blackwater (corporation) 199
Blagojevich, Rod 199
Bocchi, Alessandro Magnoli 135
Boston, corruption in 198
Bouazizi, Mohammad 86–8
Boudou, Amado 161, 182
boundaries, public–private 81, 200
  and Influence Market corruption
    208–9
Bourguiba, Habib 92–3
Bribe Payers Index (BPI, Transparency
    International) 201
bribery, international treaties against
    204–5
bureaucrats, in Official Mogul
    corruption 112
Burundi Leadership Training Program
    (BLTP) 77–8
business sector
  in Philippines 135
  see also private sector
business-style government 13–14

La Cámpora youth organization
    (Argentina) 171
capital
  concealment/illicit export of,
    prevention of 113
  trap of low equilibrium of, in
    Philippines 135

Index

Carballo, Marita 172
Carrefour de Développement (France), corruption scandal associated with 195
Catholic Church, in Philippines, corrupt bishops in 127
changes *see* reforms
Chavez, Rebecca Bill 178–9
Chayes, Sarah 93–4
China, corruption in 27
Chirac, Jacques 195–6
Chua, Yvonne T. 128–9
citizen advocates 142
citizens
  expectations of
    indicators of 80, 81, 82
    managing/changing of 108, 116–17, 149–50
    and quality of government 78–83
    and syndromes of corruption 79, 81
  participation of 17–18, 215–16
    incentives for 223–30
    and Influence Market corruption 188–9
    and institutions 18–19
    in measurements of government performance 75–6, 111–12, 115–16, 147–8
civil liberties, assurance of 108, 174
civil society
  anti-corruption reforms based on 145
  components of 223
  revival of 173–4
  strength of 232
coalitions, promotion of reforms by 46
collective action challenges, and anti-corruption reform 15
Committee on Privileges (House of Commons, UK) 39
competition, political *see* political contention/competition
conflict-of-interest rules, needs for 182
Connecticut, corruption in 198–9
constitutional monarchy, in England 38–9
contention *see* political contention/competition
Coronel, Sheila S. 128–9
corruption xi–xii, 6–9, 10, 11, 12, 31–2
  benefits of 10–11
  comparative analysis of 235
    see also Syndromes of Corruption
  costs of 161–2
  and democracy 3–4, 189
  globalization of 11, 187–8, 200–5, 212
  and inequalities 207–8
  and lobbying 199–200
  and local government 184
  measuring of 1–2, 66–8, 107–8, 201
    see also indices of corruption
  and politics 8, 12–14, 248–9
  and power 1, 10
  prosecution of 55, 61, 144–5
  reduction of *see* anti-corruption movement; anti-corruption reforms; reform activism
  research on xii
  syndromes of 5, 16–17, 18–19, 20, 27–8, 52–3, 235, 241, 246
    and anti-corruption reforms 54–5, 84, 223
    citizen participation/civil society role 145, 221–2, 223
    and citizen expectations 79, 81
    and deep democratization efforts 48–52, 54–5
    development of 53
    examples of 84–5
      see also individual countries
    and fragility 59–60
    identification of 56, 243, 244–5, 249–51
    and measurements of government performance 74
    and politics 248–9
    see also Elite Cartel corruption; Influence Market corruption; Official Mogul corruption; Oligarch-and-Clan corruption
corruption-free states, illusion of 11–12
Corruption Perceptions Index (CPI) 190, 201
Costigan Commission (Australia) 191–2
costs
  of corruption, in Argentina 161–2
  of political contention 44
countermeasures, against poor government performance 71

CPI *see* Corruption Perceptions Index
Cruz, Boomba B. 128–9
customs-farming 32–3

data, on government performance 70, 71
debts, public, of United States 210
democracy/democracies
 and corruption 3–4, 189
 emerging 12, 14
 in United States 35
democratization 34
 deep 4–5, 28, 29, 35, 36, 47
  and anti-corruption reform 234–5, 236–7, 239–40
  disguises of 56
  and reform activism 234–5, 236–7, 239–40
  and syndromes of corruption 48–52, 54–5
   Elite Cartel corruption 51
   Influence Market corruption 52, 188–9, 214–15
   Official Mogul corruption 49, 91
   Oligarch-and-Clan corruption 49–51
 tasks of 47–8, 54
demokrasya concept 133–4
deregulation, judicious 111
De Soto, Hernando 88
developed societies, and corruption 235–6
development aid, misuse of
 monitoring of 111
 and Official Mogul corruption 99–100
 prevention of 112–13
deviance perspectives, on corruption 12
Dijk, Oege 209–10
DiJohn, Jonathan 79
de Dios Pueblos, Juan 127
disclosures
 of assets, obligations to 148–9
 financial, rules for elected officials 180
Dix, Sarah 65
Dobel, J. Patrick 31
Dominican Republic, trust in 65

economic competition 164
economic crises
 of 2008, causes of 200
 in Argentina 153–4

economic growth, and citizen expectations 83
economic opportunities, creation of 112–13
economic power
 of Argentine military 156
 of Egyptian military 97–8
 and political competition 178–9
economic reforms
 in Argentina 157–8, 167–9
 in Influence Market corruption societies 217–18
economic transparency, needs for 113, 182–3
education, anti-corruption 143–4
efficiency, of government 72
Egypt 96–7
 anti-corruption reforms in 89–91
 after Arab Spring 89, 101–2
 Mubarak regime in 96
  corruption of 97–100
  research into stolen assets of 100–1
 political pluralism needed in 103–5
elections
 in Argentina 155, 166
 fairness of 175–6, 214–15
 in Philippines 124–5, 132, 135
  and community project funding 133
  and vote-buying 132–3, 141
Elf-Aquitaine corruption scandal 202–3
Elite Cartel corruption 16, 18, 22–3, 243, 244, 246–7, 248
 anti-corruption reforms in 23, 51, 154, 170–3
 accountability among elites 179–80, 182
 and citizen participation 221
 extension of economic interests 178–9
 political reforms 173, 175–6
 success of 181–5
 in Argentina 151–2, 154–61, 169–70
 adaptability of 162–3
 costs of 161–2
 and citizen expectations 82
 and deep democratization efforts 51
 developments toward 53, 146, 150
 as interim goal 62, 238–9
 and fragility 60

Index 289

elites
  in Argentina 154–5
    accountability among 179–80, 182
    international 188, 212
  in Zambia 79
emerging democracies 12, 14
England
  anti-corruption struggles in 29–30, 36–9
  freeholder offices in 32–3
  patronage systems in 33
  Putney debates in 33
  see also United Kingdom
Espinal, Rosario 65
Estrada, Joseph "Erap" 132
ethics, political 7
expectations of citizens
  indicators of 80, 81, 82
  managing/changing of 108, 116–17, 149–50
  and quality of government 78–83
  and syndromes of corruption 79, 81
  trap, in Philippines 135, 150
expert assessments 73

fairness 214
  of elections 175–6, 214–15
  in provision of basic services 64
Federated Ship Painters and Dockers Union (Australia) 191–2
financial crisis (2008), causes of 200
financial disclosure rules, for elected officials 180
financial transparency, needs for 113, 182–3
financing of politics
  and inequalities 210–11
  transparency of 142–3, 176–7, 214–15
  and US corruption 8, 197–8
Fitzgerald Inquiry (Australia) 192
fixers, role of 124, 202
forced-choice approach to identification of corruption syndromes 249–51
Foreign Corrupt Practices Act (FCPA, United States) 203–4
foreign exchange manipulations, in Argentina 158

Fouda, Khaled Aly 98
fragility in societies 5, 56, 58–60
  and basic services provision 63–6
  and reforms 57–8, 60–2, 83–4, 238
France
  corruption in 190, 194–7, 201, 202–3
  politics in 203
Frank, Robert H. 209–10
freeholder offices 32–3
Friedrich, Carl J. 32
fry-a-big-fish anti-corruption strategy 61, 144–5

gaming of performance indicators 75
Gezira Tower/Hotel (Cairo), controversies over 98
globalization, of corruption 11, 187–8, 200–5, 212
goals
  of anti-corruption reforms 62, 107–11, 121–2, 238–9
  of government 64
  of reform activism 234–5
GONGOs (Government-sponsored NGOs) 234
good-government movements 45
Goodin, Robert E. 36
governance 59
  good
    and corruption 7–8
    in emerging democracies 12
    movements for 45
  good enough 62, 108
government 34
  business-style 13–14
  extractive 64–5
  and international corruption 202–3
  local, and corruption 184
  measuring performance of 68–9, 239
    benchmarks/indicators 69–76
    citizen participation in 75–6, 111–12, 115–16, 147–8
    risks 76–7
  quality of 35–6
    and basic services provision 63–6
    citizen expectations dilemma 78–83

government (cont.)
    improvement of 62–3, 76
    transparency of 172
    see also state
Grey, Charles, 2nd Earl 44
Grindle, Merilee 62, 108
Guillan Montero, Aranzazu 156, 160
Guthrie, Woody 186

Hartlyn, Jonathan 65
Hazare, Anna 221
Heilbrunn, John R. 203
historical anti-corruption struggles 29–30
    in England 29–30, 36–9
    in United States 39–43
Hong Kong
    anti-corruption education in 143–4
    ICAC (anti-corruption agency) in 61, 227
Hood, Christopher 75
Hope, Bradley 100–1
horizontal accountability 179–80, 182
House, James S. 210
human rights *see* civil liberties, assurance of
Huntington, Samuel 17–18
Hussmann, Karen 65

ICACs (agencies against corruption) 61
    in Australia 193–4
    drawbacks of 114
    in Hong Kong 61, 227
    in Philippines 138–9, 145
Illinois, corruption in 199
impartiality 35–6
impeachment procedures, in England 38
incentives to sustain citizen participation 223–30
    and anti-corruption reforms 225, 226–30
inclusive institutions 9, 181
inclusive politics, and perceptions of corruption 8
India, social audits in 116
indicators
    of citizen expectations 80, 81, 82
    of government performance 69–71, 74–6
    of insecurity 149
    of progress in anti-corruption reforms 115–16
indices of corruption
    Bribe Payers Index (BPI) 201
    Corruption Perceptions Index (CPI) 190, 201
    drawbacks of 67
    on France, Australia, and United States 190
    on Philippines 126
Indonesia, corruption in 27
inequalities
    adverse effects of 209–10
    and corruption 207–8
    in Philippines 129
    and political funding 210–11
Influence Market corruption 16, 18, 19–22, 186–7, 189–90, 245, 246, 248
    anti-corruption reforms in 22, 52, 205–6, 213–19
        economic reforms 217–18
        political reforms 216–17
        and reform activism/citizen participation 213–14, 221
        success of 218
    in Australia 190
    and citizen expectations 80–1, 82
    and deep democratization 52, 188–9, 214–15
    and fragility 60
    in France 190, 202–3
    identification of corrupt practices in 206–13
    international dimension of 187–8, 200–5, 212, 218–19, 235–6
    in United States 190, 206–7
insecurity
    created by anti-corruption reforms 114–15
    indicators of 149
    of oligarchs, and corruption 145
    reduction of, as goal for anti-corruption reforms 121–2
    see also security
institutions 18
    extractive 64–5
    inclusive 9, 181
    and participation 18–19

Index

interim goals, for anti-corruption reforms 62, 238–9
international dimensions, of Influence Market corruption 187–8, 200–5, 212, 218–19, 235–6
international elites 188, 212
investigations *see* measurements; research
Iraq, US peacekeeping and reconstruction efforts in, and corruption 199
Islamists, in Egypt and Tunisia 104–5
Italy, corruption in 23

James I (King of England) 37
John (King of England) 36–7
Johnston, Michael xii, 235
judiciary
  deregulation of 111
  reform of 140, 183–4
justice 55

kalayaan concept 134
Kang, David C. 130
Kaplan, George A. 210
Kelly, Jana Morgan 65
Kettle, Martin 33
Kirchner, Cristina Fernandez de 160–1, 169, 173
Kirchner, Néstor 156, 159–60, 169, 173

Ladgham, Abderrahman 95
landownership
  in Egypt 98–9
  in Philippines 129
language, of anti-corruption reforms 62–3
Lapegna, Pablo 171
Lavagna, Roberto 159
leaders, political, as anti-corruption champions 144
Lessig, Lawrence 35, 214–15
Levine, Adam Seth 209–10
limits
  of anti-corruption activism 230–1
  on power 9
lobbying, and corruption 199–200
local government, and corruption 184
Louisiana, corruption in 198

low-capital equilibrium trap, in Philippines 135
Lynch, Marc 210

Madison, James 1, 3
Magna Carta 36–7
Maguindanao massacre (Philippines, 2009) 124, 132
Manzano, Jose Louis 151, 154
Manzetti, Luigi 160
Marcos, Ferdinand 130
Marcos, Imelda 119
Marquette, Heather 65–6
Marseille, police corruption in 196
Massachusetts, corruption in 198
el-Materi, Sakher 94
material incentives to sustain citizen participation 224
  and anti-corruption reforms 226
McCoy, Alfred W. 130
McDonald, Steve 77
measurements
  of citizen expectations 80, 82
  of corruption 1–2, 66–8
    international 201
    of Official Mogul corruption 107–8
    see also indices of corruption
  of government performance 68–9, 239
    benchmarks/indicators 69–76
    citizen participation in 75–6, 111–12, 115–16, 147–8
    risks of 76–7
Menem, Carlos 157–8, 168–9
Mery, Jean-Claude 196
Mexico, corruption in 25
military, economic power of
  in Argentina 156
  in Egypt 97–8
Miller, James C. 178–9
Mindanao (Philippines), Ampatuan clan in 130–2
Mishler, William 65
modernization 68
monolithic views of corruption 11
movements
  anti-corruption xii
    accomplishments of 1, 9–10
    in United States 39–43
  for good government 45

Mubarak, Alaa and Gamal 97
Mubarak regime (Egypt) 96
　corruption of 97–100
　research into stolen assets of 100–1
Mursi, Muhammad 89
Muslim Brotherhood (Egypt) 104

al-Nadim (Egyptian human-rights
　　group) 100
Naím, Moisés 234
Nasr, Mahmoud 98
Nast, Thomas 41
NGOs 232–3
　government-sponsored (GONGOs)
　　234
　involvement in measuring
　　government performance 148
　socially rooted 233
norms
　of private sector 73
　statistical 73
al-Nur (Salafi political party, Egypt) 104

OECD, Anti-Bribery Treaty of 204–5
Official Mogul corruption 17, 19, 26–7,
　　92, 243, 247–9
　anti-corruption reforms in 27, 49,
　　89–91, 105–6, 117
　　and citizen participation 221
　　political pluralism needs 106–7
　　priorities 109
　　risks of 114–15
　　strategic goals 107–11
　　success of 115–16
　　tactical measures 111–13
　and citizen expectations 82
　and deep democratization efforts 49, 91
　developing into Elite Cartel
　　corruption 53
　developing into Oligarch-and-Clan
　　corruption 115
　in Egypt 97–100
　encounters with Influence Market
　　corruption 205
　and fragility 59
　in Tunisia 86–8, 93–5
Oklahoma, corruption in 198
Oligarch-and-Clan corruption 16–17,
　　18–19, 23–5, 118, 119–20,
　　121, 243, 247, 248

anti-corruption reforms in 49–51,
　　120–2, 135–6, 137
　amnesties for corrupt officials 140
　anti-corruption courts 139–40
　and citizen participation/reform
　　activism 141–4, 221
　ICACs 138–9, 145
　incentives for opponents of
　　corruption 140–1
　judiciary reform 140
　risks of 144–6
　"stateness" of state 192
　success of 146–50
and citizen expectations 82
and deep democratization efforts
　49–51
development toward Elite Cartel
　corruption 53, 146, 150
encounters with Influence Market
　corruption 205
and fragility 59
and measurements of government
　performance 74
other syndromes of corruption
　developing into 61–2, 115
in Philippines 122, 123–4, 126–8,
　129–30, 134–5
oligarchs
　insecurity of, and corruption 145
　in Philippines 128–30
organizations
　building of 223, 231–2, 234–5
　social, terror groups disguised as 233
Ostrom, Elinor 149–50, 224
outcomes, comparisons of 73
Oyamada, Eiji 150

Packer, Kerry 191–2
Pakistan, French arms deal with 196–7
participation see citizens,
　　participation of
patronage systems
　in Argentina 167, 171
　　needs for ending of 174
　in England 33
Performance Governance System (PGS,
　　Philippines) 148
Perón, Juan Domingo 152–3
Peronismo 171
　alternatives for 173–4

Philippines 122–3
  anti-corruption reforms in 135–6, 137
    amnesties for corrupt officials 140
    fry-a-big-fish 61, 144–5
    ICACs 138–9, 145
    incentives for opponents of corruption 140–1
    judiciary reform 140
    promotion of reform activism 141–4
    risks of 144–6
    Sandiganbayan (anti-corruption court) 139–40
    "stateness" of state 137–8
    success of 146–50
  corruption in 25, 122, 123–4, 126–8, 129–30, 134–5
  elections in *see* elections
  political culture in 133–4, 136
  powerful families (oligarchs) in 128–30
    Ampatuan clan 130–2
  presidents
    Aquino III 125–6
    Arroyo 126–7
    Estrada 132
    Marcos 130
    Ramos 132
  private sector in 135
Plunkitt, George Washington 220, 222
pluralism, political
  in Egypt and Tunisia 103–5
  to fight Official Mogul corruption 106–7
pluralistic views of corruption *see* Syndromes of Corruption
police corruption
  in Australia 192
  in France 196
political contention/competition 43
  agreements resulting from 44–7
  in Argentina 164–6, 177–8
  in Australia 194
  costs of 44
  in France 203
  see also politics
Political and Economic Risk Consultancy (PERC, Hong Kong) 126

political ethics 7
political leaders, as anti-corruption champions 144
Political Organizations (Wilson) 223–5
political parties 83
  in emerging democracies 14
  Islamist 104–5
political reforms/change
  need for
    in Argentina 173, 175–6
    in Egypt and Tunisia 103–5
    in Influence Market corruption societies 216–17
    in Official Mogul corruption societies 106–7
    in Philippines 143
  United Kingdom 44
politics 36
  in Argentina 155, 158–9, 164–6, 171, 177–8
  and corruption 8, 12–14, 248–9
  funding of
    and inequalities 210–11
    transparency of 142–3, 176–7, 214–15
  and US corruption 8, 197–8
  in Philippines 133–4, 136
  pre-modern 32–4
  see also political contention/competition
post-conflict/post-dictatorial societies, corruption in 25
poverty reduction, and anti-corruption reform 150, 184–5
power
  abuse of 9
  and corruption 1, 10
  economic
    of Argentine military 156
    of Egyptian military 97–8
    and political competition 178–9
  limits on 9
PricewaterhouseCoopers, on costs of corruption in Argentina 162
private property, public offices as 32–4
private sector
  boundaries with public sector 81, 200
  and Influence Market corruption 208–9
  norms 73

private sector (cont.)
  rent-seeking in 209
  transparency needs for 180–1
  see also business sector
privatization, in Argentina 157–8, 167–9
Procurement Watch (NGO, Philippines) 148
progress in anti-corruption reforms *see* successes
projections, statistical 73
property rights
  and political competition 178–9
  see also landownership
proportional representation
  advantages of 216–17
  in Argentina 165
prosecution of corruption 55
  fry-a-big-fish strategy 61, 144–5
public debts, of United States 210
public offices, as private property 32–4
public–private boundaries 81, 200
  and Influence Market corruption 208–9
purposive incentives to sustain citizen participation 225
  in anti-corruption reform 225
Putney Debates (England) 33

quality of government 35–6
  and basic services provision 63–6
  and citizen expectations dilemma 78–83
  improvement of 62–3, 76
Queensland (Australia), police corruption in 192

Rainborough, Thomas 33
Ramos, Fidel V. 132
reduction
  of corruption 1–2
    see also successes, of antiorruption reforms
  of poverty 150, 184–5
reform activism
  in Argentina 171, 175–7
  and deep democratization 234–5, 236–7, 239–40
  goals of 234–5
  in Influence Market corruption societies 213–14
  in Philippines 141–4
  success of 235
  tasks of 230–2
reforms
  economic
    in Argentina 157–8, 167–9
    in Influence Market corruption societies 217–18
    and fragility in societies 57–8
    in landownership 129
  political
    in Influence Market corruption societies 216–17
    needs for
      in Argentina 173
      in Egypt and Tunisia 103–5
      in Official Mogul corruption societies 106–7
      in United Kingdom 44
  see also anti-corruption reforms
renationalizations, in Argentina 169
research
  on corruption xii
  into Mubarak regime's stolen assets 100–1
  see also measurements
resources, of agencies 73
Rice, Condoleezza 199
Rimban, Luz 128–9
risks
  of anti-corruption reforms 114–15, 144–6, 237–8
  in measuring government performance 76–7
Robinson, James A.
  on Egypt 102
  on extractive governments/ institutions 64–5
  on inclusive institutions 9, 181
  on politics/political reforms 36, 44, 45, 46
Rose, Richard 65
Rothstein, Bo 12, 13, 35–6, 65, 237
Rothwells Bank (Australia) 193
Rowland, John 198–9

Index

Russia
  corruption in 25, 237
  trust in 65
Rustow, Dankwart A. 34

Salafists, in Egypt 104
Saleh, Yasmine 101–2
Salem, Hussein 98–9, 100–1
Sandiganbayan (anti-corruption court, Philippines) 139–40
Santiso, Carlos 166
Sarkozy, Nicolas 196–7
Schaffer, Frederic 133–4
Schattschneider, E. E. 14
schools, anti-corruption education in 143–4
Schwartz, Richard D. 178–9
Scott, James C. 34
security
  provision of, as goal for governments 64
  see also insecurity
Shafiq, Ahmed 97
Sidi Bouzid (Tunisia), Arab Spring starting in 86–8
Sin, Jaime 133
Singapore, corruption in 251
Smith, George Davey 210
social audits 116
social benefits, in Argentina 167
social media, and citizen participation 111–12
social organizations, terror groups disguised as 233
socially rooted NGOs 233
societies
  fragility of 5, 56, 58–60
  and basic services provision 63–6
  and reforms 57–8, 60–2, 83–4, 238
  trust in 59, 77–8
  and anti-corruption reforms 14–15, 62–3
socio-political foundations of anti-corruption reform 3, 34–5
solidary incentives to sustain citizen participation 226
  and anti-corruption reforms 227–30
South Korea, corruption in 23

speed, of government processes 69, 72
stalemates, agreements resulting from 46
standards of good governance, and corruption 7–8
state
  corruption-free 11–12
  and international corruption 202–3
  private to public evolution of 32–4
  "stateness" of 137–8
  views of 7
    minimalist 12–13
    normative 13
    pre-modern 32
  see also government
statistics
  norms of 73
  projections 73
Stiglitz, Joseph 164, 209, 210, 211
Stokes, Susan 165, 166
Strafford, Thomas Wentworth, 1st Earl of 38
strategic goals, for Official Mogul anti-corruption reforms 107–11
successes
  of anti-corruption reforms 2, 14, 15–16, 115–16, 237
  building trust 14–15, 62–3
  and collective-action challenges 15
  Elite Cartel corruption 181–5
  Influence Market corruption 218
  Official Mogul corruption 115–16
  Oligarch-and-Clan corruption 146–50
  and poverty reduction 150, 184–5
  in building trust 77–8
  of reform activism 235
Syndromes of Corruption (Johnston) xii, 235
systemic corruption 12

taxation, reliability of 81–3
tax-farming 32–3
Theobald, Robin 32
Thucydides 7, 29
de Tocqueville, Alexis 178–9
Tolstoy, Lev 57, 58
Trabelsi, Belhassen 94
Trabelsi, Leila 93

transparency
  financial/economic, needs for 113, 182–3
  of government 172
  of political funding 142–3, 176–7, 214–15
  in private sector, needs for 180–1
Transparency International, corruption indices of 190, 201
treaties, against bribery 204–5
trust
  building 77–8
    and anti-corruption reforms 14–15, 62–3
    by basic services provision 63–6
  and fragility 59
Tunisia 92–3
  anti-corruption reforms in 89–91, 95–6
  after Arab Spring 88–9
  corruption in 86–8, 93–5
  political pluralism needed in 103–5
Turner, Frederick C. 172

uncertainty *see* insecurity
United Kingdom
  civil service modernization in 68
  political reforms in 44
  see also England
United States
  anti-corruption fights/reforms 29–30, 39–43
    Foreign Corrupt Practices Act (FCPA) 203–4
  corruption in 190, 197–200, 201, 206–7
    analysis of 235–6
    and political funding 8, 197–8
  democracy in 35
  inequalities in 209–10
    and political funding 210–11
  wealth accumulation in 209
Uslaner, Eric M. 65
utilities, provision of, as goal for governments 64

Van Biezen, Ingrid 14
Van Klaveren, Jacob 33
Victoria harbor (Australia) corruption scandal 191–2
violence, in Philippine election campaigns 124
vote-buying
  in Argentina 166
  in Philippines 132–3, 141

Waisbord, Silvio R. 184
Wali, Yussef 98–9
Walton, Grant 65
Warren, Mark 189
Watergate scandal 197
Wedel, Janine R. 202
Weitz-Shapiro, Rebecca 184
West Australia, corruption in 192–3
White, Andres Dickson 40
Williams, Robert 192
Wilson, James Q. 223–5
Wolpe, Howard 77

You Jong-sung 126

Zambia, elites in 79

For EU product safety concerns, contact us at Calle de José Abascal, 56–1°, 28003 Madrid, Spain or eugpsr@cambridge.org.

www.ingramcontent.com/pod-product-compliance
Ingram Content Group UK Ltd.
Pitfield, Milton Keynes, MK11 3LW, UK
UKHW020354060825
461487UK00008B/654